Essays
by
Rosemond Tuve

Publication of this book has been
aided by a grant from the American
Association of University Women.
A portion of this grant came from
the Mrs. Adam Leroy Jones Memorial
Fund to assist publications.

EDITED BY THOMAS P. ROCHE, JR.

ESSAYS BY ROSEMOND TUVE

Spenser Herbert Milton

PRINCETON UNIVERSITY PRESS · PRINCETON
1970

LC Card: 69-18070
Standard Book Number: 691-06171-8

This book has been composed in Linotype Caslon Old Face
Printed in the United States of America
by Vail-Ballou Press, Binghamton, New York

Introduction

"... lanterne vnto late succeeding age ..."

THIS selection of essays by Rosemond Tuve is intended for two groups of readers—for those of us who regard her work in the field of Renaissance poetry as most highly persuasive, that rare combination of painstaking scholarly detail and imaginative insight, and for those of us who knew and loved Ros and would want her to be remembered. The two groups are not mutually exclusive, for those who have read her books on Elizabethan and metaphysical imagery, on Herbert and on Milton cannot have missed the intelligence and vitality of her personality, and those who knew her personally could not avoid her infectious enthusiasm for her period. For this reason I have chosen Spenser's praise of William Camden as an epigraph. It is a line that I must have read many times but had not noticed until she pointed it out in her last essay, "Spenserus," explaining why Camden should be included in *The Ruins of Time:* "the power of learning and letters to hold truth safe as in a vial." I hope that neither group of readers will find it inappropriate here.

The process of selection from among the 40 articles and reviews was difficult. I decided to exclude reviews, those articles that appear unchanged in books still in print, and those articles that seem too dated. This was done with regret, for the reviews contain some of Miss Tuve's most sprightly comments, and the double article on virtues and vices should still be consulted for some details that did not get into her *Allegorical Imagery*. (The excluded articles are listed in the bibliography.) With the exception of the three essays on education, this left the essays on Spenser, on Herbert, and on Milton, those three poets who engaged Miss Tuve's imagination more than any others.

Half of the essays included are on Spenser. They range in time from her first scholarly article in 1929 to her last in 1964. I include all of them because, read together, they show Miss Tuve's abiding and profound interest in Spenser. It is strange that she did not write a book on Spenser—strange, but understandable in that all the essays, including the long last chapter of *Allegorical Im-*

agery, show that oblique and radically tangential technique of dealing with Spenser's poetry. I once questioned Miss Tuve about the value of source studies and Spenser's possible belief in the Neoplatonic scheme of three worlds. Her reply was characteristically instructive:

> –I prefer welters of lng. [language] & let *me* pick what's relevant, & you'd better tell me WHAT scheme of "worlds" Sp. stuck to or I shall return to my conviction that he like all here-grab there-grab poets (esp. Yeats) was as 'reductive' as any later comer & damn well plucked inconsistently what he wanted. Instead of a critic that tells me what HE would have plucked I'd rather have the chaos handed me, & then read the poem myself. I don't espouse anybody but E.Sp.; I just want to be told 'hey read this & see if it might light up a alley or two' & then please let them beat it & not talk in the passage. [Letter dated "Easter Day, 3 Crick Road, Oxford," 22 April 1962.]

In all the early Spenser essays there is a purposeful shying away from specifying meanings for his poem. She sought to enrich our reading through literary and non-literary sources, but she never enroached on the right and privilege of every reader to discover meaning for himself. In the last two essays there is a breakthrough into the work that was peculiarly hers as a literary critic: the relation of pictorial and verbal imagery and the relevance of *what* books and *how* a poet might have read. One cannot resist a feeling of awe at the thought of all those hours, poring over manuscripts, which in any other critic would not have found their way into print. Miss Tuve took these manuscripts into her imagination and spilled them pell-mell on the page—with accurate citations—in all the abandon she attributes to Spenser. What other critic would have made more than a one-page note of "Spenserus"? Who else would have done the immense amount of background research? Who else would have dared to commit the tentative and imaginative suggestions to print? In these essays as in the others she does not give answers but points the way to new appreciation and further researches.

The Herbert essays present two other aspects of Miss Tuve's work. In the beautifully perceptive "Herbert and *Caritas*" she speaks more freely of her own Christian love in trying to define Herbert's. Part of the richness of the essay comes from the shared "background" of poet and critic, a "background" more valued and real for her because lived. I do not think that Miss Tuve would have liked that last statement for many reasons, but primarily because those manuscripts and early printed books, habitually categorized as "background" by us, were for her no more dead than her Christianity. One of the truly admirable things about her was her power to read each work, not to prove a point, not to add to the footnotes, but to *read* each one for itself alone. For her each work had a value in and of itself, and the greatest critical sin was to think that "poems were written for critics to earn bread and butter by." And this is why she saw more in works than most of us and could make those discriminations so nicely. Her examination of the word "parody" in the second Herbert essay with its distinctions between sacred and secular love, between words and music, is a case in point.

Her discriminations were not always directed solely at a work of art but to the decorum and rationale of critical methods. Her broadcast talk for the BBC on Milton returns to the problem she raised in *A Reading of George Herbert:* the difference between imagery and figurative language. Coupled with the distortion of what we draw out of a poem is the opposite indecorum of what we impose on the poem, our own invented terms. The second Milton essay takes up the problem of the application of art historical terms and categories to Milton's various poems. Once more we are in her debt for discriminating among our too-easy discriminations.

All the essays take up, each in its own minutely particularized way, the problems of reading literature. Even in the welter of language and masses of footnotes there is a constant and unflagging devotion to the value of literature, which is the reason I have included the three essays on education. In these essays she was most explicit about those broader humane values that directed her energetic research. It is appropriate that they come at the beginning of the volume, for we should all be reminded of the values behind those facts she taught so abundantly—"without talk in the passage."

THOMAS P. ROCHE, JR.

Princeton
1969

Contents

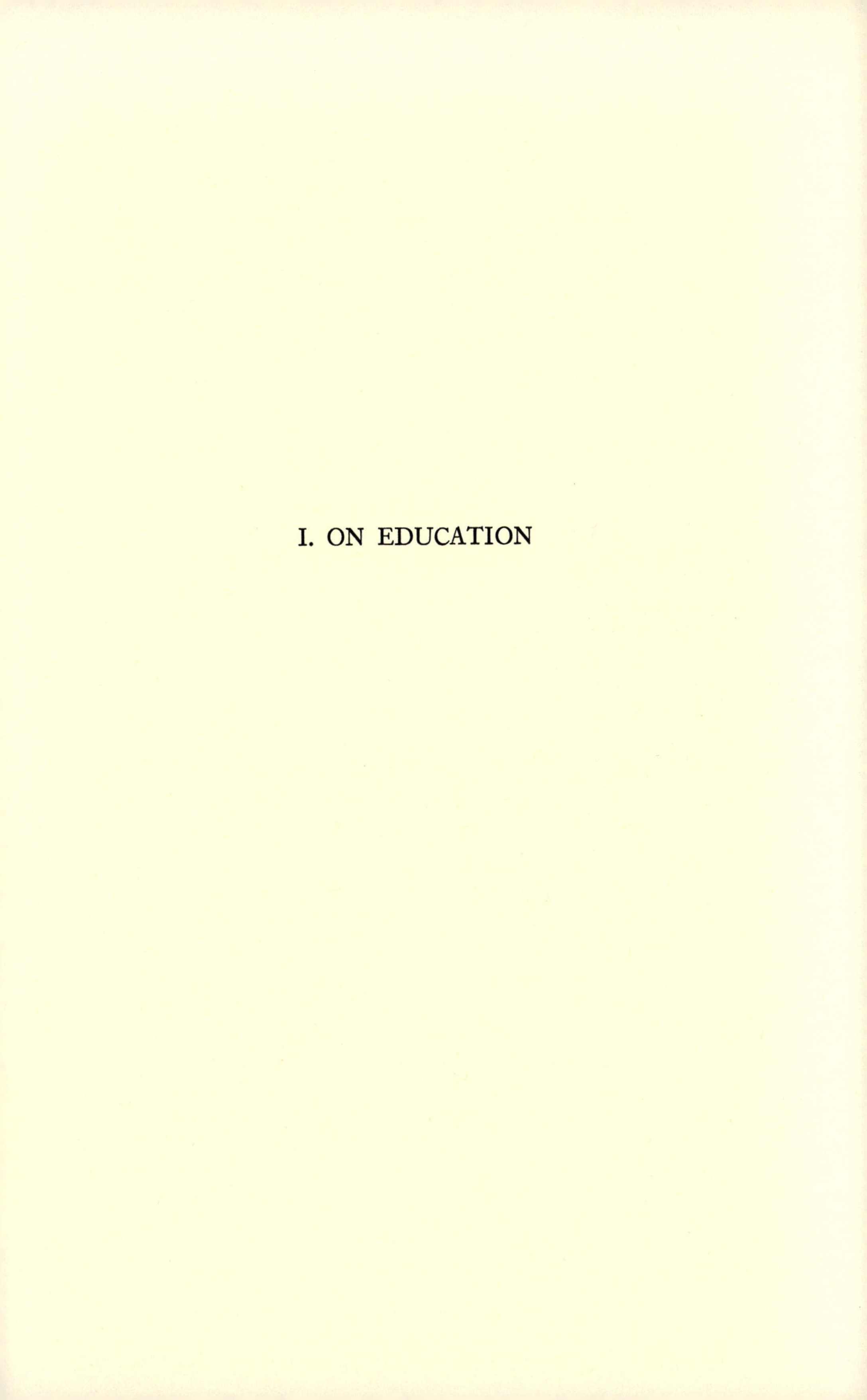

I. ON EDUCATION

More Battle Than Books*

THE traditional issue in a symposium on "the teaching of literature," the expected, the comfortable, the scarred and symbolic bone, is the place of philological, literary-historical and "research" considerations in that teaching, and in training those who are to teach. I shall pick this bone but little, and that little in whispers. I do not take it very seriously. I take seriously that unhappy figure in whose name the contentions are evoked—the student who is not taught what he needs, does not need what he is taught, and does not much enjoy what he learns. But I would put forward another worry, a cause for deeper disquiet.

This worry will sound like the mere making of excuses until I have done with fixing the responsibility for the difficulties. I have reference to the decreasing number of first-class people among those students who are to be the teachers of literature. And beyond that, to the increasing difficulty of making good teachers of literature out of those multitudes needed to "teach English" up and down America, an increasing difficulty because more and more is left to be done at the highest levels of training. Other things have increasingly supplanted, at the lower levels, those things which were fundamental to the future training of teachers of literature. These embarrassments are but a part of the larger difficulty. Literature as an aesthetic experience for students seems to have shrunk in the last hundred years. The disquiet behind all these is a disquiet about the character and values of American culture. I fear that the major obstacles to good teaching of literature lie outside the profession and outside the training, though I fear also that the profession and the training do little to counter them.

To this last point I shall return. As concerns the first, perhaps if one asks the questions, one may be saved the embarrassment of answering them. Do the colleges get the best human material (*is* the "best" in education given to the most teachable young people)? of those, do the best go on to higher studies? of those, the best go into teaching? of those, into the teaching of literature? But let that pass, let that pass, said Simon Eyre.

* Reprinted from the *Sewanee Review* 55 (1947), 571–85 (first copyrighted by the University of the South).

Teachers of literature, like the rest of the profession of which they are part, and the institutions in which literature is taught, have given over one of their professional tasks in a way which would have caused chaos had it been the practice in the professions of medicine and law. When the world, the press and the parent have laughed at scholars and literary men with the scorn of "As if the students were *professionals!* they teach as if they wanted to produce another race of scholars and critics," we have laughed loud and long as earnest of our innocence, recognized that the all-round man of this particular world could make do with but two Shakespeare sonnets, added two of Millay's to relate Shakespeare's "to the student's world," and hurried off to the meeting of the Committee on Curricular Change. What wonder if the Schools of Education have taken up with alacrity the job of squaring off all our well-rounded pegs? while the Graduate School hurriedly introduces the two pegs it gets from the lot to the problem of what a sonnet can be, and do, by pouring Petrarch, Drayton and Daniel onto the ashes of two forgotten Shakespeare items? In a very true sense, *magister nascitur non fit,* but few professions try to make it happen by laughing at their own sterility. In addition to their other responsibilities, college and university English departments face—or ought to—a strict professional task, of fearsome scope and delicacy.

Willy nilly, out of "the English major" are going to come (and they may be either good or bad): *A.* scholars and critics; *B.* college teachers; *C.* the army of high-school English teachers (1. the M.A. group, 2. the rest).[1] *A* and *B* and *C* must all also be part of a group, *D,* which covers them but which *A. B. C.* does not cover: *D.* the readers of good books, for pure love. These four have one fundamental necessity in common, as far as the teaching of literature is concerned; all must *read* decently. I shall not define it now; we all mean pretty much the same thing when we say of the Freshmen, the Ph.D. candidates, the reviewers, that they simply don't know how to read. This at least, then, we can teach everyone at once without loss, and this must be taught at all costs.

[1] I do not include the creative writer, who will be and probably should be obstreperous under any system; we cannot cut our cloth to his measure partly because he never comes twice the same size. But anyhow he is probably better off, like Yeats, in walking naked. I suppose he must in these days and times take a B.A.; it should probably not be in English but in a foreign literature, in politics or fine arts or philosophy.

There are certain reasons why the costs come so high. One of these is a fact about education in a democracy which we could think of some way around, but haven't. At each stage of the educational process the push of the crowd against the gates has weakened the standards. Enjoyment (a *sine qua non;* literature by definition should and must involve pleasure) gets defined as "liking without thinking too hard"; Steinbeck and Galsworthy begin to look safer than Pope and Spenser; and the 2 in 10 who would enjoy Pope more than Steinbeck don't know he existed; grammar disappears for similar reasons, and the syntax of any sentence written as early as Dr. Johnson becomes unmanageable except via class discussion. Spenser, Pope, Johnson, including tools to read Johnson, postponed; for handling by the Graduate School. At the college under-classman level: same process, plus the hazards involved in competing with Abnormal Psych, Marriage: how to succeed in it, and Geo-Politics; the 1 out of 25 who will in five years be teaching high-school students misses grammatical discipline, and now for the last time; since "they only *get* what you discuss," excerpts supplant epics, "Three Years She Grew" supplants a good slice of *The Prelude*, *Lear* by itself supplants (and must supplant, for comprehension; I would defend it) *Lear*-in-class, *Oedipus* and part of the *Poetics* for comparison, and *Tamburlaine* to sharpen one's points for a paper. Marlowe, Sophocles, Aristotle, also ability to construe a strange poem or play by oneself, postponed; for handling by the Graduate School. At the Senior level: have those who expect to teach the next year subtract 12 hours from total time spent reading literature, for use in learning How To Teach In General. At the M.A. level: 27,000 M.A.'s were given in 1940; of these 9,500 were in Education, 900 in English; a moment's thought will produce conclusions anent "the teaching of literature." (Reading postponed to the Ph.D.)

But: whose job *was* it to train whatever proportion teaches English out of that 18-fold increase in numbers of M.A.'s? (B.A.'s for the same dates, 1900 *cf.* 1940, increased 7-fold; Ph.D.'s 9-fold).[2] It is easy to say we have little faith in

[2] See the hair-raising and frank report in *Assoc. of Amer. Universities: Journal of Proceedings*, 46th Annual Conference (1945), pp. 112ff. To one who thinks reading the literature indispensable, there is great pathos in the committee's recommendation (despairing, perhaps) that at least two-fifths of the graduate year for the M.A. in Teaching should be given to one's subject matter, and for the

what this young army got taught, and went forth to teach to others (whom we shall teach, *ai, ai,* in six more years). But who precisely is the custodian and guard responsible for maintaining those aesthetic values we think of when we talk of "the teaching of literature"? "My God, I mean my self," said George Herbert ending his poem on *Miserie.* It doesn't lower the death rate to deprecate the capacities of those doctors who rushed into the area.

There is a worse misery still. Since I have admitted that one Indispensable for the professional groups *A. B. C.* is that non-professional one of reading-well-and-for-love, we might be cheerful if the undermining of professional training (because of the mere brute fact of numbers) were accompanied by a new strengthening of that primarily aesthetic aspect. This I doubt. We have instead allowed the entrance of two new professional risks (weeds in a cultivated public as well)—the aesthetic bigot, who has read too little and too squintingly by the rush-light of a very few literary experiences, and the literary vulgarian, who has read much carelessly but little that was good enough to shake him by the roots.

I wonder if this might be true: if we took our *professional* responsibility seriously for one generation, we might be able to *teach literature to* the next one—because it could read. I should like to think out how it would hit group *C,* and then notice whether such tactics would hurt or harm *A, B* and *D.* When I began teaching, English was Outlining and Surveys (Great Tool Age), then it became Sociology (Period of Economic Man), now it is Psychology (The Author's Sensibility). It would be exhilarating for spades to be spades, for a time. We might conserve some of the discipline of the Tool Age, and some of the discussion approaches of the others, but all in the service of *English: or, the reading of mature literature, by oneself.* As in a seventeenth-century sermon, my division is word by word.

Reading: Many possible meanings of a literary work admitted, but no substitution, for inquiry into its meaning, of vague remarks

M.A. proper, three-fifths. A comparable problem: 49 institutions gave 603 Ph.D.'s in English in 1928–32. But only 27 institutions were rated as adequately equipped to give work for the Ph.D., and only 8 rated as outstandingly well equipped, by the 67 scholars in the field approached by the Amer. Council on Educ. (see its Report of Comm. on Grad. Instruction, for April 1934). Divide either 8 or 27 into 603. (Of course "adequacy" would vanish if we did so.) But those who decide, observing its possessors, that "the Ph.D." is poor preparation for teaching might consider whether they are fighting the right dragon.

on its effect; enter *explication,* the study of words, syntax, artistic structure, metrics to catch tone of voice (part of meaning). Reading with the ear of the mind included; one is thankful for recent emphasis on the fact that poetry is a craft, thankful that we can of late years remark on Milton's pitying sternness toward Man and his caesuras in the same breath. *Caveat,* that the over-efficient student can make a trick and a technique out of this too, a substitute for honest aesthetic responses of his own. Two levels of reading admitted: one extremely meticulous, and one admittedly imperfect—to learn what the world contains. The only *verboten* on either level: a separation between what's said and how. In other words, perhaps one can only read if one makes, and stands to, the hard admission that if a poem says a stupidity, its caesuras will show it; and vice versa.

Mature: The deepest, widest, maturest writers we have, and no quarter. Shakespeare, all of Milton, all of Keats, *Troilus and Criseyde,* Yeats, James, Swift—or whatever we think is greatest, but *for* that reason. This would make English the hardest course in the curriculum, unpopular with all but serious students. *Soit;* that would include the geese that can lay golden eggs. Neglect the others, for this generation. One lucky peculiarity of English departments would operate: in most colleges, the unavoidable Waterfall, "The common pass Where, clear as glass, All must descend," is the required year of English. I think we might escape detection for ten years at the outside if we applied here the same standard of intellectual maturity. By the time our colleagues discovered why 20 per cent failed and had to take a non-credit remedial course in reading, we could lose the course, having salvaged whatever percentage of students have it in them to be "quickened by this deep and rocky grave." Bury the rest (of this generation). We might even succeed with most of them if we taught these greatest works as

Literature: Literature is not the history of ideas. (Nor even the recurring of recurrent symbols.) Some young people, at least, have become hungry for plays that have plots, poems that are enchanted music, novels that people their thin world, for literature that extends their experience—but through and because of the compelling power of form. This last relation they do not realize and must be shown. Once they have learnt it, they can "read." One generation of lower-school teachers who could read Chaucer,

Spenser, Shakespeare, Milton and Eliot aloud with passion and understanding would clear up half the reading-comprehension troubles at the Freshman level. I would even reinstate learning by heart. And keep to the best metrists and prose-writers in the elementary courses, no matter what the pressures; we have tried flouting the touchstone notion and found all hands reading the COSMOPOLITAN when the lights went up. But most of all, I would remind us that a core course in great books, *where such is substituted for literature* written in English, is no substitute, but another kettle of fish entirely. In fact, it is not fish at all. It is the New Didacticism. Eight Great Books, half or a third of them in translation, is a course in Philosophy.[3] For one thing, comparison rests upon the non-formal aspects of all the writings. Literature is experience grasped *through form;* and the first essential if we would read literature is to be quiet and listen to the very words the man uttered. (This happens to be the justification for philological and literary-historical approaches to literature as well; sometimes we can hear his words no other way, but hear instead only our own pulse-beats. When by any method we can grab in our extremity the two are one, we have read the book as literature.) If we must choose, perhaps literature has a better chance with a graduate student (or a person, or a high-school teacher) who has lived in the Middle Ages through Chaucer, or in the Eighteenth Century through Boswell's Johnson, than with one who can tell us, from discussing translations of Dante and Voltaire, "what the Middle Ages thought," or the Eighteenth Century. And which of these is more likely to be roused by curiosity to learn more about the Middle Ages? to read not only Taylor and Gilson but the Gawain poet and for that matter Dante on his own? The miracle of literature is identification, living the very life of another mind; the miracles of philosophy are otherwise.

One other danger dogs both "General Education" and "Humanities courses." We want students to have a synthesis; but we forget that a man has none until he makes his own—and that this happens about *aetat.* 28–30 at earliest. Unfortunate, no doubt,

[3] Of course most good books are didactic, and all literature is a course in philosophy. But both elements had best get into a literature course by gate-crashing, since that's how they got into the books in the first place. (I should be obliged if the reader will attach to his understanding of what I mean by these disclaimers regarding the history of ideas certain later remarks, especially about p. 12).

since students prefer to get a good fashionable synthesis off the peg. Teaching is one continual fight to keep students from parroting the teacher's synthesis, or substituting our critical judgments for their own aesthetic responses, and all the other dozen apings they try—to avoid the hard, hard task of making the relations themselves. Splendidly fitted though we find ourselves for the speedy "integrating" of others, students ought in all these matters to watch a process, not secure an opinion, or erect into truth another man's set of interpretative judgments.[4] A synthesis, like an aesthetic experience, is something one has

By oneself: I suppose flesh and blood could not resist it, but surely faculties, from the high-school to the graduate level, have followed students into the Great American Delusion: "Take a course in it." It is part of the delusion that we design courses to provide their takers here and now with the end-results of reading books, instead of to point to the entrances of all the roads we know. There is a horrid logic in the fact that the greatest need to overcome the cultural lag by teaching—instead of *expecting*—a man to read his own contemporaries has been coincident with a time of least emphasis on the *past* in all our teaching. No society matches ours for willingness to keep its young people immature, but if the American middle-class parent is the egregious security-worshipper, faculties co-operate by the lowness of their expectations, not even ostracizing the non-vacation-reader. And of course if I thought that these remarks about English courses had provided for "learning to read," I should deserve to be choked with a volume of Beowulf-to-Hemingway. How read Mann without Freud, or Whitman without American history, or Donne without Augustine, or Swift without Veblen? Literature and death are not the only things a man must learn to handle alone.

Clearly I have not talked only of group *C* in all this. But I will telescope by putting in terms of our other groups—the scholars, the critics, the teachers of most advanced work—certain approaches which seem to me not at all ruled out by emphasis on

[4] As one reads the descriptions of Humanities Courses in 57 American colleges (see Francis Shoemaker, *Aesthetic Experience and the Humanities*, Columbia University Press, 1943, pp. 156ff), one cannot but sigh to think of all the "formulations" one has had to unteach, in one's time. The younger a student, the more he is at the mercy of a formulator. The fewer facts he has to fight back with, the less he is able to learn *how to make* a generalization. Of course it always looks like success when he learns to "make" ours.

that primarily aesthetic activity, reading as a concentrated form of living.

All discoveries touching instruments complicate learning. If less complexity in the data were a prime desideratum, it were a pity that microscopes and telescopes ever opened up the world at both the small and the large end. But it can never be 1590 again. Men have developed two vast new mechanisms (among others) for finding answers to that aesthetic question, "How shall I read this poet?", and we can neither throw philology and literary history into the sea, nor parcel out our microscopes to just a few selected technicians. When we have learned to use them for critical ends (and it is far too early to expect that we should have, though the process has begun), certain dimensions of criticism and certain pleasures in the reading of books will be open to us which were not open to the man of 1590. As usual, our tools will in some instances just restore something we have lost. One generation of teachers and writers (mine) came to its training likely to have no Greek; the next came unlikely to have usable Latin; if we now cut off philological training we shall have a set of scholars, critics and teachers who have less notion than ever of language *as a phenomenon.* I refer to no mere habit of using the NED, but to a consciousness of the living nature of the very medium of that art we teach and judge. Words, syntax, rhythm, the music of verse, the meaning of meaning and the genesis of concepts are something quite different to the student of linguistics than to the innocent pre-Babel mind. Learning other modern tongues is the long way around, and only a few ever get to the destination I mean by that route. Just as a person does not so much learn about the discovery of relativity as realize it, so whenever modes of thinking are in question, slow patient mastery of information is the only road (not all travellers arrive). Critical activity will suffer most if we divide "scholars" from "critics" in this connection (a division which generally makes a worse thing of both activities, anyway); one has only to think of the pits that are open before the critic ignorant of certain relativistic assumptions imposed by linguistic knowledge (examination of the sound as fitted to the sense of a Shakespeare passage, for example). Our common primary connection between mediaeval studies proper and studying "the language" has some of the impertinence of historical accident, like the selling of seedlings in a hardware store because men who need hoes come there oftenest.

There are more pasts than there once were, and this is awkward; that they are more valuable than we had thought is a fact surely but perversely dodged by those to whom beauty is a value. Too bad, some will think it, but the music of Middle English cannot be taught by saying it is beautiful. Happily no one who can read it needs to be told; but students have a right to play their Chaucer from the score, and a fiddler hired for the hour does not teach the positions. It is moreover symptomatic that one of the greatest of twentieth-century poems finds young readers of the kind a poet dreams of in a *mediaeval* literature class (because thinking of the Fisher King is experience, not hearsay, to them); we close only at our peril those doors which modern recovery of so many literary pasts has opened to those who write what we shall read. There are also those who think *Troilus and Criseyde* and *Piers Plowman* are good books, and that to be cut off from them is a deprivation.

If, as the Harvard Report says, "science is knowledge for which an exact standard of truth exists," [5] then it is as critics, again, that we have most need of being able to judge where such knowledge pertains or doesn't pertain, with respect to a given work of art. It is the man concerned with the aesthetic question of unity who needs to know all that can be scientifically known about the state of the text, the man listening to cadences or evaluating the coherence of images who must collate variants late into the night. In this palmy age we stand upon others' shoulders, but it is no service to a graduate student and future critic to let him go on thinking that he can see from where he stands. We can see *some* things just by standing erect, and where we have confused these with, or totally ignored them for, "knowledge for which an exact standard of truth exists," this has not been done by "scientists" in the profession but by those mortals-by-Puck's-definition who in every profession will do a good thing wrong. I suppose no one is against the elimination of fools from the profession of teaching literature.

From the student's side, the graduate school is the primary place (in formal training) to learn what kinds of a fool one can avoid being, as a critic. Since many can be avoided by knowing what shoulders there are to stand upon, I would sooner not use the graduate school to practice standing erect in solitude, which is slow business, and bows the legs if tried too stubbornly too soon;

[5] *General Education in a Free Society*, Harvard University Press, 1945, p. 62.

for similar practical reasons, graduate school is late in the day to look for teacher-models. I am that rarity, the student whose graduate training was satisfactory because aesthetically fructifying even to my naked eye; the great scholars I knew were great critics (I confused this combination with "being good teachers," and I am glad I did). They did not tell me the poem was beautiful; I should have been a blind idiot not to see that they thought so, and why; but they were busy as teachers with the problem of what ways there are *to see into what a thing is*. Only so can men teach what is yet to be known, as well as what they see. I owe my chance to learn what they could not tell me, or did not believe, to their reticence and disinterested passion; thank heaven their allegiance was to their authors and to learning, and not to my welfare, for this is the condition of freedom.

If philological and "scientific" training may not safely be isolated from the teaching of "reading," literary history may take its chances in this essay. Except for one point, having to do with a kind of bigotry. It is hard to learn (so hard that I have never succeeded myself with Browning or Emerson) but it is really extremely easy to teach the notion that the process of seeing what a writer could have meant is antecedent to making the decision that he meets no need of ours. Even quite brilliant students see that though Reading the Work is the great desideratum, one has not read it if one has just read oneself as of Monday 3 June into it, and they see also that one may nevertheless not for one moment stop being oneself as of Monday 3 June. They will unselfconsciously use literary history to get themselves out of this predicament, re-visiting alien times and thought with a willingness to get beyond the tourist stage which would put more self-centered older readers to shame. But another barrier to sympathetic reading is harder to counter.

The inability of this age—so vociferously proud of its belief in the "relativity" of truth—to get outside of its own relatives erected into absolutes, goes beyond any. To most readers (and I would defend this, but that is another fight), those books mean most in which they are able to contemplate and embrace certain "absolute" values; these range from pure loveliness of sound to newly understood great ideas. The range of books which act so is for an untrained reader quite narrow, for a kind of translation is necessary. I have so to construe the author that I can see his meaning in what Sidney calls its universal consideration, not in its time-bound-ness—for a poem is an historical event, took shape in a given context. This translating is the instrument by which I (who am also time-bound) can see this "relative" thing "absolutely"; one has to get past the relative both ways, and finding what the Twentieth Century takes to be absolutes, in every Milton and Donne, is a misinterpretation of this process too. But when I have found the level on which an author, retaining his integrity, *can be believed* by me—then whatever he has is mine. Metaphor is oftenest the way of it. Pure love is the condition and the instigator of this union, but it need not be marriage at first sight. Intellectual history is Pandarus.

I return, at my close, to the unhappiest point of all. To lift one's head and look about is to fear that the major obstacles to good teaching of literature lie in certain deeply entrenched characteristics of our culture. Insofar as we are a business civilization, our values are opposed to the values inherent in aesthetic experience. Literature aesthetically considered has no cash equivalent, no advertising status; it does not Get One Anywhere. There is a distribution problem for literature as for all commodities which fill human needs; but this particular need itself is flat nonsense to a society organized for and around material profits. The postulate of literature is that life is something else entirely.

Insofar as we are a technological civilization we are not opposed to but unalert to aesthetic values. There is too much to do; being is a luxury. Literature as mere relaxation is as much a contradiction in terms as literature written to sell soap. So we thunder professionally against plain enjoyment and against rhetorical persuasion, and the technologist concludes (quite rightly) that "aesthetic" must mean something-useless-but-decorative (which is what he said all along), and that all America should buy one when things loosen up a little. And this indeed it most amiably does.

Insofar as we are a society which does what is to its interest but says what it thinks sounds well (see foreign policy or social mores, any newspaper for any day) we can nourish no sound literature, nor read any, for long. If literature (except satire) were not other-worldly in a world of arrogant acts accompanied by pious disclaimers, the more shame to it; but otherworldliness can kill an art too.

Insofar as we believe only in the active life and defend the contemplative life only in terms of it, aesthetic activity, including the writing and reading of literature, loses its touch with the impulse which gave it birth (both births; all books have two, if they find a reader). Professionally alarmed, we call names at "science"—though it is born of the same impulse, as its thoughtful exponents constantly point out. Or we deride the notions of "social relevance" or "moral purpose," as if this were not the finite world, and as if contemplation could ever end in a state of pure rest in the realm of imperfections. So we assist the break we thought to mend, and squabble with those whose glue we do not like, or who are working on some other tear in the fabric.

Insofar as we are a culture with a push-button conception of the human mechanism, the whole set of our life is inimical to aesthetic experience. "It is expected that they will be able to find the formula tomorrow morning," say the reports of our deliberations upon the most delicate problems of political and economic difference. "Push the right button and you can chart the human reaction" is no merely American delusion, yet if there are no traces of it in this essay, I am no American.

These and like limitations of the modern mind are the most serious obstacles to "the teaching of literature." These are the Common Enemy—yet like most groups not in the ascendant (like most liberals, 1947), we find more stimulating our fights with each other. Teacher against scholar, humanist against scientist, scholar against critic, the pot calling the kettle "mere" is the scrap that has life in it, that sells the book, re-hires the instructor, makes a man a hero among his own kettles. That there is pedantry among scholars, superficiality among critics, technique-worship among scientists, personality-mongering among teachers, who is not aware? But who is for it? Least of all those in the baskets wherein these staler eggs get put, looking as they do so much like other eggs. Perhaps the "teaching of literature" would be served if we dropped these groupings in American intellectual life, spoke to a man's arguments instead of to his coterie or position, paid each other the compliment of disagreement without malice, and fought instead the forces that are out and out against the love and understanding of literature. These forces are not weak; nor few.

AAUW Fellows and Their Survival*

I INTEND to talk about something which I grant no human being can achieve with any great degree of perfection, but which every human being I respect, up and down the recorded centuries, has believed in and does believe in. And I include the present company among those to whom I give this respect—for there is no conceivable other reason for working for the fellowship cause. I refer to that strange and passionate human belief: that it is necessary and good to look for the truth about things.

The American Association of University Women has put that value high. In your fellowship program you have found a means of sending out scouts where one cannot go in person, in the hope that later all men will benefit by any pushing back of the boundaries of the unknown which surrounds us on all sides—whether this unknown be the nature of the physical world, which the natural scientist investigates; the nature of man's mind, of his institutions and their success or failure, which the historian, the psychologist, the social scientist, investigates; or the nature and the validity of man's answers to his question, "what is worth doing?"—which the artist, the philosopher, the man of letters investigates.

The scouts sent out ahead by the AAUW fellowship program may not be Shakespeares or Leonardos, nor Einsteins nor Toynbees—but they are busy about the same affair. Those who send them out have discovered ways of taking advantage of those moments in some human life when the gift of a little time and a little peace can clear off just space enough to make it possible for someone to find out what the human race will be better off for knowing, or to understand better and thus give a second life to those beautiful things which the human race is better off for looking at.

The gift of Time and Peace is not a small gift. For me it meant not only a year with the illuminated manuscripts of Oxford and London, a year in an Oxford college to which I still fully belong, and twenty years later went back to live in, asked to come as a colleague and member of the Senior Common Room whenever I can.

* Reprinted from the *Journal of the American Association of University Women* 44 (1951), 201–208.

It meant also a year in an Oxford college where now English friends of mine have established a scholarship that Americans may come yearly to study—and who knows what scores of English young people and what scores of American students of mine or any of the others, may have different and truer ideas of a nation they must work with on the world's business, because the AAUW has a fellowship program? Bread upon the waters.

A firm belief in the free search for knowledge as an undisputed human good is behind the fellowship program of the American Association of University Women or any other group which promotes scholarship. But there is one necessity without which a fellowship program will fall to pieces, however wonderfully supported. We might announce tomorrow that we had two millions instead of one, and it would be simply of no use whatever without one essential: *you must have fellows.*

THE 1950–51 roster of 32 fellows of the American Association of University Women is a superb proclamation of faith in the worth-whileness of what those human beings represent and will try to do. But your one million or your two will be dead cash, and all those hours you spent in committee, running the benefit performances, planning the fellowship bridges, all will be wasted, gone down the drain—unless those human beings appear year by year, willing and capable and prepared to believe in and carry on the human adventure of the search to know, and to contemplate.

These human beings in whom you put your faith can neither be produced nor can they later bring their researches to maturity, to enrich the common life, without a society which also respects the values we have spoken of. Without such a society the fellows will simply not come to your net, ready to use your gift of Time and Peace. And on the other side of your crucial year, they will peter out, dwindle, cease to be those human emissaries into the undiscovered countries still hid to the human mind, which we have envisaged.

What kind of a society produces persons whose primary devotion is to that peculiarly human aim which we have called the desire to know truly? And what kind of a society does it take to provide them later with a growing-place, in which to replant the seeds, to bear yet more fruit in later generations? Not a society which puts power ahead of knowledge. Not a society which puts pragmatic efficiency ahead of seeing into the nature of the mystery. Not a society which puts doing things to others ahead of being something ourselves. Not a primarily profit-seeking set of citizens. Not a society whose voice is the voice of the advertiser, and whose technical achievements are put with greatest lavishness and least opposition to the service of two aims: the body's comfort, and the destruction of other human creatures and their societies and their beliefs.

Ask yourself whether in your community the life of the mind and the spirit is the good life primarily put before young people as the richest and most satisfying kind of a life to live. Whether its austerities are admitted and defended, to them. Whether in your newspapers, over your radio, at the dinner tables up and down your shady streets, the men and women of your town who have dedicated their energies to knowledge—or to power?—are those who are regarded with most pride as the town's First Citizens, its reason for considering itself an important city.

What newer American city would you name which is thought important because an *idea* was born in it? Yet behind every one of the world's imperishable cities there lies not pre-eminently an industry, nor a marvelously well planned shopping center, nor a vigorous Chamber of Commerce, but some idea, and some group of devoted men who lived, and sometimes died, to make it live.

A nation's assumptions regarding what is important, like a person's, are not always to be found in its public statements. Take one day and live it with this question in your mind. Read and listen to every word that comes into your house, printed or by radio or television; look closely at every street you pass down; and consider the implications of every conversation you have with every sort of person. At the end of that sample 24 hours, see if you can honestly claim that our society has a firm and active belief in the life of the mind, and the power of truth to make men free.

Our anti-intellectualism does not hurt first and most those who have already chosen to devote themselves to the cause of learning and the pursuit of truth. Plato, Aristotle, Dante, Spenser, Pascal, would do their work as lovingly as ever, in that small place which American society reserves for "intellectuals," for the poet, the philosopher, the thinker, even the teacher. They would not mind the snubs in the newspapers about ivory towers, "mere" theorists, and Classroom Liberals. These worthies would not mind not being serialized; or not being asked to do *The Divine Comedy* or *The Faerie Queene* for Hollywood; or not being able to keep a 15-minute commentator's place on any major network (as they assuredly could not). Aristotle would take it very lightly when he was told that those who cannot do, teach. Milton would be much crosser, when his sponsor decided that his opinions were too dangerous to allow him longer to represent pickles or soup—but it would never stop him from writing the next poem.

No, it is not they who would suffer. It is society that suffers. It suffers because in not honoring and imitating its learned men it emasculates them; it takes from them their chance to gain the ear of other men, especially of the young, and thus to produce other Platos, other Galileos, other Dantes and Miltons and Goethes.—And other AAUW fellows, and other AAUW fund-raisers. For a society which does not honor the life of the mind will cease to produce men who engage in it.

The largest reason why this happens is a very subtle one, very hard to correct. Good young people go less and less into the learned professions and the pursuit of truth because the motive which takes people into such endeavors can easily be killed before it has a chance to stir. That motive is not self-interest. It is disinterested passionate devotion to something larger than oneself. One of the tragedies of modern Western thought lies in the way we have come to believe this is more than can be expected of the human being.

The motives we confidently expect a human being to act upon you are surely very familiar with. The desire for advancement. Adjustment to the group, to ensure popularity. The desire to come out first in a competitive race. Prestige. Power. When these motives produce scholars, they do not produce good scholars.

"It is a poor centre of a man's actions, himself," says Bacon; "it is right earth." Plain dirt, he meant. He is using the medieval and Renaissance cliché, of earth as the least noble of the four elements. He probably had not forgotten (though he took it no more literally than we do) that God made Adam of a handful of dust, as far as his body is concerned. But before that body had anything in it that could make it care even to get up and go look at one of the roses of Paradise to call it pretty, He breathed into it the nobler element of air, the spirit which forever after was an inextricable motivating part of it.

THE Middle Ages and the Renaissance and the Reformation are often accused of an unfortunate dualism, dividing off the body from the soul and worshipping the soul. It often seems to me that we make a far more violent dualism by our notion that body and body's self-centered demands come first in time. We assume that we first feed and clothe body and buy overstuffed sofas and twenty-dollar toasters for it, and after that it sits down freed from tensions, rings in its spirit side, and thinks. But it thinks during, not after the comfort-buying, self-centered getting process. And its thought will be, "These are good things, these matter most." "Oh, come down to earth; how can a fellow think on an uncomfortable chair? Don't be a visionary with your head in the clouds."

Where have the heads been, that gave men what they most value: their conceptions of love and courage, of good and bad; music, poetry, and all the arts; their faiths and their sciences, their belief that man can see beyond his own need to the needs of others? In the clouds, expecting too much—and getting it.

We have vastly underestimated the human being's spiritual capacities, wantonly centralizing him around his less humane needs and desires. And one form of this underestimation is the assumption that the main way to appeal to him is through his self-interest, that he has little capacity for disinterested devotion to something larger than himself.

No other motive than this last can produce a decent scholar. Moreover, it is too late even by the time he gets to college. The conception of a devoted and unselfish search for what is true because truth is a good, is not possible to a young person who has grown up in communities, in homes, in schools, reading magazines and ads, wherein the expected human motives are: Desire for advancement. Adjustment to the group, to ensure popularity. The desire to come first in a competitive race. Prestige. Power. These describe with woeful incompleteness the possible motivations of the human being—yet this incomplete human being we are coming to accept. He will be no scholar. He will give his energy to no fund-raising.

The methods which accompany these motives are equally unsuitable to the pursuit of truth. "Get in on the ground floor." "Win friends and influence people." "Find out what the person you have to please wants." "Look a little better than you are."

The acceptability of such motives and such methods—by very

many of my students, for example, who come from such communities and from the social stratum which you and I too represent—is a sad but an accurate commentary on the extent to which our society is giving up its firm and active belief in the life of the mind as a good life, and in the power of truth, even such relative truth as we can grasp, to make men free.

Perhaps one of the most shocking evidences of our growing disbelief in the power of man to come closer to the truth by inquiry is the growing number of cases in which freedom of scholarly inquiry is being denied even in that last haven of such freedom, the American college and university. Academic freedom is not only under fire; there have been some deaths.

At California, members of an entire faculty were asked to sign not only a loyalty oath upholding the Constitution, which they did, but an oath of conformity as regards political beliefs and affiliations, and refusal to sign the latter was judged by the Regents as justifying dismissal. In other words, those whose stated business it is to examine the validity of ideas, rather than simply to embrace sets of ideas as absolutes certainly established, were asked to swear conformity of belief before being considered fit to examine ideas with their students.

THEY were asked to do so by regents or trustees, representatives of a state (though a state to which they had already sworn loyalty). Not asked to swear conformity of belief by an institution like a church, the nature of which gives it some right to claim access to absolute truth through revelation, but by a state—an institution which, unless it tries also to be a religion, has no basis for such a claim. A man-made institution can never hope to transcend the necessarily fallible set of truths it once found, if even those whose job it is to watch for the possibility of errors in those supposed truths are asked first and foremost for conformity.

The relevance of all this to our present point lies in the fact that it is direct evidence of a growing disbelief in the capacity of man's combined rational powers to get at what is true, by looking, always with freedom to see what he sees.

I have seen no rising up of public opinion in the great mass of the college-educated American public, to protest against these cases where adults must be certified conformers before they can teach even other adults. We have advanced to a point where our people no longer dare say with John Milton—

> And though all the winds of doctrine were let loose to play upon the earth, so Truth be in the field, we do injuriously by licensing and prohibiting to misdoubt her strength. Let her and Falsehood grapple; who ever knew Truth put to the worse in a free and open encounter?

The demand for conformity, and the narrowing and vulgarizing of our conceptions of man's possible motivations to action, which we examined earlier, are both forms of disbelief in man's rational powers. Both have invaded the very centers of learning. As an example of how the notion of measurable profit to oneself as the only sure appeal has come to characterize even the thinking of people within educational institutions I would quote from a recent article in the *Bulletin* of the American Association of University Professors, stressing the need for "salesmanship" for higher education:

> The public relations task of higher education—in common with all public education—is to reach each individual citizen and convince him of the significance and importance of education to him in terms of his own self-interest, and thus persuade him to protect and to pay for education.[1]

This "self-interest" phrase crept into this author's defense of "public relations"; he did not really mean quite this. But why did it creep in, and why is the American citizen assumed to be only movable if as for a donkey you can hold up a carrot that he himself is going to be able to grab? When did we decide that the American citizen can only see as donkeys see, move for the reasons donkeys do? I do not believe it.

I am now going to say something shocking, and you may mistake my full meaning. I shall have to run the risk, for I have not time to be careful.

Those AAUW fellows, year by year in the many years to come, are to be women. There is a new set of reasons why those women may not be there, asking for your awards. Women's education already suffers more than does men's from this danger of assuming that human beings are not capable of being motivated by disinterested devotion to the finding out of what is true. And it suffers more from the danger of an underlying assumption that the intel-

[1] Scott M. Cutlip, "Effective Public Relations for Higher Education," *Bulletin* of the American Association of University Professors, Vol. 36, No. 4 (Winter 1950).

lectual life, however rich, is somehow merely tangential when we are thinking of a full life for the whole personality, that the life of the mind is somehow a pretty thin thing.

It suffers more for many reasons: because women, who bear the children of a society, must in fewer numbers devote themselves gainfully to the professional pursuit of knowledge; because modern thinking has not learned how to make intellect and emotion mutually serviceable but divides people into these two parts as though thoughts and drives were forever occupied in a tug-of-war with each other; and most relevantly of all perhaps, because vulgarized and misconceived notions of modern psychology have often led to defining the Good Life primarily as the biologically normal life.

The abnormality, for the human creature, of a life in which biological satisfactions permanently bear the burden of making a complex personality satisfied, is not regarded. Granted that for women the usual way of satisfying certain basic needs, including that of being of use in her society, is through bearing and training children, which is a biological function even more obviously than it is a social contribution and a moral responsibility. But the net result of the modern over-emphasis on the human being as a biologically functioning animal has been to think of women, and make young women think of themselves, as so first and foremost female that they are lucky if they can squeeze in even an occasional glimpse of themselves as human beings, with all the complicated reasons-for-being that any fully alive human being has.

You would be shocked to the teeth if you knew the extent to which the young women I see every day have been pressed by their society toward a state of fairly constant anxiety for fear they may fail at achieving this *sine qua non.* Never taught by this society to see that being a success as a woman is inextricably connected with being a success as a human being, and beaten on by advertisements, competing other girls, parents, movies, radio, magazines, and their own need to see themselves as up to whatever the others can do, they inevitably translate all these pressures into one: *capture him.* Marriage is the immediate hurdle, though engagement will do to show that one is not on the road to failure.

This emphasis on a single standard of personal success is not only injurious to the 25 percent or so of women graduates who will not marry; it is out of square with the stage of development of many who will. They are all interested in men and they all should be. But they are not yet ready, any more than men of seventeen to twenty-one, to bend everything toward the focal point of a home and children. That is why they translate these pressures into the one form in which they do honestly experience them—capturing someone.

The compulsions are for many more outer than inner, and more related to prestige than to satisfaction of basic needs, and they work to deprive young women of a right we should give to every human being—the right to find out what the human responsibilities are, what human beings have thought and done and hoped and created, and how to be a good one.

It is obvious that this pressure in women's education to stress women's sex more than their humanity, pushes them regardless of individual endowment toward one particular mode of creativity before they have even found out what kinds there are, or tested their own capacity for two or three kinds. And one of the kinds we thus deliberately close to them too early is that adventurous discovery of truth which I have called the peculiarly human adventure. How should they know what it is if they are never with seriousness called upon to think of themselves as possible sharers in it?

There are signs that this modern form of the old attempt to fit women's education to their particular sex instead of to their basic humanity is becoming especially prevalent in precisely the quarters where it can do most harm. I pick up a book by a women's-college president, and find that curricula should be remolded to place primary emphasis upon "a truly feminine higher education." That government, for example, should be taught "in a woman's way," i.e. "in terms of how one gets specific jobs done through political machinery at the local, state, national and international levels, with plenty of case histories." I find that this truly feminine higher education will highlight all practical skills—everything from cooking and ceramics to costume design—partly on the ground that we have taught literature in colleges because we thought that "cookery" was more "elementary" than the study of literature. A ground which seems to me a kind of bogus democracy, assuming that all subjects of study are on an equal footing regardless of whether they do or do not deal directly (as literature does, for instance) with the deepest questions man faces, his reason for being and his values and motives and spiritual possibilities.

This is not unrelated to a salient error in Western thinking—that techniques are wisdom and that know-how can save. We forget that knowing how to do still leaves one utterly at sea as to how to pick what it is best to do. This is what man so desperately needs to know, and what some subjects deal with.

A new danger confronts us when this prevalent error of substituting training for a true education in reflecting upon the meaning of human life is to be integrated into the college experience of half the young people of a nation—the half which most of all educates both sexes in their impressionable years on this very matter of what human life can mean. The prospect of a nation whose college-educated mothers have been siphoned off and taught (my verbs are quoted) to "cherish" and "conserve" existing values, who have been denied the tools of thought which enable human beings to criticize and transcend existing values, by our substituting for such values, skills and techniques, is to me a dismaying spectacle.

No MATTER how much lip service we pay to breadth and depth—and Mr. Lynn White duly pays it in the book I have been quoting from, *Educating Our Daughters*—there is only so much space and time in any young person's four years. Moreover, the second ground (besides their value and dignity as skills) on which this book is ready to substitute various techniques for the ancient truth-seeking and truth-examining disciplines in the "distinctively feminine higher education" is a much hoarier assumption, concerning the difference between men's and women's minds. It will be apparent to you if I tell you that the reason implied for girls having done less well at analyzing a certain poem than boys, is this: "Of all the ways of using words, poetry is *the most abstract.*" . . . Women succeed better in writing novels than other things because it is "the least abstract" form. Our girls will feel equal to men only in "an intellectual atmosphere" where cultural creativity is not too much stressed; rather it is important to encourage "those who wish to conserve, as well as those who wish to originate, what is good, true, beautiful, useful and holy."

There go your AAUW fellows, because there goes your conception that women naturally are interested to know what is true, to contemplate, to use the mind as an instrument for originating, for the discovery of truth—simply because the human mind is ineradicably given to thinking it is good to know, and to know truly.

The signs of abdication of the human creature as the thinker are very numerous and widespread, but they are very tiny, each by itself the merest straw in the wind. In conclusion, therefore, I plead that you do something besides raise fellowships, difficult and valuable as that is. Raise future fellows too, and make a society in which they can both be born and be useful. Talk to the young people you know as if every human being were capable of passionate devotion to something bigger than himself. Somewhere in every young person there is a desire to find that something and pursue it—expect it of him. And of her. Have the courage to emphasize the austere side of study. We vastly underestimate the austerity young people will embrace if they see that they are needed, and that disciplined knowledge in any area is so valuable, and society so stuck for decent workers, that every ounce of responsible and well trained strength they can put behind some wheel is desperately needed. Ask them to take more responsibility than you think they can take; they will rise to meet it.

And here comes a string of little straws-in-the-wind set in motion not by any AAUW fellowship fund raiser, but perhaps by her neighbor. I will call your neighbor Mamie. Please work on Mamie. Don't let Mamie throw off on professors. If Mamie doesn't honor teaching as a profession, why doesn't she? Don't let Mamie make fun of Ph.D. thesis subjects. Some are more important than others, but neither you nor I nor Mamie knows which, and human curiosity is the safest guide to what might be worth learning.

Tell Mamie to remain shocked at what we pay teachers as compared say with owners of cleaning establishments—and to do something about it. The best teacher is a learner too, and if Mamie is caught up by the current tendency to oppose "good teacher" to "research," tell her to stop and think and not let herself say it, or you'll drop her, being a friend of scholars and fellows. Don't let Mamie talk to young women as if they had to choose between marrying and caring intensely about scholarship. If this society cannot evolve ways to let women both bear children and bear ideas, we have come to a poor pass. And for heaven's sake, get Mamie to drop the cliché "career woman." A "career man" is a thing to run from.

There's lots more to be done on Mamie, but I'm leaving her to you. For this is addressed to those who already believe in and support the adventure of learning. If you belong to a PTA, or if your AAUW branch can have influence, ask the schools to teach the basic disciplines. The future enquirers into the truth of things are in that schoolroom full of children; guard their chance to master the tools that will help them. If you belong to any poor soul who's still in school or college, tell them you wouldn't for anything have missed Dr. A., that stimulating teacher, but tell them that you'd give two years of your life if you hadn't missed X and X and X, those stimulating subjects. For teachers help, or hinder, but it's subjects students have to learn to be set on fire by—the things learned and learnable, and the very ideal itself of being excited by learning the truth about something.

I could count the years in which any seventeen-year-old has come into my classes already prepared from school and home with the conception of cooperating with me to find out something true, preparing herself to be an active and forceful unit in this whole great cooperative human endeavor, and already regarding herself as a responsible, adult part of the adventure. That idea is news to them. This is a travesty. And an injustice to these students. It is done by just the clichés you have heard so often: "It's the best four years of your life, don't work too hard." "Contacts, of course the studying is only part of it." Of course it is. But it's the part at the center.

If we give up belief in true knowledge, that is in the controlling human personality, humble before what it cannot know and control, but not the slave of its own controllable insufficiencies, and if we supplant this ancient human faith by the equally ancient human heresy, belief in power, we may simply go down in defeat before those whose belief in their ideas will give them a spiritual power we lack.

As one of the fellows who has benefited by your allegiance to this faith in the peculiarly human search, the search to know—humbly but still with hope—what is true and therefore good, my charge to you would be: do not give it up, even in the littlest things, do not give it up. Wherever you can, help to make this society one which will produce better and wiser fellows for you to endow, and one in which these fellows, women or men, can serve this cause without apology and without fear.

The Race Not to the Swift*

THIS is not my kind of speech. In fact, the only way I can reconcile myself to being here is to remind us both that it certainly is not I that the AAUW is honoring. The achievements to which the award's title refers were completed, in the case of this award, at latest by 1675.

Bacon says in that great treatise, *The Advancement of Learning*, which he wrote in 1605 to persuade King James to look into the parlous state of studies in the England of that time:

> it may be truly affirmed, that no kind of men love working for itself but those that are learned; for other persons love it for profit, as an hireling, that loves the work for the wages, or for honour, as because it beareth them up in the eyes of men, and refresheth their reputation; . . . or because it exercisesth some faculty wherein they take pride, and so entertaineth them in good humour and pleasing conceits towards themselves;—or because it advanceth any other their ends. . . . Only learned men love working as an action according to nature, taking pleasure in the action itself, and not in the purchase.

Now I do not agree with Bacon, that learned men are the only ones who do things for the sake of what is done, not for the sake of the doer. But I do think that with our competitive emphasis, our worship of "enterprise" and our exaltation of "ambition" (a sin, not a virtue, in the age I study), and with our blind over-attention to individual rewards, we have come close to making the values of the tradesman, the buyer and seller of goods, obtain almost in every province save that of tonight's subject—"The Pursuit of Truth." They will never obtain there. You cannot buy one ounce of "truth." The man whose thoughts are bought cannot think.

There is in all thinking a thinker involved, who cannot be both a thinker and a reward-getter, and may as well face the fact early that he is going to have to choose the former, or else become only the latter.

This does not mean that we cannot support thinking with mate-

*Reprinted from the *Journal of the Association of University Women* 49 (1955), 23–27.

rial aids—only that if the material aids cost anything, you'll get farther in the end without them. No money in the wide world can produce Dr. Salk's idea; or the sense of responsibility and devotion that led him to take the steps that brought him to it.

At the heart of every discovery and every piece of scholarship there is one key ingredient or component: an indispensable human mind, working without thought of reward or gain or of anything except finding out. Lose this, and no amount of money can buy you another. The most shocking aspect of the Oppenheimer case was the attitude taken in some remarks by persons in authority, that one could just go out and buy another Oppenheimer somewhere. It doesn't happen. The very sensitivity and super-honesty that more vulgar minds find dangerous in such an open and questioning intelligence may be the very quality without which we should for generations miss out on what that intelligence could find.

The saving grace in the whole situation is the one I think illustrated in, for one thing, the AAUW's Fellowship Program. You don't give money to people in whom you have faith. You give it to the thing they have faith in because you have faith in it too. It isn't that we have faith in Dr. Salk; our faith lies in that marvelous orderliness of reality, by virtue of which we are led to believe that there is a cause behind that effect we call polio, that there is a rational structure into which the questing mind of man, who has his rational side, can unwearyingly search, until he comes upon that which is our tonight's subject: the truth that will free him.

It is this common belief, held by both supporter and worker, that there is such a thing as truth, and that man should put all lesser considerations in a lower place and go out and look for it—this is the faith that has enabled man to find out things.

The zeal to find things out is reborn with every new human being—but it is easily squelched and easily perverted. It is not the major motive of our culture. It is not even as characteristic a motive in ours as it has been in many others. I would emphasize again that you can get along for a while without everyone who supports learning having this zeal, but you can't get along overnight without workers who have it. The only way a worker can hang onto it is that society's support to the inquiry into truth comes as an absolutely free gift—given not to some thinker for something he does in return but simply put back into the common pool to ensure that learning and the pursuit of truth should not vanish from the world.

This is what I mean by saying that the achievements your award recognizes are certainly not achievements of the person to whom you are entrusting the grant. The achievements were in this case put into the world, to make it a better one, by at least the seventeenth century. You are supporting the poetry of Edmund Spenser, John Milton, the religious poets of the late Middle Ages and the seventeenth century, the beautiful prose and the profoundly humane ideas of Francis Bacon and John Donne and Sir Philip Sidney.

There is even a sense in which we cannot "give" to men of this size, who have done things of the magnitude and the loveliness that these have done. We but give them their due. We announce our gratefulness that they in their day put all lower considerations in a lesser place, and served the things of the spirit. And we try to make it possible for what they left to go on in its centuries-long habitual way of enriching the lives of those who read them.

THERE is no paying for some things. You just give money away, and hope that some of what you give will keep the evils of impermanence from attacking the things that are permanent and inviolable. For these things can get hidden from men if they do not look out. The permanent things can get lost if no one takes care.

Scholars in the fields I represent keep our past alive. And it is true that without a past a human race, like a human being, is a poor thin thing. Consider your own life, and see. Imagine yourself confined to thoughts of your own thinking, religions of your own finding, symphonies of your own writing, language of your own inventing, landscapes of your own pruning, even trees of your own planting. So the human race itself. And in my kind of area some of the things most necessary to be kept alive are not the kind of thoughts or beauties we would naturally think or see, but the ones unpopular in our times, the ones that don't look self-evident, the unfashionable points of view and the kind of tastes that aren't in the current magazines.

One of the results of this is that intellectuals generally support what looks useless to others. What earthly difference does it make if I don't know exactly what form Spenser read a mediaeval romance in? Only this, that I might make some tiny little error in trying to figure out how he got in the habit of using romance situations to symbolize certain important moral problems.

And am I going to make a big contribution to literature and morals by knowing this? Not at all. I'm going to see whether some ideas about symbols and allegory that came out in somebody's book nineteen years ago, and which I've been gradually questioning over a period of eighteen years, might need a little adjusting and correcting. That little adjusting might turn out to make us realize that the great power of allegory in the Middle Ages results from the fact that allegories were understood as vast metaphors, not little old Bunyan-like picture-language tricks. When we understand that, we read the great Spenserian metaphors as figures of our own state, and suddenly he is more beautiful than he ever was, and more gripping.

But this is much too useful for my purposes as an example. Doing something of which I myself can see the moral and aesthetic uses, right in my own lifetime—that doesn't take much devotion. The far more usual situation is that scholars look up things they don't know the precise usefulness of either, just because they want to know them. I would warn you, if I didn't think you knew it already and acted on it, that this odd activity is what you have to work your fingers to the bone getting money to give away for. Your faith has to be in the great postulate that there are relations between things which it's good for us to find out, because in the great super-web of truth, especially historical truth (what did really happen and what was it like?), a knowledge of multitudinous relations will sometime lead someone to see *pattern.*

To see that pattern, significance, what we call "meaning"—that is the end, in itself.

You can't sell a "meaning" in the market; yet you know yourself that those moments when you have suddenly thought you came upon something of the significance of life are precious beyond rubies. That is the human experience par excellence.

Your only safe emissary into that endless adventure of finding the things that sometime may lead to the meanings is the curious person. He will be one who doesn't care whether things are useful or not—he just wants to know. He has a different definition of "useful"; a thing feels useful to him if it's something he can know for sure. He simply enjoys that. Scholars, and children, and students, and artists aren't so "all-fired sure" of what is useful as other people in a society are. So this makes for struggles and fights.

I WOULD assume that this group does not belong in that segment of our society which raises the old bogey of "Ivory Tower." The scholar who doesn't live in an ivory tower at least part of every day is likely to lose sight of the ideals that make him a thinker, and also to see no more than everyone else can see, down on the plain, of what life can be. I should think most of you are anxious that at least professors in universities and colleges give your young people some notion of what can be seen in and from the Tower of Ivory, some notion of what it means to transcend this small and transitory life, how a man can get past being "confined and pestered in this pinfold here." "And be not conformed to this world: but be ye transformed by the renewing of your mind, that ye may prove what is that good, and acceptable and perfect, will of God."

Who ever thought we could get at the true nature of the good by staying down in the rabbit-warren of what looks to our century as if it would be useful? The man with a real tower of ivory, whence he can evaluate truly some of the fake towers that fall so unexpectedly, doesn't need to go to a mental hospital to get over the shock of seeing towers fall. It's the nature of non-ivory towers to fall. But their glory is that they copy the ivory ones.

So I take it for granted that this group understands about the so-called "uselessness" of knowledge that doesn't look useful. And supports that knowledge against its detractors. But it can be very annoying when the intellectual, the scholar and artist, has this seemingly irresponsible attitude toward getting the work of the world done. You call her up to serve on a rummage-sale committee. "Oh, I haven't got time." This is part of the price. If society wants to see farther than its own nose, it has to value and support those who "haven't got time" to do what looks like their duty, because they are hell-bent on finding out what exactly Abraham Fleming said about Virgil's Eclogues in his translation of the mid 1500's.

Because although a great deal is made of old Nero fiddling

while Rome burned, it is essential that someone fiddles while cities burn. I grant you that if Nero were responsible for the fire and for not curbing it, I see some evil in his violin, but by and large unless we dedicate ourselves to the principle that somebody has to keep on with the violin instead of waiting till the fires are out, we won't have any cities worth saving. "Life," naked and unqualified, isn't valuable. What life? Beetles have life. So—

~ *Point 1.*—Scholars, artists, writers, and intellectuals generally are an annoyance to their society because they do what looks useless, and may even prove to be so, who knows. If your faith is real, support them.

I cannot help interpolating that the support I should best like would be: produce some to carry on. The lack of devoted students is one of the major causes of inanition in college faculties. They don't have anybody who values what they value. Who cares about helping a student to get a grade, to satisfy a parent? That is only, in Wordsworth's phrase, to become, as a teacher (that is, a senior student) "the witless shepherd who persists to drive . . . A flock that thirsts not to a pool disliked." I will not do it; I have too much respect for my pool. It is a common complaint; we want students who don't want to get somewhere, who don't care what is thought of them, who simply like to study. Parents, and all early teachers, can produce them. Without any, scholarship will die, and money will not save it.

I think myself that this is part and parcel of a larger problem. The disinterestedness that produces scholars produces also the great humanitarians, the great helpers of others. It all comes out of the same root: a generous unself-centered vision of the thing outside one, from which one stands to gain nothing—merely to pitch in and do what one was made to do. They used to put this more simply: Man is created for the glory of God. Is there some nobler end?

~ *Point 2.*—This kind of eccentric nonconformist behavior annoys, in an acquisitive, materialistic, individualistic culture like our own. . . . There is not much to wonder at in the fact that the old friendship between Scholar and Student, between old enthusiast and young neophyte, is becoming a thing we meet chiefly in memoirs. Friendship disregards age, but it does require common zeal to pursue common ends, love of the same things.

Scholars on campuses do not want disciples; they want co-workers, young minds who do not want to be told what to like and do, but out of love for the same things pitch in to pursue truth in their way.

Not all the "faculty-student relations" busy work in the world can produce this comradeship—and since most young students now ask a faculty member to be another parent (to guide, reassure, help, cherish when bumped), the scholar backs off. This is not only because he thinks nineteen-year-olds should cherish their own bumps, or at most ask it of each other. It is because he knows that only love of the subject will produce decent work. Love of the professor's approval produces nothing; an empty B here and there. Because it is a veiled form of love-of-self.

A scholar is only a student; he likes all true fellow-students —those are whom he should like. He will nourish them in his bosom, feed them of his dish, and give them of his drink. The present tendency to ask him to nourish everybody in his bosom, fellow-students or not, is only going to result in crowded bosoms, and no ewe lamb in the end.

~ *Point 3.*—Scholarship is the slowest form of productive work known to man. Nothing is more usual than that one throws the work of a year right down the drain. Not that there isn't a residuum; one of your ideas may have moved over from northwest to north-northwest. Besides, you enjoyed doing the work, so what matter if there are no results that show? But there is always a judge sitting ready to say, after eight months of hard labor and giving up your swim and your dinner: "No. Not good enough. Probably not true. Scrap it." That judge is oneself.

This sounds like frustration; it isn't at all. It is exhilarating. The pursuit which is the subject of this evening's examination is the race Milton spoke of when he said he could not praise a fugitive and cloistered virtue, unexercised and unbreathed, that never sallies out and sees her adversary, but slinks out of the race where that immortal garland is to be run for, not without dust and heat.

Hence this kind of thoughtless spouting tonight is just not my kind of thing. I prefer dust and heat. I wish to run after the immortal garland—not to wear it, heaven forbid such presumption —just to run after it, and put one flower straight that might otherwise fall and get trampled. I have complete faith in the immortality of the garland, and in the value to mankind of those who do wear it.

Milton himself is one. He began to plan his greatest epic in the early 1640's, having trained himself to be such a man as could write one, from about 1620 onward; he lived a full political life in Cromwell's commonwealth, blinded himself knowingly writing the *Defensio pro Populo Anglicano* (the defense of the action of the English people in bringing their king to judgment), began the writing of his epic poem, blind, continued it though meanwhile witnessing the complete failure of all he had spent his political life to bring about, and published it in 1667.

Then along about 1955 the AAUW added their recognition of his achievement by an award that honors his devotion and his poetry, among others of his time and craft.

He needed no reward; he had it. We can give him nothing, can only recognize with gratitude what he gave us. For he did nothing for honor, his motives were the same time-honored ones that are still the true motives of any scholar. I shall read them as Bacon said them, stating the false ones and the true, the incomplete ones and the full:

> But the greatest error of all the rest is the mistaking or misplacing of the last or furthest end of knowledge. For men have entered into a desire of learning and knowledge, sometimes upon a natural curiosity and inquisitive appetite—as if there were sought in knowledge a couch whereupon to rest a searching and restless spirit. Sometimes to entertain their minds with variety and delight—a terrace for a wandering and variable mind to walk up and down with a fair prospect. Sometimes for ornament and reputation, and sometimes to enable them to victory of wit and contradiction—as if there were sought in knowledge a tower of state for a proud mind to raise itself upon, or a fort or commanding ground for strife and contention. And most times for lucre and profession—as of a shop for profit and sale. And seldom sincerely to give a true account of their gift of reason, to the benefit and use of men—for this is knowledge truly, a rich storehouse for the glory of the creator and the relief of man's estate.

This then is what I assume you and I honor tonight—nothing we possess or achieve, but something we know exists and have seen men die for in the past: knowledge, a storehouse of truth that attests to the glory of its creator, and that asks every student old or young to give account of his gift of reason to the benefit and relief of man's estate.

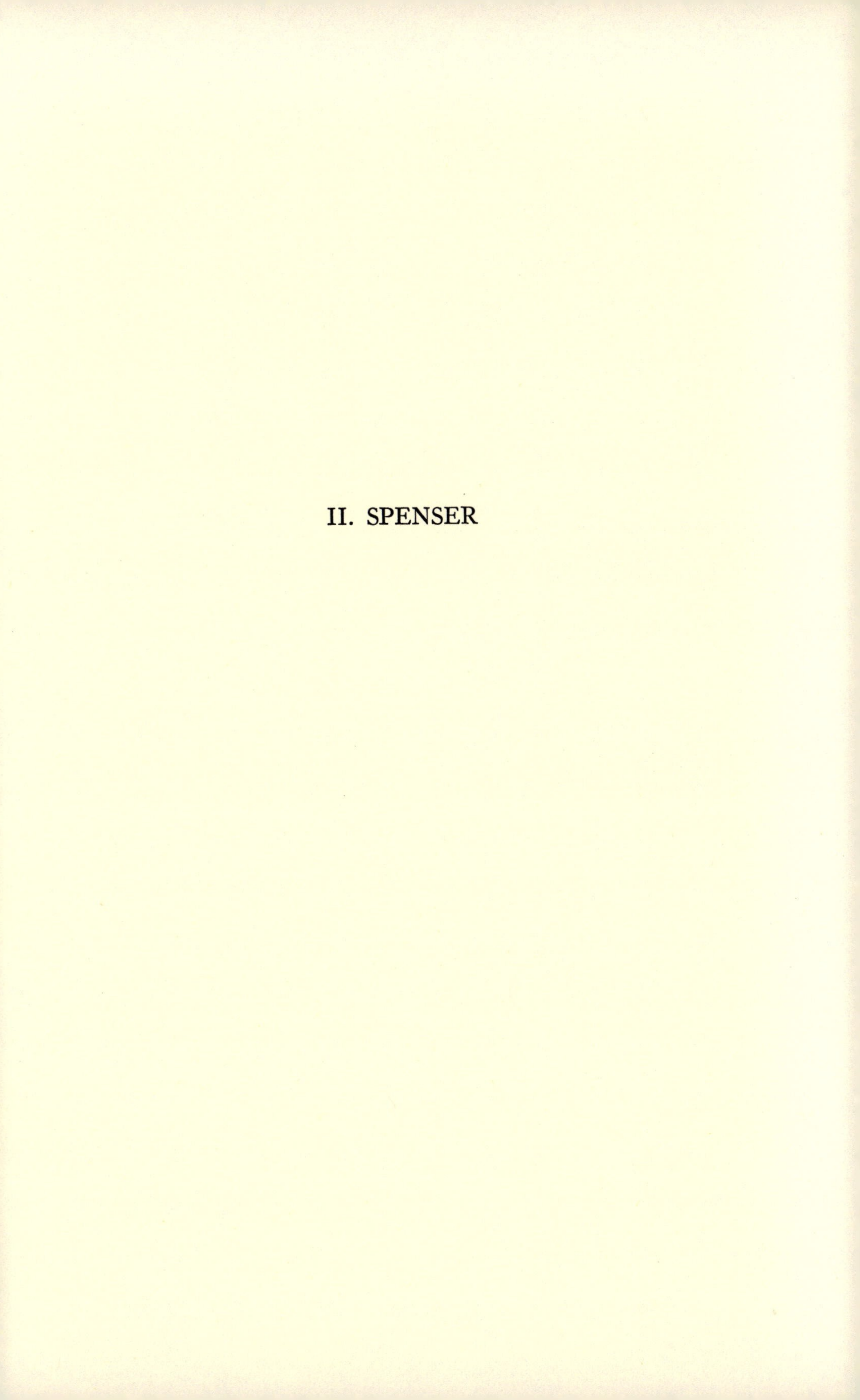

II. SPENSER

The Red Crosse Knight and Mediaeval Demon Stories*

THREE times in Canto X of the First Book of the *Faerie Queene* the "godly aged Sire" impresses upon Red Crosse the fact of his earthly, rather than elfin, lineage.

> Then come, *thou man of earth*, and see the way,
> That neuer yet was seene of Faeries sonne (*F.Q.* I, x, 52).

Stanza 60 has:

> And thou faire ymp, sprong out from English race,
> *How euer now accompted Elfins sonne*,

and stanza 65 gives the reason for this misconception—the story of the theft of Red Crosse while yet "in tender swadling band," and of the "chaungeling" who "vnweeting" takes his place during his upbringing in "Faerie lond."

Now so wondrous quick and persant a spright as the old man of the Hermitage would not thus carefully establish a distinction which had no point. And we shall see that for the Gentle Knight mortality is not a limitation and a curse, but a divinely planned prerequisite to an "aspiration for the infinite." We have to do with some power, some privilege which is given to the hero because he is *not* of supernatural birth, but an ordinary mortal—in this case it is a sight of the New Jerusalem, entrance into the heavenly kingdom where there are mansions prepared for men but cold shrift for Merlin, Puck, Lucifer, Grendel, and the Tuatha da Danann.

In that numerous class of devil-commitment, supernatural-parent, or orchard-stranger stories and romances, which clearly show the intricate interweaving of pagan and Christian conceptions, the gradual contamination of the non-Christian tale of a wonder-child with folk beliefs and patristic warnings against *incubi* and *succubae*, one of the most arresting motifs is the bitter repentance and difficult penance of the hero, victim of his mother's rash vow committing her child to the devil and his service if only her Kin-

* Reprinted by permission of the Modern Language Association from *PMLA*, 44 (1929), 706–14.

derwünsch may be fulfilled. By a curious contamination with the older story, which accounted for the exploits of a hero by really giving him one supernatural parent—no devil, but a warrior and a gentleman (Tydorel, Finn, Mongan, Alexander, Arthur)—the poor hero is actually made the son of the devil (as in *Sir Gowther;* Robert the Devil has merely commitment). This, of course, confuses the motif by taking responsibility from the sinful mother (still portrayed, illogically, as remorseful), and by making the repentance and penance impossible—according to all right and proper demonology. For it is only a sentimental generation which gives moments of pity to the Principle of Evil; the author of *Sir Gowther* was only confused, and no willful defender of Cain, like Blake and Leconte de Lisle and others of the devil's party.

For the devil-committed child the way is hard. Unaware of his tragic law, he perpetrates innumerable and awful crimes. No gentle Fidelia is it who opens "his dull eyes, that light mote in them shine," but instead the bitter discovery of all men's enmity toward him. Then is he, like Red Crosse, "prickt with anguish of his sinnes so sore" *F.Q.* I, x, 21); he swoons "for very grete sorowe," and "bytterly wepes[s] and complayne[s]" for his sins, "whiche are innumerable and abhomynable to recounte," and can only be assoiled by the Pope himself, in Rome.[1] The monks of the Abbey where he first rests, "fayne thereof" though they were "when they hearde hym pitteously complayne"[2] still seem to have had none of the "words of wondrous might" of the Leech Patience, who gives Red Crosse his first consolation (st. 24), perhaps because Robert had as yet no Una to plead with a Cœlia for him. Like Red Crosse, he must go on for more potent shrift. It is at this point that Spenser's penitent hero undergoes the mortification which reminds us of certain details in that which is undergone by the devil-child because of his "*inward* corruption and *infected* sin" (*F.Q.* I, x, 15). The romance of *Robert the Devil* (and of *Sir Gowther*, its variant) has attached to it the motif of that *Gesta Romanorum* exemplum against pride (the story of Emperor Jovinian)[3]—the Male Cinderella motif, by which Robert, for penance, must put an antic disposition on under circumstances far more like,

[1] *Robert the Deuyll*, ed. Thoms, *Early Engl. Prose Rom*, I, pp. 21–22.

[2] *Lyfe of Roberte the Deuyll*, ed. Hazlitt, *Early Pop. Poetry*, I, p. 244.

[3] *Gesta Romanorum*, ed. *Early Engl. Text Soc.*, ex. ser. 33, p. 75.

in discomfort, to Red Crosse's than to either Hamlet's or the proud Emperor's. "Downe in a darkesome lowly place farre in," "with streight diet," with "ashes and sack-cloth" arraying "His daintie corse," with "fasting" "the swelling of his wounds to mitigate," praying "both earely and eke late," Red Crosse roars like a lion, rends his flesh and "his owne synewes" eats, while Una, hearing him, "often tore Her guiltlesse garments, and her golden heare, For pitty" yet must wisely bear all.[4] Robert lies "vnder a stayre at nyght,"[5] can eat only what is thrown to the dogs, gives up his "dylycate metes and drynkes, . . . his raymentes and wordely pleasure" (Thoms, 35), to "Covertement ses pechies pleure En pensant Jhesu Crist aeure, Et por avoir redemsion Li prie . . . ,"[6] is forced to act with all the extravagant wildness of a natural fool, yet contrives to deliver his benefactor from the Saracens, only identified as the mysterious white knight by the wounds he suffers from, in his hiding-place,[7] and the testimony of the princess who wept with pity for him,[8] and who, for love of Robert, "tare her hare from her head, and all to tare her clothes,"[9] upon learning that she must marry the seneschal.

Red Crosse is guided by Mercie, by way of the holy Hospitall with its seven Bead-men (we rejoice that they are not the "vii hooly heremytes" whom Robert sent to heaven), "Forth to an hill, that was both steepe and hy," whereon was a "sacred chappell" attended by the hermit Comtemplation, a man favored of God—Whom he even miraculously "often saw from heauens hight,"—an "aged holy man," with "snowy lockes," who, saluted by Red Crosse and Mercie, greets them courteously because of his great respect for Mercie, who gives as their purpose "that same end . . . high heauen to attaine," although the hermit protests that Red Crosse could have no better guide to heaven than Mercie, who does "the prayers of the righteous sead Present before the maiestie diuine." Then, after Red Crosse has fulfilled the command, for a season to "fast and pray Till from her bands the spright assoiled is," he is shown that heavenly sight accorded to

[4] *F.Q.* I, x, 25–27.

[5] Hazlitt, 252; also Thoms, 34, *Robert le Diable,* ed. Löseth, *Soc. Anc. Textes Fr.*, 1903, v. 1265.

[6] *Robert le Diable,* v. 1268.

[7] *R. le D.*, 3495ff, Thoms, 44, Hazlitt, 256.

[8] *R. le D.*, 3548.

[9] Thoms, 47.

no *real* Faeries sonne.[10] Robert is commanded by the Pope "t'en iras vers les *montaignes*" where he will find, by "une chapele," the "plus saint hermite" in the world, "Car n'est jors qu'en son abitacle Ne fache Dieus por lui miracle." Robert goes to this "saint home, chenu, ferant," salutes him "par l'apostoile de Rome Qui son saiel li a tramis"; [11] however, "as yet" the hermit will not "assoylle" him, till he has lain without meat or drink all night in the chapel, in penitence for his sins.[12] Robert fulfills the difficult penance given him in the morning; then must he, also, "aide a virgin desolate foredonne," win famous victorie, and hang his shield "high emongst all knights" (*F.Q.* I, x, 60). And then is he, as well, ready to "shonne" all earthly conquest, and would not "turne againe Backe to the world whose ioyes so fruitlesse are" but would rather "here for aye in peace remaine" (*F.Q.* I, x, 63), for as he puts it, "de nul deduit n'avrai cure," and he will "en la forest grant abite. Jamais ne quier de lui partir" but "al siecle un jor ne seroie." [13] In the French version he dies in the odor of sanctity; in the English he is forever happy with the princess.

The legend of Robert the Devil was as well-known and popular as a universally appealing character and a tinge of supernatural melodrama could make it, for it had the same attraction, as a story of the spiritual regeneration of a hero, which gave the theme of the morality play its hold upon the English imagination, from *Everyman* to the House of Holiness. We have used references from a French metrical version of the thirteenth century.[14] The French prose "volksbuch" was published in 1496, 1497, etc.[15] Its derivative, the English prose version in Thoms' collection, was printed by Wynkyn de Worde in 1514.[16] The English metrical version printed by Hazlitt is based on the prose, and is of the sixteenth century.[17] Lodge published his *Robin the Diuell* in 1591. There are numerous contaminations and variants of the legend—*Sir Gowther, Tydorel, Orfeo, Yonec, The Voyage of the Húi*

[10] *F.Q.* I, x, 46–52.

[11] *R. le D.*, 638, 656, 706, 720. Upton "remarks that the residence of Contemplation on a hill seems imaged from the Table of Cebes. . . ." (Todd, III, 134).

[12] Hazlitt, 248. [13] *R. le D.*, 4961, 4986. [14] *R. le D.*, introd., i.

[15] Breul, *Sir Gowther* (1886), p. 57.

[16] Gordon Duff (*Hand-lists*, p. 24) assigns this date with a query; Breul (*op. cit.*, p. 62) and Wells (*Manual of Writings in Mid. Eng.*, p. 137) give the date as "*c.* 1510."

[17] Breul, 63; Wells, 137.

Corra.[18] In the fifteenth century Book of Fermoy, possibly a much older tale,[19] is the same story, with an interesting parallel to Fidelia's instruction in her sacred Booke, in the instruction ("in the canonical scriptures") of the three "smooth-delightful, greatly famous" devil-committed sons of Caerderg.

There are certain other sons of ambiguous parentage whose romantic *enfances* remind us of that of Georgos, and whose pedigree, unknown to them, gives them the right of entrance into marvellous places. In the *Bel Inconnu* group, the hero is admitted to a sight of the isle, or the palace—typical otherworlds—because of some characteristic peculiar to him; he is of Gawain's race (*Libeaus Desconus*) or he is come "le dame aidier" (*B. I.* 2880).[20] In *Thomas of Erceldoune* (Cambridge MS., mid-1400's) [21] the lady calls Thomas "Man of molde" (p. 7), but nevertheless shows him the "fayre way" over the "mountayne," the "fayre castell" upon the "hill" that "of towne and toure . . . berith þe bell." Oberon himself, curiously enough, has only half claim to his title of fée, and even that, as we shall see, is questioned, in that strange thirteenth-century prologue to *Huon of Bordeaux*, the French *Auberon.*[22] As has been noted in the case of *Huon,*[23] this same *Auberon* has more than one familiar figure. There is the giant Orguilleus, incited by Satan to steal Auberon's famous hauberk, get possession of the castle of Dunostre and mew up there the daughter of Guilemer until Huon shall deliver her. This dazzling white hauberk, which was a chastity test, and at the same time rendered its wearer invulnerable, was originally the property of Brunehaut (*Aub.* 1067), who was queen of the faerye (*Aub.* 663). We are not quite told, as of Arthur's shield, that

> the Faerie Queene it brought
> To Faerie lond, where yet it may be seene, if sought
> (*F.Q.* I, vii, 36),

[18] Printed by Whitley Stokes in *Rev. Celt.*, XIV, 22ff.

[19] Hibbard, *Med. Rom. in Eng.*, 53: "possibly 11th century."

[20] Schofield, *Studies on the Libeaus Desconus, Harvard Studies and Notes in Philol. and Lit.*, IV (1895), 48, 52.

[21] *Thomas of Erceldoune, EETS,* orig. ser. 60–61, lvi.

[22] Ed. Graf, *I Complementi della Chanson d'Huon de Bordeaux*, I.

[23] The article of J. B. Fletcher in *JEGP,* ii concerns itself chiefly with parallels in general action, but various details have been noted by J. R. Macarthur in an article on the "Influence of *Huon of Burdeux* upon the *F.Q.*," in *JEGP,* iv, 215–38, and by Miss Winstanley in the introduction to her edition of Book I.

yet it *is* this same "good harnays," Oberon's gift from Brunehaut which is delivered over to Huon with his realme and dygnite, after which they "taryed styll in the fayrey, and shal do unto the day of Iugemente." [24] There are the copper automata, at the door, each with his flail, long ago noted as the predecessors of Talus.[25] Brunehaut, into whose especial service Auberon comes, has the same sort of wonder-working powers that make of Fidelia such a curious, almost mythical character; Oberon himself can make a path through the river for his men to pass,[26] but the "flouds" he parts "in tway" (*F.Q.* I, x, 20) do not, after all, seem quite so much like the Red Sea. There are certain interesting castle descriptions in the *Huon* and in the *Libeaus Desconus* group [27] which sound curiously as though Spenser were putting his Jerusalem in England's green and pleasant land. The other-world palace of Oberon, whose inhabitants have such "great marueyle to se any mortal persons to enter" [28] is perhaps not that same "goodly Citie" "Whose wals and towres were builded high and strong Of perle and precious stone" seen from the top of the "highest Mount," at the end of a "little path, that was both steepe and long," nor yet that Cleopolis with its "bright towre all built of christall cleene" (*F.Q.* I, x, 55–58), yet it is at least seen in very much the same manner—from the "mountayne whereon they mou*n*ted with great payne and trauayle,"—a "great citye . . . the walles and towers of the citye and paleys . . . of whyghte marble polysshed, the which stone [*sic*] so bryght agaynst the sonne as thoughe it had bene al of christall" [29]—and seen, after all, by just such another mere "man of earth."

For Robert the Devil is only one of many half-mortal sons

[24] *Huon of Burdeux, EETS,* ex. ser. 41, p. 606.

[25] By Miss Winstanley and by Macarthur, who also notes the parallel in the castle descriptions.

[26] *Huon of Burdeux, EETS,* ex. ser. 40, p. 78.

[27] The parallel in general action between the stories of *Libeaus Desconus* and of the Red Crosse Knight has of course been frequently noted, e.g. in Ker, *Epic and Romance,* 392, Cambridge *History* I, 295; Broadus in *MLN,* XVIII, 202–204, Maynadier, *The Arthur of the English Poets,* 263. Miss Paton (*Studies in Fairy Mythology of Arth. Rom.,* 134) compares Dunostre, which in *Fergus* receives its light from a miraculous shield (cf. Auberon's hauberk) with Dun-an-Oir in the *Lay of the Great Fool,* with the Il d'Or in *Bel Inconnu,* and the Chef d'Oire of *Partonopeus* (v. Gaston Paris' connection of *oire* with the *portae aureae* of Jerusalem).

[28] *Huon of Burdeux, EETS,* ex. ser. 41, p. 597.

[29] *Ibid.,* p. 596.

whose mortality insures their participation in joys otherwise never yet seen of Faeries sonne. Oberon, known in Huon of Bordeaux as the son of Julius Caesar and the lady of the "pryuey Isle," endowed with marvellous gifts at his birth, by many ladies of the Fayrrey, nevertheless has "a place *aperrelyd* in paradyce," for "all thynges creatyd in this *mortall* world must nedys haue an ende."[30] He explains his peculiarly unfairylike behaviour once more when he gives Huon his kingdom: "lordes and ladyes who be here assembeled all, ye knowe that euery mortall thynge connot always endure / I speke it for my owne selfe who am sone to a mortall man, and was engendered on the ladye of the preuye Ile who can neuer dye, because she is one of the fairy engendered of a man of the fayrey and doughter to a woman of the fayrey, and where so it was so that Iulius Seser was a mortall man, therfore it behouethe me to pas out of this worlde by the co*m*mandement of our lorde god, who hathe ordeined that it shulde so be."[30a]

To have been redeemed for the Christian heaven through Iulius Seser is no small matter. But even Oberon himself is far from exhaustive, in *Huon*, on the subject of his fairy forbears. The definitive edition of his complicated genealogy, properly connected with all the important events in human, divine and elfin history is to be found in that same *Auberon*[31] which we have already noticed. Therein we learn that Judas Macacbeus and the daughter of king Bandifort have a daughter Brunehaut, gifted at her birth by four fées, taken at the age of seven into fairy land, where she becomes queen, marries Caesar and gives birth to Julius Caesar. When he is to marry, Brunehaut selects Morgue:

> Suer est Artu qui tant est de grant pris:/ Tex est li rois c'onours li croist tous dis (v. 1209).

And this "Morgue" has a history that is distinctly apropos:

> Morgue sa suer, quant enfes fu petis/ *De gens faees ful li siens cors rauis;*/ Vns rois faes, qui uix ert et flouris,/ Le nourri tant qu'ele ot ans dusc' a.X. (vv. 1211–1214).

It is from this old fée that "Morgain tous ses engiens apris." This seems a sorry disturbance of the Fata Morgana, "euer now

[30] *Ibid.*, p. 74. [30a] *Ibid.*, p. 599.

[31] Ed. Arturo Graf, *op. cit.* For convenient summary see Gautier, *Les Epopées Francaises*, III, 725ff.

accompted Elfins race." So Oberon is born, in the land of Faerye, of Julius Caesar and of the sister of Arthur—thus "vnweeting reft." The next item in the genealogy is more astounding. Morgan gives birth to twin boys. One of these is Auberon le fae, dowered at birth as we have come to expect; he shall be king of the fairies, yet "quant li ame de son cors partira/ Em paradis seurement ira" (v. 1421). But the other, son of Julius Caesar and of Morgue suer d'Artus, shall be "*saintefies* en paradis," and *he* is none other than Saint *George* the Dragonkiller! And more than that, for in this curious hodge-podge, he is, as well, voyager into strange Eastern lands, protector of all things—of the daughter of the king of Persia, the infant Jesus en route to Egypt, and the miraculously re-attached beard of poor Saint Joseph. It is again the same story of him "that is accompted Elfins sonne," who wins many a "famous victorie" "To aide a virgin desolate foredonne," whose blessed end is to "be a Saint" "emongst those Saints"—and whose name is "Saint George of mery England" (*F.Q.* I, x, 60–61).[32]

This Saint George has an enfance curiously parallel to that given to his mother in the Auberon. "Reft," as he slept "in tender swadling band," by a Faerie: "Thence she thee brought into this Faerie lond, And in a heaped furrow did thee hyde" (*F.Q.* I, x, 65–66).[33] We find remnants in other of the St. George legends of what may have been a traditional attachment to motifs of su-

[32] It is perhaps more than interesting to note that in that book of the "*Antiquitie of Faerie* lond" (*F.Q.* II, x) in which Guyon reads the high history of the elfin line which was to give the Faerie Queene to England, which had built the Cleopolis, and the Panthea "all of Christall," whose glory Red Crosse had known (*F.Q.* I, x, 55),—in this complicated genealogy, that same Oberon whose political counterpart (Henry VIII) has sometimes been connected with the Red Crosse knight is also the half-mortal descendant of a Fay. Inescapably, a Celtic Fairy Mistress in the royal family. This Fay had been met in the gardens of Adonis by that anomalous creature, the "man so made [by Prometheus] . . . called *Elfe,* to weet Quick, the first authour of all Elfin kind," as he wandered "through the world with wearie feet" (*F.Q.* II, x, 71).

[33] Upton explains "Georgos" as follows: "*Georgos* in the Greek language signifying a *husbandman,* our poet hence takes occasion . . . of introducing the marvellous tale of Tages . . . the son of the earth: a ploughman found him" (Todd, III, 146). He also notes the legend in the *Seven Champions* (Todd, III, 145). Padelford and O'Connor in an article on "Spenser's Use of the St. George Legend" (*SP,* XXIII, 142–56) stress other parallels in the legend, but do not mention the birth story.

pernatural conception and fairy enfances. In the *Seven Champions of Christendom*[34] the lady "never was in hope of child till now"; however, the mysterious dragon birth is only in her dreams; although George can only accomplish the deed because he is a "Christian knight, never born of a woman," the motif has been completely rationalized. When the child is born, however, the fell enchantress Kalyb steals it from the careless nurses, brings it up in a cave, unaware of its parentage, for twice seven years. A late ballad in Percy's *Reliques*, the *Birth of St. George*,[35] stresses the grief of the old father, who, like Spenser's hermit, "So withers on the mountain top A fair and stately oake," because of the loss of the infant George.

> Meantime amid the lonely wilds/ His little son was bred./ There the weird lady of the woods,/ Had borne him far away,/ And train'd him up in feates of arms/ And every martial play.

Selden, in his notes to Drayton's *Polyolbion*, says (with regard to the legend which connected George with the Perseus-Andromeda motif): "But you may better beleeue the Legend then that he was a Couentry man borne, with his Caleb Lady of the Woods, or that he descended from the Saxon race and such like, which some English fictions deliver."[36] We can only quote "sprong out from English race," "from ancient race Of Saxon kings" (*F.Q.* I, x, 60–65), and regret the "English fictions," with a *maledicat* for some nameless analogue of Warburton's cook. That there must have been a traditional enfance story for Saint George, we recognize; but the late remnants that are left to us are highly rationalized, and are mere echoes of the primitive tendency to endow a hero (as in a sort of pourquoi story) with a truly supernatural conception, such as Spenser may have known in Irish story (for example, Mongan, begotten upon the wife of Fiachna by Manannan mac Ler in Fiachna's shape, and kept by his supernatural father in the Land of Promise from his third day until his twelfth year).[37]

The stanzas which tell the story of the infant George are full

[34] Richard Johnson, *Seven Champions of Christendom*, ed. 1670, ch. 1.

[35] Percy's *Reliques of Ancient Poetry*, III, 223–24.

[36] Drayton's *Polyolbion*, Spenser Society new ser. 1, 2, 3, p. 68. I am indebted for this note to Professor Edwin Greenlaw.

[37] See Nutt's discussion, *Voyage of Bran*, II, 22ff.

of reminiscences of often-recurring romantic enfances—the shreds and patches gathered by an eclectic imagination and fused, as was Spenser's habit, into a new whole, coherent, convincing, true, yet none the less suggestive of those tales of other foundlings—from Romulus and Remus, Valentin and Orson, down to *Libeaus Desconus* and the young Perceval—which were Spenser's unrealized literary inheritance. It is only as we are aware of this unconsciously eclectic temper that such considerations as these have any importance in the study of a poet's "sources." For if by that may be implied only the conscious adaptation, into a consistent parallel, of material carefully scrutinized and deliberately selected—only the making over of a *Rosalynde* into an *As You Like It*—if "sources" may include that process only, then indeed we must admit *this* sacred river to be flung up momently from no source whatever. But there were caverns through which it ran, and though perhaps they are, to our sorrow, measureless to man, they are, after all, surely worth our remarking.

A Mediaeval Commonplace in Spenser's Cosmology*

RECENT discussions have called attention to the importance of certain "Empedoclean" doctrines in Spenser's exposition of the creation of the world by Love. The conception of "Love and Strife as combining and disintegrating forces working the changes among the four elements" has been pointed to as "the distinctive doctrine which Spenser took over from Empedocles."[1] Spenser's important passages on the creation (*Colin Clout,* 839ff; *Hymne of Loue,* 57ff) expound this doctrine with many details —Love's separation and ordering of the parts of the world, the discord of the elements and their reconciliation by Love, the continuing of life and of forms through Love's power.

It seems improbable that Spenser followed any one "source" for such conceptions as these. He rather absorbed them from seeing them in various places and connections, read many statements of them which, though often inconsistent with each other, underlined these ideas in his mind until they took definite form and became his own. Their particular clothing, setting, or color was given to them from his own predispositions, or as he used them for his own purposes. The idea of creation here outlined is frequently stated in mediaeval or late mediaeval books which Spenser almost certainly read; often a different aspect of the idea is stressed, of course. It is important to recognize that to Spenser much of this mediaeval background was near and ordinary; he selected and took over ideas from it not for their quaintness or their historical importance but for their truth. He does not collect curiosities, as did later "Romantic" antiquarians, but criticizes seriously, chooses materials and converts them to his uses. Accordingly, the following parallels are not given as sources. However, they serve to indicate the commonness of such cosmological ideas, and the kind of material in which Spenser may well have found them. Love as a motivating force for the creation of the world is

* Reprinted from *Studies in Philology,* 30 (1933), 133–47.

[1] *V.* Albright, "Spenser's Cosmic Philosophy and his Religion," *PMLA,* XLIV (1929), 737, 759.

familiar enough in mediaeval Neo-Platonic Christianity; the physical theory of the separation and reconciliation of the elements is just as familiar. The examples given are typical mediaeval statements of a common idea of rather complicated provenance, which had been turned by various authors to their uses as Spenser turned it to his.

In Spenser's exposition, Love was before "this worlds still mouing mightie masse, Out of great *Chaos* vgly prison crept." This mass "had lyen confused euer"; the world "was not till he did it make"; its "sundrie parts he from them selues did seuer" (*HL,* 57ff). The elements are in discord; they were and are "great enemies" (*CC,* 844); "The earth, the ayre, the water, and the fyre, Then gan to raunge them selues in huge array, And with contrary forces to conspyre Each against other, . . . Threatning their owne confusion and decay" (*HL,* 77). But Love reconciled them, and thus "the world was made"; "how should else things so far from attone . . . Be euer drawne together into one, And taught in such accordance to agree?" (*CC,* 841); "Ayre hated earth, and water hated fyre, Till Loue relented their rebellious yre" (*HL,* 83). He made "cold . . . couet heat, And water fire" (*CC,* 847). He tempered "goodly well Their contrary dislikes with loued meanes" (*HL,* 85). He made "the light to mount on hie, And th'heauie downe to peize" (*CC,* 848); he did "place them all in order, and compell To keepe them selues within their sundrie raines" (*HL,* 87). He "linkt" them together "with Adamantine chaines" (*HL,* 89); "So being former foes, they wexed friends" (*CC,* 851). And thus "being knit," they "brought forth other kynds" (*CC,* 853); "in euery liuing wight" they "mixe themselues, and shew their kindly might" (*HL,* 91); and "euer since" they have observed Love's behest, "through which" all things "their being haue, and dayly are increast" (*HL,* 92; *v. CC,* 853ff).

Practically all mediaeval encyclopedic compilations include, of course, descriptions of the creation. The following description is a typical example; it is found in *Batman vppon Bartholome,*[2] the

[2] I take quotations from the copy in the Pierpont Morgan Library, with title page as follows: BATMAN / vppon Bartholome, / His Booke / *De proprietatibus Rerum,* / Newly corrected, enlarged and amended: / with such Additions as are requi- / site, vnto euery seuerall / Booke: / Taken foorth of the most approued Authors, the like here- / tofore not translated in English. / *Profitable for all*

famous Renaissance recension of Bartholomaeus Anglicus' *De proprietatibus rerum.* Bartholomaeus wrote his encyclopedia probably *c.* 1230, and from the latter part of that century on it was widely used as textbook and reference book. There are over a hundred copies of the Latin text still extant, *c.* thirty-five MSS in French, six of Trevisa's English translation (finished 1398); there were English editions in 1495 (?), 1535, and (Batman's) 1582.[3] The first quotation comes from a chapter "What is the world" (Bk. VIII, ch. 1, "De Coelo et Mundo"), the second from "Of Elements" (Bk. X, ch. 3, "De Materia et Forma"):[4]

> The vertue of God made & ordained Primordial matter, in ye which as it were in a massie thing, the foure Elements were potentially, and not distinguished in tale and number, as they are now: but they were meddeled. . . . And thereof the wisedome of God made and brought forth all the Elements, and all that is made of Elementes, & ordayned them in their owne qualyties & place. For that which was hot and drye, in that manner passed into kinde of fire, and because of lyghtnes thereof, the wisdome of God set it aboue other. And such as was most colde and drye, passed into kinde of earth: and for heauinesse and sadnesse thereof, he set it beneth that was hot. And moyst he put into kinde of aire, and such as was cold and moyst, passed into kinde of water. And as these two Elementes be more light, cleere and subtill, he set them betweene fire and earth. . . . (f. 118^{v}, 119^{r})
>
> Euen betweene the qualities of elements, is contrariousnes and strife, by reason whereof they work togethers, and suffer, and ingender, and corrupt. And though the Elementes bee neuer so contrarye, euery each to other: yet by influence of heauen, and vertue of Planets, they be reconciled in their dooings, and brought to accord: and

---

Estates, as well for the benefite of / the Mind as the Bodie. / 1 5 8 2. / [type ornament] / LONDON / Imprinted by Thomas East, dwel- / *ling by Paules wharfe.* /

[3] There were Latin editions in 1470?, 1480, 1481, 1483, 1491, 1492, 1505, 1519, etc., French editions in 1482, 1485, 1498?, 1525, 1556, 1539 (*B. Mus. Cat. s. v.* Barth. de Glanvilla). For dates and other information *v.* Thorndike, *Hist. of Magic and Experimental Science*, II, ch. LIV, esp. pp. 404–406; See Boyar, "Barth. Angl. and his Encyclopedia," *JEGP* XIX (1920), 168ff, esp. 185ff.

[4] These passages, in the Wynkyn de Worde edition of 1495 (?)—also in the Morgan Library—are parallel almost word for word with the text as quoted above from the 1582 edition (VIII, 1, and X, 3, in both editions). They are therefore not among the "requisite additions" referred to on Batman's title page.

> therefore they be onyd & ioyned with a wonderfull bond in kinde. For fire and aire accorde in heate, though they discorde in drinesse and moystnesse: and ayre and water accord in moysture, but they discorde in heate and coldnesse. And water and earth accord in coldnesse, though they discord in moysture and drinesse. Fire and earth that be elements in place most farre asunder, accord. . . . [etc.] [Fire and air] be more high in place and stead. . . . And the two neather Elements, water & earth, be kindly more heauie, than the other twaine, . . . And elements be neuer idle: but be continually in doing & suffering: & so they neuer rest, nor cease off generation & mouing (f. 154^{r}).

These parts of Bartholomaeus' exposition include many of Spenser's important points.[5] It is true that here the creator is not "Love," but "the vertue of God." Nevertheless there are, in Bartholomaeus as in Spenser, descriptions of the confusion of the mass of chaos, of the distinction, separation, and ordering of the various parts, of the "contrariousness and strife" between the "qualities of elements" (i.e., Spenser's "contrary forces"), of their uniting (they are "onyd," cf. "drawne . . . into one"), of their reconciliation and accord, as some are set above and some below, and as their discordant qualities are tempered by their accordant qualities (Spenser's "loued meanes"), of the "bond" (cf. "chaines") which joins them together, in a harmony out of which comes mutable life with its eternal succession of generation and corruption. The most significant generalization proceeding from this description of creation is neatly summed up in Book XI: [6]

> It now resteth to see that all things have betweene them loue and discord . . . : So in Elements, fire is contrary to the water, & the

[5] I hope to discuss in another article the further relationships between Spenser and Bartholomaeus Anglicus (in the characterization of the first "substaunce," in certain Neo-Platonic conceptions, etc.); one on Spenser and the *Zodiacus Vitae* of Palingenius, referred to below, will appear shortly in *JEGP*. [See following article.]

[6] Book XI is "De aere et eius impressionibus"; this passage is part of a long one occurring after ch. 16, with the rubric, "Of the foure Elements, and their qualities and mixtures togethers, forth of Henrie. C. Agrippa, de occ. Phi. Which are newly added." Spenser's tempering of "contrary dislikes with loued meanes" is also paralleled in this passage: "And euery one of the Elements hath two speciall qualities, the first of which it keepeth to it selfe, in the other as a meane, it agreeth with the qualitie following. For the fire is hot and dry, the earth dry and colde, the water colde . . ." etc. This addition after ch. 16 does not appear in the Wynkyn de Worde edition of 1495. For a literary statement of this same detail *v.* e.g. the late xiv. c. *Testament of Love*, in Skeat, *Chaucer*, VII, 75.

aire to the earth, but yet they all agree together: againe in heauenly bodies. . . . [etc.] Wherefore these friendshippes and enmities are nothing else but certaine inclinations of things among thēselues, in desiring such a thing or such a thing, . . . or to repose it selfe in that it hath gotten, in shunning the contrarye. . . . Wherfore Heraclitus being lead with this opinion, did confesse that all things were made by strife and friendship (f. 174^r, 174^v).

Also interesting, in connection with Spenser's idea of the function of Love in creation, is an addition to Book I (on "God") from the "first ladder of Henry Cornelius Agrippa" in his "booke, tituled, De Occulta philosophia": [7]

Let us first consider what one is, . . . [the fountain of all numbers] . . . Wherefore it is multiplied, not into parts, but into it selfe, and therefore some haue called this Concord, some Pietie, some friendship, because it is so knit, y it cannot be cut into parts, & Marcianus after Aristotle affirmeth, that Cupid is so named, because it is one alone, & wold euer haue himselfe to be sought, & hath nothing besides, but being voide of all elation or couple, doth wrest his owne heates to himselfe: wherefore one, is the beginning, and end of all things, hauing no beginning nor end . . . and things that are, desire the very one, because all things proceed of one . . . wherefore one is referred to almightie God, who forasmuch as he is one, and innumerable, doth create innumberable things of himselfe, and containeth them within himselfe: wherefore there is one God, one world of one God, one Sunne of one worlde: . . . There is one Element ouercomming & pearcing all things, which is fire. . . . (f. 2^r, 2^v)

The Neo-Platonism of this passage would be interesting to Spenser, and has certain similarities to his own.[8] There is the same reconciliation between the two conceptions—of "friendship" or "Cupid" as the fountain of all things, or the Christian God, the world's great workmaster, that high "eternall powre, which now

[7] Not in the edition of 1495(?).

[8] A familiar source for concepts similar to these is the popular treatise of Macrobius, *Comm. in Somn. Scip.* I, vi, 7, 8, 9 (ed. Eyssenhardt, Leipzig, 1893, p. 497; *v.* also p. 500, on the reconciliation of inimical elements by their mean qualities). Cf. the *Timaeus*, tr. Taylor (London, 1929), 27–29, 52, 57, for various points similar to those discussed. There are of course near parallels in the Italian Renaissance Platonists. This study does not try to substitute other sources for the Platonic and Neo-Platonic sources pointed out, for example, in Miss Winstanley's edition of the *Fowre Hymnes*, but to stress the commonness of certain ideas in Spenser's complicated inheritance, and to give typical examples of earlier statements of ideas similar to his, in places where he was likely to have come upon them.

doth moue In all these things" (*HHL*, 27). As a pictorial figure, this "Cupid" is rather different from that Cupid in the *Hymne of Loue* who took "to him wings of his owne heate" and gives all things being through "his infused fyre," or from the Cupid who "his owne perfection wrought" and created the world, in *Colin Clout*. But as a concept, this Cupid is strikingly similar to Spenser's. The same thing is true of the "Concord" of this passage as compared with that in the *Faerie Queene*, IV, x[9] (*v.* below p. 59). Spenser's "Concord" is a more effective figure, more clearly visualized; nevertheless, she is really only the symbol for an idea very similar to that of "Concord" in the passage quoted above.

There are frequent references in the *Roman de la Rose* to similar cosmological theories. One may take as an example the speech of Nature in confession to her priest Genius.[10] She tells of all her powers, of how stars, planets, seas, were created, how they obey her laws. In this description as in Spenser's, we find the motivation of the creator by love, the confused mass of chaos, separated into its parts and ordered by the creator (who makes "the light to mount on hie, And th'heauie downe to peize," as in *Colin Clout*). Nature says she is "conestable e . . . vicaire"; she holds the chain of the elements, and through them continues all forms in perpetuity:

Cil Deus qui de beautez abonde,
Quant il trés beaus fist cet beau monde, . . .
N'onc riens ne l'esmut a ce faire,

[9] She has much the same functions as "Love"; for a similar figure cf. also the "Dame Pees" who sat "soberly" before the temple-door in the *Parlement of Foules* (240).

[10] The dialogue between Genius and Nature comes out of a situation obscured by many digressions. After a speech by the God of Love, his barons swear their oath, on "Love's implements of war." Nature goes into her workshop; this oath "brought to her Great solace" but nevertheless she cries to Genius, and confesses to him (the speech above, *Cil deus* . . . comes here). Cf. the discussion in *Colin Clout* of "loues perfection," of his nature which "needs his priest t'expresse his powre diuine" (835). Long digressions or "exempla" separate the parts of the story from each other, e.g., the description of Nature working at her forge to ensure the continuity of life: "she doth mould things so" that no species shall die; "as one dies Forthwith another may arise To fill his place" (various examples are given; cf. Spenser, *Mut.* VII, 18). There is also a long passage on Art and Nature; and Genius' tirade on women is part of his "comfort." For the many editions of this poem, *v.* Bourdillon, *The Early Edit. of the R. de la R.*, esp. 13ff, 35ff.

Fors sa volenté debonaire,
Large, courteise, senz envie,
Qui fontaine est de toute vie.
Et le fist au comencement
Une masse tant seulement,
Qui toute iert en confusion,
Senz ordre et senz distinccion,
Puis le devisa par parties,
Qui puis ne furent departies, . . .
E les mist en leus couvenables, . . .
Les legieres en haut volerent,
Les pesanz au centre en alerent
E les meienes ou mileu. . . .
(ed. Langlois, IV, 16729ff)

Si gart, tant m'a Deus enouree,
La bele chaeine doree
Qui les quatre elemenz enlace . . .
E me bailla toutes les choses
Qui sont en la chaeine encloses,
E comanda que jes gardasse
E leur fourmes continuasse, . . .
(IV, 16781ff)

There are other references in the *Roman de la Rose* to the reconciled discord of the four elements. See, for example, a passage on the influence of the stars, which tells how the four opposed qualities are yet included in one body, "E freit e chaut e sec e moiste, Tout ausinc come en une boiste, Font il en chascun cors venir . . ." Through the harmony thus brought about Nature can create forms: "Si font pais de quatre anemis. . . . Pour fourmer en la meilleur fourme Toutes les choses que je fourme" (IV, 16961ff). These are direct likenesses with Spenser's description of the creation and continuing of life; there are other cosmological discussions in the poem with similar details. There were of course many manuscripts and many editions of the *Roman de la Rose* (21 editions between *c.* 1480 and 1538).[10a]

One can hardly believe that Spenser did not read Chaucer's translation of Boethius. At least he could have found there various statements of the points which he himself makes in the two

[10a] Passages quoted here in English are from Ellis's translation, III 43–44 (London, 1900); those in French from the edition by Langlois for the *Société des anciens textes français*, vol. IV, refs. to verses (Paris, 1922).

passages being discussed. In Boethius' Book II, metre viii, certain powers of "according" are given to Love (in Chaucer's translation, which I use throughout); Love sees "that the contrarious qualitee of elements holden among hem-self aliaunce perdurable." Love provides "that the see, greedy to flowen, constreyneth with a certein ende hise flodes, so that it is nat leveful to strecche hise brode termes or boundes up-on the erthes . . ." (cf. the *Hymne of Loue,* in which Love reconciles the elements and "compell[s them] To keepe them selues within their sundrie raines"). Boethius concludes, "al this acordaunce of thinges is bounden with Love, that governeth erthe and see, and hath also commaundements to the hevenes." It is true that Boethius' "Love" would hardly have taken form and shape in the figure of Cupid, as does Spenser's. However, the functions of Love are much the same in both expositions; and Spenser was using (consciously, no doubt) a figure who had come to have allegorical, almost philosophical significance in mediaeval literature—as son of Venus (goddess and planet), and God of Love. Boethius and Spenser give the same importance to the preservation of this harmony between the elements. Boethius says that "yif this Love slakede the brydeles, alle thinges that now loven hem to-gederes wolden maken a bataile continuely, and stryven to fordoon the fasoun of this worlde." In Spenser this is included as part of the creation story: the elements, ranged "in huge array," began "to conspyre Each against other, by all meanes they may, Threatning their owne confusion and decay"; [11] Love placed them in order, since when "they firmely haue remained, And duly well obserued his beheast" (*HL,* 79ff). The steps by which this accord is accomplished are parallel in the two texts. Spenser gives as parts of this process: making the cold to "couet" heat, and water fire; appointing their own "raines" to the several elements; tempering their dislikes with "meanes"; placing the light above and heavy below. Chaucer's *Boece,* in an apostrophe to the creator, has: "Thou bindest the elements by noumbres proporcionables, that the colde thinges mowen acorden with the hote thinges, and the drye thinges with the moiste thinges: that the fyr . . . ne flee nat over

[11] Cf. also *Boece,* IV, m. vi: "For yif that he ne clepede ayein the right goinge of thinges, and yif that he ne constreinede hem . . . , the things that ben now continued by stable ordinaunce, they sholden departen from hir welle, *that is to seyn, from hir beginninge,* and faylen, *that is to seyn, torne in-to nought.*"

hye, ne that the hevinesse ne drawe nat adoun over-lowe the erthes . . . Thou knittest to-gider the mene sowle of treble kinde . . ." (III, m. ix). In a passage on the stars keeping "hir olde pees" through Love, we find:

> This acordaunce atempreth by evenlyk maneres the elements, that the moiste things stryving with the drye thinges, yeven place by stoundes; and the colde thinges joynen hem by feyth to the hote thinges; and that the lighte fyr aryseth in-to heighte; and the hevy erthes avalen by hir weightes (IV, m. vi).

The generalization which follows is familiar in Spenser:[12] "This atempraunce norissheth and bringeth forth al thing that bretheth lyf in this world; and thilke same atempraunce . . . drencheth under the laste deeth, alle thinges y-born"; "This is the comune Love to alle thinges." Troilus' hymn to "Love, that of erthe and see hath governaunce" is of course dependent on the Boethian passage (*Troil.* III, 1744ff). Love is he who so orders things "That elements that been so discordable Holden a bond perpetuely duringe"; he constrains the greedy sea's "flodes" "to a certeyn ende"; if he "lete his brydel go" all would leap asunder, "And lost were al, that Love halt now to-hepe." Naturally, in this context, the strong "bond" of Love is more important as it will "cerclen hertes" than as it chains together the elements; both functions are accomplished by the same force, however.

This linking or knitting together of the elements often occurs as one of the powers or responsibilities of "Nature."[13] For exam-

[12] The illustration directly following is that of the procession of the seasons, a common mediaeval illustration for the permanence of God's and Nature's law and for the changefulness of human life. The end of this metre, and the other Boethian statements on the government of the eternal flux by this "atempraunce" or Love, may be compared to ideas in Spenser's *Mutability*. For some differences (and also a reference to Alanus) *v.* note 24, pp. 336–37 in Greenlaw, "Spenser's Influence on *Paradise Lost*," *SP*, XVII (1920); this article (esp. section 3) shows the far-reaching importance of certain concepts developed by Spenser into a philosophy of nature. The present article attempts only to note a few of the possible "sources for Spenser's ideas" which Dr. Greenlaw says "have not yet been systematically studied."

[13] These are typical statements of the idea of Nature quelling the strife of the elements. A speech of Nature's in Lydagte's translation of Guillaume's *Pilgrimage:* "Off ellementys I am maystresse . . . ffor I ha the gouernaunce Off fyr, of heyr, (as ye may se,) Off erthe, and off the largë se, Off ther accord & ther debate; I leue no thyng in on estat, . . ." (she makes each thing "to drawë to his ffyn," etc.); *EETS*, extra ser. 77, 83, 92, *v.* 3437ff; various MSS and edi-

ple, in the *Parlement of Foules* Nature, "the vicaire of th'almyghty lorde," is she "That hoot, cold, hevy, light, [and] moist and dreye Hath knit by even noumbre of acorde . . ." (379). The idea is stated more clearly and with more of the details which Spenser uses, in Chaucer's source, the *De planctus naturae* of Alanus de Insulis. There we find the discord of the elements and their reconciliation, the appointing of their proper places, the mediating or "mean" quality, the "chain," bond, knot of peace, the continuance of life upon the basis of this harmony, with "Nature" as the mother of all things and of all forms. Nature's description of the "abundance of [her] power" which "shines out" in all things, in Prose III, includes some of these details; see also the apostrophe to her in metre IV:[14]

> For just as, of the four elements, the concordant discord, the single plurality, the dissonant consonance, the dissenting agreement, produce the structures of the palace of earth, so, of four ingredients, the similar unsimilarity, the unequal equality, the unformed conformity, the separate identity, firmly erect the building of the human body. And those qualities which come together as mediators among the elements—these establish a firm peace among the four humors. (Prose III)
>
> O offspring of God, mother of all things, bond and firm chain of the universe. . . . ! Peace, love, virtue, . . . order, . . . source, life, . . . beauty, form, pattern of the world! Thou who, guiding the universe with thy reins, dost join all things in firmness with the knot of concord . . . ; who . . . dost shape the cloak of form with thy finger; . . . who dost repress and increase the threatening sea, . . . lest the seething of the flood should prevail to bury the region of earth! (Metre IV)

---

tions, *v.* p. lxiii * ff. Nature's speech in the *Roman de la Rose* 18967: "Ne ne me plaing des elemenz: Bien gardent mes comandemenz, Bien font entre aus leur mixtions, Tournant en resolucions; . . ."; ed. Langlois, IV. Nature's first speech in Medwall's play *Nature:* "Atwyxt thelementys / that whylom were at stryfe, I haue swaged / the old repugnaunce and knyt theym togeder / in maner of alyaunce" (*c.* 1516–20, ed. Farmer, *Tudor Facsimile Texts,* 1908). The ascription of such powers to Nature is thoroughly commonplace, in Latin and vernacular texts.

[14] These passages are at pp. 451, 458 of Wright's edition of Alanus' poem (*Rolls Series* 59 pt. 2); I quote from the translation by Moffat, *Yale Stud.* 36, pp. 25, 32–3. For evidence as to the knowledge of Alanus by Spenser *v.* Greenlaw's discussion in "Some Old Religious Cults," *SP,* XX (1923), 216ff.

A third Spenserian passage is interesting in connection with the attribution of these functions to Dame Nature. In *Faerie Queene* IV, x, Scudamour crosses the bridge into the island where the temple of Venus stands. In the porch "sate an amiable Dame" of "sober mood," "Mother of blessed *Peace,* and *Friendship* trew"; "*Concord* she cleeped was in common reed." Her duties are those ordinarily given to Nature: [15]

> By her the heauen is in his course contained,
> And all the world in state vnmoued stands,
> As their Almightie maker first ordained,
> And bound them with inuiolable bands;
> Else would the waters ouerflow the lands,
> And fire deuoure the ayre, and hell them quight,
> But that she holds them with her blessed hands (st. 35).

This passage and those quoted above from mediaeval texts obviously draw from a common tradition.

Another later parallel is interesting in connection with both this passage on Concord and other Spenserian passages. In a translation by Barnabe Googe of Palingenius Stellatus' *Zodiacus Vitae* [16] the Fourth Book (Cancer) is chiefly taken up with discussions of Love. The guiding dame Arete sends to the quester a young man who explains that without Venus "the use of earth would cease" (cf. the hymn to Venus in *F. Q.* IV, x); all creatures are subject to that Cupid who made even Jove obey him (cf. *Col. Cl.* 809). "Wherefore who seekes this loue, a thing of fame He seekes: for if the king, and Lord of all the world, should not All things created here retayne in loues assured knot," then "The worlde should straight be at an end, and the elements decay." God's love is everlasting, "Wherefore the order of all things shall last continually"; he does not care for the bodies, but

[15] See note 9 above.

[16] I use the Library of Congress copy, edition of 1588, with title page as follows: The Zodiake of life, written / by the excellent and Christian Poet, / *Marcellus Palingenius / Stellatus.* / Wherein are conteined twelue seuerall / labours, painting out most liuely the whole com- / *passe of the world,* [. . . etc.] Translated out of Latine into English, by Barnabie / Googe and by him newly recognished/[. . .] *Imprinted at London by Robert Robinson / dwelling in Feter Lane neere / Holborne. 1588.* / The first quotation is taken from pp. 50, 62—these are contiguous, signatures D1^v, D2^r, pagination mistaken. The second quotation is from p. 120; the fourth line is not in black letter, unlike the rest (therefore my italics).

"Though all things made doe fall and fade, the kindes yet neuer slide."[17] Through Love there is permanence and order:

The skie, the ground, the seas and ayre, and raging fiers flame,
And eke in fine, the world it selfe (by loues enduring knot)
So many yeares doth stande and last, for if this loue were not:
The elements altogether would with bursten bonds goe fight.
Nor downe to earth, the Heauens would shew forth their blisseful
    light,
And beames so warm: No seede should growe, and eke the fierie
    flame
This Ayre his neighbor, would consume. . . .
The seas should quench the fire quite, or rather fire boyle
And waste away the fishie seas. . . .

Then comes praise of peace, and of powerful love in whom this harmony subsists. This is surely the same huge elemental battle array which Spenser describes in the *Hymne of Loue*, when he tells how Love linked together the elements and restrained them from bringing on their own "confusion and decay." Googe states this notion of creation more baldly in his Seventh Book (Libra):

The world in such a wondrous sort the almightie Lord did frame,
That many things doe well agree as ioyned in the same.
And many things doe disagree, and keepe continuall fight,
Whereby some mē haue surely thought, that strife and friendship might
Be iustly calde beginnings chiefe, by which are all things wrought.
    . . .

Palingenius' book was printed in 1537; Googe's translation, the *Zodiake of Life*, came out in 1565, with later editions in 1576 and 1588. Gabriel Harvey remarks that Digges knows Palingenius' Book Aquarius (XI) by heart, and that "M. Spenser conceiues the like pleasure in the fourth day of the first Weeke of Bartas."[18] Spenser also knew Googe, in all probability.[19]

Lydgate, who was honorably regarded by sixteenth-century lovers of Chaucer, is most likely to include his similar cosmologi-

[17] This close connection between the power of Love (Peace, Natura, Harmony, the Providence or Wisdom of God) and the power of Mutability, is the mediaeval connection. The traditional resolution of apparent change in the world into the real changelessness of eternal law and of God's love is also that of Spenser's *Mutability* and, in different terms, of his Garden of Adonis passage.

[18] *Gabriel Harvey's Marginalia*, ed. Moore Smith (Stratford, 1913), p. 161.

[19] V. Carpenter, *Reference Guide*, 91; Jones, *Sp. Handbook*, 31.

cal ideas in discussions of the functions of "Nature," although he sometimes stresses other aspects of the theory. A typical passage is one in *Reson and Sensuallyte*.[20] Dame Nature, through her eternal power, "The elementez dothe gouerne In ther werkyng ful contrayre"; this "lady debonayre" accords them "in oon," and "after severeth hem anoon, And devydeth hem a-sonder: The ton here and the tother yonder." She repairs new each earthly thing, "By naturel reuolucion And new[e] generacion"; she continues the kinds, however the single creature may "By naturel disposicion, . . . tourne to corrupcion." The notion of the strife between the elements is the very basis for the poem "On the Mutability of Human Affairs,"[21] with refrain "How shuld man than be stedfast in livyng." Man has the various contrary qualities of the four elements from which he is made; he is "complexionat of sondryfold coloures"; he has the contrary dispositions of the four seasons with their opposing qualities; he is influenced by the mutable moon and all the different planets; he is a pilgrim from Youth to Age; "How shuld he than be stedfast of lyvyng?" (A passage in Gower's *Confessio Amantis* has the same argument).[22] Other common developments of the idea are shown conveniently together in this poem. In discussing the changeableness of the elements, for example, it includes statements about the changing of one element into another, similar to those of Spenser's *Mutability*, VII, 25, and introduced for the same purpose. Spenser has: "Thus, all these fower (the which the ground-work bee Of all the world, and of all liuing wights) . . . Yet are they

[20] *EETS*, ex. ser. 84, 89, *v.* 283ff. This poem is adapted from the French *Échecs Amoureux*. See also the first quotation in note 13 above.

[21] *Minor Poems*, ed. Halliwell, *Percy Soc.* II, 193ff; not listed as spurious in MacCracken, *EETS*, ex. ser. 107, xlvii. Somewhat the same point is made in Lydgate's "Al stant in chaunge like a mydsomer rose" (*ibid.*, xxii; *Percy Soc.* II, 22ff); the seasons are used as illustration and the poem ends with an *ubi sunt* catalogue.

[22] Prol. 971, in a passage on 'Division' (ed. Macaulay, II, 31):

It may ferst proeve upon a man;
The which, for his complexioun
Is mad upon divisioun
Of cold, of hot, of moist, of drye,
He mot be verray kynde dye:
For the contraire of his astat
Stant evermore in such debat, . . .

This is a common notion, of course.

chang'd . . . The Fire to Aire, and th'Ayre to Water sheere, And Water into Earth: yet Water fights With Fire, . . . Yet all are in one body, and as one appeare"; cf. Lydgate: "Fyr resolvethe erthe by watry, And watry thynges fyr turneth into hayr." These four changing elements were "compact in our makyng" (pp. 195–96); Spenser's last sentence is the theme of Lydgate's whole poem.[23] In Spenser, this comes after a review of the powers of Mutability—of how all things that spring from earth must decay and "turne again vnto their earthly slime," of how men change from "youth to eld, from wealth to pouerty," of the inconstancy of water, the flitting of the subtle air, the shifting changes from sunshine to bitter storm. The procession of seasons and months follows. In Lydgate, the changing elements are part of a similar universe of change—the four elements thus "flettyng," the air "so remevable," "sotil" fire and "mutable" earth, the "watir nevir in oon," unsteadfast man, made of these, and returning "To erthe ageyn by processe corumpable," sharing in the variable qualities of each season and in those of each planet. A stanza of description is given to each of the seasons; there is no steadfastness in any of them, in the "brihte shynyng" of "Titan" in summer, or in winter's cold that despoils the earth. Man's life in the world is unsure—"an ebbe of povert next ffloodys of richesse," and a continual "transmutacioun," from "the sesoun of greene lusty age" to manhood and old age. The poem ends with an appeal which is the common mediaeval answer to the question of mutability, and which (though far simpler in its implications) is not unlike Spenser's "stedfast rest of all things . . . Vpon the pillours of Eternity" when all shall rest "With Him that is the God of Sabbaoth hight" (*Mut.* VIII):

> Man! left up thyn eye to the hevene,
> And pray the Lord, which is eternal!
> That sitt so ferre above the sterrys sevene,
> In his paleys moost Imperyal!
> To graunt the grace heer in this liff mortal, . . .
> And, or thu passe, remyssioun fynal,
> Toward that lyf wher joye is ay lastyng!
>
> (*Minor Poems,* p. 198)

[23] Cf. also, *e.g. Roman de la Rose,* 16961ff; *v.* above pp. 54–55. On the changing of the elements into each other *v.* Albright, *op. cit.,* 732.

This is the traditional solution to the familiar mediaeval problem which finds shallow and commonplace but still fairly typical statement in this poem.

These quotations from mediaeval texts do not represent the particularly advanced or complicated theories peculiar to any one thinker or to any one school of thought. They merely state with clarity certain widely prevailing generalizations of the cosmology and physics of the period. These are typical contexts; it is quite natural that these ideas should appear in courtly romances set in the garden of the God of Love, or in praises sung to the power of Love, of Venus, or of Dame Nature, or that they should find place in half-scientific, half-philosophical treatises with a Neo-Platonic cast of thought, or in didactic poetry intent (like the treatises) upon preaching certain tenets of Christian theology. That Spenser presents the same generalizations in similar contexts and with similar coloring or imaginative "machinery" of figures and setting, is indicative of a closer relationship than we commonly recognize between his thought and that of the mediaeval period. The Cambridge education of Spenser's day was still a mediaeval as well as a Renaissance education; a sixteenth-century poet must still have been influenced in his ideas of a Christian philosophical poetry by the literature and philosophy of the age which had preceded him, in a period when much of this was still regarded quite unselfconsciously as the truthful findings of previous Christian philosophers. Harvey's famous reference to the poet as a "curious vniuersal scholler" is part of a passage in praise of the astronomical learning of certain mediaeval poets; he did not regard their works as Early English Texts, but as part of the available body of information and ideas, to be made use of wherever necessary, like all information. We need not expect to find any particular mediaeval document or author whom Spenser followed assiduously as a source for his Mutability, or his Dame Nature, or his ideas of the creation. However, we can find and note statements of similar ideas in places where he was likely to have read them and taken them for truth. We may thus at least try and distinguish what Spenser chose from the common heritage to make into the tissue of what we call his own thought.

Spenser and the Zodiake of Life*

THE reference to Spenser's devotion to the "proper profession of Urania" and his pleasure in the first week of Du Bartas is one of the most familiar of Gabriel Harvey's observations about him. Harvey remarks upon a certain Palingenius, whose "Aquarius" "M. Digges hath . . . bie hart: & takes mutch delight to repeate . . . often"; he then adds that "M. Spenser conceiues the like pleasure in the fourth day of the first Weeke of Bartas." He goes on to say that "Excellent Doctor Gesner made as singular account of the most learned Zodiacus of Palingenius Stellatus, as owre worthie Mr Thomas Digges. Who esteemes him abooue all moderne poets, for a pregnant introduction into Astronomie, & both philosophies. With a fine touch of the philosophers stone itself, the quintessence of nature, & art sublimed." Again, Harvey puts "learned Palingenius" into a list of authors who had not been "wronged" by their English translators.[1] Barnabe Googe's translation, the *Zodiake of Life,* came out in 1565,[2] Palingenius' original in 1537. It would seem natural that Spenser (whose *Calender* was to be published in 1579) should be interested in a book like Palingenius, *Zodiacus,* commented on by Harvey in 1574, translated by Googe (whom Spenser apparently knew).[3] According to Googe's title page,[4] "The Zodiake of life,

* Reprinted from the *Journal of English and Germanic Philology,* XXXIV (1935), 1–19.

[1] Moore Smith, *Gabriel Harvey's Marginalia* (Stratford, 1913), p. 161 (in his Twine, *Surueye of the World, v.* below), p. 231, note p. 307 (in his Chaucer, 1598). Palingenius is also mentioned by Harvey, p. 162. 6, 163. 2.

[2] Later editions in 1576, 1588. The first three books came out in 1560, the first six in 1561, but the year starts with March, so that Aquarius is Book XI—in the full editions at least.

[3] V. Carpenter, *Reference Guide,* p. 91, Jones, *Spenser Handbook,* p. 31; F. F. Covington, Jr., "Biog. Notes on Spenser," *MP,* XXII (1924–1925), 65–66. One of Grindal's statutes for St. Begh's School, of his foundation (and from which he sent scholars to Pembroke) is: "The master is advised to teach his scholars *Palingenius, Sedulius* and *Prudentius*" (Strype, *Life of Grindal,* Oxford, 1821, p. 463). William Chaderton, an old Pembroke man, disputant with Cartwright and Harvey's friend Clerke in 1564, Leicester's chaplain, and President of Queens', 1568, prefixed a Latin elegy to Googe's 1561 edition (*Ath. Cantab.,* II, 482–83).

[4] I use the 1588 edition (Library of Congress): *Imprinted at London by Robert Robinson* | *dwelling in Feter Lane neere* | *Holborne. 1588.* |

written | by the excellent and Christian Poet, | *Marcellus Palingenius* | *Stellatus,*" contains "twelue seuerall labours, painting out most liuely, the whole compasse of the world, the reformation of manners, the miseries of mankinde, the pathway to vertue & vice, . . . the misteries of nature, and diuers other circumstances of great learning. . . ." Spenser's *Calender* has purposes much like these; the "generall end" of the *Faerie Queene* is still more definitely this "painting out lively" the pathway to virtue; we may believe from his works that Spenser would have poetry be just such a learned Christian survey of "the whole compasse of the world." He could hardly have missed hearing of the *Zodiake of Life;* and it seems very unlikely that he would have left it unread.

A writer of Spenser's predispositions would have noted in the *Zodiake* discussions of certain familiar ideas: of strife and friendship as the chief beginnings of the world, of Love as the principle which keeps the elements in harmony, brings order in the world and thus growth and continuity, of God as the "workeman" of the world, of chance and law and mutability, of seeming change but real stability, of inspiration through God's "sacred spright," inflaming the mind with "heauenly loue" and causing it to mount up through the spheres to join itself to the divine, of Urania who helps the poet to "disclose Dame Nature's face." He would also have found certain settings and motifs—a dark garden of Proserpina, a paradise where the lady Voluptuousness dwells, who changes men into beasts (so at least the hero is warned).

These similar settings and motifs are perhaps most immediately striking. I shall take them up first because I think they show definite relationships with Spenser's similar descriptions. Nevertheless they seem to me less important than the stress upon philosophical, "astronomical" knowledge, which parallels certain preoccupations of Spenser's. I may make clear here before examining the two texts the limitations and particular nature of the relationship which one may expect to find between Spenser and Palingenius; it is not one of those which suddenly illuminate a whole phase of a poet's thought, explain his obscurities and justify his inconsistencies. But the relationship between what a poet reads and what he produces appears in many less complete degrees than actual borrowing or reproducing; we may even know of some definite "source" for the conceptions or descriptions which show similarity.

I have taken it here as part of the study of a poet's sources to examine (in books which we have reason to think he knew) whatever common habits we find in the disposition of material, whatever settings we know he was fond of, whatever reiterations we find of "conceipts" we know were sympathetic to him. To do this is only to try to follow the poet in the reading of a book—to find, as he may have, re-emphasis and new warrant for ideas and manner already familiar and loved, to be struck as he was struck, in vulnerable places. Obviously, we can repeat with only an attempt at fullness the process by which what went into the poet's mind was tempered, combined, remade, into what we know as "his."

Certain descriptions in Googe's Palingenius, not themselves beautiful, nevertheless show themselves (I think) to have been suggestive to Spenser. For example: Spenser's source for the "direfull deadly blacke" *Gardin of Proserpina* into which Guyon is led by Mammon is supposed to be Claudian's *De raptu Proserpinae*.[5] The passage in Claudian is part of a promise made by Pluto to Proserpina; she shall have "soft meads," "everblooming flowers," "gentler zephyrs," great power over many things, and—most striking—a precious tree with golden fruit.[6] This is all we find in Claudian. Here is Spenser's passage:

> [Mammon] . . . him forth thence led
> Through griesly shadowes by a beaten path,
> Into a gardin goodly garnished
> With hearbs and fruits, whose kinds mote not be red: . .
> But direfull deadly blacke both leafe and bloom,
> Fit to adorne the dead, and decke the drery toombe.
> There mournfull *Cypresse* grew in greatest store,
> And trees of bitter *Gall*, and *Heben* sad,
> Dead sleeping *Poppy*, and blacke *Hellebore*,
> Cold *Coloquintida*, and *Tetra* mad,
> Mortall *Samnitis*, and *Cicuta* bad, . . .
> The *Gardin* of *Proserpina* this hight;
> And in the midst thereof a siluer seat, . . .
> Next thereunto did grow a goodly tree,

[5] *FQ*, ed. Todd (London, 1805), III, 459–60, Warton's note; ed. Winstanley (Cambridge, 1919), introd. xxxix; ed. Kitchin (9th ed., Oxford, 1903), note p. 208.

[6] Claudian, *De raptu Proserpinae*, Loeb ed., II, 338 (Bk. II, vv. 287ff). Also, to her feet shall come "purple-clothed kings" now rendered equal with other men, by death; cf. the Googe passage.

With braunches broad dispred and body great,
Clothed with leaues, that none the wood mote see
And loaden all with fruit as thicke as it might bee.
Their fruit were golden apples glistring bright, . . .
And his broad braunches, laden with rich fee, . . .
. . . ouer-hanging, they themselues did steepe,
In a blacke flood which flow'd about it round;
This is the riuer of *Cocytus* deepe,
In which full many soules do endlesse waile and weepe.
(*FQ* II, vii, 51ff)

Spenser is supposed to have added to Claudian's account, "by giving details of the plants in the garden; he makes them all gloomy and poisonous."[7] He also makes "another use" of the river Cocytus—"that the shores of this river eternally resounded with the shrieks of damned ghosts," immersed in its waters.[8]

Certain passages in the *Zodiake of Life* will fill out this idea of the origin of the *Gardin of Proserpina.* Suppose Spenser to have had in mind the Claudian passage. We think of him as having the kind of mind which made very real that familiar process by which, as poetry is read, the impressions seized upon by the imagination are embodied—realized almost actually as sensuous experiences—and almost simultaneously given color, texture, and elaboration by what is subconsciously associated with them in the reader's mind. To this vivid inward sight, Claudian's garden is a garden in hell, under the black earth, promised to the dark god of the underworld—taking on, too, the devil's darkness. He is wed to Proserpina; two shining things in his garden—fair Proserpina and the bright gold gleaming tree: "est etiam lucis arbor praedives opacis fulgentes viridi ramos curvata metallo. . . ." If one may judge by the qualities of his writing, Spenser made sharp visual images as he read—these images come out in his poetry, with black-and-white definiteness, flat coloring, "statuesque groupings," careful detail of line.[9] Suppose that before his own vision of what he read in Claudian was gone from his mind he had picked up the *Zodiake of Life* and had read, under the sign Virgo (VI), how the quester, seeking Dame Virtue, had a vision of Death, how he was taught, in a dark death-like garden, the sad end of mortal life:

[7] ed. Winstanley, xxxix. [8] ed. Todd, III, 460.
[9] J. B. Fletcher, "The Painter of the Poets," *SP*, XIV (1917), 153–66.

Beholde, I enter nowe the way which with a lothsome shade:
The Cipresse and the Yeutree hides, with leaues that neuer fade.
The doubtfull fieldes and darkesome raigne of Proserpine I see:
Wherein the Letheus riuer runs, with streames that darkned be.
Amyd the poysoned fields abroad, doth slepy Popie spring
On silent shores, Calliope whereto dost thou me bring? . . .
With doleful noyse of yrkesome Owles, sounds all the woods so darke,
The scrichowles cry with woefull tunes, and loud lamenting noyse,
O Muse, whereto dost thou me bring? behold, with wayling voyce
The hilles and valleis all doe rore, and Eccho backe doth beat
The mourning tunes: An answere giue, what griefe is this so
great? . . .
What men are they that thus in blacke, with weeping fill the skies?
Alas, what sight of bodies slayne, lie here before myne eyes? . . .
How many Kings and Bishops bones lie here? . . .

[Death comes, with bloody scythe, and speaks of his power; the quester trembles; he is told by "Ioue his daughter deare" that fear is beastly, that man must search beyond the shadow of things for their truth]

It is not easie for eche one the truth it selfe to know,
This is the selfe same bowe that doth amid the great wood grow,
With trees of order thicke embraste, that misty errors hide,
Nor euer might this golden twig of many men be spide, . . .

(*ZL*, pp. 84ff)

There is no word here which says that this garden of Proserpina was "deadly blacke both leafe and bloom." These leaves are unfading because they are ever green. But into the picture that Spenser was making from what he already had from Claudian, no green could come; nor does it for us as we re-read Googe's description—the only color and light come from the gold twigs of the tree. These very fields are "poysoned," fed by the darkened river, whose black streams are layers of dark within dark. It runs without sound; the poppy grows on the silent black shores. It is not very strange that this "*darkesome* raigne," these "woods so *darke*," with leaves that never fade, never whiten, should become to Spenser "direfull deadly blacke," trees "of bitter *Gall*, and *Heben* sad," black "both leafe and bloom" (*FQ* II, vii, 51–52). In the *Zodiake* description, "Amyd the poysoned fields . . . doth slepy Popie spring. On silent shores"; to Spenser this is the silence of death—cold, swift, deliberate death, accurately dealt, creeping into the veins from "Dead sleeping *Poppy*, and blacke *Hellebore,* Cold *Coloquintida,* and *Tetra* mad, Mortall *Samnitis* . . ." (*FQ* II, vii, 52). Pluto's promise ends darkly. Claudian's "soft meads," Googe's "*doubtfull* fieldes and . . . raigne of *Proserpine,*" have become in Spenser's *Gardin of Proserpina* black as death, full of dire fear. Googe's "raigne" is come upon by a way hidden by Cipresse and Yeutree "with a lothsome shade"; Guyon is led to Spenser's *Gardin* "Through griesly shadowes by a beaten path," "There mournfull *Cypresse* grew in greatest store." These *griesly shadowes* and *lothsome shade* are—by way of *shade: phantom* and other reverberations of this almost symbolic word—evil and horrid not only by their physical darkness.

With Googe's next line this silence is broken. "With *doleful* noyse of yrkesome Owles," with the scrich owl's "*woefull* tunes, and loud *lamenting* noyse" "sounds all the woods"; "behold, with *wayling voyce* The hilles and valleis all doe rore, and *Eccho backe doth beat* The *mourning* tunes." The quester asks what "is the cause of mischiefe such, what kinde of people those" in "wayling vesture," what men "in blacke, with *weeping* fill the skies." In Spenser's *Gardin,* Guyon sees in the "*blacke* flood" many damned wights; in those "*sad* waues" "full many soules do endlesse *waile and weepe,*" plunged therein by "cruell Sprights"; "with their pitteous cryes and yelling shrights, They made the further *shore resounden* wide."[10] Guyon asks of these "*ruefull* sights" who they are, what they "ment thereby." They are cursed examples—greedy Tantalus and false Pilate, damned into hell for frail intemperance. Accurst of the Lord of Life, they are the tormented examples of man's endless end, in a Proserpina's garden that is also hell-mouth. In the *Zodiake of Life* the combination of Lethean fields and Christian hell is more inept. "Calliope whereto dost thou me bring?"[11] asks the quester; not the Muse

[10] I italicize words which are possible echoes (unconscious, of course), if it is true, as I think, that the sights and sounds of the Googe passage were in Spenser's subconscious remembrance, as an imagined sense-experience closely associated with the one which he was at the moment imaging.

[11] The fact that Calliope is the muse called upon is interesting in connection with Dr. Padelford's article on "The Muse of the *Faerie Queene*" (*SP*, XXVII [1930], 111–24), holding that Calliope, not Clio, is Spenser's "greater Muse." Spenser's characterization of Calliope as "the nurse of vertue . . . And golden Trompet of eternitie" by whom the fame of mortal men is made immortal (*Teares of Muses,* 457) is definitely a fitting one for the Calliope of the *ZL*—the Muse

comes to explain, but the mediaeval figure of Death himself, a "Ghastly fiend" who cuts down all, even mighty Kings and the pompous pride of prelates. The morality-like speech of Death brings forth the quester's soliloquy on "time that euermore doth chaunge," on "fading human kinde."[12] Spenser's "ensamples" to teach "all that liue in high degree" "how to vse their present state" are not, as these are, mere opportunities to play upon the conventional stops—but both authors are making the same point with similar machinery. Googe's visitor to the otherworld has learned as Guyon did what is the end of man, who is but dust.

There was not much that was new for Spenser to learn from this Proserpina passage. There is no group of striking details, surely peculiar to this description, which he added to his known source. The golden twig that cuts across the blackness of Googe's description typifies truth rather than the "sinfull bayt" of Spenser's golden-fruited tree; the wood of error, though interesting, is out of place. And yet, given the picture Spenser already had,

who shows the way in the quest of Dame Vertue's dwelling, and who brings the quester to Proserpina's Raigne where he is shown the sad fate of those great ones whose mortal pride gave them so false an idea of fame and greatness. Cf. the nature of this quest and this lesson with Spenser's lament of Calliope in *TM*, and then with his address to his muse in *FQ* I, xi, 5: "The Nourse of time, and euerlasting fame . . ." (*v.* Padelford, esp. 114–5). Cf. also the resemblance in cadence between the two questions in *ZL* (esp. "O M u s e , whereto dost thou me bring? behold," etc.) and Spenser's "Ah! whither doost thou now thou greater Muse | Me from these woods and pleasing forrests bring?" (VII, vii, 1).

12 "Much like to Roses that doe shewe a gorgeous gaudy face | When sunne doth rise, and when the night appears do lose their grace"—which would only have suggested to Spenser the passage which is his source for the lovely stanzas in *FQ* II, xii. He could have noted (unconsciously, again) in Googe new emphasis for several old commonplaces like this. *V.*, *e.g.*, Envy, snake in bosom, chewing a toad, the poison running about his maw (*FQ* I, iv. 30–31); cf. *ZL* 21—Covetousness, with ugly adders, her "greedy iawes" never sated "with bloud of men," "churlish chaps deuouring meat"; the familiar figure of a boat at stages of its journey, for the introductions of cantos (books, in *ZL*); the fatal birds in the Proserpina passage; the long eulogies of Friendship, of the virtuous man, of Reason; the shepherds' eclogue contests; the fiery-eyed King of Pride, whose men have hooks and bellows to blow up men's minds. Perhaps a reading of Goorge's vivid description of Proserpina's dark and woeful Raigne may have some connection with Spenser's confusion of Persephone and Tisiphone in *TM* 164, *VGnat* 422; cf. *Sh. Cal.* gloss for November (*v. Minor Poems*, ed. de Sélincourt, 516). The *Zodiake* passage would fit well enough the description in *TM* of the "sad sights" of man's life and death: "So all with rufull spectacles is fild, Fit for *Megera* or *Persephone.*"

given his quality of imagination, and his predispositions, it seems logical to see a source-connection here, and an example of Spenser's way of transforming the shoddy material of conventional moralizing and shallow "allegory" into the lovely stuff of his own poetry.

Another description in the *Zodiake*—of the paradise of Voluptuousness—may be related to such descriptions in Spenser as the House of Pride or the Bower of Bliss (more complicated however in their provenance than his *Gardin of Proserpina*). In the *Zodiake,* Book III (Gemini), the hero meets an old man, Epicure, who says that men should enjoy this life, for death is the end; not far from here Voluptuousness, "that lusty Lady, dwels," so hand-in-hand they set out to seek her. They go by "strange unhaunted waies"; suddenly, "Behold appeares a sumptuous house." The quester asks of his guide, "What owner keepes that precious gem, and princely palace wide?" "Plutus . . . possesseth this," answers the old man; he says that an armed knight keeps the way so that none can pass without a gift to Plutus, who holds "his hall amid yon towry clift." Plutus has three daughters—"Filthy excesse," "Swelling pride," and "Foolish ignorance" (p. 28). The two decide to go a different way; it is stony and grown with thorns, but leads them to the paradise where dwells the "worthy Queene" they seek. This is surrounded by the "water cleare" of a river, full of "scaley beasts" and with banks a deer's leap apart; it has for a wall lofty pines with "crabbed bark"; there are roses, pansies, a thousand kinds of birds and trees, odors of frankincense and spices, a space in the center with tables covered with dainties. As they look on, the Queen comes walking in the field, with her train; at her right hand is Venus with her pleasant face and her blind boy. At the left hand of the Queen is another woman, Gluttony—

> Whose chaps doe alwaies chaw the cud her golles they greasy beene:
> With musty, dusty, lothsome clothes, whose stinke doth all anoy:
> . . .
> Great tankards deepe she turneth quite the bottoms vpside downe:
> And in her hand a boy she leads, with drousy drouping crowne,
> And winking eies: he scarce could wake nor would his dame permit
> With meate and drinke thus ouerchargde to haue a waking fit:
>
> (*ZL*, p. 31)

As they watch, a Dame runs from the wood to warn them; this Queen is no goddess, though she has gold and gems. Let not her face deceive them; she has spots within. As did Circe, so doth this Queen "change them that her regard. For dish in hand to them she giues, of pleasant poyson full, Of which who drinkes is straight transformde in Lion, Bore or Bull. . . ."

Each single detail in the description of the Garden itself—and even many in the procession of figures—could be found in half a dozen other paradises of pleasure. But their combination here is very interesting if we reflect that Spenser, with Lucifera, Philotime, Acrasia still only partly realized in his mind, might easily have come upon this paradise too, in addition to those in Tasso, in mediaeval garden-of-love poems, etc. Besides the garden and temple of Venus herself in Book IV Spenser has other important uses of this motif: the Bower of Bliss, whose mistress turns her lovers into beasts; the palace of Pride, daughter of Pluto and Proserpina; the palace of Mammon's daughter Philotime (less related to the tradition). We may look at Spenser's descriptions to see what evidences there are that he had read, portrayed in his imagination and half-remembered the deceiving pleasaunce described by Googe.

The difference between Googe's earthly paradise and those in Spenser seem to represent the kind of changes that would have been made in Spenser's imagination as he read. The motif remaining the same, in general outline and purpose, certain details would have been seized on and retained (especially if striking to the eye), certain others vivified, certain figures brought to life and given symbolical or philosophical significance. We may look first at the palace of Pride in Book I. In Googe, the "sumptuous house"—the "precious gem, and princely palace wide"—which the bad guide Epicure and the quester saw on their way, belonged to Plutus. He lived "amid yon towry clift" with his daughters (one of them S w e l l i n g p r i d e). Spenser's Red Crosse Knight, guided by the false Duessa, comes to the house of Pride, a "stately Pallace" on a sandy hill, bright with "golden foile," high with "loftie towres." Proud Lucifera has "made her selfe a Queene" and claimed descent from Jove, "with pride so did she swell." This Pride is daughter "Of griesly *Pluto* . . . And sad *Proserpina* the Queene of hell"[13] (Googe's description of the

[13] Cf. Lowes, in "Spenser and the *Mirour de l'Omme*": "Moreover, Spenser gives Pride (so far as I know) a unique parentage: 'Of griesly *Pluto* . . . And

"raigne of Proserpine" comes in a later book as the setting for a moral lesson against Pride, as we have seen). Forth comes this "royall Dame . . . with Princely pace" to her coach. Her sage counsellors ride upon the beasts which draw her; first comes sluggish Idlenesse "Stil drownd in sleepe," "Scarse could he once vphold his heauie hed, To looken, whether it were night or day." By his side comes "loathsome" Gluttony, still eating, in his hand "a bouzing can" of which he sups too often. Compare Googe's always-chewing Gluttony, with her loathsome clothes, her tankards deep, her drowsy boy whose head will not stay up nor eyes stay open.

These pictures are of course not the same. Gluttony is a woman, she has musty clothes, not vine leaves; the slothful sleepy boy is not the monk Idlenesse. But still the similarities in idea and in picturesque detail are of a kind which would naturally result from Spenser's reading Googe's description and (unconsciously, almost) keeping scraps of it in his mind. The obvious verbal similarities are also such as would result from this unrealized retention of visible or very "pat" detail. *Swelling Pride*, daughter of Pluto, made Spenser a fitting kind of Lucifera, with the satanic qualities of both her underworld fathers. Lucifera's classical parentage and her train of Christian vices are part of the characteristic superimposing of Christian upon pagan underworld so common in the Middle Ages and still natural to both Palingenius and Spenser. The ways in which Spenser and the *Zodiake* juxtapose the two kinds of material are exactly parallel (as also in the Proserpina passages). Googe's parentage of Pride and his quester's adventure would have strengthened notions familiar to Spenser, and helped to suggest the machinery of pictorial detail in which Spenser liked to envelop his ideas. This detail, in Googe, is of a sort that Spenser liked and remembered. He would have seen with an almost actual sight the palace outlined high up on the "towry clift," the hall being held, the processional group with the queen at its head,

---

sad *Proserpina* the Queene of hell' " (*PMLA*, XXIX [1914], 403). Googe does not make Proserpina mother of Pride, but he makes Pluto father of her—and the union of "Pluto, and his quene, Proserpina" was as familiar a mythographers' commonplace to Googe and Spenser as it was to Chaucer's Merchant. There is in Googe a vivid description of the *reign* of Proserpina, and a reference to the palace of Pluto and his daughters—among them Pride; it is like Spenser to store his imagination with pictures and as he uses them, unthinkingly to relate Pluto, Proserpina, and Pride in this more orderly way.

the queen's grotesque attendants—to which were to be added all his multitudinous remembrances of Seven Sins processions, read or seen. The small details which are similar in the two accounts are of the kind likely to persist in Spenser's vision—for example, the sleepy boy whose drowsy head droops heavily (deliberately changed into a monk). Spenser's figures are carefully line-drawn —such ones he would also most clearly picture to himself as he read; he catches them in an act and pins them down in it much as illustration does. So his Gluttony forever drinks from his "bouzing can," as Googe's forever shows the bottom of the tankard.[14]

The underworld palace of Mammon's daughter Philotime may possibly be comparable with that of Pluto and his daughters. We know that an idea, a phrase, or a visual detail lodged in Spenser's mind brought forth many things, not one; and these variations on the theme of *underworld god*: *proud daughter* are striking. However, if there is a relationship here it is a faint one, and certainly unintended by Spenser.[15]

The end of the adventure in Googe seems to me to have gone into Spenser's imagination not as a mental image but as a notion, to be combined with other impressions from many sources and come out as part not of another picture but of another moral exemplum, in the Bower of Bliss. It is possible that as Spenser described the appearance of the bower, he remembered, as a picture, the similar garden in Googe; however, he had read of dozens of them, and the two settings are chiefly alike in having the same conventional paraphernalia.[16] In Googe the quester on his way to

[14] Cf. Lowes, *op. cit.*, p. 415: "The 'bouzing can' has been identified with the 'cantharus' in Vergil's description of Silenus. But Gower's 'beau cop de vin envesselé' may certainly have been the intermediary, if not the sole suggestion."

[15] Any likeness to Googe's palace of Pluto would be interesting here because in a few stanzas we come to the *Gardin* of Proserpina. Suggestive references in Googe may have had something to do with these details: the "darksome narrow strait" through which the quester Guyon is led, the guardian of the castle, the magnificent hall, pompous proud Philotime, the striving of the people to rise in degree by "vnrighteous reward," "base regard" or through friends (the three maids of whom Googe's quester is told—Fraud, Usury and Chance—may have helped to fill out Spenser's idea of what things went on in Pluto's stronghold).

[16] Almost all such conventional gardens—Googe's with them—had the same earthly-paradise characteristics as Acrasia's: the spacious green plain, the soft and fragrant air, the "painted flowres," the "trembling groues, the Christall running by," the sweet sounds of birds and water, the "blanket houses," the wanton lovely Lady (*FQ* II, xii). Even similarly stressed details, like the high trees and the

the garden of Pleasure is led past the palace where "Filthy excesse" lives; in Spenser he pauses by the porch kept by *Excesse* "fowle disordered" (supposedly original with Spenser, surely original as a vividly seen figure). Neither garden is quite the conventional *Roman de la Rose* pleasaunce; both teach the same moral lesson with the same device. The Dame who runs to Googe's quester and his guide warns them that this Lady is only beautiful without, and foul within; she changes her men into beasts, she ensnares them like a spider. This Dame then talks to the quester and tells him how Reason should guide the "affections of the minde," how lusts of the body (drunkenness, sleep, luxury) must be controlled. Googe's "lusty Lady," "Voluptuousnesse," in Spenser is "Pleasure," Acrasia the "Enchauntresse"; Guyon and his old guide (very different in character from old Epicure) find out the same deception. Both authors tell the story as a pointed example of the "sad end . . . of life intemperate, And mournefull meed of ioyes delicious" (*FQ* II, xii, 85). It is true that this is not an extraordinary aim for a Christian philosophical poet of the age of Gosson; and these two gardens, though alike in appearance, in purpose, and in their Circe-like ladies, coincide in details that are often commonplace and never peculiar to them alone. But still the similarities are interesting if we may think of Spenser (his mind already stocked with Gardens of Love from other sources) reading Googe and merging that use of the motif with the others, making it (as usual) more carefully drawn, more seeable with the eye, but using his Garden of Love likewise as an exemplum of Intemperance.

The description of the Garden and Temple of Venus in *FQ* IV, x is in a different temper. Spenser here shows a conception of Love which is neither the Reason-and-Sensuality motif of Book II nor the *service des dames* of the mediaeval courtly romances. Spenser's conception of Love in the Garden of Venus, especially as seen in the figure of Concord and in the hymn to Venus, is more like the idea of Love as a cosmic principle or creating force, found in the *Hymnes* and in *Colin Clout.* I shall only outline briefly

laurels, are common (cf. Spenser's "trees vpshooting hye," Googe's "trees so hie Which with their tops doe seeme to touch the . . . sky" [p. 29]; Spenser's "all the margent round about was set, With shady Laurell trees," Googe's ". . . round about . . . beset, with bowes of laurell tree"—and a comparison of this garden with another).

here [17] the similarities between Spenser's cosmological conception of Love and that found in the *Zodiake.* In Googe's fourth book (which follows that treating of the garden of pleasure) the guiding Dame sends her son down from the sky to discourse upon Venus, "without whom the use of earth would cease" ("this loue, a thing of fame" it is, he says). If all things were not held together by "loues assured knot," "if this loue were not," then "The elements altogether would with bursten bonds goe fight." No seed would grow, the elements would decay, "The worlde should straight be at an end" (*ZL,* 47ff; cf. the description in the first *Hymne* of the linking together of the inimical elements with "Adamantine chaines," by Love). This marvellous according of the discordant qualities in all things is discussed again in the *Zodiake,* Book VII; Googe says that therefore "some me*n* haue surely thought, that strife and friendship might Be iustly calde beginnings chiefe, by which are all things wrought." He goes on to explain why and how there is growth in the world:

> How liuing things doe waxe so great, what causeth them to growe:
> And why at certayne time they cease. A fiery spirit doth raigne,
> Which quickneth euery liuing thing . . .
> This heate doth liuely moysture feede . . . (*ZL,* p. 122)

Compare the *Hymne to Loue,* after the description of Love's according of the elements in the creation: "[through Love's behest] now all these things that are contained Within this goodly cope, . . . Their being haue, and dayly are increast, Through secret sparks of his infused fyre." (In the Garden of Adonis passage it is the Sun which makes matter when "tempred right With heate and humour" conceive life; Googe also makes this identification between the Sun and the "fire," "spirit"—but according to him *God* so "framde it" that his light might be "fixed in the Sunne" "And shine, creating day and life, and goodly things beside" [p. 231]).

Thus, according to Googe, the world's stability and growth as well as its coming-to-be result from the harmony and balance in which all things are held by "loues enduring knot" (*v.* esp. *ZL,* p. 62—mistaken pagination for 51). This is the same conception of

[17] I have treated more fully elsewhere the similar statement by Spenser and the *Zodiake* of this familiar conception of the functions of Love ("A Mediaeval Commonplace in Spenser's Cosmology," *SP,* XXX [1933], 143). [Cf. pp. 49–63 above.]

Love's creative function in the world and of Love as the principle of growth that Spenser shows in the passages in the *Hymne to Loue* and *Colin Clout* on the creation and ordering of the universe, in the figure of Concord seen by Scudamour as he goes into the Garden of Venus, and in the hymn to Venus which he hears there. Scudamour's description of the temple of Venus and of the altar itself, of the flock of little loves and the complaining lovers, is on the other hand the usual "courtly" use of Love, with all the familar paraphernalia of the *service des dames* conception.

In connection with the intimations of a philosophical idea of Love in Googe's Palingenius we find certain other interesting notions which would have been remarked by Spenser, as he was trying to weave conflicting concepts into a patterned whole.[18] In general, the problems are similar in statement and implication, the conclusions different in scope and in emphasis. I do not think that Spenser found either new problems or new solutions in Googe's book, but it seems plausible that these discussions by the "learned Palingenius" were among the infinite number of pricks and compulsions to thought which finally impelled Spenser to handle these problems in his own great philosophical cantos. Googe's discussion of the lasting order of things through Love includes a passage on the eternity of the "kindes," which "neuer slide" "Though all things made doe fall and fade." In the Garden of Adonis passage Spenser states his conception of the continuity of life in terms of transient particular form and eternal "substaunce"; Googe uses the traditional terms of transient individual form and lasting kinds (the usual mediaeval terms, popularized especially by the *Roman de la Rose* and the encyclopedists). God lets the bodies die, says Googe, "But not the kinds he so permits from their estate to flie"; the potter does not care if "this or that his pot be burst," he merely makes "A newer sort of them" (p. 62, mistake for 51). This is all adduced to prove how Love makes "the order of all things" to "last continually"; there follows immediately the description of the terrible things which would happen through the enmity of the elements if Love's bond did not hold all things together in a harmony which permits growth.

[18] Since the writing of this article Mrs. Josephine Bennett has treated some of the Platonic conceptions in Palingenius (not covered here) which show similarity to Spenser's, in her article on "Spenser's Garden of Adonis," *PMLA*, XLVI (1932), 46–80.

One other discussion of this problem Spenser would have read with interest, though he would have learned nothing new from it either. Googe's book Scorpius (VIII) is a discussion of chance, fortune, and cause and their ruling of the world. There is no chance, he says; there is a chain of causes which none can break—"Thalmightie workeman of the worlde hath all things vnder cast Assured lawes, and measure delt to all the thinges he past." In reality all things are certain and law-abiding. This is the answer given in mediaeval discussions of change and permanence, especially since Boethius's; as in them (and as in Spenser, with a different emphasis) so in Googe the procession of the seasons is the chief example of how all things "by their change their being doe dilate":

> . . . all things are certaine tho.
> For with one sort of mouing round the heauens alwayes goe,
> Like seede, like frute, and elements, in ancient order reigne,
> And keepe their kinde. And wonted course the yeare doth stil reteyne.
> For after S p r i n g, the S u m m e r hot himselfe hath straightwayes plaste,
> And after him with Apples thicke, and Grapes doth H a r u e s t hast,
> Next after that his nipping frostes the W i n t e r bringeth in,
> And with his Isye northern blastes all things to droupe begin.
> No herbe doth euer change his force. . . .
>
> (*ZL*, pp. 136–37)

This is not the great argument of the Mutability cantos. But Spenser's concluding words also answer the question by reference to the great workmaster of the world; all things hate steadfastness, yet their moving is eternally of one sort; "rightly wayd They are not changed from their first estate." It is possible to think that such a restatement as Googe's of the traditional argument, so convenient to Spenser's hand, may have helped to decide the final form and clothing of Spenser's exposition of the idea.

Certain other fairly commonplace elements in Spenser's conception of Love are found in the *Zodiake.* "Beauty" is emphasized as the force which allures men into subjection to Love ("beauty cause of burning flame hath louers linckes procurde"—Spenser's metaphor is the same [*CC*, 871]). As in Spenser this is part of a semi-conventional praise of "Dame Venus sonne, whos force doth cause both man & God obay"—even the "thūdring God"; but both authors go on to the larger idea of Love as the creative and ordering principle (the passage following in Googe is that explaining the power of "loues assured knot" to keep the elements from destroying the world; for all this cf. *ZL*, 48–50 with the first *Hymne* and the *CC* passage on Love). Love is a prick to lead the mind on to heavenly things; this "heauenly loue" according to Googe comes to us through God's holy Spirit, which adorns the mind of man, inflames and inspires it to mount above the things of this world, up through the various heavenly spheres, to join itself to the divine. God's "sacred Spright"—

> . . . adournes the minde, & heart doth vpward moue,
> This cuttes away the worldly cares, & breedeth heauenly loue:
> Wherewith the minde inflamed once, all things doth easie seeme,
> . . .
> Wherewith the minde inspirde may mount, aboue the starry skye,
> Despising much the world, and ioyes, that vaine doe please the eye,
> And striue to ioyne it selfe to God, with all the force and might.
> (*ZL*, p. 195)

Googe's next book is Aquarius, in which the poet with Urania's help discloses "N a t u r e s face"—in the earth below and in the various circles of heaven; in the next (Pisces) he describes the highest heaven, which is the seat of God and the abode of the angels, and compares the divine eternal kingdom with the "Chery fayre" of this earth. Here ignorant man rejoices "to lie in dong" and takes foolish comfort in this fading life. There, where God is, surrounded by light far brighter than the sun's, is eternal joy; there the Sprites and Angels, many as leaves, rejoice forever. (There is an earlier passage on the happiness of the angels, in the book treating of Proserpina's Raigne and the Tree of Truth; they know all hid causes, are not thrall to grief, for "Sapience to angels doth belong.")

These are familiar elements in Spenser's conception of Love; the last two *Hymnes* have many of the emphases found in Googe—the inspiration through the "almightie Spright" from whom come "all guifts of wit and knowledge" and the sparkling light of eternal truth, the mind inflamed with heavenly love, inspired with heavenly thoughts "farre aboue humane skil," renouncing the vain glory of this world, beginning with "th'easie vew Of this base world" and through contemplation of the Earth, the Skye sown with stars, the other heavens, mounting "vp aloft" to where God sits, amid light far exceeding that from Titan's flaming head, attended by bright Angels—who can unfold the most sacred mysteries of this fair Love, gazing at will upon that Sapience who sits in the bosom of the Deity. As I have said, these are common ideas which could hardly have been new to Spenser when he read Googe, but would have been emphasized in his mind by that reading, and whose wording would have called up many others. They are simply and often inconsistently stated; their statement is in terms familiar from mediaeval neo-Platonic discussions; they are scattered notions brought in when convenient rather than organically related members of a whole concept. Nevertheless, for us to interpret these statements and inter-relate these notions is not to read the book falsely, since that is how Spenser would have read it, relating smaller points or vivid pictures to what he already believed, building a reasoned whole out of scattered bits.

The book Aquarius was that which Digges had by heart and took "mutch delight to repeate . . . often"—perhaps to a group of curious universal scholars which included Spenser. However, this book is less interesting for direct correspondences than the others; it is perhaps chiefly important as an example of the kind of reading which helped to form Spenser's idea of the proper concerns of poetry. Invoking the muse Urania, the poet purposes "Dame Natures face for to disclose"; he discusses all natural phenomena, the heavens, Matter and Form, the great principles of Moving and Rest. It will be remembered that Harvey's reference to Spenser's love of Bartas, the parallel to Digges' love of Palingenius, includes Spenser's judgment of Bartas' fourth Day as the "proper profession of Urania." The obvious connection to be made here is that with Spenser's lament of Urania in the *Teares of the Muses.* He there makes her the same figure as the Urania of the Aquarius, with the same powers, the same delights, the same knowledge got in the same way. She is invoked as follows in the *Zodiake:*

> But first we must Vrania call, my verses herevnto,
> That she may ayde and succour sende, such secrets to vndo.
> Vrania, thou that knowest the things, aloft that hidden lie,
> That walkest oft by seates of God, and starrie temples hie:
> Vrania beautifull, drawe nere, and open vnto me,
> The secret seates of Gods aboue, and things that hidden be,
> And helpe thy Poet, that in song, thy Scepters seekes to shewe,
> And graunt the whirling Skies aboue, in minde that I may knowe.
>
> (*ZL*, p. 211)

The work for which the poet invokes Urania's aid is a review of the same knowledge which Spenser's Urania professes to believe in and to have—"of Natures cunning operation," of the skies, the stars, the "spheres swift mouement," the majesty of God, the angels "waighting on th'Almighties chayre," the precepts of a "heauenlie discipline" gained by delighted "contemplation of things heauenlie wrought." Thus this book of the *Zodiake* was like Bartas, the "proper profession of Urania" in a very definite and meaningful sense.

Harvey's reference to Palingenius and Spenser's love of Bartas is one of a significant group, occurring in his copy of Twine's *Surueye of the World* (1572; on title page "Gabrielis Harueij. 1574"). Harvey is discussing poets who are learned particularly in natural philosophy, listing various "Notable Astronomical descriptions" found in earlier English poets. "I specially note their Astronomie, philosophie, & other parts of profound or cunning art," he says at the conclusion of his list; thereupon follows immediately his famous dictum: "It is not sufficient for poets, to be superficial humanists: but they must be exquisite artists, & curious vniuersal schollers." His list of learned descriptions worthy of emulation includes references to many passages on spring, on winter, on the hours of the day, on the months, on astrology and astrologers, to be found in Lydgate, in Chaucer (many references), in the *Romance of the Rose,* the *Assembly of Ladies,* the *Testament of Cressid,* and many others. Then comes the Palingenius reference, and a list of Latin poets, then "The like fine, & gallant astrological descriptions" in Italian and French. He goes on to speak of the favorite books of astrologers; he includes among these the "Shepherds Kalendar, their primer," "The Compost of Ptolemeus, their Bible," "Albertus secrets, . . . & wonderfull Secreta secretorum," and other cosmological or "scientific compilations familiar to mediaeval writers.

The fact that Palingenius and his learned poem are referred to in this company is significant. It is important to remember the nature of the material which surrounds Harvey's dictum on the poet as scholar, if we may think of his choice of authors and his ideas of poetry as influencing Spenser's. It is interesting if there are in Spenser's poetry (as I hope I have made plausible in this article) incidents or descriptions influenced by those in Googe's Palingenius; this itself is not of exceeding importance. It would be more important if we were able to find in Harvey's recommendation of a book, in Spenser's reasons for reading it and way of using it, some clarification of their ideas on the nature and function of poetry, or something of the process by which their ideas were formed and re-formed. The ideal of the learned philosophical poet is familiar enough in Renaissance poetics; the ideas which the two philosophical poets examined here have in common are familiar too. But I think that for Harvey and Spenser, among others, the forming of this ideal of learned Christian "astronomical" poetry results in part from a familiarity with such "scientific" poets and treatises as Harvey mentions, mediaeval and late mediaeval. The connection between "philosophy" and poetry which they found in mediaeval books like the computs, the encyclopedias, the *Secreta Secretorum* and other regimens, seems to me to have definable relations with the existence and form of the *Shepheardes Calender*, perhaps even to have helped determine the character and purposes of the first three books of the *Faerie Queene*. Just as the ordinary people were familiar with much of the traditional story material now known only to learned investigators, so the "scholars" must surely have read widely in the great still unclassified mass of "scientific" and "philosophical" materials that had accumulated during the period which we now call "mediaeval" but from which they did not so definitely separate themselves. The "auncient Poetes" whose words rang in Spenser's ears are to be thought of as delightful to him partly because they were serious philosophical poets trying to explain the riddles of this world, with all "science" as their proper field. The *Zodiake of Life* carried on this learned tradition. Like them—indeed in almost precisely the same way, making use of their material and their methods—it fulfilled the high function of Christian philosophical poetry; it treated of great matters—of God, Nature and Man: his end on earth, his temptations, his virtues, and his possible helps. And it presented these in ways which Spenser approved of and often used—astronomical framework, didactic allegory, quests, dream-visions, gardens-of-love, and all the familiar devices of mediaeval romance.

Spenser's Reading: The De Claris Mulieribus*

THIS article will deal with a small but fairly simple and clear example of the relationship between Spenser and Boccaccio: with what traces there are of Spenser's having read the *De Claris Mulieribus,* with the question of which form (and in fact which edition) he read it in, and (the most significant point to be made) with the way in which this reading, often betrayed by mere phrases which it is quite unimportant to remark upon as far as source study is concerned, affected his notion of the significance of his material, pointed and directed it, and gave extra values, emotional "loading," to certain names, figures, or stories. It has importance not as a study of Spenser's borrowings, but as an attempt to see what part was played by mediaeval tradition of this kind in building a background for Spenser's almost symbolic use of certain story-figures and motifs.

In such a consideration, both the probability that Spenser would come across the *De Claris* and his attitude toward such books should be examined. To the sixteenth-century gentleman scholar or university man, the name of Boccaccio had a very different connotation from what it has to his modern equivalent. It had none of the flavour of "correlative reading in source materials" which it has for the modern student in a Chaucer course, little of the slightly salacious suggestion which modern de luxe editions and locked cases in the library have given it for the average undergraduate. Rather, he was to be thought of on one side as a Latin moralist,[1] on the other as an Italian story-writer. To the young

* Reprinted from *Studies in Philology* 33 (1936), 147–65.

[1] Bodleian MS Rawlinson A 338, 15th century, with 16th century title "English politicks," and containing advice to those interested in the State to read Boccaccio, presents an interesting example of several points in this connection: that the 16th century conceived of the later Middle Ages as part of the immediate and usable past, that MSS were part of the ordinary literary heritage just as were printed books, that Boccaccio and other mediaeval writers were quite unselfconsciously ranked with classical theorists among the authorities to be mastered. This MS belonged to the Earl of Leicester (as did also a 15th-century English version of the *Brut,* B. Mus. MS Addit. 12030, with marginalia in a hand temptingly like Spenser's, but finally thought not to be his, by Mr. Flower, head of the Dept.

litterateur of the Renaissance, alertly (if cautiously) Italianate, he would have appealed on the last of these counts, to the moral Christian poet on the first of them. He preached against sinful pride, he exposed the deceits of Fortune, he told sad stories of the falls of princes, drawing the moral from each; he spoke pointedly to his own time. But also he preached in fables, he overflowed with just sufficiently moralized histories, he made glorified *exempla* collections from extended and interesting sources, he utilized all classical materials to his purpose, he was at once learned, correct, and romantic in his attitude toward history, story material, the pastoral, and the pagan gods. He wrote novels about a society now beginning to seem archaic and picturesque, novels that were both impassioned and analytically penetrating; these novels were moreover poems. He wrote on poetics, he was interested in language, and in the modes for making writing powerful to action—the almost desperate concern of certain English Renaissance poets, among them Spenser. He stood only just behind Tasso and Ariosto, the writers of the new Italy; as sophisticated and learned as they, he yet wrote in the idiom and costume of the Middle Ages. He was a writer of tremendous scope, and all sides of him were still alive, not eclipsing but supplementing each other. He supplied compendia of unexampled convenience in an age when handbooks and "dictionaries" were fewer and less well organized. And he was highly accessible. There were frequent editions of his Latin works, frequent reprints, frequent translations, frequent editions newly illustrated. Early and common French versions had made "Boccace" seem almost a part of French literature; these translations were abundantly available—in notoriously handsome manuscripts, in ordinary everyday editions and in richly illustrated ones. Lydgate's Bochas was familiar to readers who would

---

of MSS). It is a 15th-century translation of the *Quadrilogue*, Chartier's allegorical treatise on the woes of the state and its salvation by Faith, Sapience, and Hope, and of Chartier's *Curial*—with marginal comments in an English 16th-century hand. Readers are advised to seek out "Virgile Tytelline Orose Troye pompe Justyn ffiore valere Stace Lucan," Caesar, Brunetto Latino, Vincent; they are to read "Seneck and . . . John Bocasse" (f. 94^r-96^v). See note 5 below. Boccaccio's *De claris* was translated by Henry Parcare, Lord Morley, whose Dedication to Henry VIII praises Boccaccio for his "clerkly . . . volumes" in Latin, and commends this book as moral reading for ladies of the court (*Vide Literary Museum*, ed. Waldron, London, 1792).

never read Lydgate. It was most improbable that Spenser should have been unaffected by such an author in many indirect and unrecognized ways, both as regards matter and method.

Among the editions of the *De Claris Mulieribus* which Spenser might have read are Italian editions such as those of Venice, 1506 (with woodcuts, mere stock figures); of Florence, 1566, 1594; of Venice, 1545, 1547, 1558.[2] More interesting are the Latin editions, some of which will be described later: the remarkable one printed at Ulm, 1473,[3] with woodcuts sufficiently detailed to furnish historiation and not merely emphasis; the edition of Louvain, 1487, whose woodcuts parallel the Ulm ones in design, using a more delicate line; a Berne edition of 1539 with rectangular pictures. This will be referred to below, as "Berne, 1539." Most important are the French editions. Vérard printed a translation, in 1493, with woodcuts. The Lyons edition of 1551 professes to be translated from an Italian text. *Le plaisant liure de . . . Jehan Bocace . . . des illustres & cleres dames*, Paris, 1538,[4] can I think be shown to have been the one which Spenser read. That he also saw illuminated MSS of this text is quite possible.[5] I shall use for correlative material the three most interesting of the exemplars now at the Bibliothèque Nationale, and

[2] See lists of MSS and some prints in Hortis, *Studj sulle op. lat. del B.* (Trieste, 1879), 889–928. Editions of 1506 and 1558 have been examined; title page of the 1547 edition, from which I quote below, reads: Libro di M. Gio. | Boccaccio Delle Don- | *ne Illustri, Tradotto per Messer* | *Giuseppe Betussi* | Con vna additione fatta | *dal medesimo delle donne Famose dal tempo di* | *M. Giouanni fino a i giorni nostri,* . . . | In Venetia M. D. XLVII.

[3] See Hortis, *op. cit.*, p. 889. Editions examined. One print, Ulm, 1473 (Bodleian), has no woodcuts; colophon of the other reads: Liber Joha*n*nis boccacij de certaldo de m*ulie*ribus claris . . . Ulme . . . Anno do*mi*ni M°cccc°lxxiij. Title page of the 1539 edition, from which I quote below, reads: Ioannis Boccatii | De Certaldo insigne opus | de Claris Mulieribus. | . . . | Bernae Helvet. | Excudebat Mathias Apiarius. | [Colophon has date:] . . . Anno | M. D. XXXIX. |

[4] Title page reads: Le plaisant li-| ure de noble homme Jehan Bocace poe-| te Florentin | auquel il traicte des | faict3 & gestes des illustres & cle-| res dames / traduict de latin en | Fra*n*cois. . . . Paris . . . Lan | Mil cinq cens tren-| te et huyt. | Vérard and Lyons editions examined.

[5] Among friends of Spenser's who owned MSS still to be seen in our present collections were Raleigh, Leicester, Dee, Howard of Effingham, Derby, Cumberland, Sir Thomas Smith, the Russell family, and many others whom Spenser almost certainly knew; I hope to publish soon an article on 'Spenser and Pictorial Conventions' which will discuss the probability of his acquaintance with books in MS. [See pp. 112–138 below.]

the very fully illustrated British Museum MS Royal 16 G v.[6]

A comparison of the use to which Spenser puts the story of Hercules and Iole with this story in Boccace will be perhaps the most interesting demonstration of the kind of influence which the reading of the *Des Cleres Dames* and similar books must have had upon Spenser. We can trace in this instance the process by which Spenser's passage is built up and by which the mere use of this story as an example influences the whole of the description of the relations between Radegund and Artegall; it is important as a type of what could be done in innumerable instances if we had sufficient knowledge of Spenser's reading. His substitution of Iole for the classical Omphale as the mistress who led Hercules into an effeminate life (*FQ* V, v, 24) is called a 'mistake' by Miss Sawtelle; [7] Mustard referred it to Tasso, *Ger. Lib.*, xvi. 3; [8] in the most recent discussion of the matter, Lotspeich says: "But Boccaccio [*i.e.* in the *De Gen. Deorum*], 13. 1, makes the same confusion and his version of the story is the closest parallel to Sp." [9] The passage containing the direct comparison reads, in the *Faerie Queene:*

Who had him seene, imagine mote thereby,
That whylome hath of *Hercules* bene told,
How for *Iolas* sake he did apply
His mightie hands, the distaffe vile to hold,
For his huge club, which had subdew'd of old
So many monsters, which the world annoyed;
His Lyons skin chaungd to a pall of gold,
In which forgetting warres, he onely ioyed
In combats of sweet loue, and with his mistresse toyed.
Such is the crueltie of womenkynd,
When they have shaken off the shamefast band,
With which wise Nature did them strongly bynd, . . .
That then all rule and reason they withstand,
To purchase a licentious libertie. . . . (V, v, 24–25)

[6] A convenient example of the traditional series of pictures. One other text, the Middle English version in MS Addit. 10304, is unimportant in the present connection (ed. Schleich, G., in *Palaestra* 144, Leipzig, 1924).

[7] (Mrs. Alice Elizabeth Sawtelle Randall), *The Sources of Spenser's Classical Mythology* (New York, 1896), *s. v.* Hercules.

[8] *MLN,* XX (1905), 127. This passage in Tasso doubtless re-emphasized the incident in Spenser's mind.

[9] Henry Gibbons Lotspeich, *Classical Mythology in the Poetry of Edmund Spenser*, Princeton Studies in English 9 (Princeton University Press, 1932), *s. v.*

As we examine the matter in detail, we shall find that this is no chance comparison brought in for decorative effect, but that Hercules as the archetype of those who establish Justice in the Western world has been in Spenser's mind from the very first stanza of canto I, and that the parallels—Hercules-Iole: Artegall-Radigund: Grey-Elizabeth's archenemy—were drawn meaningfully and with subtlety. It is not by chance that it is in Spenser's book on the responsibility of great princes to express their sovereign power in the establishment of Justice (Prologue to Bk. V) that we find the clearest trace of his reading of a great mediaeval sourcebook of *exempla* of just and unjust *women-in-power.* His theme is their abuse or right use of power; so is Boccaccio's. It is significant that he uses that Iole whom Boccaccio had taken care to portray not as a mere Acrasia-temptress but as a princess whose motive is personal-political—the avenging of her father's death upon Hercules who had warred against him. Her significance to Spenser would lie in her misuse (understandable yet unquestionably to be punished) of her power, hers by virtue of both sex and position. She is an example of the subtlest, not the simplest temptation encountered by the instrument of Justice.

The Paris 1538 edition of the *Des Cleres Dames* (ff. xxxvi^r^–xxxvii^v^) tells how Iole was "aymee du noble Hercules qui estoit le chastiement et craincte du monde"; refused by her father, Hercules wars against him, and kills him. Iole, in deep resentment, will not love him; finally, however, cunningly taking the avenging of her father into her own hands, deceitfully and with calculated guile she feigns love to him. He marries her. Now completely in power, "elle attira led*it* hercules par blandices & cautelles artificieuses en si arda*n*te & si feruente amour de elle q*u*'elle contraignit . . . luy q*ui* estoit ho*m*me robuste & vestu de aspres & durs vestemens en signe des vasselages & faictȝ de armes lesquelȝ il auoit perpetreȝ" into the famous series of symbolical weaknesses; now entirely captived, he begins the sufferance of the indignities which he must undergo—to her the revenge for her father's death, to him the punishment for his unworthy willfulness. So Artegall, yielding himself to Radigund after a first vic-

Iole. Douglas Bush (*Mythology and the Renaissance Tradition,* Minneapolis, 1932, p. 91) mentions the point again, referring to Mustard's article and to the appearance of the detail in *Gerusalemme Liberata* and in the Italian works of Boccaccio.

tory, "wilfull lost, that he before attayned"; "Left to her will by his owne wilfull blame, [she] caused him to be disarmed quight, Of all the ornaments of knightly name, With which whylome he gotten had great fame: In stead whereof . . ." etc. "So was he ouercome, not ouercome, But to her yeelded of his owne accord; Yet was he iustly damned by the doome Of his owne mouth, . . . To be her thrall, and seruice her afford" (FQ V, v, 17, 20). As is characteristic of Spenser's method, the "example" (Iole is not introduced by name until stanza 24) is no mere epic simile, but is present in Spenser's mind as picture and as a pointing of the moral for some time before it appears; it has influenced in both these ways the description of Artegall's fall, from stanza 17 on.

Already visible here, the moral direction given to the whole canto, though it does not proceed from the Iole story as from an *exemplum*, is strengthened by the direct use of it and finds concrete expression in the same symbolic details (their similar visualization will be examined later). The suggestion of calculated but understandably motivated deep deceit underlying loveliness, used by a woman in high position to obtain complete power (this is the spring of Radigund's actions), is not in the other Ioles but is definitely in Boccaccio's.[10] It must have immediately connected her, for Spenser, with Delilah, with Cleopatra, with the passionate queen or great woman who wants "lawlesse regiment" and destroys Justice and virtue to get it (like Duessa, like Adicia, like the Scottish Queen), rather than with the merely seductive woman who distracts men from their duty. That Iole thus interpreted had called up in Spenser's mind the classical examples of just this kind of feminine peril to the politically great, the instru-

[10] This emphasis is not in Tasso; nor in other accounts mentioned below (p. 94); nor in the *De Genealogia* passage, the Latin original of which is quoted in Lotspeich, *op. cit.;* I quote the Italian version (the French translation is parallel): "Dice Seruio, che hauendoli Eurito Re d'Etholia promesso per mogie Iole sua figliuola: per disconforto d'i figliuoli; attento che hauea amazzato. . . . La onde Hercole presa la Città, & amazzato Eurito; ottenne Iole. Essendo adunque infiammato dell'amore di costei; per suoi commandamenti messe quella claua . . ." (Geneologia degli dei | I Quindeci | Libri di M. Giovanni | Boccaccio . . . | Vinegia . . . 1547. Translated by G. Betussi. Fol. 228^{r}). The Italian version . . . *delle Donne Illustri* (Venice, 1547; *v.* note 2 above) treats the story as "vero argomento dell'imbecillità humana, & delle astutie donnesche." "Con questa consideratione, l'artificiosa giouane, & con eterna uergogna d'Hercole uendico non con armi, ma con inganni, & lasciuia la morte del padre, & se fece degna di eterno nome . . ." (f. 27^{v}).

ments of Justice on earth, is clear from his placing her with these other great exemplars in a following canto. This re-echo of the Iole story in canto viii, where Adicia is the "mortall foe To Iustice" (st. 20), is evidence of Spenser's preoccupation with these parallels; doubly valuable, it enhances a contrast in situation; here Artegall is being praised for that strength in which he had once been found wanting. Iole's stature has become that of her more renowned sisters; the last line is significant:

> So whylome learnd that mighty Iewish swaine,
> Each of whose lockes did match a man in might,
> To lay his spoiles before his lemans traine:
> So also did that great Oetean Knight
> For his loues sake his Lions skin vndight:
> And so did warlike *Antony* neglect
> The worlds whole rule for *Cleopatras* sight
> Such wondrous powre hath wemens faire aspect,
> To captiue men, and make them all the world reiect.
>
> (*FQ* V, viii, 2)

The partially admirable or at least understandable motivation of Iole's deceit—her avenging of her father (here she is comparable with Delilah)—complicates the action and makes more ironic the man's willful bringing of himself to destruction; so in the case of Artegall and Radigund the turn of the story which makes Radigund suffer for her pride in a tormenting love for her prisoner also takes the story out of the category of the simpler seduction-from-duty motif. The protagonist is not simply decoyed into undignified softness by a temptation of mean proportions and a temptress unworthy of his yielding; the basis here is rather the *hybris* motif of a large nature brought irrevocably (but with dignity, despite the undignified symbolic form of the yielding) to disintegration and near-destruction through conflict with another of like proportions, playing upon his peculiar weakness. Radigund is no longer merely a martial Acrasia.

This enlargement and deepening of the action proceeds, I think, from the working of Spenser's imagination upon these similitudes. Radigund's situation does not parallel that of her avowed prototype Iole with exactness; the pardonableness which makes the tragic situation more poignant has a different exposition in the case of Hercules and Iole. But both heroines subdue their pride and direct their cunning toward a humanly understandable end, rooted in their pride, yet compelling our sympathy; and the complication of motive in Boccaccio's undermining of Hercules by Iole works in the mind to produce the same mingled respect, sympathy, and condemnation which Spenser produces by a similar complication of motive in Radigund—whom he expressly compares to her. To conclude because he makes no detailed parallel that he simply introduced comparable figures as rhetorical decoration, rather than that his conceptions of his characters grew in part out of his thinking about his "comparisons," is merely to accuse him of the most pedantic mode of composition. Merely another lay figure of an Amazon at first, Radigund is built up by complication and suggestion until, in the actual sensation of her conflict and pain given in stanza 28, in her gradual capitulation to her own stronger wish, the recognition of her worthiness by Artegall in stanza 41, the emphasis upon her trust in the person who insidiously betrays her, we begin to feel that forward-seeing and fearful sympathy for Radigund which we ought to feel only for a tragic heroine, and which we are meant to feel for Artegall. There is even an unlawful assent in us to her words in stanza 29—"the heauens vniust, Spighting my happie freedome, haue agreed, To thrall my looser life, or my last bale to breed." Spenser feels it too and immediately retracts, taking up again the motivation of "wandring fancie [raunging] after lust" with which he began, and stressing again the unworthiness of her motive—desire, unrightfully, for complete power. But not before he has made her someone in whom we feel a likeness to those greater heroines whose loveliness it was worth losing the world to possess. And for this person Iole would not be, as here, the type, unless we felt in both instances "sympathy" as well as awareness of power. This drawing back from Radigund as that possibly tragic figure (who in a completed tragedy adds ironic complication to the action), Spenser does not show before we have been so brought to the possibility of sympathy with her that we condemn Clarinda outright as the villainous one, and later feel not alone triumph but a certain pain at Britomart's destruction of Radigund; to be courageously proud is her essential character, and there is something over-successful about Britomart, despite the sop in vii, 36.

The development of this conception of Radigund dates from Spenser's introduction of Iole, and the rebuke administered to the latter in stanza 25, against an overweening taking of affairs into one's own hands, signals I think the fact that he conceived of their parallel relationship as something much deeper than the superficial one of similar theatrical scene. As I have said, it is significant that Spenser groups Iole in canto viii with two heroines of just the kind I have outlined. Hercules too has become a figure large with symbolical meaning. He has been in Spenser's mind since canto i as the example of those of "vertuous race" who have re-established the "*princely* rule" of Justice upon earth, have "wrong repressed, and establisht right." This is a "*soueraine* powre," like God's own, expressing the "most sacred vertue" of all, through that "powre he also doth *to Princes lend*." This is the highest trust of Princes. As Bacchus established Justice in the East,

> Next *Hercules* his like ensample shewed,
> Who all the West with equall conquest wonne,
> And *monstrous tyrants* with his club subdewed;
> The *club of Iustice* dread, with *kingly powre* endewed.
>
> (V, i, 2; my italics.)

These are no simple monsters, but types of monstrous disharmony in the body politic, examples of tyranny—great power misused. The club is an almost mystical symbol, as a king's sceptre is—or should be. Hercules captived by Iole is the instrument of princely Justice temporarily in the thrall of Injustice, overweeningly seizing power. The organic connection here between the whole conception of the Book and the comparison figuring it forth is obvious; moreover, it is an example of the way in which Spenser's imagination, fired with that conception, was set off by certain concrete story-figures which he met in a form overlaid with mediaeval interpretations, and of how he could compel within his scheme all these layers of meaning to give a figure an almost inexhaustible richness of significance.

Like Samson and Antony and like Artegall, Hercules is deflected from his great viceregal task through his own peculiar weakness. The picture of magnificent strength disarmed is at the heart of the parallel. And it is in the very terms of the images which fix that picture that Spenser seems to remember Boccaccio, and to remember him with such vividness as to re-echo Boccaccio in his selection of details to emphasize; and sometimes in his words. Hercules' heroic proportions are first forcefully summed up in the description of him as *the chastisement and fear of the world.* Boccaccio outlines the story, and goes on to describe how Iole "contraignit . . . luy . . . a premierement laisser la grande & grosse massue de laquelle *il auoit vaincue & suppedite les monstres de la terre.*" [11] This is a spacious phrase; as all symbols do, it concentrates into an image the vast power which we here see disintegrating before our eyes. Spenser consolidates it with a later image and to a certain extent weakens it:

> How for *Iolas* sake he did apply
> His mightie hands, the distaffe vile to hold,
> *For his huge club, which had subdew'd of old*
> *So many monsters, which the world annoyed;*
>
> (V, v, 24)

In the Boccace account the emphasis on the "mightie hands" comes later: "Et ses doidȝ auecques lesquelȝ luy estant encores ou berceau/il auoit occis et estrangle les serpens/ il en tiroit la laine et filoit auecques le fuseau en son aage parfaicte. . . ." [12] This is not so much a ridiculous picture as a painful and sorrowful contrast, and the antithesis of *enfance* with "*aage parfaicte*" underlines this sweepingly, and gives a dignity which is more valuable than the concentration which Spenser has effected by combining these two images. Both Latin original and Italian translation lack the quality which gives the first image its effectiveness in the 1538 Boccace and in Spenser: "ponere clauam, qua monstra domuerat"; [13] "la mazza, con laquale havea domato i Mostri"; [14] neither of these has the sudden vision of the wild places of the world wandered over by strange and monstrous creatures which only this hero could destroy, he himself now destroyed. Spenser has weakened it by changing the position of the crucial word "world," but also given it still more far-reaching quality with his "of old," and fixed our eyes upon the club as on a talisman (which it was to him), by his shift of subject. The other image is as effective in the Latin,[15] in the Italian less so, because

[11] 1538 edition, f. xxxvii^r; the italics are mine.

[12] F. xxxvii^v. This contrast is not in the *De Geneal.* account (either Latin, French, or Italian versions).

[13] Berne, 1539, f. xv^r. [14] Venice, 1547, f. 27^r.

[15] Berne, 1539, f. xv^r: "digitosque quos ad extinguendos in cunis adhuc infans angues durauerat, inualida iam imō perfecta ętate ad extenuanda fila molliret."

by interjecting "la Donna fece che"[16] the whipping scorn of the phrase which follows in the 1538 version is anticipated and weakened: ". . . filoit auecques le fuseau en son aage parfaicte et se seoit ou meilliéu dung tas de fe*m*melettes pour co*m*plaire a la voule*n*te dune ieune dame. . . ." Spenser, having already shown this picture, sharp with the same scorn, in his "Spinning and carding all in comely rew" (st. 22), contents himself with adding the heavy strength of the word "mightie" and the slight change to "hands," written from the same visual image. The exact parallel in emphasis, the similar delimitation of the image, the peculiar blending of graphic terseness with imaginative suggestion, I think point to the 1538 Boccace as the source of the sharply outlined mental picture from which Spenser has written.

The two most striking details, the "huge club" and the "mightie hands," have moreover undergone the same transformation into symbols as that by which Hercules' subduing of the monsters was made by Spenser into a symbol which he could link to his main theme of Justice. With this symbolical inference they appear constantly throughout the Book; the picture and its meaning seem to be graven in Spenser's mind. The club is the kingly emblem, "the club of Iustice dread" (i, 2); "those mighty palmes" are to Britomart (vii, 40) the symbols of Artegall's power, now lost; in great heroes' "mighty hands" resides the "manlinesse" with which they should subdue the world (viii, 1); and most striking passage of all:

> Who so vpon him selfe will take the skill
> True Iustice vnto people to diuide,
> Had neede haue *mightie hands*, . . .
> For *powre is the right hand of Iustice* truely hight.
>
> (V, iv, 1; my italics)

These recurring phrases show that the vivid pictorial image with its symbolical force, taken from the Hercules story, was constantly present in Spenser's mind and was for him tightly connected with the main conception of his Book, which strives to point out the responsibility of Princes toward true Justice, "that doth right de-

[16] Venice, 1547, f. 27r-27v: "quelle dita, che da fanciullo nella culla s'haueano auezzate a suffocar serpenti, la Donna fece che si posero con la conocchia sotto il braccio a filar lana, nel piu uerde delle forte età sua."

fine," "the skill whereof to Princes hearts [Ioue] doth reueale" that they may establish on earth a counterpart of 'his heauenly Commonweale' (vii, 1).

The other details which Spenser uses are of course in the 1538 Boccace. "Et luy fist pareillement despouiller la iacquette laq*ue*lle il auoit faict faire de la peau du lyon . . . le signe de sa noble vertu. . . . Et aussi ses trousse & sayetes"; she persuades him to ornament his fingers with rings and anoint his hair; "et ffinablement le vestit de moulȝ & delicatȝ vestemens de pourpre et autres draps de soye precieulx" (ff. xxxvi^{v}–xxxvii^{r}). This is a wordier version of Spenser's "His Lyons skin chaungd to a pall of gold"; it may have suggested Spenser's—the piling up of tactile sensations, the soft heaviness of "moulȝ" and the sibilant luxuriousness of "draps de soye," are present in the slightly mannered archaism "pall"; cloth-of-"gold" is not necessarily suggested by the inexact but shining word "precieulx"—it may more likely be a transference from the vivid splash of yellow-gold of the lion's skin which is characteristic of the conventional pictures of Hercules. It is hardly necessary to remark that such a process of suggestion is not a conscious one. It is, however, just the sort of process we should be able to trace if we knew oftener the exact form in which Spenser read his source materials. "Elle avoit ai*n*si effemine & induict a choses voluptueuses luy q*ui* estoit si robuste ho*m*me"—this is the generalized summary and contrast of Spenser's slightly more rhetorical two lines and calls up the same image to us: "In which forgetting warres, he onely ioyed In combats of sweet loue, and with his mistresse toyed." Spenser follows this with a condemnation of the "crueltie of womenkynd" when they set out "to purchase a licentious libertie." The Boccace has, "yole *con*sidera quelle ne auoit point encores assez satisfait a lindignation de son courage & quelle se vengeroit encores plus"; the scornful picture again follows of Hercules "en habit de femme entre les damoyselles . . . de ladicte yole. Et auoit . . . q*ue*nouille a son coste chargee de laine & se seoit parmy lesdictes fe*m*mes" (f. xxxvii^{r}). Spenser uses but once the picture of Artegall "In womans weedes" and "napron white," placed distaff in hand among the spinners. (Here Radigund's knights are the effeminate servants.)

The account of Iole in the *De Genealogia* (either in Latin or in the French or Italian versions which I have seen) does not show the similarities in emphasis, dramatic point, and suggestive image which we find between Spenser and the *Des Cleres Dames*, and if we suppose him to have followed the *De Genealogia*, then he must have happened by chance upon these special emphases. It reads:

> Eurito occiso, Iolem obtinuit [Hercules]. Huius enim amore ardens ea iubente leonis spolium et clavam deposuit, sertis et unguentis et purpura annulisque usus est, et quod turpius, inter pedissequas amatae iuvenis sedens, penso suscepto venit.[17]

The confusion of Iole with Omphale, noted by Mustard and Lotspeich, is no distinguishing characteristic. The story is so told in Lydgate's *Fall of Princes*,[18] in Caxton's *Recuyell*,[19] in the *Ovide moralisé* (*i.e.* Mansion's and Vérard's 15th-century prints of the mediaeval moralized Ovid) and in the 16th-century illustrated Ovids which depend upon it,[20] in Gower's *Confessio Amantis*.[21] But in none of these is there the suggestive parallel furnished by the *Des Cleres Dames*. One other medium of suggestion is less important to remember in this instance than I think it to have been in others—that of the conventional pictorial figure. However, I shall summarize briefly here the ways in which the pictured Hercules and Iole conventionally appear, stressing the *Des Cleres Dames*. Fixed early as one of the usual il-

[17] As quoted in Lotspeich, *op. cit.*, *s. v.*, Iole. This, and the Italian version (also the French), show no such suggestive parallels in image; they do not stress Iole's motive, elaborate on the same details, emphasize the contrast between Hercules' changed and his former self in their summarizing statement, nor put the very accent of scorn into the picture of Hercules among the spinners (f. 228r: "tra le seruenti dell' amata giouane si diede a filare").

[18] Bk. I, v. 5175 (ed. Henry Washington Bergen, The Carnegie Institute of Washington, 1923–27 [4 vols.]; also *EETS*, ex. ser. 121–24).

[19] Ed. H. Oskar Sommer (London, 1894), II, 469ff (a long story in which Iole is a different character, far more of a contrast than a parallel to Radigund).

[20] La bible des poetes metha-| morphoze. nouelleme*n*t | imprime a paris. | AV | [1493], f. xcvi. This parallels Mansion's 1484 version, which for the most part follows that of P. Bersuire 14th century; fairly frequent later Latin and French editions often attribute the work to Th. Waleys. The detail in question occurs also (in Bk. IX) in *e. g.*: Les xv. liures de | la Metamorphose D'ouide . . . | contenans L'olym | pe des Histoires poëtiques | . . . figuré | de nouuelles figures . . . a Paris par | Denys Ianot . . . 1539; Le Grand | Olympe des Hystoires Poeti | ques . . . Paris MDXXXIX . . . par Jehan ruelle . . . ; Les XV. Livres de la Metamorphose . . . contenants l'Olympe . . . Paris 1586.

[21] II, 2259ff (ed. Macaulay).

lustrations in MSS and prints, the recurrence of these figures perhaps served to underline and characterize them in Spenser's mind. In British Museum MS Royal 16 G v (early 15th-century, a French translation of the *De Claris*), Hercules, still in blue-gray armor, but wearing over it a *gold* cloak, clasped at the neck, and holding distaff and wool, is in a garden with "yolle" and two women (f. 24ᵛ). In the closely related MS Royal 20 C v his cloak is brownish with yellow embroidery (f. 34ᵛ).[22] In Bibl. Nationale MS. f. fr. 598, the duc de Berry's copy of the *Des Cleres Dames*, Hercules, bearded as usual, in gold-brown lion-skin shirt, with distaff and spindle, stands by Iole and a companion (f. 33ʳ); in f. fr. 599 Hercules wears a rich gold jacket in the Dyanira picture, but Iole appears alone (ff. 20ʳ, 21ʳ); in f. fr. 12420 Hercules in lion-skin tunic, with distaff, garlanded—like Iole, sports with her and three other women in a meadow (f. 32ʳ). In the Ulm edition of 1473, Hercules in garland and short lion-skin jumper, club in belt, embraces Iole; to the right are he and Iole, now both in skirts and with distaffs (f. 23ʳ). In the French moralized Ovid printed by Vérard in 1493, Hercules armed and helmeted, in skirt-like lion's skin, stands near Iole, both with distaff and yarn in hand (f. xcvᵛ). Like other conventions, pictorial convention tends to give a sort of proverbial currency to certain figures, as well as define schematically their treatment.

Flora is another of Boccace's *cleres dames*. The familiar figure who appears in the *Faerie Queene*[23] is the Flora of uncounted Old French and Middle English seasons-descriptions (of which Lydgate's are the most important for Spenser), of the *Roman de la Rose*, and of vast numbers of court-of-love romances. But E. K.'s gloss to Flora in *The Shephearde's Calender*, March, 16, shows as Lotspeich says "that strange things have been done to her." He says further that "E. K.'s material is not from Tacitus . . but originates in Lactantius . . . and is transcribed by Bocc. [*De Gen.*], 4. 61, whence E. K. probably took it."[24] E. K.'s gloss reads:

[22] Brit. Mus., *Cat. of . . . Royal and King's Coll.*, II, 208, 372. MS. 20 C v was evidently done for a Beaufort and belonged to an English owner by the xv. c.

[23] *FQ* I, i, 48; I, 4, 17; II, ii, 6; II, xii, 50; *Shep. Cal.* March 16, May 31.

[24] Lotspeich, *op. cit.*, *s. v.*, Flora. The verbal parallels, indicated by my italics above, between E. K.'s glosses on Flora and Chloris and the *Des Cleres Dames*, add force to the idea that he had read the latter rather than (or in addition to) the *De Gen.* account. Bush, *op. cit.*, 90, cites Miss Cornelia C. Coulter's article attaching these glosses to the *De Gen.* (*MLN*, XXXV [1920], 55).

> Flora) the Goddesse of flowres, but indede (as saith Tacitus) a famous harlot, which with the abuse of her body hauing gotten great riches, *made the people of Rome her heyre:* who *in remembrance of so great beneficence,* appointed a yearely feste *for the memoriall* of her, *calling her, not as she was,* nor as some doe think, Andronica, *but Flora:* making her the Goddesse of all floures, and doing yerely to her solemne sacrifice. [Italics mine.]

In the *Des Cleres Dames* the story of "Flora . . . qui fut ribaulde et riche femme" begins with a description of how she obtained her money. Then, being very cunning, she "*fist & constitua le peuple de Romme son hoir*"; thus, "quand elle eut captee la beniuolence et grace du peuple Ro*m*main elle obti*n*t legierement les ieux faitȝ *en la memoire* de son nom" (edition of 1538, f. cxviii[r]). Her third name, Andronica, is found neither in the *Des Cleres Dames* nor in the sources mentioned by Lotspeich or Mustard; [25] but E. K.'s "*calling her, not as she was, . . . but Flora*" is explained by what follows in the Boccace. He says that the Senate, ashamed of giving a yearly feast in memory of a harlot, circulated a fable—

> Cestoit que *flora iadis auoit este* vne nymphe dicelluy pays de merueilleuse beaulte no*m*mee *Clora. Et par le vent Zeph irus . . . tresardentement amee et au dernier prinse a femme.* Et par icelluy *zephirus . . . pour ung certain don de douaire* deite luy auoit este octroye Auecques cest office cest que en printemps elle ornast les arbres les montaignes & les pres *de fleurs a iceulx presidast* et dilecques en auant *fust en lieu de Clora appelee Flora . . .* icelle deesse Flora fure*n*t concedeȝ ieux & sacrifices / temples & autelȝ. [f. cxviii[v]; italics mine.]

E. K. gloss on "*Chloris,* that is the chiefest Nymph of al" (in the following month of the *Shep. Cal.* [Aprill, 122]), with its possibly reminiscent phrases (particularly "gaue her for a dowrie," "chiefedome . . . of al flowres . . .") seems to depend upon this same account, and completes the link with the *Des Cleres Dames* account of Flora.[26] The latter concludes with an emphasis upon

[25] Mustard says, "The name 'Andronica' is not given by our Latin dictionaries" (*MLN,* XXXIV [1919], 196).

[26] Though the material is not peculiar to this account. *Vide* Lotspeich, *s. v.* Chloris; he says that "E. K.'s gloss . . . is probably based on *Fasti* 5. 195 f." but quotes Bocc. *De Gen.* 4. 61, which he says "parallels E. K.'s wording." But

her deceitful ingenuity, thus "par son engin . . . et pecune mal aquise" to have got all she desired. This calculating doubleness stressed in the Boccace account, even more than the mere lasciviousness of Flora-as-harlot, makes her a fit figure for the uses of Archimago in the tricking of the Red Crosse Knight through the false Una (*FQ* I, i, 48). Traditionally pictured among garlanded dancers, the Flora of the *Des Cleres Dames* MSS is the conventional figure whom Spenser also uses; typical illustrations are the naked dancers, red-dressed woman, and fiddle players of Royal 16 G v (f. 77ᵛ), the half-undressed, loose-bodiced woman of f. fr. 599 (f. 56ᵛ), the garland-crowned woman of f. fr. 12420, at a doorway with two men, a woman holding up her skirts, and a woman naked except for veil-like shift (f. 98ᵛ).

In one other detail, involving a puzzling error or "carelessness" on the part of Spenser, I am not sure whether one sees traces of Spenser's reading of the *Des Cleres Dames* or of Boccaccio's *De Casibus Virorum* in the French translation—perhaps of both, with the detail found in one recalled to mind and stressed by its appearance in not quite the same form and connection in the other. Two of Spenser's allusions to King Ninus are provocative. In FQ I, v, 48, in the company of Nimrod, Philip and other *De Casibus* heroes,[27] and following a passage on Hippolytus which I think shows the influence of the French *Des cas des Nobles Hommes*, Spenser lists among the woeful examples of fallen pride "old *Ninus*," who even above great Nimrod "farre did pas In princely pompe, of all the world obayd." The *Des Cleres Dames* treats of Ninus in the article on Semiramis his wife; as usual it stresses his "ferocite & puissa*n*ce de armes,"[28] but also more particularly his pride: "[Nine] . . . auoit vng appetit desordo*n*ne de regner & seigneurier sur ses voysins"; it does not extend his conquests quite so widely as does Spenser, but says that he had "toute la terre de Ase & empire de orient . . . a luy submis & asubiecte" (1538 edition, f. viᵛ). The Boccace goes on to

neither of these is so close a parallel verbally nor so circumstantial a story as the *Des Cleres Dames* account. The Italian De Gen. is a little closer than the Latin text quoted by L. (Venice, 1581, f. 78ᵛ).

27 *Vide The Works of Edmund Spenser*, A Variorum Edition (Baltimore, 1932), I, 237, where the passage is referred to Chaucer's *Monkes Tale*. I hope to publish soon some materials on Spenser's possible use of some form of the *De Casibus*; this detail will be examined.

28 Spenser's stress again in II, ix, 56.

tell how Semiramis the wife of Ninus restored the walls of the city of Babylon, which "Nemroth le geant avoit des pieca edifiee es champs et terre de Sannaer," "lesquelʒ murs elle fist faire de tuylles cuytes/ sablon/ chaux et cyment mesleʒ ensemble de si gra*n*de haulteur et espesseur . . . que cestoit chose esmerueillable . . ." (f. viii^v^). Spenser describes the walls of the castle of Alma thus:

> Not built of bricke, ne yet of stone and lime,
> But of thing like to that *Ægyptian* slime,
> Whereof king *Nine* whilome built *Babell* towre;
> But O great pitty, that no lenger time
> So goodly workemanship should not endure:
> Soone it must turne to earth; no earthly thing is sure.
>
> (II, ix, 21)

The "*Ægyptian* slime" has long been a puzzle. Jortin "can't conceive" why Spenser confuses it with "Assyrian bitumen"; Upton says conciliatingly that "even historians confound neighbouring nations, much more so poets." Miss Sawtelle refers to Diodorus Siculus, who "mentions the Assyrian bitumen abounding in the region around Babylon, of which the walls of the city were built." [29] Spenser's placing of Babel in Egypt instead of Assyria resulted I think from his reading of another favorite mediaeval text—the *Orose en français*—in a 15th- or 16th-century print. But his reading of the *Des Cleres Dames* may account for the puzzling *slime.* Its word *chaux* is sometimes so translated—*e.g.* in Diodorus Siculus' description of the Nile.[30] The *Des cas des Nobles Hommes* passage on the tower of Babel is more striking in one way, though unfortunately it ascribes the tower to Nembroth. It reads: ". . . laq*ue*lle tour fu f*ai*te de pierre cuitte a ciment de chaux viue et de sablon." [31] If *chaux* meant *slime* to Spenser, *chaux viue* is of course an even better material for the house of Alma. It looks as though Spenser, with Babel-on-the-Nile in his mind, had read the French *De Casibus,* envisaged the tower built of this strange living slime by the great Eastern warrior-king,

[29] *Vide The Works of Edmund Spenser,* A Variorum Edition (Baltimore, 1933), II, 288–9, for these various notes.

[30] *Vide* descriptions of the inundations of the Nile in French 16th-century translations of Diod. Sic. (Paris editions of 1541, 1554, first three chapters); English editions translate *slime* for *chaux.*

[31] B. Mus. MS Addit. 35321, f. 5^r^; Paris, 1538 edition (f. iii^r^), is parallel.

read again in the *Des Cleres Dames* of how Semiramis and her husband rebuilt Babylon with tiles, sand, slime and cement [32]—and from the image constructed by amalgamation of these two, made insensibly one image of the building of Babel out of material like to that of Alma's perishable temple.

Meanwhile he had picked up from another source the information that Babel was built in Egypt. The mediaeval historical compilation *Orose en français* is common in MS; it uses Orosius but is not as its title implies a translation of his History; it was printed in 1491, 1503, 1509, and 1526.[33] It tells a long tale of how Nimrod in his vain pride against God assembled his companions to discuss the building of a tower and to decide upon the best place to build it, concluding: "ilʒ ordonnerent quelle seroit faicte en vne grande place sur le fleuue du nil qui descent degipte." [34] There are then descriptions of its building (with a woodcut), of the confusion of tongues, and of Nimrod's further exploits.[35] This placing of the tower of Babel in Egypt is not in Orosius' account,[36] but is peculiar to the later refurbishing.

Thus Spenser's "Ægyptian slime," [37] though commentators have been unable to account for it by reference to any single source, is not necessarily evidence of confusion or gross ignorance

[32] The "sablon" of Boccace may have been another link to remind Spenser of Babel when in the *Ruins of Time* 509 he compares it with his Towre built on "sandie ground." The "close connection" between "the achievements of Ninus and his wife" by which Miss Sawtelle excuses Spenser's false attribution is made very close in the *Des Cleres Dames*, where the two are treated together (under Semiramis).

[33] *Vide* P. Meyer's study, "Les premières compilations fr. d'histoire ancienne," *Romania*, XIV (1885), 1–81. Other details which Spenser may have seen in this text in a particularly suggestive form will be spoken of in connection with the materials referred to in note 5 above.

[34] [Le premier volume de Orose, Paris, A. Vérard, 1491], f. xii^r (Watkinson Library, Hartford, t. p. missing).

[35] Including his introduction of fire-worship (f. xiii^r); *cf.* Spenser's '*Nimrod* . . . That first the world with sword and fire warrayd,' I, v, 48.

[36] Migne, *Patrol. Lat.* XXXI, *vide* cols. 669, 745ff, 758ff.

[37] A 15th-century parallel to Spenser's *slime* in a description of Babel in a short extract from a chronicle, in B. Mus. MS Addit. 37049, indicates either that other writers translated their sources in a similar way, or that this was a traditional building material for Babel; it reads "þe syme*n*t was mengyd *with* terre" (f. 9^v, last word substituted for "pyke"). According to the *Cat. of Addit. MSS* this text is "chiefly perhaps" from Higden's *Polychronicon*, but the latter does not parallel this detail (Rolls Ser. edit.).

on Spenser's part, but may well have resulted from a process such as I have outlined, associative rather than deliberate, and indicating wide and attentive reading.

It is also perhaps a very small example of the point which this article tries to make—that in innumerable hidden ways the Renaissance writer, and Spenser particularly, was dependent upon and consciously in touch with the learning of the "Middle" Ages which had preceded him; to him they were not "Middle," and he had far less than we have the habit of sharply delimiting that period and of relegating its knowledge to a category approached only by the curious historian of knowledge. Learning was usable wherever one found it; Spenser's imagination found a point of departure in that of the age preceding his far oftener than we have thought, in materials of more varying kinds. It is not important to find a mediaeval source for this stray fact and that. But it is important to our idea both of Spenser's mind and method to discover that he read widely, reflectively, and with an imagination so alert that casually encountered figures (like Hercules and Iole) were not only raised to an organic relationship with the themes which preoccupied him, but served to clarify and enrich those themes. It goes without saying that for every instance in which we can trace this process a hundred must remain hidden from us. It is therefore all the more important to follow the process in detail when we have reasonable cause to believe we are not inventing it.

Spenser and Mediaeval Mazers

WITH A NOTE ON JASON IN IVORY *

IN the August eclogue of the *Shepheardes Calender* Willye and Perigot, as is proper for Theocritean and Virgilian shepherds, sing against each other for plighted "pledges." Willye's pledge is a carved mazer bowl, E. K.'s excuse for commenting on the way Theocritus's "booke is ful" of such "shapes or pictures" of things—whence his eclogues are termed Idyllia. Spenser's description of Willye's mazer has always been accepted as thoroughly conventional and derivative as are the figures of the shepherds themselves, the idea of their striving against each other in song, or the notion that they would wish thus to contest for the possession of a carved wooden bowl. Theocritus's ivy-bordered bowl and Virgil's two beechen cups have always been thought to account sufficiently for the introduction of a carved mazer, especially since E. K. compares in a gloss this "pretie description" of Spenser's with those of Theocritus.

Here is Spenser's "picture":

> Then loe *Perigot* the Pledge, which I plight:
> A mazer ywrought of the Maple warre:
> Wherein is enchased many a fayre sight
> Of Beres and Tygers, that maken fiers warre:
> And ouer them spred a goodly wild vine,
> Entrailed with a wanton Yuie twine.
>
> Thereby is a Lambe in the Wolues iawes:
> But see, how fast renneth the shepheard swayne,
> To saue the innocent from the beastes pawes:
> And here with his shepehooke hath him slayne.
> Tell me, such a cup hast thou euer sene?
> Well mought it beseme any haruest Queene.
>
> (*SC*, August, 25ff)

In Theocritus' first eclogue the bowl which is to be sung for has a *lip* "hanged about with curling ivy, ivy freaked with a cassidony"; "within this *bordure*" is a woman mocking her two swains,

* Reprinted from *Studies in Philology*, 34 (1937), 138–47.

also an old fisher, a vineyard, a lad and some foxes; "*spread all about* the cup" are the "writhen leaves" of the bear's-foot.[1] Virgil's Menalcas (in the third eclogue) stakes two beechen cups; "*on* these a pliant vine . . . is entwined with spreading clusters of pale ivy"; "in the midst" are two figures of astronomers. The *handles* of Damoetas' cups are "clasped . . . with . . . acanthus, and in the centre" is Orpheus.[2] Professor Herford says in his notes to *August:* "Spenser's description of the cup is but a rude sketch from the finished picture of Theocritus, copied in slighter detail by Virgil; he doubtless felt their more elaborate art out of place in the homely style adopted in this eclogue. The twining vine and ivy carved on the edge is from Vergil. . . . The scenes carved within the bowl are taken from neither; but the secund . . . corresponds, according to Reissert, to a woodcut . . . in the 1519 edition of Sannazaro's *Arcadia.*"[3]

It is obviously true that no Renaissance pastoral writer would put a carved bowl into one of his eclogues without having these literary bowls in his mind. I think, however, that these "sources" were vivified to Spenser by familiarity with actual English mazer bowls. And moreover, that these matters of his changes in their "elaborate art," his additions, and difference in descriptive technique, his "homelier style," are immediately clarified when we examine English mazers. The point is significant as a type case, first of Spenser's imaginative use of suggestions from other than literary materials, and secondly of the process by which Spenser anglicized his poetic material and turned what was learned and polite into what was rustic and "old English," and "mought beseme any haruest Queene."

It is particularly significant that we should find a description of a wooden bowl called a *mazer* and made of *maple warre* in a poet known to have been interested in "antiquities." One of the most charming groups of mediaeval *objets d'art* is that of the late mediaeval drinking-bowls called mazers, made out of mottled maple

[1] Theocritus, Eclogue I, *The Greek Bucolic Poets,* Loeb Classical Library (London and New York, 1912), pp. 8–23.

[2] Virgil, Eclogue III, *Virgil,* Loeb Classical Library (London and New York, 1916), pp. 19, 21.

[3] Edmund Spenser, *The Shepheards Calendar,* ed. by C. H. Herford (London, 1895), p. 155. Herford points out the fact that Boccaccio and Sannazaro also imitate Theocritus and Virgil in this detail. In Spenser's bowl, the vine and ivy are not "on the edge," a departure explained below.

wood, particularly popular in the fourteenth and fifteenth centuries, and once possessed in what seem to us surprising numbers, especially by monastic establishments. There were 182 of these bowls at Canterbury in 1328; Westminister had as many as 40 left in 1540. They are frequent in late mediaeval wills and inventories; guilds often owned rather elaborate mazers, as did colleges. There is a famous one at Pembroke College, called the "Mary Valence cup" after the foundress; Spenser must have seen it there, if an interest in mediaeval customs made his notice of the traditional possessions of his College sharper than is customary among undergraduates, or even among prospective M. A.'s with friends among the Fellows.[4] One may look idly at the lists of mazers with Spenser's connections in mind and see, for example, that a 1512 inventory of the Merchant Taylors' Company mentions a standing mazer, a mazer at King Edward's Alms-houses in Saffron Walden was there in 1524,[5] one now privately owned has an inscription which shows it to have belonged to Rochester frater-house, several were owned by Corpus Christi College. A *mazer bowl* of "*Maple* warre" (*cf.* Virgil's "beechen"), was thus a very particular object. It would surely have been so to a young antiquarian interested in the archaic, particularly in the mediaeval archaic, and more particularly still in the *English* middle ages. Moreover, there were still a good many such bowls to be seen.

Inside such a maple-wood bowl there is a "print." This is a medallion, usually silver-gilt, "enchased" with a figure or a scene. At St. Nicholas' Hospital at Harbledown, just outside Canterbury, there are—and evidently were when Spenser was secretary to the Bishop of the neighboring diocese of Rochester—two especially interesting maple-wood mazers. The print of one of them has a very spirited Guy of Warwick, killing a bright shining dragon with a gracefully looped tail and a "bras-scaly backe" like that of Red Crosse's enemy; the grateful lion is at one side. On the other, "the print of silver-gilt [is] embossed with a lion attacking a monster (late XIIIth century") [6] (described as lioness

[4] St. John Hope, "On the English mediaeval drinking bowls called Mazers," *Archaeologia,* L (1887), 130, 152–53. The Pembroke mazer, listed in a 1491 inventory in the College Register, is recorded as having a cover as late as 1546.

[5] *Ibid.*, pp. 191, 163–64, 134.

[6] *Catalogue of Exhibition of English Mediaeval Art,* South Kensington Museum, No. 177, London, 1930, p. 36.

and dragon in St. John Hope's article on mazers).[7] The two animals fight, like Spenser's, against a background of vine tendrils, "entrailed" in spirals. The bosses made by the leaves of the vine stand out in relief; the spirals made by the twined double tendrils are sinuous and delicate, in admirable contrast to the strong solidity of the lion's body. There is a good deal of vigor and movement in the two fighting beasts, especially in the taut thigh of the lion and in the fierceness of his eyes and mouth. The "monster" or dragon is chiefly striking by the brightness of its burnished side; standing on two legs of much the same kind and length as the lion's, it is rather nondescript as to species—indeed both are. It turns around an angry head towards the other beast, so that the attention is drawn first to the two fierce heads with their glowing eyes, then balanced by the volumes of their two bodies, standing out against the delicate whorls of the vine, which fills the spaces above and to the side with rather finely-managed curves.

These are not a fighting "bere" and "Tygre," it is true. Nevertheless, the bowl one pictures from Spenser's description is so much more like this one than it is like Theocritus's and Virgil's (with their different material, different shape, differently placed ornament, and historiated scenes), that it seems almost to have been described with the eye upon the object. Theocritus's cup has a "*lip . . . hanged about* with" ivy—Spenser's vine is twined about over his fighting beasts (not "on the edge" as Herford says, thinking of Virgil's cup; the specifying of ivy and vine, however, doubtless did come "from Virgil"); the Greek bowl has "*within this bordure*" a complicated series of scenes; it is more like Keats' Grecian urn than like Spenser's bowl, "*wherein*" a simple picture is enchased. Virgil's scenes, too, are indeterminate in position—the vine "*on*" the beechen cups, the acanthus clasping the *handles*.

Undoubtedly Spenser wanted to imitate the "pretie descriptions" of Theocritus and Virgil. But it seems to me indubitable, and an interesting sidelight on the way his "descriptions" took definite form, that as he pictured in his mind the shepherds' cups of these literary sources, their shapes and the position and detail of their decoration were altered, made definite, and added to, by the images which he also had in his mind of other different and more actual bowls. If Spenser read attentively, he also observed

[7] St. John Hope, *op. cit.*, pp. 138ff. The mount which holds the medallion in place is dated 1603, at which time this portion must have been renewed.

carefully. And if as Reissert says the details in the second picture parallel those in a woodcut in the *Arcadia* of 1519,[8] it is particularly interesting to discover that for the first picture, and for the shape and kind and name as well as for the material of the bowl, we find more striking suggestions in actual things seen than in literary sources. The process would not seem to have been one of conscious selection from a literary source of a proper decorative detail, of which the poet deliberately presents (because he is writing in a homely style) only a rude sketch instead of the finished picture which he found in his reading. More plausibly was it a process in which, from a mind filled with vivid and accurate visual images both of things seen and read about—the one insensibly modifying and amplifying the other—the poet chooses for his descriptions "shapes or pictures of things" without actually deciding upon their fitness but presenting them with striking dramatic fidelity because of the definiteness to him of both these kinds of images. Had Spenser had only the Theocritus and Virgil pictures in his mind I think we should have had no more "finished" a picture —but only a rather different one. Obviously this is only a small instance of Spenser's way of combining for his own purposes many things from many places. But it is nevertheless significant of a certain habit of mind and of a particular texture of imagination. Any scrap of information is to the point if it helps to fill out our idea, necessarily so imperfect, of how Spenser saw and read—with what emphases and in what connections he took impressions into his mind, and why they appear in his poetry in their particular guise and connection and with one emphasis rather than another. Such instances as these show in little the kind of unconscious combination of impressions of different provenance and stress which must have gone on continuously in a far more complicated way than we can attempt to reconstruct, in Spenser's mind. The very mingling of literary and actual, of classical and contemporary, of ancient form and present comment, which makes the pastoral idyl a difficult form for us to accept made it a meaningful one for a sixteenth-century poet.

Of the date of the *Shepheardes Calender,* Professor Padelford says that though Spenser may have incorporated certain verses written earlier, "all of the evidence goes to show that . . . [it]

[8] O. Reissert, "Bemerkungen über Spenser's *Shepherd's Calendar* und die frühere Bukolik," *Anglia,* IX (1886), 218.

was conceived, written, and finished, and the gloss to the same prepared by his friend E. K., while the poet was secretary to Bishop Young."[9] That is to say partially resident, at least, in Rochester. One doubts if the secretaries of Elizabeth's bishops spent much time in the adjoining dioceses, but it is conceivable that Spenser went to Canterbury, whence one can walk amiably to Harbledown, and even that he saw the same maplewood bowl that one sees there now. It is not necessary to suppose this; there must have been many to see, and another would do (though not so temptingly) to make my point—that the multitudinous crowd of impressions which went into Spenser's mind to remain in his inward sight and determine the character of his descriptions must have been from a great many sources, chiefly undiscoverable. Indeed, as for any poet, they were surely of almost infinite kinds, differing minutely and in complicated ways from each other—in intensity, in "direction" of reference, in stress of one quality rather than another—and differing thus especially by reason of difference in medium and in provenance. As always, the danger is in oversimplification; if Spenser saw this very mazer, even so it is no more than Virgil or Theocritus the "source" for his description of a mazer. All these things plus all we have lost make up that "source." Nevertheless it is part of our reading of him to make all three annotations.

A Note on Jason in Ivory

This mingling in the poet's mind during the process of composition of suggestions from things actually seen with suggestions imaged in the mind when reading is possibly exemplified in another of Spenser's more famous descriptions: the story of Jason and Medea in ivory on the gates of the Bower of Blisse.

> Yt framed was of precious yuory,
> That seemd a worke of admirable wit;
> And therein all the famous history
> Of *Iason* and *Medœa* was ywrit;
> *Her mighty charmes, her furious louing fit,*
> *His goodly conquest of the golden fleece,*
> His falsed faith, and loue too lightly flit,

[9] F. M. Padelford, "Spenser and the Puritan Propaganda," *MP*, XI (1913), 98.

The wondred *Argo*, which in venturous peece
First through the *Euxine* seas bore all the flowr of *Greece*.

Ye might haue seene *the frothy billowes fry*
Vnder the ship, as thorough them she went,
That seemd the waues were into yuory,
Or yuory into the waues were sent;
And other where the snowy substance *sprent*
With vermell, like the boyes bloud therein shed,
A piteous spectacle did represent,
And otherwhiles *with gold besprinkeled;*
Yt seemd th'enchaunted flame, which did *Creüsa* wed.

(*FQ* II, xii, 44–5)

Upton says that Spenser had in mind here Tasso's description of the silver gates of Armida's palace (which however portray not this story but two others).[10] So he doubtless did. That Tasso's gates are of silver, not of ivory, and that they picture the stories of Hercules and Iole and of Antony and Cleopatra, not that of Jason and Medea, need not make us look about uneasily for a second source. But after all, though alike in moral point, these two gates differ both in subject matter and in medium. Spenser had some reason for substituting the Jason story. And moreover, the fact of their being worked in *ivory* is no mere chance detail, put in for allegorical neatness or for some irrelevant reason such as the rhyme scheme. It is the most striking thing about the passage. Spenser *saw* them in ivory; the whiteness of it lit with gold and made startling with vermilion shows us one of the rare instances in which he is writing from an image whose salient effect is one of color rather than one of light or of line. In texture and tactile quality the image has the softened cold smoothness of an ivory; there is no hint left of the hard metallic light-flashing brilliance of silver. And the series of scenes is told off like a list of tableaux or illustrations.

It is quite possible for Spenser to have seen the story of Jason and Medea in ivory. It was a fairly well-known subject for carvings in that medium. There are, for instance, four elaborate examples of it among the ivories at the Victoria and Albert Museum.

One of the most striking of these portrays the story on a series

[10] Edmund Spenser, *Works*, Variorum Edition, II (Baltimore, 1933), 372; Tasso, *Gerusalemme Liberata*, canto xvi, stanzas 2–7.

of six plaques, set into a marriage casket of wood inlaid with marqueterie; it is of Italian workmanship of the beginning of the 15th century.[11] The plaques on the casket depict in quick succession the high moments of the story; as in tapestries or glass, two scenes are sometimes incorporated into one panel, without division, and their order (as in Spenser) is not accurately kept to. There is much use of gold on the bone plaques: for hair, buttons or decoration on the clothing, or to touch the edges of the waves. As in Spenser, this sprinkled gold, and occasional touches of vermilion, furnish the only color. The most interesting panels in this portrayal are the following: Jason, helmeted, in gold-decorated armour, fights the two bulls, the insides of whose mouths are touched with red; an angry dragon guards the fleece in the wood nearby; a waiting figure sits in a fine crescent-shaped boat which rides the gilded waves to the left. Ram and vermilion-mouthed dragon occur on other panels, as does Medea holding a child.[12] There are four scenes which stress Medea's "louing fit"; in one the queenly Medea in her gold-besprinkled dress touches Jason on the forehead, in another she appears accompanied by Jason carrying the Fleece, in a boat riding upon crisply outlined waves; they are frothy, touched with gold, and "fry" under the boat as Spenser's do. The version of the story used is the mediaeval one in Benoit de Sainte-Maure's *Roman de Troie*. As with Spenser's use of the story, this is merely a series of striking episodes vividly carved, for a purely decorative purpose, in a pleasing and opulent medium.

Another marriage casket,[13] also of inlaid wood, is set with eight plaques; an impressive object, it stands about a foot and a half high. It has an interesting lid, also set with plaques. With that fondness for the emblematic juxtaposition of story and moral point which is characteristic and conventional in the later Middle

[11] Victoria and Albert Museum, no. 3265—1856; Margaret H. Longhurst, *Catalogue of Carvings in Ivory* (London, 1926), p. 65, Plate LIX; Julius von Schlosser, "Die Werkstatt der Embriachi in Venedig," *Jahrbuch der Kunsthistorischen sammlungen des Allerhöchsten kaiserhauses,* XX (Vienna, 1899), 220ff.

[12] Von Schlosser, in describing a similar plaque on a Cluny casket, interprets the child's figure as the "Zauberbild" with which Jason was protected against the dangers of the dragon-island (*v.* pp. 260ff). But *v.* below, and note 15.

[13] No. 4304—1857; Longhurst, *op. cit.,* p. 65, Pls. LX, LXI; *v.* Schlosser, *op. cit.,* no. 53. Also of Italian workmanship; beginning of fifteenth century.

Ages as in Spenser, the series chosen is that of the personified Virtues (Fortitude with sword and shield above the dragon fight, Prudence with snake and mirror above Jason on his way to the combat, Faith above the plaque with Jason and Medea at the grove, Charity suckling a child—like Spenser's, both conventional of course). The most striking pictures on this casket are: that of the conquest of the Fleece (the dragon vermilion-mouthed and wide-winged); that whose three divisions show a handsome Jason in scalloped doublet carrying the Fleece, Jason talking to a very tall, queenly Medea who points upward and hands him an object —this is the Medea of "mighty charmes," and Medea holding up the child. Another plaque incorporates the two charging bulls, the doubleted Jason, kneeling, and Medea observing or counselling him from a boat rowed by two other figures—again here the waves are charmingly done, splashing and breaking in crisp whiteness against either side of the boat.

A third casket [14] has a similar lid set with plaques of the Virtues. The pictures showing the most striking variation are those which portray Medea and the child; in one three women hand it over to her, in another a woman with set face strides before us carrying the child, in her right hand a drawn dagger. A casual interpreter of the pictures would most naturally relate these to Medea's murder of her children or of the "boy" her brother.[15] The original confusion was perhaps with the Paris story, as in another plaque showing a man carrying off a woman, her skirts swirling as he lifts her, three other women looking back aghast.[16] On still another casket,[17] similar "high moments" of the story appear: Medea with the child, the bulls, Jason fighting the dragon at the wood, with the ram in a tree above, Jason talking amorously to Medea, who smiles at him as they make off in the boat, a follower holding the Fleece. The boat has a handsome spread sail, the ivory waves are crisply carved and break to the right upon a coast with a castle.

These are not isolated examples. Dr. von Schlosser lists nine

[14] Victoria and Albert Museum, Hildburgh Loan 15. Italian; fifteenth century.

[15] A "petit enfant" in, for example, the *Fall of Princes* version of the story (John Lydgate, *Fall of princes*, ed. by Henry Bergen, Washington, 1923–1927, IV, 147).

[16] There has doutbless been a confusion here with the Paris story; cf. one of the plaques in von Schlosser's no. 124, Tafel XXXVIII.

[17] Victoria and Albert Museum, Hildburgh Loan 405. Italian; *ca.* 1400.

caskets of the Embriachi school with the Jason and Medea story in ivory, and a treatment in relief.[18] In the present connection, I wish only to point out the facts that the story was a fairly familiar one for treatment in the medium into which Spenser puts it (here departing from his source, which treats of *different* stories in *silver*), that such ivories were of a suitable date, and that ivories of various types were possessed in large numbers in England.[19] In certain descriptions of tapestries Spenser seems to have written "with his mind's eye upon examples which he had actually seen." [20] So, in this instance, the change in story-subject and that from silver to ivory, certain particularly vivid descriptive details such as the color and the frothy ivory waves, and the descriptive method used (the telling-off of tableau-like episodic moments of the story, in a series), may result from Spenser's having at some time or other been struck by a beautiful treatment of the Jason story, actually seen, carved in the medium in which he describes it. It does not detract from the imaginative quality of the passage to think that he had really seen, in an ivory such as these I have described, those waves that seemed as if they "into yuory, Or yuory into the waves were sent," that "snowy substance sprent with vermell" or "with gold besprinkeled."

THESE two examples of possible relations between Spenser's descriptive technique and the objects which did at least exist for him to see, though we cannot prove that he saw them, are as I have said only suggested as a subsidiary element in the full story of what made Spenser's descriptions what they are. But one reason for his extraordinary clarity of descriptive technique may lie in this combination of literary and visual "sources"—a combination which I think could be pointed out far oftener if we knew as much about his artistic interests—or took as much cognizance of them—as we do of his literary sources.

[18] *Op. cit.*, p. 260; Adolfo Venturi (*Storia dell'arte italiana*, Milano, 1901, IV, 893, n. 1 and illustration) adds examples in Pistoia and Laurino; O. M. Dalton (*Catalogue of the Ivory Carvings of the Christian Era*, London, 1909) describes one in the British Museum.

[19] *V.* general treatments with references from inventories and wills in Alfred Maskell, *Ivories* (New York, 1877); Margaret H. Longhurst, *English Ivories* (London, 1926).

[20] F. Hard, "Spenser's 'Clothes of Arras and of Toure,'" *SP*, XXVII (1930), 176.

Spenser and Some Pictorial Conventions

WITH PARTICULAR REFERENCE TO ILLUMINATED MANUSCRIPTS *

THIS article will treat of certain figures which receive markedly pictorial descriptive treatment in Spenser, and of certain figures which he uses almost as descriptive "counters," flashing a picture of them before us for associative (or decorative) purposes, much as modern film technique uses "symbolic" insets. It will describe the form in which such figures appear in actual picture, in texts which it is either certain or highly likely that Spenser read. I think that pictures helped form his conceptions. I shall not point to particular illustrations which he saw and copied; rather I shall show the character of a pictorial tradition which was vivid, rich, and available to him. One tries to read a poet's sources with continuous attention to how they may have acted as spurs to his imagination, especially to his visual imagination and hence to his descriptive power. And one must recognize that the reading of a text in such different forms as a "modern" French print, an early English black-letter with woodcuts, or a fifteenth-century manuscript with illuminations, makes correspondingly different impressions; the variation in form almost constitutes a variation in the text itself. We perhaps tend to forget that these differing forms were all of them accessible and familiar to the Elizabethan reader. Illuminated manuscripts particularly may seem to us difficult to come at; to the Elizabethan they were ordinary and available. A rich pictorial tradition lay to Spenser's hand in these varying forms in which he could read his sources, and particularly in manuscripts, the least examined of them. And the points at which Spenser's descriptions relate themselves to this rich pictorial tradition are frequent and often most striking.

The figures to be considered are conventional figures in book illustration. Not only is their very occurrence in manuscript illumination traditional, but also certain recurrent details of their representation are fixed by tradition, i.e., there are two constants, convention enters in two ways. In the first place, the mention of such

* Reprinted from *Studies in Philology* 37 (1940), 149–76.

figures in a work is a signal for the punctuation of the text with a picture. This results not only in pictorial stress on the same figures in many different works, but also in a conventional series in the many exemplars of a given work. This is true of most texts commonly illustrated in manuscript; moreover, such a series is oftenest the basis for the number and character of the woodcuts in early editions. Secondly, there also developed quite early and hardened into convention a norm, fairly firmly adhered to, for the representation of particular figures or story-moments; only certain minor details are fluctuating. Other details are fixed, not changing even from text to text. So also in Spenser, convention enters in the same ways: certain figures habitually receive "picturesque" treatment; and certain details are an habitual part of the description of given figures. These details are often identical with the fixed details of illuminations and illustrations.

The treatment of such a source relationship as this cannot be exhaustive. I shall attempt to show the probability and define the character of the relationship by an examination of certain type cases of such conventional figures or details—how and where they appear, how continuously, in what contexts. Though one cannot say that Spenser's use of them resulted from his seeing them in such and such a book, in such and such colours, still there must emerge from such an examination a richer and more nearly true notion of the process by which they came to be in their conventional aspects part of the furniture of his mind, in those aspects to find their way into his poetry.

That Spenser looked at and read some books in manuscript is inherently probable not only because of his proved attention to "antiquities," but also because of the zeal with which many great collections were then beginning to be formed, the already fine collections in Cambridge colleges with which he or Harvey had connections, the numbers of his friends who owned manuscripts—as proved by the stray signed examples we can still turn up in the great public libraries. The most striking instance is the huge number of manuscripts, read and annotated by that friend of the Sidneys and connection of Harvey's, John Dee.[1] But, for lesser ex-

[1] I have looked at some 60 or 70 of the MSS formerly owned by Dee now at Corpus Christi College, Oxford, the British Museum, various Cambridge libraries, Trinity College, Dublin, etc. They vary in character, including not only the vast number of scientific treatises we should expect but also such books as Alain de

amples of proved interest in manuscripts among connections or friends of Spenser's: Charles Lord Howard of Effingham (Marinell?) owned some dozen and a half mediaeval manuscripts of various kinds,[2] now in Bodley, many of them remarkable for decoration. A Horae manuscript of Sir Walter Ralegh's, with not undistinguished illuminations,[3] his signature on f. 1^r, is now Bodl. Add. A 185. Leicester's 15th-century *Brut* in English,[4] and

---

Lille's *Anticlaudianus*, Lydgate's *Fall of Princes*, the *Brut* in French, chronicles, legends of St. Brendan in French and Latin, Robert Rolle's *Incendium Amoris* in English, etc. Marginal annotations are of course by far most frequent in the cosmological, alchemical, or other scientific works, but again vary, from occasional synonyms for archaic words in the Rolle MS (Corpus Christi 236) to mere underscorings, hands marking points to be noted, quick marginal summaries. On Dee's MS collections see M. R. James, *List of MSS formerly owned by Dr. John Dee, Supplement to Bibliographical Society's Transactions*, No. I (Oxford, 1921), especially the list at pp. 35ff of the many now available at various places. References to evidence for Dee's connections with Sidney, Spenser, Harvey, Rogers, *et al.* may be conveniently found in C. B. Millican, *Spenser and the Table Round* (Cambridge, 1932), pp. 42ff, notes and index.

2 See the Slip Catalogue in the Bodleian for MSS given by Lord Howard. They include, *e.g.*, a Bede in Carolingian minuscule which had belonged to Henry VIII (Bodl. 218, *Summary Cat. of MSS in the Bodleian Library*, Oxford, 1895–1937, no. 2054), 13th- and 14th-century MSS of the Psalms with grotesques or with miniatures (*Summ. Cat.* 2730, 2339), a 15th-century treatise on maritime law (3341), saints' lives in English, 13th-century, with illuminated capitals (2432), Middle English devotional treatises (2676), etc.

3 The Ralegh *Horae* MS is French, 15th-century (*Summ. Cat.* 3077); besides the St. George described later in this article, its many miniatures include for example the vision of the shining-roofed new Jerusalem such as that seen by Red Crosse, the usual golden-plumed angels, curly-golden-haired young Michael, Margaret on her spotted dragon, with its coiled tail and rows of teeth and conventional resemblances to Spenser's. With echoes in mind of Ralegh's famous "Give me my scallop-shell of quiet" one cannot help noticing the miniature of James the pilgrim-saint, with his gold-shaded *gown*, his *staff*, his red *scrip* with a white *shell* painted upon it (as also upon his flat pilgrim's hat; f. 59^v). A chance corroboration of Ralegh's interest in MSS occurs in the letter to Cotton reproduced by Greg as an example of Ralegh's hand (*English Literary Autographs*, Part III, London, 1932): "Sr Robert Cotton if yow haue any of thes old books or any manuscrips wherein j [cann reade any] of our Brittan antiquitee . . ."—requesting the loan of such MSS.

4 B. Mus. Addit. 12030; the marginal summaries and marks are probably in neither Leicester's hand nor (though temptingly like) in Spenser's. The second MS (Bodl. Rawl. A 338), though a translation of the *Quadrilogue*, is boldly inscribed "English ploiticks"; I intend in some more fitting place (for the MS

his Alain Chartier in English (handsomely bound with his arms; both manuscripts bear his name), show by their marginal notes evidence of having been read with some care at this later period. An illuminated Psalter belonging to the Sidneys (with birth and marriage of Philip, Mary, *et al.*, recorded in the calendar) and a Sidney *Horae* manuscript (coarsely illuminated, with similar records) are now Trin. Coll. Cambridge R. 17.2, and Bodleian MS 850. Harvey's and Spenser's friend Daniel Rogers [5] gave some ten manuscripts to Corpus Christi, Cambridge, and owned some now at Lambeth; Lancelot Andrewes gave two to Pembroke. The Russell-Clifford-Stanley family group, so many of whose members had connections with Spenser, owned handsome and interesting manuscripts, wrote their names and their verses into them, gave them as presents. Ambrose Dudley's wife Anne Russell, one of the dedicatees of the *Fowre Hymnes*, and a friend and patron of Dee's, owned a large and very legible manuscript of Gower's *Confessio Amantis* (Bodl. 902), among the 16th-century annotations of which appears one bracketed "Spenserus." [6] Her brother-in-law George Clifford, 3rd Earl of Cumberland (Dedicatory Sonnet, *FQ;* his wife was Spenser's "Marian" and the other dedicatee of the *Fowre Hymnes*), owned and gave to the collector Lumley in 1599 an elaborate copy of Lydgate's *Fall of Princes* (Brit. Mus. Royal 18 D iv; he also owned the beautiful Vienna cod. 1840; *v.* also Bodl. 3). Clifford's sister Margaret, wife of Henry Stanley, Earl of Derby (mother of Spenser's Amintas, Ferdinando, Lord Strange and Derby, whose wife was Spenser's

has no pictures) to call attention to certain allegorical figures and arguments showing similarities to Spenser's.

[5] See Harvey's mention of Rogers in his letter of May 1580, Carpenter's list of Spenser's friends (*Reference Guide*, Chicago, 1923, p. 86), and the descriptive catalogues by M. R. James of the MS collections referred to. Convenient references to the sources which show Rogers to be the friend of Sidney, Languet, and Camden, and quotations of Languet's remarks to Sidney on him, are to be found in Millican *op. citi.*, p. 45 and note. See also J. J. Higginson, *Spenser's Shepherd's Calender* (N.Y., 1912), p. 316 note.

[6] A consideration of the very great likelihood that the four Latin lines thus signed were written in the MS by Spenser, and of Spenser's relationships with the Russell and Clifford families, will be found in my article " 'Spenserus' in in a Mediaeval Manuscript," forthcoming. [See pp. 139–63 below.] Lady Warwick was a patron of Dee's; *v.* Charlotte Fell Smith, *John Dee* (London, 1909), p. 247 and index.

Amaryllis, dedicatee of the *Teares of the Muses*) owned several manuscripts of which the most interesting is an illustrated Hardyng's Chronicle; [7] she also owned two Gowers.

I seize on the most striking examples among known connections of Spenser's. One must remember that such famous collectors as Arundel and Lumley,[8] who selected finely illuminated manuscripts but evidently read them as well,[9] were at this time active. So also was Henry Percy, 9th Earl of Northumberland, Ralegh's friend.[10] Cambridge libraries were being swelled by such gifts as that astounding one of Archbishop Parker's four hundred and thirty manuscripts, many of them extraordinarily fine, left by him in 1575 to Corpus Christi, with restrictions which involved Trinity Hall, where Harvey and Spenser had connections.[11] Cra-

[7] Bodl. Arch. Selden B 10; it contains provocative verses upon and diagrammatic representation of the "palais of pride" of "Pluto king of hel neighbore to Scottez"—not found in the printed versions of Hardyng, who was one of Spenser's sources. See the article referred to in note 6. Her Gower MSS are B. Mus. Royal 18 C 22; Cambr. Mm. 2. 21.

[8] John Lord Lumley (d. 1609), son-in-law of the collector Arundel, owned some 300 of the Royal MSS now in the British Museum (including many of the handsomest ones), as well as a good number now in other collections. *V.* introd. to *Catalogue of . . . MSS. in the Royal . . . Collection* (London, 1921), xix, catalogues of Cambridge and Oxford libraries, and for more general points Seymour de Ricci, *English Collectors of Books and MSS, 1530–1930* (Cambridge, 1930), pp. 19–20. Henry Fitzalan, Earl of Arundel (d. 1580), was nephew of "the magnificent 5th earl of Northumberland" (who not only collected MSS and books but had MSS completed and illuminated for him—as e.g. Royal 18 D ii, referred to below, note 37); Arundel was himself a noted collector. [See *The Lumley Library*, *The Catalogue of 1609*, eds. Sears Jayne, and Francis Johnson, London, 1956.]

[9] Evidenced, for example, by the fairly careful textual notes and comparisons in B. Mus. MS Royal 18 D iv, of the *Fall of Princess* "probably written while the MS was in Lumley's possession" (*Catalogue*, *op. cit.*, II, 312).

[10] For MSS owned by him see Sotheby's catalogue of the sale April 23–24, 1928, by Lord Leconfield, of some of the books from Petsworth. The majority of the books and MSS were associated with the 9th Earl; included for example is a 15th-century MS with 26 miniatures of Guillaume de Deguileville's *Pilgrimage* (translated), referred to later in this article.

[11] The Master of Trinity Hall was one of the yearly inspectors of the collection, and it was to revert to Trinity Hall or Caius College in case of neglect by Corpus Christi. Harvey was Fellow of Trinity Hall in 1578; Thomas Preston, made its Master in 1584, was a connection of his and Spenser's. So also was John Still (see Carpenter's list, *Ref. Guide*, p. 86; G. C. Moore Smith, *Gabriel Harvey's Marginalia*, Stratford, 1913, p. 21, note); Parker was friend and

shaw's collection, to come to St. John's through the Earl of Southampton, was forming, as was Robert Hare's comparatively tiny but interesting collection, given to Trinity Hall (probably actually given later than Harvey's connection there).[12] Also important are the antiquarians like Camden, or Stowe, or the Anglo-Saxon scholar Lambarde, whom Spenser possibly knew,[13] or Lumley's brother-in-law Humphrey Lluyd, whom the Sidneys encouraged.[14] One must remember that these and many others like them owned and were actively and unselfconsciously interested in manuscripts as sources of knowledge, and moreover that Spenser's connections and interests make his knowledge of these activities highly probable. The sixteenth-century gentleman of literary tastes did not ignore manuscripts, nor could he find all he wished to read reprinted by an *Early English Text Society* or a *Société des anciens textes français.* Perhaps he chiefly read the earlier works which interested him in the reprints of the prolific

patron to Still, formerly his domestic chaplain (Strype, *Life and Acts of Matthew Parker*, London, 1711, p. 510; on all these Cambridge figures see not only *DNB* but C. Cooper, *Athenae Cantabrigienses*, Cambridge, 1858, 1913). On Parker's vast and important collection, its extent, nature, provenance, and conditions of gift, see M. R. James, *Descriptive Cat. of MSS in the Library of Corpus Christi College* (Cambridge, 1912), I, xivff. Others of Parker's MSS are at University Library Cambridge, British Museum (Royal Collection), Lambeth, Trinity College Cambridge.

[12] On this group of MSS one of which is described later in this article, see M. R. James, *Descriptive Cat. of MSS . . . in Trinity Hall* (Cambridge, 1907), preface p. vi and descriptions; Hare's own college was Caius, to which he also gave MSS; others are in Lambeth, the Bodleian, St. Paul's. In 1571 he retired and worked on Cambridge history and antiquities; for Hare's life see esp. Cooper, *op. cit.*, III, 47.

[13] According to Renwick in his edition of the *Veue* (London, 1934), p. 297. On this antiquarian scholar see Eleanor Adams, *Old English Scholarship* (New Haven, 1917), pp. 27ff; de Ricci, *op. cit.*, p. 16. For MSS owned by him see the Slip Catalogue at the Bodleian, catalogue of owners in the British Museum MSS room; his MSS show not only historical and linguistic interests but include patristic works, a couple of copies each of the *Secreta Secretorum* and the *Brut*, etc. Another "Saxonist" connected with Lambarde and Parker was Laurence Nowell, brother of the Alexander Nowell who with Grindal was examiner at Merchant Taylors School, and of Robert, from whose money Spenser got aid at College (*v.* P. Long, "Spenser and the Bishop of Rochester," *PMLA*, XXXI [1916], 716).

[14] On Humphrey Lluyd the antiquarian, collector, and author, who owned several MSS now in the Royal collection, British Museum, and who assisted Lord Lumley in the formation of his great collection, see Millican, *op. cit.*, pp. 69ff; note 8 above and the references there; *DNB.*

French and other printing presses; nevertheless he did not yet regard manuscripts as a closed province, and he assuredly looked at the illustrated originals of his printed texts with interest and attention whenever he came upon them. And this need not have been seldom. For the most part unselfconsciously regarded, though valued, manuscripts were not as now locked up as unread curiosities in libraries difficult of access, or considered as a *recherché* field of the especially prepared scholar.

The emphasis here, however, is not upon which texts we have reason to think Spenser saw in this form or that, particularly in manuscript. The stress is rather upon certain figures and story motifs for which there was—in manuscript or in prints pictorially dependent upon them—a widespread pictorial tradition that may account for his use of them and his manner of presenting them. I shall therefore take them up figure by figure rather than text by text, keeping however to such examples as appeared either in texts almost surely known to Spenser or in books owned by those who had some connection with him.

One may distinguish various types of relationship between Spenser's figures and those in the pictorial tradition. The relationship is sometimes a matter of the physical appearance of the figure, plain and simple: Spenser's Belphoebe and Radigund are the typical pictured Amazon (the quality of Spenser's additions is interesting); his Cupid is the God of Love figure as usually painted; his Sapience is the traditional Sapience or Wisdom figure of illustrated allegories or the *Bible historiale;* his Disdain is the churlish dark porter pictured with his club in vast numbers of romance manuscripts. Or, sometimes, his divergence from the facts as presented in his proper source is accounted for by the pictorial conventions: his Penthesilea killed by *Pirrus,* instead of by Achilles as the sources relate, his Argus with eyes strewn over his *whole* body. Sometimes it is a question merely of the choice of a conventional figure which would not have sprung so inescapably to his mind had it not been so familiar in illustration—the proud charioted Oriental king, the helpful lion. Similarly, it is sometimes a question of the introduction of a story or allusion which, but for its frequent appearance pictorially and therefore vividly, would not have been marked down in his mind as the natural choice when he needed an exemplum. Such favorite stories, which had become through incessant pictorial stress common associational "counters," like *cliché* rhetorical figures, are those of Hercules and Iole, of Nimrod, of Semiramis, of Hippolytus, of Phrixus and Helle, of Ino, of Bellerophon and his stepmother. When Spenser's figures are commonplaces of classical literature, it is often the traditional *illustrational* emphasis which has helped to give them a non-classical emotional content, a new allegorical significance or direction: Pluto in Spenser has become also the mediaeval Christian's devil-figure; Flora is less goddess than *ribaulde*—the lascivious attendant of Venus in a garden-of-love romance; Hercules is exponent of justice, club in hand, and just as importantly, tied always to Iole, the type of strength become effeminate through a woman. The gradual accretion of emphasis through hundreds of years of conventional pictorial appearance must have been important in determining also Spenser's choice of such traditionally symbolic figures as the St. George with maiden, lamb, and dragon. Richness and immediacy as symbols depend in part upon a long artistic—as complementary to literary—history. These types of relationship to the traditions of book-illustration are fairly tangible; other possible results are less so. It is possible that a simple but eternally reiterated story, given always the emphasis of pictures, was stressed above its importance in his mind, its main figure becoming the genesis for a connected but much-changed story or story-situation—for example, there may be in Busyrane a half-realized reincarnation of the cruel Busiris. The thought is suggestive (and applicable to other Elizabethans) that Spenser's addiction to a style rich with allusion comes—in part only, and neatly attached to a theory—from the fact that a mind capable of minute observation and remembrance of pictured detail was thus presented over and over again with hosts of familiar but vivid pictured "examples"—swarms of proud "fallen princes," bevies of strongminded "cleres dames," the stereotypes of mythology, the inevitable vices and virtues, the inevitable symbolic god-planets.

In specifying particular figures which through long and conventional use had come to have this rich connotative value and immediacy of effect, it is necessary to describe typical appearances of the figure rather carefully. These descriptions may seem for the moment rather unconnected with Spenser, but this cannot be helped when one is outlining a background. Parallelisms in details will be shown later.

The Amazon is one of the most firmly pictorial of figures. She is ubiquitous, she reappears with the same yellow hair, the same clothing, bows and arrows, processional train, in text after text, manuscript after manuscript.[15] The Marpesie of B. Nat. MS f. fr. 599 (15th century), Boccaccio's *Des cleres dames* (a work we have reason to think Spenser read),[16] shows the familiar type of Amazon-figure: her crisped "golden wyre" hair, distinctly drawn—almost strand by strand—hangs down her shoulders, she wears a red baldric, gold-dotted, an elaborate gold-patterned belt, a red skirt and jacket of armour, a jewelled crown, and carries sword and feathered lance; Lampedon has her hair trussed up in ribbons, and a gold chain baldric (f. 12^{r}). Orichie (f. 18^{v}) has her yellow hair gathered at the nape of her neck; Antiope again has trimmed gold belt and shield. B. Mus. MS Royal 16 G v, of the same text (early 15th century), has a Penthesilea in "mayled habergeon," red skirt elaborately trimmed at the hips, with curved gold shield, yellow curls, a caparisoned white horse; of her troop of damsels most are helmeted, one with loose hair (f. 35^{v}). Hippsicrate is similarly dressed and accompanied, she has a grey quiver (f. 91^{v}); Lampedon and Marpesie (f. 14^{r}) have a shield-carrying damsel, the latter is distinguished by a blue robe adorned with gold stars. In B. Nat. MS f. fr. 598 (15th century) Penthesilea in red with gold belt carries bow and arrows, her attendants have helmets and banner (f. 46^{r}); Hippsicrate, armed to the waist, has a huge bow and green quiver (f. 116^{r}). The Penthesilea of MS f. fr. 12420, on her caparisoned horse as usual, carries bow and arrows, wears a gold belt and armor showing through her mantle; her followers carry pennons and gold shields, embossed (f. 46^{r}). Thamilis, fighting, is helmed and wears a red baldric elaborated with several orders of gold design; Semiramis' red baldric, shoulder to knee, is decorated and hung with tassels or balls (f. 74^{v}, 8^{r}).

In addition to lending them to other queens, the Amazon carries her accoutrements with her from text to text (and to *FQ*—my justification for repeated mentions of minute detail). The com-

[15] She is substantially the same whether she is Penthesilea, Orithia, Marpesia, Lampedon; and the powerful queen not an Amazon (Semiramis, Thamiris, Hippsicrate) took on characteristic details of her appearance.

[16] I have given support for this elsewhere; *v.* "Spenser's Reading: The *De claris mulieribus*," *SP*, XXXIII (1936), 147–65. [See pp. 83–101 above.]

mon mediaeval historical compilation usually titled *Orose en français* (only in part a redoing of Orosius) [17] is another of the texts which practically always has pictures of Penthesilea, and more important ones, because they are pictures of Penthesilea's fight with Pyrrus and her death at his hands. Spenser's attribution of her death to Pyrrus instead of Achilles is one of his departures from his classical sources; the reference follows upon that description in which Belphoebe point for point resembles her (*FQ* II, iii). The *Orose* was a popular text; the B. Nat. has some twenty manuscripts of the first redaction and four of the second; the British Museum has seven; there were editions in 1491, 1503, 1509, 1515, 1526. In the illuminated *Orose* manuscripts the story of the Pyrrus-Penthesilea conflict is usually illustrated with a series of two to eight pictures. For example in B. Mus. MS Royal 20 D i,[18] the most striking of the eight are those two story-moments which also lodged themselves in Spenser's memory, her arrival and her death. On f. 153^r Priam is formally greeted by Penthesilea, an earnest-faced lady in brocade, the ranked heads of damsels behind her, all mounted; this moment is commonly chosen for illustration, and might receive its title from Spenser's "Did shew her selfe in great triumphant ioy, The day that first of Priame she was seene" (II, iii, 31).[19] In the great *melée* of the death-picture (f. 158^r) Penthesilea's face is strong and outstanding; blood spurts, from the wound being made by Pyrrus, over her clothing, half-feminine, half-armor; her yellow braids escape from a flat helmet (in the battle-pictures also she is distinguished by these yellow braids flying out from her head in great curves, so also are the Amazons of the Theseus story earlier, f. 25^r). In B. Nat. MS f. fr. 301 the series of fine pictures (ff. 133^v to 139) begins with Priam being greeted with an embrace from Penthesilea, her yellow hair falling down her back under her crown, her damsels following her; then come two battle-pictures—a crowd of Amazons with swords, two yellow braids flying out from under each helmet, are led by Penthesilea in a mantle shining with gold

[17] V. P. Meyer, "Les premières compilations françaises d'histoire ancienne," *Romania*, XIV (1885), 1–87.

[18] 14th century; in the Richmond Palace list of 1535, probably no. 104.

[19] This MS and that following are of the second redaction; in copies of the first and less elaborate form the appearance of the figure is parallel (*v.*, *e.g.*, f. fr. 64, f. 84^r, in which the shield is particularly striking).

bell-figures. Several other pictures show her prowess; her gold hair comes undone and flies out straight behind her in the wind. In the picture of her wounding and death, blood streams down her face, her hair loose around it; last she is carried off in her magnificent gold-figured robe by her damsels. In MS f. fr. 254, in the greeting-Priam picture, Penthesilea beautifully mounted as usual, leading her train, with shield, armor to the waist, has fine shiny gold hair falling down below her waist—her "cheueulx . . . plus reluisans que fin or," according to the description in this elaborate form of the text (f. 128^{r}). Ordinarily these figures are labelled or there are rubrics which arrest the attention and emphasize the story to the casual observer.[20] Woodcuts in the early prints follow the MS tradition—the hair flying out free from under the helmet, the partial armor, troop of followers, bow, shield adorned with gems (e.g., A. Vérard's edition, Paris, 1491, f. 121).[21] With its careful descriptions, its stress on Pyrrus' shame at Penthesilea's taunts (cf. Artegall), its strong emphases through rubrics and series of striking pictures, this text shows up figures and story more saliently than any other. I shall show in a moment how much more closely Spenser's Amazons resemble this figure than, e.g., the Penthesilea of the *Aeneid* whom Lotspeich mentions as a source.[22] Penthesilea's story, with the detail of her death at Pyrrus' hands, is also found in Raoul Lefevre's *Recueil des histoires de troyes,* illustrated in manuscripts and in prints; it was composed in 1464, is partially dependent upon Dares, was translated by Caxton. His edition and later ones make this detail clear enough in rubrics or chapter headings; the Wynkyn de Worde edition, 1503, has woodcuts but none for this story; French editions however (Lyons, 1494, 1510, 1529) emphasize it with a woodcut of the labelled protagonists, portrayed

20 This attention-factor is important, if we are to think of Spenser as looking over de luxe copies of texts he knew, with casual interest, in other people's libraries—as anyone who has looked swiftly at unfamiliar MSS. of familiar texts well knows. Rubrics also in the prints, or even in the less elaborate version, *e.g.* B. Mus. Addit. 19669 (*v.* f. 89^{r}).

21 The familiar details are of course stressed in the text as well: "Priam . . . et toute la cheualerie la receut en gra*n*t ioye . . . tant estoit ceste royne triomphante et toutes ses damoiselles . . . les heaulmes dorez et couuers de pierrerie/ et toutes leurs armures estoient fort precieuses et riches" (ff. 120^{v}–121).

22 *Aeneid* I, 490; *v.* H. G. Lotspeich, *Classical Mythology in the Poetry of Edmund Spenser* (Princeton, 1932), *s.v. Penthesilea.*

with the conventional details established by manuscript tradition —streaming hair, baldric, armed followers, blood-spurting wound. As always, illuminations are more striking; compare, in B. Mus. Royal 17 E ii,[23] Penthesilea with long golden hair and armor to hips leading her mounted followers.

Spenser too, like the *Orose* and the *Recueil*, may have got the bare fact of Pyrrus' killing of Penthesilea straight from Dares' *De Excidio*, as many commentators have said he did.[24] But if details about the Amazon queen came to Spenser through Dares, instead of secondhand as above described, they came far less emphatically. Had he looked at printed editions of Dares, he would have found little to make him see the story vividly and keep the figure in mind for his own several uses; Pyrrus is called "Neoptolomo," there are not pictures.[25] There is no tradition of illumination in the Dares manuscripts.[26] And of course the notion that Spenser read these other later mediaeval works does not hinge on this one detail.[27]

Another text treating this famous Amazon, and other figures I shall mention later, is Christine de Pisan's *Othea*. Of this there is a very lovely example in B. Mus. MS Harleian 4431; another fine copy at St. John's College Cambridge was evidently there when Spenser was up. This series of a hundred "moralized" figures, each with picture and "allegorie," is exactly the kind of storehouse of classical commonplaces in a mediaeval presentation which one would think Spenser likeliest to look at with interest. His reading of it cannot be proved. Christine was highly praised by Clément Marot; [28] a prolific writer, frequently reprinted and translated, she must have been fairly well known in the 16th cen-

[23] A 15th-century MS; in the Richmond Palace list of 1535.

[24] See Lotspeich, *op. cit.*, *s.v. Penthesilea;* Alice E. Sawtelle (Mrs. Randall), *Sources of Spenser's Classical Mythology* (New York, 1896), *s.v. Amazon; The Works of Edmund Spenser*, A Variorum Edition (Baltimore, 1933), II, 218. Upton mentioned the Caxton parallel.

[25] See editions of Venice, 1472?, f. 22^v; Venice, 1499, sg. I 7; Leipzig, 1498, sg. C ii; Paris, 1527, sg. D^v; or portion included in Diodorus Siculus, *Bibliotheca Historica* (Basle, 1559), p. 221.

[26] For example, in the 17 examples listed by Ward in his *Catalogue of Romances in the . . . MSS. of the British Museum* (London, 1883), I, 12ff, there is no example with pictures.

[27] See other figures treated below, and my article cited in note 16. [See pp. 83–101 above.]

[28] See E. Nys, *Christine de Pisan* (La Haye, 1914), p. 77.

tury. The *Othea,* which is far from rare in manuscript,[29] was written about 1400, appeared as *Les cent histoires / de troye. /* , Paris, *c.* 1490, 1522; Lyons, 1497, 1519; was translated as *The C. Hystoryes of Troye, c.* 1540–50.[30] In MS Harl. 4431 (f. 103ᵛ), the golden-haired Penthesilea leads her gaily-accoutred host of damsels; her clothing ornate with gold and the curved and decorated shields stand out most; she figures forth bounty or charity (Belphoebe, though assuredly not Radigund!). Her death by Pyrrus' hand is not told here; but in the translation of Christine's *Cyte of Ladyes,* London, 1521, chapter xix treats at length of Pyrrus' humiliation at her hands, his plot against her, and conquest of her.[31]

It is thus obvious that Spenser's Amazon-figures are not to be traced to any single "source." It may be true that Spenser used for his Radigund "quite specific material" from Diodorus Siculus 2.45 and 3.51, as Lotspeich says,[32] and that he was imitating in his Belphoebe Ariosto's Alcina and Tasso's Clarice.[33] It is true that he was writing out of the commonplaces of his day. More particularly, I think it is also true that he was writing from a store of impressions, vividly remembered because they had been seen as well as read—not necessarily in the examples here enumerated but in the many like them which must have fallen in his way, and

[29] There are, for example, 12 in the Bibliothèque Nationale, 6 at Brussels, 4 in the British Museum. See the edition by George F. Warner, *Epistle of Othea* (London, 1904), introd., esp. p. xxxv. For history and owners of MS Harl. 4431, described above, *v.* p. xxxvi. B. Nat. MS f. fr. 606 parallels the Harley MS; its illustrator appears to have made a bad copy of the latter or of its prototype. MS Bodl. 421 has a yellow-haired Penthesilea in embroidered surcoat and belt, distinguished by her red "bauldricke" (Spenser's is golden).

[30] See Warner, *op. cit.,* pp. xli, xxvii. Warner's edition is of another translation (by Stephen Scrope), which did not attain print.

[31] Sg. Hh v-vᵛ; "when he sawe yᵉ heed bare by whiche her yelowe heere appered" he cleft head and brain in sunder.

[32] See Lotspeich, *op. cit., s. v.* Amazons, and his references to Gough's edition of *FQ* V (comparisons there are general and undetailed). But if Spenser used these Diodorus passages, he not only failed to utilize some of the most vivid details there given but also he did not find there the salient details of appearance which make his description striking and which are closely paralleled by the conventional pictured Amazon.

[33] See the Variorum Spenser, *op. cit.,* II, 212–13, and the articles there referred to, by R. E. N. Dodge and H. H. Blanchard, on imitations from Ariosto and Tasso, respectively.

which moreover are the background for "the commonplaces of his day." The alteration and recreation which a conventional figure undergoes at the hands of a great poet is often even more revealing than are the figures he makes out of his own whole cloth. This relation of the artist to "tradition" can be examined in Spenser's Amazons. We look again at those definitely outlined figures of his, with the crowd of conventional Amazons in our mind's eye, remembering that those described are but a few examples. There is scarcely a detail in Spenser's picturesque figure that has not been long a part of the convention, widespread as our examples have been in time, place, and authorship. Details are elaborated upon, made more splendid, but they are not *invented*, by Spenser. Moreover these agreeing details are of the sort which are *pictorially* impressive; the *words* of the two texts (Spenser and any given other) show nowhere nearly the same closely parallel imaging of the figure. The "convention" lies not in the words themselves, for these coincident details are seldom mentioned, but in the illustrations which accompany them.

We have looked above at typical examples of these illustrations; I will re-enumerate the details as Spenser gives them.[34] Again, in Spenser, we see the martial woman pictured with feminine overgarment and a shorter "mayled habergeon," the "camis" white or "purple" (i.e. crimson, probably, *purpurea*), and gleaming with metallic figures (the glint of brocaded pattern is more surprising and rich in illuminations than in any real brocade), "wouen vppon with siluer, subtly wrought" or "besprinckled . . . With golden aygulets, that glistred bright, Like twinckling starres" (a most usual type of enrichment in manuscript decoration, in gold or red; our examples have shown stars or bell-figures), reaching to her heel or tucked up (in the pictures often trimmed or otherwise held up at hip or waist). Here again are the "bow and quiver gay," the spear (or lance); Spenser makes the darts "steele-headed," or for Radigund orientalizes the usual sword into a "Cemitare" (though her "swarming" followers fight with arrows in just such a disorderly battle scene as those we have reviewed). She wears a "golden bauldricke, . . . Athwart her snowy brest"—in the manuscripts made noticeable by gold

[34] Quotations are from the descriptions of Belphoebe in *FQ* II, iii, and of Radigund in *FQ* V, v.

trimming, as is the patterned or "embrodered belt of mickell pride." [35] Shield too is "bedeckt" with shining gems. Most striking of all are her "yellow lockes," "crisped," drawn carefully separate "like golden wyre," or flying "like a penon wide dispred" in the swift wind of pursuit or battle. It is the first detail one's eye notes in any pictured Amazon—this frequently rather amusing sort of *carte d'identité*, her flying hair—and it is the most vivid one in Spenser's description. "Guarded with many damzels," Radigund's "stately port" is matched in picture after picture. Though Spenser refers directly to Penthesilea in the Belphoebe description, we scarcely need this rubric for our identification of her. The figure of Diana simultaneously present in Spenser's imagination (naturally enough) has added one significant detail the elaborate laced buskins—and the Diana-figure remains in Spenser's mind through the stanza which follows the elaboration of this detail in II, ii, 27–28. Here he had also in his memory the appearance of Venus to Aeneas. It is a general rule that Spenser keeps to the conventional appearance of a figure except where he is led off by some such subsidiary memory, once led off he frequently combines details from several sources for which association-links are quite perceptible—as here, the buskins are paralleled in *Rinaldo* V, 13.[36]

I have looked at this figure in detail because I wished to demonstrate what I think is Spenser's *characteristic* relation to traditional materials—an important and constantly recurring point. He does not invent nor change radically as far as picturesque descriptive detail is concerned. He saw vividly and remembered accurately, he reproduces almost without loss. He merely adds, characteristically, more opulence or more sensitive feeling in the sense-images, and, also characteristically, occasional associated details from similar pictures in his mind. The link is with striking consistency the linking of picture to similar picture in the mind. He seems to have written almost at the command of the visual images or visual associations in his memory. It is notable that

[35] It would seem hardly necessary to suppose, as Lotspeich does (*op. cit., s. v. Camilla*), that Belphoebe's quiver and baldric 'seem to derive from the description of Camilla' in the *Aeneid*.

[36] See Merritt Hughes, *Virgil and Spenser* (Univ. of California Publications in English 2, 1929), pp. 359ff. For the *Rinaldo* parallels see H. H. Blanchard, "Imitations from Tasso in the *FQ*," *SP*, XXII (1925), 207.

proven literary sources frequently do not show verbal parallels in pictorially descriptive detail. The Diodorus Siculus passages which Lotspeich points to as sources are full of historical and topographical details about Amazons; Diodorus' concrete details however are ignored by Spenser in favor of the conventional pictured details. Details which he deliberately took from Tasso are heightenings through abstractions: Belphoebe's *portance,* the Platonic suggestion of her eyes "kindled aboue," etc. (The yellow hair occurs in both, but Tasso's image is different from Spenser's, which parallels the actual pictures.) That is, Spenser is extraordinarily closely dependent upon accurately remembered tradition for visualized detail; he superimposes additional such details in case an associated picture works simultaneously upon his mind; what he imitates consciously from literary sources is not visual descriptive detail but abstract tags which serve to heighten the significance (as cf. the vividness) of the visualized figure. For his initial *choice* of a particular figure (i.e. of an Amazon guise for his heroine or for the beautiful enemy) I think the impetus came very largely from long-built-up tradition.

These generalizations, which it was necessary to show up in detail by the exposition of a particular example, apply justly to Spenser's descriptive technique as a whole. The inferences to be made about his qualities of mind, his methods of composition, and the nature of his dependence upon source material are important ones. The connections with Spenser's famous "richness" and "painter-like" qualities are patent. I shall take up other conventional figures far more rapidly. They simply re-illustrate the generalizations I have made.

Of other cases of possible parallels in detail of physical appearance between Spenser's figures and conventional pictured figures, one of the simplest is the well-worn figure of the God of Love. The strange angelic apparition which the palmer finds beside Guyon is less like to the "Cupido on Idœan hill" (II, viii, 6) of classical tradition than to the beautiful young God of Love who is his descendant, and who appears with just such beauty in very many illuminated romance manuscripts. The God of Love figure in the manuscripts is given the physical attributes which traditionally characterize pictured angels—a peculiar loveliness which they possessed long before Fra Angelico—heads "curled with golden heares," wings with "diuerse plumes, like painted Iayes" (blue, yellow, and green, melting into pink, tipped with gold feathers; [37] Spenser's *golden*-pinioned angels appear and reappear in manuscripts). Guyon's angel justly enough puts his creator in mind of "Cupido," for that "faire young man, Of wondrous beautie" and "painted nimble wings" appearing in a "shady delue" had appeared just so in one Garden of Love after another —most commonly of all, naturally, in manuscripts of the *Romance of the Rose.* There were of course an exceedingly large number of manuscripts of this text; even now there are some eighty-five in the three great libraries. The God of Love appears to the quester as a beautiful youth, blue- red- or silver-winged, clad in gold, fine stuffs, or the usual angel's robes, golden-haired, often appearing in a cloud.[38] Spenser's comparison to "*Phoebus* face adorned with sunny rayes" is a good example of similarity in pictorial tradition acting as an association-link. The visual image here is a sharp and well-defined one, especially against a background of illustration, for the bright red-gold locks rayed out from Phoebus' handsome face, in pictures,[39] link one's image of him to that of the other figure in much the same way as they evidently did in Spenser's mind's eye. The God of Love figure occurs of course in a great number of other texts in MS.[40] To exemplify: In Christine de Pisan's *Epitre au dieu d'amours,* he sits in a meadow by a fountain, a young man with bright curly hair, a red gown patterned with wing figures, beautiful yellow-gold wings

[37] A convenient example in a romance MS of this conventional angel-figure who came to share his characteristics with the conventional God of Love figure, is the Michael of B. Mus. Royal 18 D ii, a MS of Lydgate's *Siege of Thebes* which belonged to Arundel and Lumley. He has lovely rainbow wings and frizzly hair, and a red-cross banner, and drives down to a rocky burning hell a spotted Lucifer with huge dragon-like wings and burning, gleaming eyes (f. 161^{v}). The Michael of *Horae* MSS is often such a figure; that in Ralegh's *Horae* (Bodl. Add. A 185) has an aureole of gold curly hair.

[38] See such MSS as Bodl. E. Museo 65, Selden supra 57, Douce 195, Brit. Mus. Royal 19 B xiii, Harl. 4425. For the great numbers of MSS and illustrated editions see E. Langlois, *Les MSS du Roman de la Rose* (Paris, 1910), Bourdillon, *Early Editions of the R. de la R.* (London, 1906).

[39] I have treated elsewhere of calendar illustrations; see *Seasons and Months: Studies in a Tradition of Middle English Poetry* (Paris, 1933), esp. pp. 175, 185–86. The *Othea* MSS for example have a particularly striking Phoebus; see Harl. 4431, f. 101^{r}, Bodl. 421, f. 40^{r}.

[40] With the God of Love as a literary rather than a pictorial convention a great deal of source study has of course been concerned; see e. g., Variorum Spenser, *op. cit.*, III, commentary on cantos xi, xii, Appendix IV.

brushed with red, like flaming plumes.[41] The "Cupido" of Marot's translation and moralization of the *Metamorphoses* Book I, in Bodl. MS Douce 117, has red rings pricked out with gold plumes (f. 26ʳ; with quiver and bow—frequent, of course). Spenser's Love with "winges of purple and blewe," hidden in the bush (*Sh. Cal.*, March), the loves playing about Venus' throne (*FQ* IV, x, 42), "Whose shapes seem'd not like to terrestriall boyes, But like to Angels . . . ," their wings "of gold and purple hew" (*purple* again I think *purpurea*, crimson)—these two are typical of his several Cupids, red-, gold-, changeful-, or peacock-winged. Although the plethora of source materials is confusing in the case of this figure, yet, as with other simpler figures, it is pertinent to remember that in just the shape in which Spenser visualizes him, just so he was frequently and strikingly to be seen, pictured (for the pictures here described are typical ones). Again similar color stress, and coincident details not mentioned in the sources being followed (e.g. *Sh. Cal.*, March); again Spenser does not invent picturesque detail, but, keeping the figure's traditional appearance in the later materials, pushes further in a reinterpretation of its significance, along lines suggested rather by his mediaeval than his classical sources.

Another romance figure who became a pictorial counter is the villein porter—Spenser's Disdaine, Daunger, Turpine's "rude Porter."[42] In mediaeval romance he is usually "Daunger," i.e. haughty arrogance, or disdain; he is large, grim and churlish, ill-dressed, with shaggy hair, sometimes with a knotted turban about his head, he carries a craggy club. Spenser uses the tradition as we by now expect; his Porter starts out as the same figure *physically*, and receives only such additions as add to his *allegorical* stature —is made of golden mould in the Mammon story, is given deformed hinder parts where vices lurk, in the Temple of Venus. In romance, as in Spenser, who liked and chose figures with allegori-

[41] B. Mus. Harl. 4431, f. 51ʳ (see also *Othea*, f. 117ʳ, with brilliant red wings). I note the wings particularly in these descriptions because they are perhaps the most salient visual detail used by Spenser. Love in a MS of Guillaume de Machaut's poems (B. Nat. f. fr. 1584) is a beautiful bright-haired youth in gold clothing patterned in red; on f. 1ᵛ, 80ʳ he sits in a bush or tree; cf. *R. de la R.*, Bodl. MS Douce 195, f. 13ʳ, red-, blue-, and gold-winged, behind a tree.

[42] Spenser's uses of this figure and those which follow may be so conveniently traced through C. H. Whitman, *Subject-Index to the Poems of Edmund Spenser* (New Haven, 1918), that I shall not crowd the discussions of minor figures with minute references.

cal possibilities, the Porter is an obstruction to the good quester. Such is the function of the ugly churl "Dangier" with his knobbed club, in the many *Romance of the Rose* manuscripts (see citations in note 38 above). The villein who obstructs the path of the Pilgrim in Guillaume de Deguileville's *Pélerinage de la vie humaine* (or in Lydgate's translation of it) appears in the illustrations with knotted stick and evil aspect.[43] The fierce skin-clad Daunger of the Masque of Cupid (III, xii, 11), the bold grim Daunger of Venus' stronghold (IV, x), show the character at his traditional post, in the latter not only huge, but gigantic. The giant "Carle" Disdaine who is part of proud Mirabella's punishment[44] is in part a moralized magnification of this villein, by now almost the personification of this particular kind of Pride: glaring-eyed, turbanned, black-haired, without weapon save his club, now one of iron.

The opulent, intolerant Persian king is another counter. He appears as Darius, as Philip, as any paynim souldan whose chariot immediately connotes "rich Orient" and "proud tyranny." The most telling illustrations of such "Persian Monarks antique guize" come in MSS of Boccaccio's *Des cas des nobles hommes*—a text which I think we may believe Spenser knew.[45] The terrible souldan figure in V, viii, mounted, as in pictures,[46] in his "charret

[43] See for example MSS Harl. 4399, f. 34^r, B. Nat. f. fr. 9196, f. 35^r, Bodl. Douce 300 (in the latter for example his face is ugly and deformed like a mask, his hair stands straight up from his head; f. 45^v, 46^v). Lydgate's translation of this well known work is edited in *EETS*, extra ser. 77, 83, 92 (London, 1899–1904); for the numerous MSS and prints see vol. 92, pp. lxiii * ff. On Spenser's possible knowledge of it see F. M. Padelford, "Spenser and the Pilgrimage of the Life of Man," *SP*, XXVIII (1931), 211–18.

[44] Cf. Lotspeich, *op. cit.*, *s. v.* Giants: "Disdain . . . seems to be developed chiefly from the idea of Pride, inherent in Spenser's conception of giants." I think that the process was the reverse: that the visual image of the proud figure of Disdain, familiar in picture and poem, came first; then came its magnification and its connection with the more comprehensive abstraction Pride.

[45] Support for this will be given in a later article; another divergence of Spenser's from his sources—Phedra's suicide by the knife in the Hippolytus story—is partially explained by the illustrators' choice of that detail for striking pictorial presentation, in the text referred to.

[46] See B. Nat. MS f. fr. 235–36, f. 146^v, B. Mus. Royal 14 E v, f. 192^r. The chariot is oftenest a kind of gold covered-wagon, large-wheeled, with a canopy roof under which a king sits (see, e. g., B. Mus. Addit, 35321, Laurence de Premierfait's translation of the *De casibus*, Darius, f. 120^r; Philip "le roy persa," f. 169^v—his gold cart, drawn by white horses, is canopied with red brocade).

hye," represents another Philip unfortunately not yet a Fallen Prince—again we see a possible example of how potent to Spenser was the connection through conventional visual image, between that earlier proud Philip and him whom his souldan represents.

It is characteristic that Spenser's taking over of certain romance figures and ignoring of others seems to depend either on their allegorical possibilities or on their visual strikingness, this last often evidenced by the fact that they were regarded as "opportunities" by the illuminators (and thence by illustrators), and frequently appeared in pictorial form. The Salvage Man is another of these mediaeval counters, familiar in fable or marginal grotesque. The motif of the Helpful Lion is another frequently illustrated one. This familiar romance creature is of course kin to St. Jerome's, pictorially at least, however widely differing in his choice of patrons. Una's Lion belongs to the same species, and one of the reasons why there is never a helpful tiger or bear lies in the vividness with which these wide-grinning pictured lions, with their tails curved over their backs, stay in the visual memory.[47]

There are other examples than that of Pyrrus and Penthesilea of a possible explanation in pictorial convention for Spenser's divergence from classical sources. Spenser gives Argus eyes over his whole body; Miss Sawtelle refers to this detail in Apollodorus.[48] But the pictures of Argus do usually show him so (instead of with the head-covered-with-eyes which he is given in *Met.* I, 625)—see pictures in the moralized Ovid, in sixteenth-century editions of "farced" Ovids, or in manuscripts of Christine's *Othea.*[49] This picture is particularly striking; once so seen, Argus stays in the mind, pock-marked with eyes. Or again, Spenser's Perseus freeing Andromeda *mounted upon* his flying horse is both more conven-

[47] For example the smirking lion who kneels before the lady in Machaut's *Dit du Lyon,* B. Nat. MS f. fr. 1584, f. 84 etc.

[48] Sawtelle, *op. cit., s. v.* Argus.

[49] In Bodl. MS Rawl. B 214, "Expositio fabularum 15. librorum Ovidii Metamorphoseos," with colored drawings, 15th century, Mercury stands on an Argus all over eyes (f. 198^v–199). In the 1539 edition of the French prose *Met.* (descended from the mediaeval translation and moralization of the text), "Les xv. liures de | la Metamorphose . . . contenans L'olym | pe des Histoires poëtiques . . . imprimé a Paris par | Denys Ianot . . . 1539," f. 18^v, Mercury holds the head in his hand, there are eyes all over the body. In MSS of the *Othea,* Mercury plays his flute into the ear of a standing sleeping Argus with eyes closely sown over his whole naked body (Harl. 4431, f. 109^v; B. Nat. f. fr. 606, f. 15^v).

tional and more effective pictorially than the classical version from which he departs.[50] Perseus is usually so portrayed. A very beautiful example is in the St. John's College Cambridge manuscript of Christine de Pisan's *Othea* (no. 208, a Manuscript which was a treasure of St. John's when its Master was a friend of Harvey's and evidently of Spenser's).[51] Perseus in plate armor is mounted on a caparisoned winged horse; he brandishes a scimitar-like weapon over the head of a scaled sea-monster emerging from the curled waves; Andromeda kneels on a stony rock. It is tempting to describe the Perseus pictured in MS Harl. 4431, where it is perhaps the loveliest in the whole manuscript; properly armed for "Dan" Perseus, even to the visor over his face, he is mounted upon a white horse with blue-grey plated armour on its head, chain armour, chevron-edged, on its upper body, and beautiful brilliant red wings. The monster raises a bony fin out of curled green waves; Andromeda kneels, yellow-haired. Perseus is pictured *on* his winged steed in various late refurbishings of Ovid: in the mediaeval moralized version printed by Vérard in 1493 (as *La bible des poetes. metha* | *morphoze;* f. xlix), in the collection of rhymes-with-illustrations printed as *La Metamor-* | *phose d'Ovide* | *figuree,* Lyon, 1557, in the verse and prose redoings of 1573 and 1586, respectively.[52]

[50] Sawtelle, *op. cit., s. v.* Andromeda: "no classical authority." So also Lotspeich (*op. cit., s. v.* Perseus), who says that Spenser is following Boccaccio's *De genealogia* 10. 27; but the passage as quoted in Latin by Lotspeich, or as it appears in Italian (*Della* | *geneologia* | *degli dei* | . . . Venetia . . . MDCXXVII, f. 157^{v}) gives the suggestion only obliquely or by inference; cf. the directness and vividness of the pictures.

[51] John Still became Master in 1574. See note 11 above. Spenser was in Cambridge until 1576. This MS, coming to St. John's through its foundress, and being an impressive example of MS decoration, would not be lightly regarded by anyone interested in mediaeval antiquities (Still's connection with the enthusiast Parker is as pertinent here as Spenser's interest and Harvey's connection). See M. R. James, *Descriptive Cat. of MSS. . . . St. John's Coll.* (Cambridge, 1913); and *Collegium Divi Johannis Evangelistae,* ed. Seward (Cambridge, 1911), Pl. XV and p. 86.

[52] These two translations, though each presents the poem in a form completely different from the 1557 "Ovid picture-book," use its illustrations—a familiar practice which partially explains why these figures became pictorial *conventions.* The 1573 edition is the French verse translation of Fr. Habert, "Les | quinze livres | de la Metamorphose" (p. 255); the 1586 edition is in French prose (as of the 1539 edition), "Les XV. | Livres . . . con- | tenants L'Olympe des histoires Poétiques" (p. 181). Other *Othea* MSS are B. Nat. f. fr. 606, f. 4^{v},

Another type of link between tradition and the individual poet is that process in which a ubiquitously pictured figure became so definitely a symbol—as Busiris was for faithless and bloody cruelty, or Flora for lascivious excess—that when Spenser fashioned a character or sought for an allusion which was to have this emotional content or connotation, these were the images which came alive in his mind and to some extent (and chiefly unconsciously) helped to determine the direction of his story. Though as a generalization this can hardly be doubted, in any given case it must be somewhat problematical since the nature of the process precludes complete proof. Warton said of Busyrane, that Spenser "seems to have drawn this name from Busiris, the king of Aegypt, famous for his cruelty and inhospitality." [53] More than this, the pictures of Busiris stress the peculiarly bloody cruelty and connection with strange gods which characterize the enchanter Busyrane. In B. Mus. MS Royal 17 E ii, of Lefevre's *Receuil*, the white-bearded "Busire," very wizard-like in appearance, with long gown and pointed cap and sceptre, stands watching two soldiers lance a victim in the breast and hold a sword over a woman with a child; an infant bleeds on the floor and two figures kneel before images on two golden pillars; the room is ornate, encircled with pillars (f. 151). He is similarly pictured in other texts: in the *Othea* (in MS Harl. 4431 "Busierres" surveys the headless bodies of his three victims, whose heads have been placed on the altar of two golden gods with shields [conventional for pagan images, in manuscripts], f. 114ʳ); in a Boethius in French given by the Cambridge antiquarian Robert Hare to Trinity Hall (where Harvey became Fellow in 1578).[54] As pictures may help to form vivid associations for certain names or figures, like Busiris, similarly a single characteristic of a given figure may be so stressed in illustrations as to determine, narrow, or change that figure's sym-

Bodl. 421, f. 8ʳ, Brussels, Bibl. royale 9392, f. 8ᵛ (see *Christine de Pisan: Epitre d'Othéa*, reproduction des 100 miniatures du MS 9392, by J. van den Gheyn, Brussels, 1913).

[53] Variorum Spenser, *op. cit.*, III, 287.

[54] See also Bodl. 421, f. 33ᵛ, or Brussels 9392, f. 44ᵛ. That Busiris thus pictured had been fastened upon as a conventional figure for illustration is evidenced not only by his appearance in the *Receuil*, but in the totally different sort of text in Trin. Hall MS. 12, a fully illustrated Boethius in French. Again Busiris, kneeling, offers a man's head to an idol (f. 26ʳ, illustrating the 6th Prose of Book II, on the misuse of power).

bolical meaning for later users. Flora as a *ribaulde,* the Flora who crowns the false Una with ivy, is the Flora of patristic condemnation, as E. K. shows clearly enough (*Sh. Cal.,* March), but she is still more vividly narrowed down to this characteristic of lasciviousness in such pictorial representations as those of a widely spread text like Boccaccio's *Des cleres dames;* various manuscripts show her dressed in red and accompanied by naked dancers, or loose-bodiced and half-clothed, or garland-crowned, with lascivious companions.[55]

By a somewhat similar process, a pictorial tradition for an allegorical figure may work unconsciously upon the poet to help determine just which abstractions he selects for portrayal and just what concrete guise his imagination confers upon them. In the case of personified abstractions, where it is a commonplace to remark that mediaeval literature was rife with (illustrated) figures which Spenser found thus vivid and useful, the pictorial tradition merges so confusingly with that in the other arts, and the materials are so disparate, that the point can hardly be "covered." It may be exemplified by a less common figure like that fair bright one of Sapience, sitting in the bosom of the enthroned Deity, in the *Hymne of Heavenly Beautie.* However complicated her literary and philosophical background,[56] this crowned and sceptered feminine figure, royal in attire and in her function as God's agent, is also the same figure as that beautiful pictured "Sapience" who illustrates the book of Wisdom in, for example, the exceedingly common text known as the *Bible hystoriale.* Like Spenser's majestic figure "menaging the euer-mouing sky" and bright with an all-surpassing light, gold-crowned and sceptered, adorned with

[55] See p. 98 of the article referred to in note 16 above.

[56] This is scarcely meant as a contribution to the complicated question of the sources of Spenser's Sapience; as is my point throughout, Spenser did not find new figures in pictorial tradition, he found them re-emphasized there together with an habitual concrete mode for their presentation. Such facts as I give help to indicate wherefore Spenser was impelled to describe "the *appearance* of Sapience from Hebrew sources," however much more complicated her metaphysical heritage (see J. W. Bennett, "Spenser's *Fowre Hymnes:* Addenda," *SP,* XXXII [1935], 141; my italics). References to discussions of Sapience are conveniently listed in Bennett, "The Theme of Spenser's *Fowre Hymnes,*" *SP,* XXVIII (1931), p. 43 note. Osgood's parallels with the Book of Wisdom are of course highly pertinent here; see "Spenser's Sapience," *SP,* XIV (1917), esp. p. 169; the verbal parallels are somewhat less striking than the pictured ones.

"gemmes and iewels," she appears in a series of illuminations, a woman beautifully apparelled, with scepter and gold crown jewel-set.[57] She is the same figure as the Lady Sapience who instructs the quester in the *Horologium Sapientiae*, or *L'Horloge de Sapience* (illustrations show "la divine Sapience" gloriously enthroned, showing the pilgrim the Trinity, etc.).[58] Other figures, in texts less definitely theological have been influenced by representations of this one: Othea, goddess of wisdom (as she appears in the sky, Harl. 4431, f. 95ᵛ), the "Grace Dieu" of the first, and the Sapience who herself appears in the last, of Guillaume de Deguileville's *Pélerinages;* [59] or the personified Wisdom or Sapience of late romances.[60] As I have said, the pictorial convention becomes too confused to follow accurately but with the tradition especially in illustrated Bibles in mind we can scarcely be surprised that Spenser's Sapience, whatever his sources, should be a feminine figure, nor doubt that he conceived of her quite vividly and quite traditionally as such.

In all of these latter examples, the effect of convention upon the individual poet was not one in which he was particularly conscious of utilizing a rich tradition for poetic purposes. They are simply cases in which I believe pictorial convention to be responsible for lodging or emphasizing in Spenser's mind certain images or associations which became a rather potent part of the rich store of materials whence his allusions, his characters or his descriptions of figures derive. More important perhaps is the way in which tradition worked upon him to make him choose certain figures, heavily weighted symbols, for crucially important roles in his allegory.

[57] See B. Mus. Royal 19 D ii, "Livre de Sapience," series of pictures, *ibid.*, Royal 15 D iii, 17 E vii.

[58] By Henricus Suso; the discourse of a disciple with a Dame Sapience showing some parallels with Spenser's. A fairly common text, though not always illustrated, in MS and print, in Latin, French, and English (e. g. B. Nat. has 4 French MSS; the Bodleian has 4 in Latin, 3 in English, 1 17th-century Italian translation, etc.); there are several Latin and French editions, of which the most interesting is the illustrated *Vérard* edition of 1493 (the other French editions I have seen: 1580?, 1535?, 1582, are not illustrated). The Middle English version is published from MS Douce 114 by K. Horstmann, in *Anglia*, X (1888), 323–89. Illustrations as mentioned in e. g. B. Nat. f. fr. 22922, f. fr. 458.

[59] See the illumination for "Sapience parle" in e. g. B. Nat f. fr. 9196, f. 148ᵛ; this is widespread text of course—see note 43.

[60] Take an example like the Lady Sapience of the *Chemin de Vaillance*, Royal 14 B ii, where the pictured figure happens to resemble Spenser's rather neatly.

It is of course a commonplace to point out that the Red Crosse Knight, with his maiden and her lamb, is a ubiquitous and traditional figure. But this article is concerned with the pictorial emphasis within such traditions which helped make the choice of a given figure natural, and his appearance in a particular way almost obligatory; hence it is to the point to mention even for the Red Crosse Knight a few of his most striking parallel pictorial appearances.[61] These few selected examples are typical ones. St. George is particularly the symbol of Christian English chivalry in a manuscript treatise on the Order of the Garter, in B. Mus. MS Royal 15 E vi; [62] he is within an oratory, but mounted, with red cross on breastplate and each arm, and turns backward to thrust a red lance into the throat of a yellow ridge-backed dragon, who has the usual emphasized claws, tongue, and looped tail. The princess stands praying near, with the lamb on a gold string (f. 439ʳ); king and knights kneel on either side. In Bodl. MS Auct. D infra 2 13 the dragon has great spreading burnished claws and ribbed wings, the princess has a lamb on a red string; king and queen stand in a turret-balcony before massed white buildings (*Horae;* St. George f. 37ᵛ). In Royal 2 A xviii (which descended to the father of three of Harvey's friends [63]) the St. George has gold armor, a red-cross shield; the princess, a crown over her yellow hair, kneels holding up her hands, the lamb on a string near her. The *Horae* manuscript owned by Sir Walter Ralegh, which

[61] No attempt is being made to do what as Greenlaw says there is "no need" to do—postulate one source for Spenser's version, which was "part and parcel of folk belief and courtly entertainment." The material presented is another part of the background from which sprang the persistent conventions that characterize the courtly entertainments and the folk beliefs. References to and excerpts from Greenlaw's article ("Una and Her Lamb") and that of Padelford and O'Connor, also pertinent, on "Spenser's Use of the St. George Legend," will be found in the Variorum Spenser, *op. cit.*, I, pp. 379ff.

[62] This MS is in the Richmond Palace list of 1535.

[63] I give occasional details of the provenance and history of MSS not because they establish sure relationship between Spenser and specific MSS, but because such details are often hard to come on, and cumulatively build up for us a notion of the extent to which MSS were owned by persons in the group of Spenser's probable connections, and how they were esteemed. Royal 2 A xviii evidently belonged to the father of Gabriel Harvey's "owld Mr. Withypoll." The *Cat. of . . . MSS. in the . . . Royal Collections* I, 33, Moore Smith, *Gabriel Harvey's Marginalia*, p. 91 and note, and W. Metcalfe, *Visitation of Suffolk* (Exeter, 1882), p. 82, give facts from which this identification is made.

Spenser very likely saw, now Bodl. Add. A. 185, has a St. George picture (f. 61^{v}) with kneeling princess, the gold-spotted dragon has looped tail, red forked tongue out between two rows of teeth, and ribbed wings; St. Margaret's dragon has the same shiny gold-spotted back. In a *Horae* manuscript which belonged in 1589 to John Morphe of Dublin,[64] Brit. Mus. Addit. 17012 (f. 30^{v}), St. George is caparisoned in red, on a prancing horse; the dragon is properly fitted with two rows of teeth, pointed tongue, looped tail and claws; the princess kneels on the hillside with the lamb lying beside her. In an elaborate George picture in Fitzwilliam Museum (Cambridge) MS 49, the princess with reddish-gold hair kneels on a rock praying with the lamb on a red string; the dragon is red-eyed and has the banner-trimmed broken spearhead stuck in its cavernous red tusked mouth (f. 10^{v}). The dragon of Fitzwilliam Museum MS 57 (St. George, f. 21^{v}) is black and red with gold glints and shadings on the back; it has glowing gold eyes, two rows of teeth, long looped tail. I mention here only St. George's dragon; of course a good many other stock stories gave to illustrators opportunities for pictures which helped to solidify notions of what was proper to dragons.[65] The conventional dragon of manuscript illuminations, as may be seen, shows with vivid reiteration a good many of the details which Spenser found in his literary sources,[66] and is another instance of a mode of transmission for these "commonplaces" which has never been properly considered; just so this little handful of typical St. George pictures exemplifies one side of the process by which the Red Crosse Knight became a figure who was both vivid and endowed with distinct value as a poetic symbol.

[64] The catalogue description (*Cat. of Additions to MSS. in the B. Mus.*, 1846–1847, p. 347), though it lists a long line of noble owners, gives no light on the identity of "one awrellyve an ytallyan" who gave the MS to Morphe—according to his inscription in the MS.

[65] The dragon of Jason—in the *Fall of Princes* (*e. g.* MS Harl. 1766, f. 31^{r}, cf. f. 156^{v}), or in the *Othea* (e. g. Bodl. 421, f. 41^{r}, where like Perseus' monster he is spotted, ribbed-winged, and spouts fire, or Harl. 4431, f. 120^{r}, where he has red and black spots like Spenser's and particularly strong wings). Or that of Cadmus (e. g. in the *Othea*); or Hercules' dragon-like monsters (in the *Orose*, e. g. B. Nat. MS f. fr. 254, or in the *Othea*). Or the dragon of St. Margaret, in innumerable *Horae*, or Michael's dragon-like Lucifer.

[66] See the summary of literary sources and analogues in the Variorum Spenser, *op. cit.*, I, App. IV, and cf. especially the dragon of the *Vision of Tundale*, as described in the article by W. Wells there cited ("Spenser's Dragon").

The conclusions postulated, as to the nature of the poet's relation to these pictorial conventions, have I think been clear as I proceeded. It was a delicate, often an unconscious relationship; it shows us Spenser's mind as alert to visual detail, as tenacious and exact in his memory of it; it shows him not so much consciously imitative as sensitively retentive of images which, stamped in his mind by actual sight, were enriched by association and by his use of literary sources. As far as actual descriptive technique is concerned, when he paints what he has seen, he paints it as he saw it. But he saw more completely, retained more accurately, and interrelated more fruitfully, than most. I do not attempt to draw the noose tight, binding Spenser's figures to particular manuscript appearances of them, excluding other influences—from the classics, from other literatures, from pageantry. But one must perceive again, as so often, that "the classical" in Spenser is the classical as it had lived through and been coloured by the Middle Ages which helped transmit it to him. And that to find one source, *or* to say "it was a commonplace" does not finish the question; there were vast numbers of commonplaces which he did not elect to use, and the commonplaces which did have life in them, to him, had more than their commonplaceness to recommend them.

The background of which I have outlined one small corner was not Spenser's alone. The Renaissance writer drew on a rich deposit. Probably in no era have the riches been more disorderly. This is true both of literary and artistic resources. But some of the riches lay nearer to hand then than later, had not yet become sophisticated and precious, to the cultivated Elizabethan Englishman. The limited store so far piled up by the English printing presses, the actual text of printed books—these contributed but a portion to the furnishings of his mind. Simultaneously, in an age not bombarded with posters nor smothered in comic strips, pictures seen were more attentively seen. I have attempted to examine but one corner of one area in the rich deposit of literary-artistic tradition, the pictorial conventions particularly to be seen in manuscripts, and, keeping availability always in mind on the one hand, and specific possible connections with a certain poet's work on the other, to show the accessibility and possible significance of such traditional materials to an Elizabethan poet.

"Spenserus"*

ON the last page of a Bodleian manuscript of Gower's *Confessio Amantis* written in a clear early fifteenth-century hand, and bearing the signature of a dedicatee of Spenser's, we encounter the following Ovidian album-sentiment, written in an Italian hand too ordinary to identify as Spenser's or not Spenser's:

Tempore foelici multi numerantur amici Cum fortuna perit nullus amicus erit	} Spenserus

This is not likely as a mistaken attribution; Spenser nowhere translates, quotes, or puts forward as his own the two lines from Ovid's *Tristia* (I.ix.5) which are the proper form of the tag. The closest it ever came to the Spenser canon—and this is interesting enough—is that it is the "Theame out of Ovid" which Harvey says he set as an exercise, and of which he gives all three English versions alleged to be done by his brother John, in one of the *Three Proper and Wittie Familiar Letters* printed in 1580 as having been exchanged between Harvey and Spenser.

What other "Spenserus" would inscribe sentiments in Lady Warwick's Gower, or rather the Russell Gower in which she wrote while she was still a Russell? And sentiments, moreover, which arose out of the famous Ovidian punishment for having written what Spenser was reproved for, too-amorous love poems? For we remember that the dedication to Lady Warwick (jointly with her sister) was the one to the *Fowre Hymnes* wherein we learn about that reproof. Though Ovid's exile was far harsher than anything which happened to make Spenser feel the cold wind of loss of support when one wrote the wrong thing, we recall that the snub may have been quite noticeably discouraging in an age of patronage, when "one of you two most excellent Ladies," either Lady Warwick or her sister, actually urged the call-

* Reprinted from *Essays in English Literature from the Renaissance to the Victorian Age, Presented to A. S. P. Woodhouse.* Edited by Millar MacLure and F. W. Watt. Toronto: University of Toronto Press, 1964, pp. 3–25.

ing-in of two hymns in praise of Love and Beauty, because they overmuch pleased young readers "vehemently caried with that kind of affection." Ovid's *Ars Amatoria* of course *was* called in (expelled from libraries), and the quoted bit comes from that poem, the *Tristia,* in which he makes the same several excuses for it that Spenser was to make when he addressed to the two ladies a "retractation" for *his* unfortunate love poems.

But this puzzling dedication is not the only token of Spenser's connections with the family whose Gower volume was inscribed by "Spenserus" and by "Anne Russell." Anne, Lady Warwick, shares with her sister Margaret Russell Clifford, Lady Cumberland, the dedication of the *Hymnes,* is the Theana of *Colin Clouts Come Home Againe,* and is addressed throughout several stanzas of the *Ruines of Time;* her father the second Earl of Bedford and his grandson and heir Edward are praised in the same poem; Anne was sister to a Lord Deputy of Ireland (1594–1597; Sir William Russell) whom Spenser mentions in the *Veue* and could not but know; she was step-sister to Lord Grey's wife; she was married in 1565 to Leicester's brother Ambrose Dudley, Earl of Warwick, and was thus Leicester's and Lady Sidney's sister-in-law; she was a member by birth of one, by marriage of another, of two great houses (closely and continuously associated) who outstandingly represented the Protestant faction to which Spenser gave lifelong allegiance, and he had early connections with both.

This *Confessio Amantis* in MS Bodl. 902, its easy Middle English as legible as blackletter, at least had enough sixteenth-century attention to be inscribed several times, but it belonged to a very bookish family. On f.80^{v} we find in a sixteenth-century hand "Be me Anne Russell." [1] The Anne Russell who became Lady Warwick and Spenser's friend and dedicatee did not break off her Bedford connections when she married into the allied and congenial Dudley-Sidney connection; her husband died in 1589/90 but she herself continued to be an influential court figure until 1604. She

[1] No description remarks upon the Latin "Spenserus" note. See the otherwise full description in Macaulay's edition of Gower, II, cxxxix, mentioning Anne Russell's signature and identifying d'Annebaut's. If we may suppose Macaulay's description correct, two errors may be amended in that of the *Summary Catalogue* (no. 27573)—Anne Russell's name and that of the donor: Gilbert *Dolben,* grandnephew of Archbishop Sheldon.

was eldest daughter to Sir Francis Russell, second Earl. The family was an important one in the annals of Protestant statesmanship and literary patronage in England.[2] Her grandfather John, the great first Earl of Bedford (d. 1555), was Lord Privy Seal and Lord High Admiral, after decades of varied services, was an important official in the West, an "encourager of literature" and author of two Latin treatises (Wiffen, I, 395). Her father (?1527–1585) was an important Protestant servant of the state; imprisoned for his religious opinions and (evidently largely by his own choice) forming ties with the group of reformers in Switzerland during Mary's reign, he was one of Elizabeth's first Privy Council, helped to remodel the religious establishment, was sent on important missions to France and Scotland, was associated continuously with the Sidneys and the Leicester group (*v.* Wiffen, I, 397ff), and was the owner of one of the most extensive Elizabethan libraries of whose contents we have record.[3] In fact, the recent discovery of the importance among Elizabethan patrons of this family, to whose various members Spenser gives such repeated attention, calls for some new observation of relations, and "a Bedford book" or "a Bedford copy of a mediaeval author" becomes something more interesting than it was. The outstanding collector, the second Earl, lost his son on the day before his own death in July, 1585, and the heir and young grandson Edward was the ward of his influential aunt, Anne—a relation on which Spenser comments in the *Ruines of Time* passage (1591). Of Anne's sister and co-dedicatee, Margaret Lady Cumberland (Spenser's Marian, also), and of their brother Lord William Russell of Thornhaugh, the Lord Deputy mentioned in the *Veue,* we may speak more particularly later.

Did Spenser read some of the mediaeval books he knew, in

[2] Biographical facts on the Bedfords are taken from the *DNB* articles and from Jeremiah Wiffen, *Historical Memoirs of the House of Russell* (London, 1833); corrections and additions are made from G. Scott Thomson, *Two Centuries of Family History* (London, 1930).

[3] See M. Byrne and G. Scott Thomson, "My Lord's Books," *RES,* VII (1931), 385–405, for a contemporary list of the printed books in this library, with identifications, dedications, and other useful materials. The reference to the uncatalogued earlier MSS is at 385; some may have been kept in his house in the West. The patronage and interest in "reformer" authors is noteworthy. Some information above (e.g. on Francis Bedford's religious opinions) is to be found in Scott Thomson, *Two Centuries,* 204–11.

manuscript? What we know about the attitudes of Elizabethans toward manuscript books is likely to be confined to the great collectors—the Arundels and the Archbishop Parkers and the Dr. Dees. I should say at once that in this case it makes very little practical difference, for Gower's famous poem could be read by men of Spenser's time—when it had very much more prestige than now—in three editions. Caxton printed it in 1483, Berthelet provided two editions, 1532 and 1554. Still it would be pleasant to envisage Spenser as having access to the Bedford books, including "all my auncient written englishe bookes . . ." not in the list of 1584, and reading or turning over this Gower with its miniature of the old poet, and writing his name (as did another visitor) on a flyleaf at the end. There are several obstructions to be removed before one would dare enjoy this pleasant picture even as conjecture.

To previous describers of the MS, the signature on f.80^{v} was simply that of any sixteenth-century "Anne Russell," and at first there seemed to be nothing to connect the book indisputably with the Bedford Russells. But on f.184^{v} there appears several times in an early sixteenth-century hand the name "John Browghton"—and Sir John Bedford, later first Earl, married in 1526 Anne Sapcote the widow of Sir John Broughton. So this was undeniably a Bedford book. It probably came to them with the manor of Chenies, a Broughton property that became the Russell family's chief seat and was a favoured residence of Lady Warwick; she was buried there.[4] Here then is an earlier "Anne Russell" if one thinks the signature thus early, but one is more interested in the fact that we may surely connect this volume with this family.

In addition, however: Bodleian MS Ballard 43 contains (f.133) a letter from Anne Lady Warwick, 1579. A mild complication occurred here in Ballard's appended (eighteenth-century) identification of its writer with Anne *Seymour*, Lady Warwick; but this lady had been mad for twenty-three years. Moreover, a scrap of endorsement proves the letter to be written to the wife of Sir Nicholas Malbie in Ireland—formerly secretary to Ambrose Dudley—and its contents fit in with our Lady Warwick's impor-

[4] See Wiffen, I, 272, 396n; II, 61; the book probably passed to the Bedfords, like Chenies or with it, in consequence of the death of Lady Bedford's son "young Mr. Broughton"; Sir John Bedford became Baron Russell of Chenies (1538) and passed on the Broughton properties, to his son the second earl, Lady Warwick's father.

tance at court as favour-dispenser for Elizabeth, and her friendship with the correspondent, a previous dependent.[5] These facts are another tie between Spenser and this whole set of people, especially perhaps Lady Warwick; he too evidently knew Malbie.[6] It is safe to assume that Spenser's friend Anne Russell wrote this letter; though a signature is too little for proof, the similarities between this one and that in the Gower MS[7] are persuasive enough, added to the rest of the circumstances, to convince us that at least one learned lady whom Spenser knew did not leave a Gower in manuscript untouched on her father's shelves. It must have been got out to show to interested visitors—a not unfamiliar habit of bookish men in their libraries—if we are to explain another sixteenth-century inscription on the same leaf as the little squib labelled "Spenserus" (f.184^{r}). For down the side we read "Annibalis·Admiralis·dominicalis" in a sixteenth-century hand, and this can hardly be any other than Claude d'Annebaut; the Broughton connection puts ownership by him out of the question, and the signature or inscription must belong to Sir John Bedford's time.[8] Or it may have been written in later for some reason we could not now hope to guess.

The importance of the Bedford family as possible patrons for a

[5] Lady Warwick's letter thanks Lady Nicholas Malbie for a gift of linen, praises Sir Nicholas' services in Ireland, and protests willingness to further their prospects if she can. The Bodleian *Summary Cat.* (no. 10829) identification depends solely upon Ballard's note, I am told, but his statement is a far from likely one; Anne Seymour married John Dudley (Earl of Warwick 1552, who died in 1554 when the title became extinct); his lady remarried, and became insane 1556 (G.E.C., *Complete Peerage*). None of this fits the letter's date and contents.

[6] Malbi or Malby belonged to the Leicester faction, had Sir Henry Sidney's approval, came to Grey's aid at Glenmalure (Spenser was there, 1580), was interested in "undertaking," and as President of Connaught was criticized much as was Grey for too free use of the sword. See an account of a 1581 consultation at which Spenser was present (*View,* ed. Renwick [London, 1934], 240). On all these Irish matters I use the apparatus to the *Var. Sp.* prose volume, but also very frequently the articles of R. Jenkins based on letters in Spenser's hand (as here the one touching on Spenser and Connaught, in *PLMA*, LII [1937], 338–53, "Spenser with Lord Grey in Ireland"). Judson's *Life* in the *Var. Sp.* is the source of some connections and dates.

[7] In the capital *A*, in the *n* penstroke; allowance made for the difference in the writer's age and for that between writing on the margin of a large parchment book and on a sheet of letter-paper.

[8] Claude d'Annebaut or d'Hanybal, Admiral of France, after his inept expedition against England in 1545, came over to sign the peace of June 7, 1546 (Ch. de la Roncière, *Histoire de la marine française* [Paris, 1906], III, 417–31). The

poet and civil servant like Spenser to look to, despite their lack of male scions who could stay alive, was not apparent until the discovery of his 1584 book-list revealed Sir Francis the second Earl as an outstanding support to letters. Even if the twenty-three dedications discovered by editors of the book-list were his total, no one approaches him but that famous dedicatee Leicester.* They discovered also ten dedications to members of the Earl's immediate family; and of the other most famous patrons, Hatton, Walsingham, Sidney, Lord Oxford, three (with Leicester) must be accounted as attached to this interrelated and congenial group of families. The web of relationships is of course especially pertinent for Spenser, with his early tie to Leicester, particularly if Ambrose Dudley's wife Anne Russell had connections with the poet for some time before the late dedication to her (1596). Several books in the list were dedicated to the Earl's son-in-law Lord Warwick, some jointly to him and his wife Anne.[9] The size and solidity of the Earl's book-list (162 separate mostly "current" books, 221 with duplicates), the continued close interest in religious and theological affairs shown in patronage and in ownership, the cultivated variety (given this date), remind us of the owner's distinguished past services and his firm connection, like this whole knot of families, with the Protestant faction we think of most as Sidney's and Leicester's. For the Earl had been an important court figure. Aside from the businesses with which she entrusted him, Elizabeth evidently maintained cordial relations with the family: she

Earl of Bedford would no longer officially represent England for he had ceased to be Lord High Admiral in 1542, but he had taken an active part in the affair as President of the four southwest counties (see Wiffen, I, 336, 347, and letter in W. L. Clowes, *Royal Navy* [London, 1897], I, 465), was Privy Councillor 1546–1547 and Lord Privy Seal 1542 till his death; Clowes describes a state visit of d'Annebaut to England August 24, 1547 (I, 466).

[9] See numbers 11, 18, 48, 103, 113, 115 in the article referred to in n. 3; discussions of the character of the books and of some of the Earl's interests and patronage may be found especially at 391, 388–89. *Leicester Patron of Letters* has been thoroughly studied by E. Rosenberg (New York, 1955), extending vastly the number of known works dedicated to him (from the 22 known to the earlier scholars, to a list of 94). Also noticed and clarified are the relations with the reforming Protestant party of this group of patrons—Bedford, Warwick, Walsingham, Huntingdon (another brother-in-law of Anne Russell's), etc.; see Index, or, for example, 22–23, 229.

* [See additional material in Franklin B. Williams, Jr., *Index of Dedications and Commendatory Verses,* London, 1962, p. 161.]

visited him (with her court, for several days) at Chenies, at Woburn,[10] quartered her foreign guests upon him, stayed with his daughter-in-law; she attended her maid of honor Anne Russell's wedding, in state, to see Leicester give the bride away and view the two days of jousting and tourneys; she was godmother to Lady Warwick's niece by Lady Warwick her deputy.

Yet for all their marks of worldly success and the unassailable prestige of their connections, the Bedfords remained a family which stood for learning and for militant but dignified piety. The hope of poetry, to Spenser's eye, lay in such families. Lady Warwick was an exponent par excellence of the combination, and it is what Spenser stresses in his many praises. She had power and court prestige as her family had had before her. She was reputed Queen Elizabeth's chief feminine favourite (Wiffen, I, 430), having remained in attendance since the time when she was maid of honour, before her marriage in 1565. She had lived at court over a long period of years; the famous diary of her niece Lady Anne Clifford contains many references to her influential court connections. She evidently had the ear of the Queen. She acted, for example, as go-between for Essex, advising him to take lodgings in Greenwich while she would apprise him of the Queen's good moods that he might board her to his advantage (Wiffen, II, 56). There is often an accent of surprise in conveying the fact that it was Anne Clifford who put up the belated monument to Spenser in Westminster. But this is the Anne Clifford who tells of going up to court to festivities when she was fourteen or thereabouts, and being lodged on a pallet in her aunt Warwick's chamber, for she is the daughter of Anne Russell's favorite younger sister Margaret (not married until 1577), and great shoals of her aunts and uncles dead and alive had had connections with the poet. No mere half-forgotten dedication to mother and aunt is behind this act of *pietas,* and it would be strange if Anne as a girl had never met Spenser, say at some such time as when he dates his letter from Greenwich where the court lay, and mentions the "great graces and honourable favours" which her aunt and mother "*dayly shew*" unto him.

Recent years have seen vigorous and badly needed correction of

[10] There Elizabeth was entertained with great liberality and the usual reluctance; see letters to Burleigh in Wiffen, I, 474, 479; for descripion of following events see *ibid.*, I, 426ff, II, 13, I, 502.

the old ideas about the appointment under Lord Grey, when it was thought correct to talk much about "exile" and "disappointment." We have been brought to realize that things may not have looked thus at all, especially to anyone who had been for a year or more in close contact with the Dudley circle; also, a sharper look at the Bedford connections with Grey shows us some other attitudes and possibilities, while Anne Russell, married to a Dudley, typifies the way these tight family groups, congenial in politics, pulled things together. Even long before, at Lady Warwick's wedding, Grey had been one of the knights chosen to "answer the challenge" (Wiffen, I, 426); he resided many years —from 1562 through the 1570's—at Whaddon, in the same county as Chenies (about twenty-five miles as the crow flies), where the Bedfords then chiefly resided. But whichever house they were living in, Grey probably came to court his wife in it, for she was Jane Sibylla Morison and her mother had become Lady Bedford in 1566 (after the death of her husband Sir Richard Morison, and the death in 1561 of the mother of the numerous Russell children). Moreover Jane Morison had gone from being step-sister to Anne, Margaret, William, and the others, to being their sister-in-law, for her first marriage was to Edward Lord Russell their brother, probably about 1572; he must have died soon after 1573, since the marriage to Grey took place *ca.* 1574–1575. Grey was at Whaddon; and his son and heir was born there *ca.* 1575–1576.[11] It must be remembered that this twice-related Lady Grey was soon, beyond doubt, known well by Spenser; for the closeness with which Spenser worked with his chief has been very much illuminated by the discovered letters, and Ireland (and danger) drew men together. We need not question Judson's idea (71) that the Sidneys had much to do with Spenser's being recommended to Grey, but we begin to see that there is little need to wonder how well these various benefactors and friends knew each other.

In fact, a family contribution to the struggle in Ireland was made practically at the same time as Spenser in his different capacity was attached to Grey, for William Russell, the Earl's fourth and youngest son, just down from Oxford and back from the grand tour, went to Ireland in 1580—but in October, not August

[11] He was 17 in 1592/93 (G.E.C. *Complete Peerage*). See *DNB*, and Wiffen, I, 430–80, on these marriages.

—and was knighted by Grey the next September. He was later to be Lord Deputy of Ireland (1594) and be mentioned in the *Veue* as "the honorable gentleman that nowe governethe theare," but there was an interlude in the Netherlands, with Leicester; he evidently had been intimate with Sidney, who had bequeathed him his best gilt armour and before as governor of Flushing had supported Leicester in his quarrel with the estates. He was to become Baron Russell of Thornhaugh, but it would be hard to believe that the two young men of 1580 remained strangers to each other, considering what ties there were between those interested in their futures, and considering what the older of the two had done and was doing. And to persons familiar with the milieu we have been delineating, an appointment in Ireland under Lord Grey would not seem either like losing touch with the civilized world or like burying the talents with which one had meant to serve one's country.

Spenser's esteem for the Russell family is most circumstantially evidenced by the long passages in *The Ruines of Time*. The context is important. Anne Russell, Lady Warwick, is addressed with praise and trust in several stanzas (240ff), in the voice of the woman who figures the destroyed, dead, forgotten Roman city of Verulam, once so proud and strong. This direct address is drawn in quite properly by the lament for Ambrose Dudley's death, which follows naturally the lament for his brother Leicester who so deserved the gratitude of poets, and of this poet; and thereafter follow references to Anne's father Lord Bedford, her nephew Edward the heir, Lady Sidney sister of the two Dudleys, dead before them, in the same year as her husband, and her son their nephew Sir Philip, who is lamented in the climax to this sad heap, that only makes one ask,

> What booteth it to have beene rich alive?
> What to be great? what to be gracious? . . .
>
> How manie great ones may remembred be,
> Which in their daies most famouslie did florish;
> Of whom no word we heare. . . .

The direct address and eulogy of Anne Russell has all one burden, and with it comes the consolatory turn we expect in this pastoral elegy. She will defeat the death of her own Lord, of his brother, of his sister, of her father Lord Bedford; she will teach the sole "bud" yet spared, the "Brave Impe of *Bedford*" her nephew, the one way to defy the ruins of time. The turn from mortality and its sad proofs to the hope and trust of immortality comes in a motif as conventional as the visions of heaven that we find instead in a *Lycidas* or a "November." There is only one everlasting monument: frail words. It is interesting that Spenser's poem addresses Lady Warwick in order to make one thing of the devotion and love of the living and the famed power of poetry to immortalize the dead—rehearsing their "worthie praise," keeping their vertues from ever dying *though* death do soul from body sever (255). "So whilst that thou . . . Dost live, by thee thy Lord shall never die"; and the very personification of vanished greatness, wasted "through spoyle of time"—Verulam—cries "Thy Lord shall never die, the whiles this verse Shall live . . ."; "Ne shall his sister, ne thy father die."

This may be a platitude but Spenser believed it. To wisdom, learning, poetry, he granted immortality; all his poetry says so time and again, and nowhere says otherwise. It is as a protector of learning and godly wisdom that Lord Bedford is praised—and we have lately seen the support brought by other facts to Spenser's choice here when he ignores the many dramatic and pious actions that had filled Russell's busy life as servant of the state, and chooses to eternize rather this man within that public figure, who collected books and patronized authors. He was a "noble Patrone of weake povertie" (261); quite particular "steps of his" are to be followed by his grandson. Spenser knows whose ward Edward is; it is "under the shadow of" Anne Russell's countenance (272) that he

> Now ginnes to shoote up fast, and flourish fayre
> In learned artes and goodlie governaunce, . . .
> Brave Impe of *Bedford*, grow apace in bountie,
> *And count of wisedome more than of thy Countie.*

One is at a loss to see why there has been so much complaint about the lack of unity of this poem, and its disjointed organization. "O trustlesse state of miserable men." Its theme, which is single, is just what its title declares, the ruins of time, and the one single remedy (in time) which man has found for this universal destruction and oblivion—the celebration of greatness in letters. Nothing could be more germane to the subject as it is here seen than the praise of Camden (169); indeed it is startlingly relevant, supplying that one little thin frail thread upon which a remembrance of busy living Verulam, as she once was, so tenuously hangs—just as the greatness and goodness of all the long list of the dead depends for remembrance on the breath of friends, a breath which can crystallize into poetry and so outwit time. Commentators have asked for more connection between Verulam and Leicester; he has the supreme connection with her (all but identity) which we shall all have: dead, under ground, "and all his glorie gone, And all his greatnes vapoured to nought."

All these are the one subject of Spenser's poem; there runs as a uniting thread through all the sections of the poem, so often pulled apart and scorned as ill-planned and disunified, not only the lament but the answering confidence in man's recording and celebration of greatness and goodness. The poet whom Spenser looks to see aided by young Bedford's "bountie" will be just what Camden was, a "lanterne unto late succeeding age," to see the truth (170), to undo what Time does—bury and re-bury in ruins, obscure all monuments, raze even memories. Of the early patriotic antiquarian authors who tried to hold their lights up to the buried and recovered face of old Britain and distinguish what she had been, Camden is of course the rightly chosen type. It is idle to remark that Spenser is "more indebted to Harrison and Holinshed"; [12] they would do, but Camden includes them, in standing for something which had Spenser's ardent faith in a way we cannot but catch: the power of learning and letters to hold truth safe as in a vial.

The early antiquarians and later chroniclers of whom Camden is the type—the Saxonists, the manuscript collectors, Bale, Leland, Parker, Lambarde [13]—found their special justification in this attempt which Spenser praises: to uncover and show by their

[12] These comments and others later are made against the background of the collected commentary easily to hand in *Var. Sp.*, Minor Poems II. This quotation is a reference to 291 (Osgood); of course the error of thinking that the poet has been caught out is based on the error "Spenser is praising Camden as the only worthy commentator of Verulam." Camden meant a good deal more to Spenser than that, and does to us; he is not a bibliographical item but the epitome of faith in that one way of defeating time which is the hope of this poem: to record the very truth of the life that was once so fair, and so cheat the mortality that awaits it. Camden's life, motives, and works declare this as no others could; the parallel with the poet's tasks was apparent to any reader of *The Faerie Queene*.

[13] The last man Spenser possibly knew, besides his books; see *View*, ed. Renwick, 297; also *Var. Sp.*, edition *passim*, and 411.

lanterns an earlier "simple veritie," become obscured by time's defacements and by frivolous false evaluations. And *The Ruines of Time* finds its prototype not only in the *Musophilus* kind of literature in-defense-of-poetry but in the harangues of a John Bale calling on the noble families of England to preserve her antiquities, safeguard her primitive religious purity, listen to the words of her ancient writers.[14] It is entirely natural that Spenser's plea for poetry, and faithful naming over of those who will live on because they supported her, should have this patriotic and archaizing cast, for his greatest poem shows that this power of ancient truth, wisdom, and beauty to defy mutability is all of a piece to him with the perennial argument that poets confer immortality. If he ever read any of his favoured words of ancient English writers, his charmed archaisms, in Lady Warwick's Gower, all the more natural that he should speak of "bountie" to the now owner of it, and consider whether some might come from the Bedford treasuries of power, to give such a plea strength in a world occupied with the ephemeral, forgetful of goodness as soon as the vital thread was cut, and destined to the oblivion of silence. But no such neat little connection is necessary to recall that the author of *The Faerie Queene*, with his sense of the extreme significance of British history, linked all the three together as actors in the discovery and keeping-alive of truth: poets, and patrons, and restorers of antiquities.

This not only unmistakably unified *The Ruines of Time* but it is one reason why hopefulness predominated in the sections given to the Dudley-Russell-Sidney families. There is a firm and proper coherence as we enter upon the Philip Sidney passage proper (280), which has no longer the heavy bitterness of the laments over transience but carries the mood of its later line, "So thou both here and there immortall art" (342). The transition seems to me careful and poetical, not awkward, disconnected, pedestrian or any of the other hard things said of it. At line 260 Lady Sidney and Lord Bedford enter, the former properly fol-

[14] Some such typical adjurations as that in Bale's *Laboryouse Journey*, and other such defenses showing motives for the new "Modern" learning of antiquarian research, are given or cited in R. Tuve, "Ancients, Moderns, and Saxons," *ELH*, VI (1939), 165–90. The didactic Protestant patriotism which motivated the early students of Gothic antiquities and especially of early English stands in amusing contrast to the nostalgic romanticism which we tend to fasten indiscriminately upon all "revival of the medieval."

lowing her brothers as a third Dudley just dead, the Earl as the first (1585) of that pitiful tally of deaths among these patrons that were all close connections of the addressee here, Anne Russell. Then in the reverse order which befits their dates he treats in relation to his theme the ruins of time, first Lord Bedford and his services as patron, and his heir, and then Lady Sidney and her far greater service—she bore the poet-patron-knight who is the apotheosis of all these praised foes of decay and mortality. Thereupon the dedicatee Mary Sidney, niece of the Dudleys, and Anne Russell, closest literary heir of her brother, come to the fore. And with that last most recent death of Walsingham (Sidney's father-in-law, proverbially generous to him), already celebrated in poetry (435) and not depending on the vanity of pyramids and brass pillars (410), the figure who as Verulam usually speaks of this vanity which was her own case, states it piteously once more (465) and with her warning vanishes.

We do well to notice that Spenser believes his "consolation." [15] It is common to think ill of this poem, "mainly official verse, melodious and uninspired," and see a spark only when Sidney is mentioned, though its most careful editorial commentator went far to readjust the balance. It is true that the visions, even with Renwick's help on the "double structure," seem

[15] So engrained is the idea that the only consolation of a Christian is the final heavenly harping that this traditional division has been located in the few lines picturing Sidney in heaven (332–42; see *Var. Sp.*, 522, from Erskine). Of course much more of the poem treats the consolatory ideas, and all the instances of mortality, including that of Verulam, are set in opposition to the suggested hopes of immortality. The mediaeval commonplace reappearing in Pegasus as carrying "a good fame" (426) is discussed with extreme acumen in M. Lascelles, "The Rider on the Winged Horse," in *Elizabethan and Jacobean Studies Presented to F. P. Wilson* (Oxford, 1959).

Probably more should be made here of the fact that Vision 5 is most likely another form of this image (625, to be connected with Renwick's larger significances of the vision-images; see, e.g., *Var. Sp.*, 309); the interpretation was fairly widespread which read *the soul* as she whom Perseus delivered to eternal life, mounted on his virtuous steed (uses in Christine de Pisan and others will be described in a forthcoming book by the writer). [See *Allegorical Imagery*, pp. 34–35, 292, 332n.] The difference in tone and point of the suggested Ariosto source remains no matter how often we read Harington on the "senses" of Perseus (ed. Gregory Smith, *Elizabethan Critical Essays*, II, 202; referred to by Renwick). For a similar reason one may refrain from bringing in Rosalind's friend, whom she is asserted to have christened "her Segnior Pegaso" (Oxford *Spenser*, ed. de Selincourt, 625).

singular as poetic method for this date. But it is a different *genre* of poem from those lyrics we are likeliest to think of as characterizing the nineties; and even much later in that rapidly moving decade, not all poems were created as direct presentations of psychological experiences. The poem's first section presents a large and important subject with more passion than is given to any single human being who enters into it; it is sobering and salutary to realize that, sniff and cry humph as we may at the notion of an immortality in letters for virtue, Spenser really believed that

> . . . deeds doe die, how ever noblie donne,
> And thoughts of men do as themselves decay,
> But wise wordes taught in numbers for to runne,
> Recorded by the Muses, *live for ay;* . . .
> *Nor age, nor envie, shall them ever waste.* (400–406)

If we can disabuse ourselves of accepted modern assumptions long enough to follow sympathetically in each of its steps the long argument which Spenser states and re-states, claiming that letters, truth, learning, poetry are among things indestructible, we see the nobility of this lengthy and passionate protestation of faith. It sheds a new light on his series of eulogized noble persons, so often denigrated.

He holds this hard faith in the teeth of a stubborn set of painful facts, and so did those he addressed. When Spenser came to England for the visit that began in 1589/90, Lord Bedford's death was a fact of four years since; though a great and hopeful patron he was not young (in his late fifties), was an ill man, and left an heir, though one too young to help any current poet. But in 1586 came the death which Spenser says cut off his young Muses' "hope of anie further fruit"; in October Sidney died, of the wound received a month after his mother died in August 1586. His father Sir Henry had died three months before her; three deaths shockingly clustered in the summer of 1586. In 1588 Leicester died. In February of 1589/90 his brother Ambrose died. In April 1590 Walsingham died. Two of these deaths came after Spenser arrived in England; the last is ironic in the face of the dedicatory sonnet to the still living man. In an era when patronage was not only a plain fact but the idealized fact Spenser presents to us, the women who still remained of this great three-

or-four-family fortress of active defenders of virtue and truth, and the Bedford youth, still a ward, must have seemed a pitiful remainder of once solid hopes.

Not only the fact of his Muses' blossoms being "nipped and quite dead," but the other narrated events of the dedication to *The Ruines of Time* may be quite simply true. Though we have no need to guess who the "friends" were, the Russells, Anne especially, obviously suit particularly well:

> Yet sithens my late cumming into England, some frends of mine (which might much prevaile with me, and indeede commaund me) knowing with how straight bandes of duetie I was tied to him: as *also bound unto that noble house,* (of which the chiefe hope then rested in him) *have sought to revive them* [the blossoms and the hope of further fruit] *by upbraiding me:* for that I have not shewed anie thankefull remembrance towards *him or any of them;* but suffer their names to sleep in silence and forgetfulnesse. Whome chiefly to satisfie, or els to avoide that fowle blot of unthankefulnesse, I have conceived this small Poeme . . . speciallie intended to the renowming of that noble race, from which both you and he sprong, and to the eternizing of *some of the chiefe of them late deceased.* . . .

Spenser's connection with Lady Pembroke is obviously bound up with the web of connections he writes about, and since Sidney's death is climactic she is a fitting choice.

It is proper to the ideas we have outlined that wisdom and support of learning are stressed in Spenser's praises of each successive member of the group so cruelly decimated in these years, when he was becoming a poet whose patron would be important—an unforeseen "ruin" of time which endangered the cause he had at heart, surely alarmingly and discouragingly. Each utterance on Lady Warwick stresses this zeal for things of the mind rather than her beauty or more generalized virtue. Comparison of the *Colin Clout* passage on her with the praises of the other nymphs would point the contrast. The widow Theana is introduced (492) as one who is "Ne lesse praise worthie" than Urania, Lady Pembroke, "In whose brave mynd" as in a coffer all gifts and riches are locked; she in turn is herself praised as "the well of bountie and brave mynd." Excelling in "glorie and great light," her advancement at court is the just reward of "her great worth and noble governance," for she is one who has power—but virtue with it:

> She is the ornament of womankind,
> And Courts chief garlond with all vertues dight.
> Therefore great Cynthia her *in chiefest grace*
> Doth hold, and *next unto her selfe advance,*
> Well worthie of so honourable place. . . .

It will be remembered that in this poem Spenser plays very heavily on his old theme of the false values of courts, the "enormities" he saw there that sent him back (650ff) to the "barrein soyle" and penury and "rude fields" and sheep of his adopted island; any honest shepherd's life is better than the climbing over others, the filed tongues and wits applied only to pleasing, of the court where "each mans worth is measured by his weed" and gain motivates all (despite Cynthia's attempt to support "sciences" and learned arts). Then comes the famous section ironically describing false love, "and love, and love my deare," and the opposing of it to "loves perfection" that created the world, which is so much more fully delineated in the *Hymnes.*

This theme of gain not virtue as the spring of action in the world of the powerful is also the theme of much of the earlier letters of Harvey to Immerito, which had dictated his use of the cynical remark from Ovid which we noticed. Harvey gives an edge to a similar mood of ironic disillusionment by quoting the idea in four (rather than two) lines from Ovid, and in the form as found in the Ovidian text, a little different from our first quotation:

> Dum fueris foelix, multos numerabis Amicos,
> Tempora si fuerint nubila, solus eris. . . .[16]

This and the three verse variations in English follow upon the exasperated and biting satire of the court in the *Speculum Tuscanismi,* giving an opportunity for some three pages of ironic comment on the "Theame out of Ovid" and much ironical advice to young Immerito. He will probably learn, as Harvey has, to employ his "travayle, and tyme wholly or chiefely on those studies

[16] This is in Letter V, published in App. I of the *Prose Works* (*Var. Spenser,* 468), and supposed to be an answer to Spenser's Letter III; in the Oxford *Spenser*, the passages described are at 626–28. My attention was first called to this reference by Dr. Mary Parmenter. The variant *felix* comes from good MSS and is common in Renaissance quotations.

and practizes, that carrie as they saye, meate in their mouth." Of course "Master *Collin Cloute* is not every body," and albeit his old companions may lose favor with Mistress Poetrie, "yet he peradventure, by the meanes of hir special favour, and some personall priviledge, may happely live by *dying Pellicanes,* and purchase great landes, and Lordshippes" by what his *Calendar* and *Dreames* bring in. We cannot conjecture all that these remarks implied, in the days of 1580, with friends all still alive and *The Faerie Queene* under way (this is the famous letter discussing it). But it must have read ironically when in such different circumstances, not a lifetime later but some eleven years, the Printer of *The Ruines of Time* is hunting for copies of *The Dying Pellican* and other oddments to publish, and *The Faerie Queene* is well launched, but Spenser's poems lament such long lists of those he had not guessed would never read it.

But Spenser's harsh words are not all kept for impersonal Death. There is an element that we did not notice in our first description, in the complaint against the ruins which time assists. Not all mutability and oblivion and impermanence comes of the irrational working of forces men cannot control; for also "*Spite* bites the dead." The "painted faces" that flatter, the "courting masker"—"*All is but fained*" (204). This satirical tone and acrid disillusionment are most apparent when the bitter generalization that "after death all friendship doth decaie" is applied to Leicester:

> . . . the Foxe is crept
> Into the hole, the which the Badger swept.
>
> He now is dead, and all his glorie gone,
> And all his greatness vapoured to nought, . . .
> His name is worne alreadie out of thought,
> Ne anie Poet seekes him to revive;
> Yet manie Poets honourd him alive.

The little squib from Ovid about how many our friends are, *tempore foelici,* and how in bad times not one remains, was evidently in the later Middle Ages a common *sentence,* or conventional tag for indicating two states of mind. One, that just exemplified, is especially clear in the embittered English verses Harvey's letter quotes. The venomous sarcasm is as vehement in a two-stanza poem in the *Paradise of Dainty Devises* which is given the title, "Donec eris Felix multos numerabis amicos. . . ." It begins with an image: "Even as the Raven, the Crowe, and greedie Kite" swarm about carrion, tear the carcass to and fro, then go on to more—so where gold grows friends resort full thick, but when mischance changes wealth to want, "They packe them thence, to place of ritcher haunt." [17] The other less bitter notion is indicated in the phrase to which this and two other poems are assigned in the *Paradise.* All are signed, "My Luck is losse."

I would only call attention to the pertinence of these evidently almost proverbial meanings of the tag from Ovid to the whole history of Spenser's relations with the noble houses whose members he makes Anne Russell typify and represent. Especially the latter sad sense, the turn of events so that good fortune and hope become nothing but a flat record of pure loss, fits what had happened in the half-decade while *The Faerie Queene* was being seriously got ready, and it is no special addition to the train of mishaps that the *Stemmata Dudleiana* was lost too. The living scions were barren in their graves; why take great care of the withering stalk? Meanwhile it is at least a nice little morsel that somebody called "Spenserus" either wrote in, or was felt to be obviously connected with, the Ovidian tag which signified "my Luck is losse"—on a page of a Russell manuscript, one even signed by the particular almost last active Russell he did finally dedicate something to; it did appear in 1596 at last, and it was his "retractation," pretending at least that he like more famous authors before him is apologizing for something indiscreet written in the greener times of his youth. Though it scarcely lost him all his friends, still whatever did happen must have seemed one more case of "my Luck is losse."

Questions have always arisen regarding the dedication to the *Fowre Hymnes.* Perhaps it came as late as 1596, despite the early ties, for the simple reason that time's ruins left few alive of this once large group, to receive dedications or help poets. We may put aside immediately the fact that it unaccountably calls Lady

[17] See H. Rollins' edition (Cambridge, 1927). This is no. 44; the notes at p. 213 add information. The title appears also in the *Gorgious Gallery of Gallant Inventions,* where (100) the proper next line follows as in Ovid; the *Paradise* title gets its second line by skipping five lines to *nullus* . . . (*Tristia,* I, ix. 5, 10). Elyot in Bk. II, ch. 12 of *The Governour* translates seven lines from "sweet Ovid," beginning with our two but in the form they show in *Tristia* texts.

Warwick "Marie," acknowledged by everyone to be an inexplicable slip and not due to distance or formality in the relation. The dedication jointly to the two sisters (the other Margaret, Lady Cumberland, Anne Clifford's mother), signalizes a friendship between them that is apparently typical of the close relationship most members of these families seem to have kept up with each other; [18] hence as everyone is aware we shall never know which one of "you two most excellent Ladies" moved Spenser to call in his first two hymns. Yet he is very exact. It was but one. The stress has been on Lady Warwick in earlier poems, but Lady Cumberland was the more famous for serious-minded piety. Spenser's wording implies that it is not quite to be laid at the author's door that readers "do rather sucke out poyson to their strong passion, then hony to their honest delight"; yet he claims to have attempted calling in his copies, is willing to admit some need for an excuse by assigning them to "greener times," and resolves "at least to amend, and by way of retractation to reforme them" by adding the two final Hymnes.

Much is made of the fact that having admitted this he nevertheless publishes the four, and slurs are also sometimes cast upon ladies, surely only prigs, who could take exception to the two first hymns we have. But it is typical of the retractation (and Spenser surely knew Dante's, Chaucer's, Sidney's) that it does not answer an accusation of lasciviousness by repairing phrases, but answers an objection of misplaced Love by substituting Heavenly Love for earthly love idolized. It would be quite possible, where a literary convention is so usual, for all these to be largely made-up situations and phrases; however, the author's publication of all the four, and the Lady's request that human and natural love should not usurp Love's title, seem to me to indicate neither lip-service and pretense on the one side nor priggish piety on the other. A true retractation is the more effective if what is retracted remains extant; we possess it in all the famous cases. We need not make the whole matter too solemn; if some hesitation or reproof intervened, there may have been just enough bite in what happened to

[18] *Diary of Lady Anne Clifford*, *passim*, and Wiffen—see, e.g., I, 509–10. Both these also support the character of Lady Cumberland presently mentioned, well known through other poets too; see Lady Anne on her mother's own writings, 84, 90, or dedicated books such as Christopher Shutt's *Sermon* (no. 141 of Lord Bedford's library).

bring home the truth of "Cum fortuna perit, nullus amicus erit." Similarly, there must have been something of the feeling of "my Luck is losse" in the fact that one's patrons no sooner lent support than they fell from favor—Ralegh was out of favor, Grey was out of favor. Nothing lasts, friends least of all, and one false step is enough.

Far more seriously, this is the actual situation responsible for Ovid's poem whence the tag is drawn. The famous and pathetic exile, or rather *relegatio*, to the rigors of Tomis among the barbaric Getes on the shores of the Black Sea, was Ovid's punishment for a truly erotic poem, the *Ars Amatoria*, teaching not merely describing these arts; he lost all hope of favor with Augustus, and the book was expelled from public libraries. He did not live in Rome again, and the *Tristia* are written to discuss his misfortune, his defenses, his virtuous present ideas on the matters where youthful indiscretion had caused a fault. They show with pitiful seriousness what may be mostly pose and allusion in the later writer, that is, the love poet declaring his basic innocency though admitting enough guilt to make a form of retraction. When the *Tristia* are not taken up with Ovid's lamenting his misfortune in that his conceptions of love have been misread, he is apologizing for such "songs of his youth" ("id quoque, quod viridi quondam male lusit in aevo").[19] Ovid makes these defenses in the very section, written to a "steadfast friend," whence come the two lines that we have seen plucked out often; the context must have been familiar to every Latin reader, for the *Tristia* were thoroughly popular and their moving quality much appreciated.

The bitter sentiment about loss of friends by those who have lost credit, which fits Ovid's case so well and became a tag phrase for that situation, fits only with the obliqueness of most literary allusion an author who has lost friend after friend through death, in the quarter where he thought them surest, only to feel finally the smart of some disapproval where it was not deserved. Spenser had written pieces and passages certain to be unpalatable to those in authority, often enough to have tasted the truth of Ovid's cynical observation. But any subterranean connection such as we now speak of is of a different order, and much less serious. For there is no question of a real similarity between the poems of Spenser and

[19] The text used (and translation when quoted) is that in the Loeb Classics, ed. A. L. Wheeler (London, 1924). The extracted or adapted lines are at I.ix.5, 6, quotations in the text above from the rest of that section, or II.339, or III.i.7.

Ovid asserted to be *lusus iuveni,* as there is none between what the two poets paid, in losses; the recognized reference would merely make a delightful, and pointed, highly educated joke out of such a proverbial sentiment inscribed at the close of a benefactress's book titled *Confessio amantis.* Someone wrote it there.

If the joke we are looking at was never made, one hopes there was another as good. For showing the conspiratorial obligingness that facts often show when there is some hypothesis in the offing toward which they can bend themselves, there is also the fact that the close of Gower's *Confessio* is a recantation of earthly love in favor of heavenly love. Presenting his book to the king, this writer on love takes his "fynal leve" of earthly love,—"but *thilke* love," that other which "stant of charite confermed," charges no man's conscience; God grant us *that* "love and alle pes" and bring us to heaven where it is enjoyed.[20] Gower too excuses his writing, begun earlier, in that though tending to "lust and game," seen another way "It mai be wisdom to the wise." The contents of this framework-poem-on-love, organized around the virtues, are of no great importance to our present concerns, however, since one would think anyhow that Spenser read Gower. He was printed; he and Chaucer and Lydgate make up the commonly mentioned trio of mediaeval poets; Harvey read him; so must anyone have done who had a large interest in Chaucer. I append nevertheless, to be tidy, a note on some of Spenser's preoccupations which would be enforced by greater attention to the *Confessio*.[21] The most interesting, the attachment to a virtues-framework, using not

[20] *Works,* ed. Macaulay, III, vv. 3088* ff., 3061*; MS Bodl. 902 is a very good manuscript of the first-recension-revised text (see introd., clxx).

[21] It has always been necessary to be more chary about Lowes's suggestions touching "Spenser and the *Miroir de l'Omme*" (*PMLA*, XXIX)—unprinted and in a single MS—though connections would be more attractive; on large debts to widespread virtues-materials see articles in *JWCI*, and *Allegorical Imagery*. The *Confessio* has a long discourse on Justice as the important *princely* virtue, in a section on the education of kings (vii, 2695ff). And a Renaissance reader would have noticed in the Prologue (hence not engulfed in the long text; such attention-factors are important in MS reading) the comparison of earlier times with the stony present (Prol. 100 *et al.*, with the usual contrasts as in *FQ*, V, Prol.); there are numerous treatments of the law of continuous change which all things obey (e.g., Prol. 930, seas, seasons, etc.), treatments as expected of Envie and Detraccioun (beg. Bk. II), the world weighing with deceit in his balance and countered with the firm blandness of platitudes (Prol. 540), visions of Venus, of Cupid with his meynee (Bk. VIII). It is always sensible to note how long some things for which we seek sources have been commonplaces. All these are commonplaces.

the four-plus-three (cardinal and theological) but the "other virtues" usually opposed to the sins, with their suggestive connections with Spenser's alterations, is part of a much larger mediaeval inheritance and is being treated elsewhere [*Allegorical Imagery*].

There is another little oddity about actual mediaeval use of this tag, in ways which explain its appearance as a commonplace in the Renaissance. We may chance to read that romance of the 1450's, Antoine de la Sale's *Le Petit Jehan de Saintré*, with its many chapters of instructions to the squire by "My Lady" who is enamoured of him. In chapter 16, when the story promotes some discourse on largesse, Fortune, and friends, the squire is told never to forget that "Tempore felici multi numerantur amici . . ." and so on. Our curiosity is especially wide awake because we notice that instead of the strictly Ovidian form of all the other Renaissance references, we meet here Spenserus's exact wording. Our curiosity is not likely to be satisfied, though the only other example I know of precisely this wording is the citation in Richard Hill's Commonplace Book; this is in a Balliol MS, about 1520, but these bunches of "Latin proverbs" represent earlier forms and popularity. Without a word about Ovid, here too sits "Tempore felici . . . ," ending "Cum fortuna perit, nullus amicus erit" like the other "mediaeval" citation.[22] In the *Petit Jehan* we are directed to a properly mediaeval source for its popularity, for the squire is not to forget that which *Alanus* says in *Anti-Claudiano* . . . and the quotation follows. But Alanus does not say it. The reference is to 7.351–55, where the chief idea of the Ovidian tag is put into similar phrases, and the editor duly cites *Tristia*.[23] So we are left with our mystery, and are likely to be, and as with the many other loose ends in this set of observa-

[22] Not having the Champion-Desonay edition of *Le Petit Jehan* to hand, I use I. Gray's translation based on it (London, 1931; see 103). The romance customarily uses Latin *sententiae* to bolster advices in these instructional chapters, which significantly follow, partially, the pattern set for pious virtues-treatises by thirteenth-century ecclesiastical constitutions (7 sins with 7 corresponding virtues, 10 commandments, etc.); other similar mixtures of idealized profane love with courtly etiquette and moral advice remind us that courtier literature did not begin with Castiglione. The variant *evit-erit* is likely in any hand (not in the French texts I know). Hill's Commonplace Book is edited in *EETS*, extra ser. 101 (1907), by R. Dyboski; see 133 and introd. 27 (5th proverb). It is described by H. A. Mason, *Humanism and Poetry in the Early Tudor Period* (London, 1959), 145–55.

[23] By an error referring to *Tr.* III.ix instead of I.ix (Alain de Lille, *Anticlaudianus*, ed. Bossuat [Paris, 1955], 167). The passage does not appear to be in

tions, it is of no importance that we cannot find out reasons for these variants and these implications and private allusions that only mattered to those who made them. The small things about periods and connections and groups and "common" knowledge which we *are* reliably led to perceive are no less interesting.

No doubt it would be pleasing to sew the whole trifle up with bright thread by identifying the hand beyond question; then a paragraph would be forthcoming on Spenser's hours among the mediaeval MSS of Lord Bedford's library, with some speculations perhaps on a handsome *Fall of Princes* MS owned by Lady Cumberland's husband George Clifford,[24] or his sister Lady Strange's MSS[25] (mother of Spenser's Amyntas, mother-in-law of his Amaryllis, claimed as kinswoman). Unfortunately we are not sure of Spenser's Italian hand. Scraps like that on the back of Grey's letter of July 10, 1581, are too small for certainty; there are definite resemblances to the Italian hand of *State Papers* 78:29, said by Renwick to be Spenser's. One *can* say definitely that the Spenserus passage could with great probability have been written by the same hand which wrote the scraps we know are Spenser's.[26] But certainty on this point would not explain for us other and

---

the Ellebaut O.F. thirteenth-century *Anticlaudien* (ed. Creighton [Washington, 1944]).

[24] B.Mus. MS Royal 18 D iv; this former ward of Lord Bedford owned the illustrated Latin book of prayers Vienna cod. 1840, and MS Bodl. 3 (Summary Cat. 1843) of the *Pore Caitif*.

[25] This other Margaret Clifford, Lady Strange, apparently owned two Gower *Confessio* MSS (Royal 18 C xxii and Camb. Mm. 2. 21); especially interesting is the strange copy of Hardyng's Chronicle, Bodl. MS Arch. Selden B. 10, with a provocative illustration and set of verses on "The palais of Pluto," beginning "Blak by thy bankes and thy Ripes also" (f.185^{r}). The four black streams of hell ebb and flow and blow misrule *thurgh Scotland*. This connection between Scotland and Pluto's "palais of *pride*," *his daughter*, in one of Spenser's chronicle sources, is not in the printed copies (the material would occur at f.234^{r}).

[26] See H. R. Plomer, "Edmund Spenser's Handwriting," *MP*, XXI (1923–1924), 201–07, and R. Jenkins, "Spenser with Lord Grey in Ireland," *PMLA*, LII (1937), 338–53, particularly the notes to the latter. Dr. Jenkins has seen a rotograph of the Spenserus inscription and agrees with my statement about the quite possible identity of the hands. If the letter from Grey to Elizabeth, from Smerwick, in *State Papers* 78, no. 29, is in Spenser's cursive Italian hand, as Renwick says in his edition of the *View*, similarities include: the long-tailed *s* and *f* (as in his secretary hand), the straight upstanding capital *T*, the slender narrow oval *o*, the shape of the *e*, the *m*, *r*, *l*, *a*, *s*. If the letter in *State Papers* 87:29 is also in Spenser's hand, as is possible, there occur in it similar capital *S* and *p*.

more teasing puzzles of where this sixteenth-century annotator got the "mediaeval" wording, whether its proverbial status came of its being perhaps elsewhere in Alanus, whether we are helped to more knowledge of the *Fowre Hymnes'* earlier history.[27] Though the whole curious little set of connected facts helps us to remarkably little provable knowledge, we see as much as we were meant to, at that, of our betters' allusions and feelings and ironies, and think chiefly how lost are the implications which make facts important, in the ruins of time, while ideas and persons the poet did set out to "eternize" still shine brightly as he promised, if we look. His volume too was one written to honor and extol, but by a series of sad interferences his grateful reasons for celebration of those he honors were never permitted to have the reality of ours.

[27] Though there is some possible implication of these discussions with old puzzles such as the matter of date (two "earlier" hymns, early relations with Russells and Dudleys, etc.), the points are not capable enough of being fixed. Meanwhile arguments are cogent for late dates based on Spenser's not using more "technical" Platonism in pieces of earlier date (as in Ellrodt, *Neoplatonism in the Poetry of Spenser* [Geneva, 1960]), and in general I think the half-knowable facts of the present article are more valuable if we use them for suggestions, not proofs.

MS. Bodl. 902, Gower's *Confessio Amantis*, early fifteenth century, f.184[r].

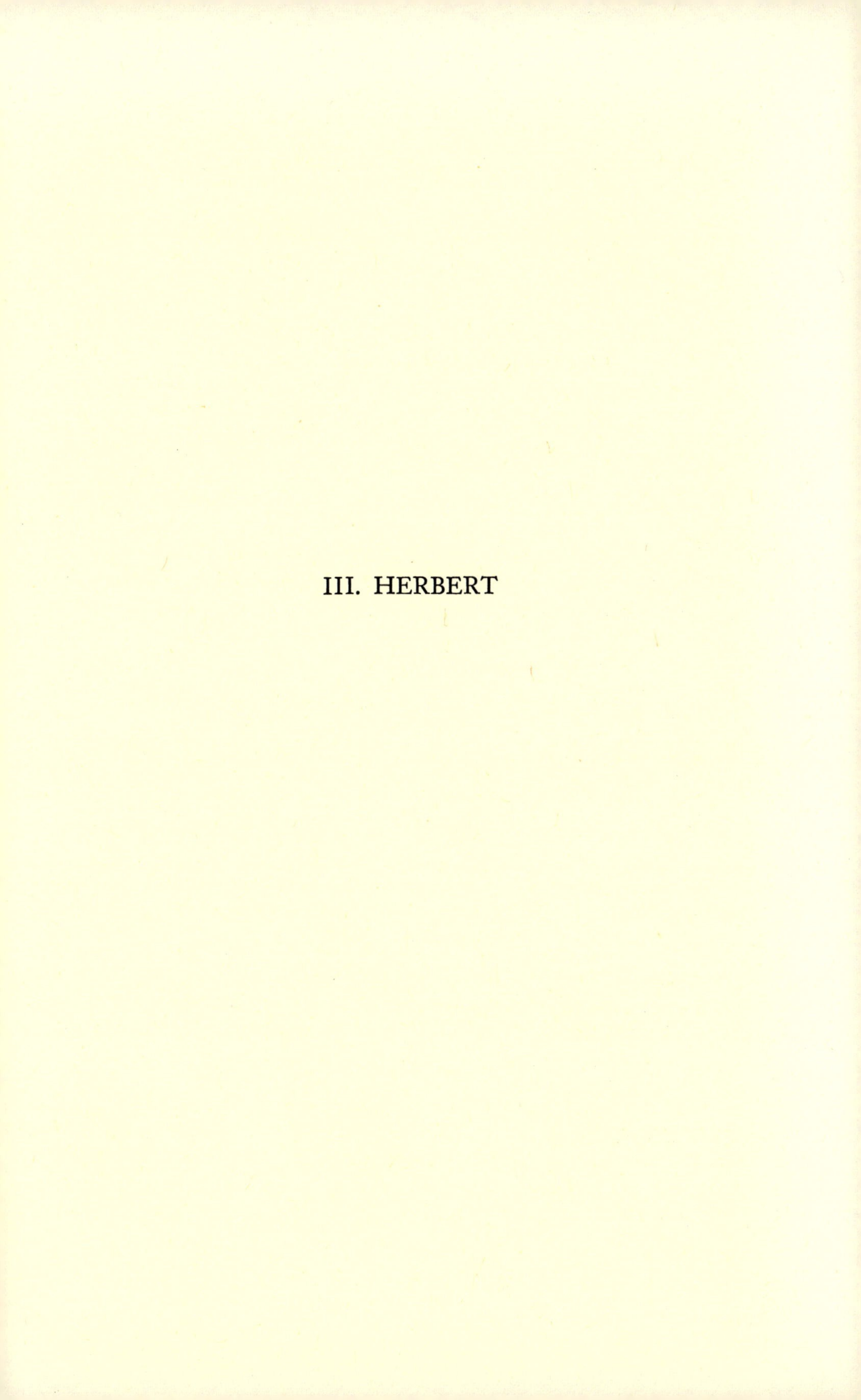

III. HERBERT

George Herbert and Caritas*

HOW much did Crashaw mean, when he said with a copy of Herbert's *The Temple* "sent to a Gentlewoman": "*Divinest love* lyes in this booke"? We may ask ourselves whether this has any close relation to what Herbert himself said we should find there, in the well-known words to Ferrar: "a picture of the many spiritual Conflicts that have past betwixt God and my Soul, before I could subject mine to the will of Jesus my Master, in whose service I have now found perfect freedom." When Herbert's conflicts of the will are spoken of, it is often too easily assumed that these concern renunciations made with difficulty as he decided to pursue "Court-hopes" no longer and as he lived with the results of his decision. But freedom from such relatively simple conflicts characterizes the majority of Herbert's poems. The paradoxical free subjection he found so difficult surely refers us to problems more complex theologically, great ancient riddles which many minds have wrestled with before him. There is nothing new in a near approach between conflicts touching the will and doctrines about the nature of "Divinest" love. "The soul's movement," Augustine calls Love, nor can love in the soul of the lover rest "idle," but must needs draw it on.[1] Seeing the problems of Christian love as problems of the will is familiar in Bonaventura and

* Reprinted from the *Journal of the Warburg and Courtauld Institutes* 22 (1959), 303–331.

This essay was originally a lecture given at the Cathedral of St. John the Divine, New York City, in 1956, in a series directed by the Rev. Canon John W. Pyle; the author's thanks are also due to Prof. F. Edward Cranz and Dr. D. P. Walker.

[1] On such connections in Augustine, see John Burnaby, *Amor Dei* (Hulsean Lectures, London, 1938), p. 94, where references are given to *Ennar. in Ps.* cxxi. 1 (i.e. 122) and to *De Trin.* xv. 38 ("For charity is strictly a form of willing"; but note context, and cf. xv. 27–28). Cf. the same author's translation of *De Trin.* xiv. 8 and p. 36. See also H. Arendt, *Der Liebesbegriff bei Aug.*, Berlin, 1929, pp. 63, 66. On Bonaventura see E. Gilson, *The Philosophy of St. Bonaventure*, p. 468. It goes without saying that when I refer to an idea as found in this thinker or that, or quote from one only, I do not intend to fasten ideas upon one writer as peculiar to him.

many another, and we may find that the connection is so close, between the conflicts of which Herbert speaks and his hard-won definition of "Divinest love," that not a few of his poems, rather almost all of them, are illuminated by considering it.

Defining the nature of love is a central problem of Christian theology, even as Crashaw's phrase points to a central mystery of Christian faith. To examine it, we must discuss outright the Christian doctrinal positions enunciated or implicit in Herbert's poems —which to my way of thinking does not preclude our looking at them "as poems," as the phrase goes. In this assumption I think I should have Herbert's agreement, if we may trust his several remarks on the subject in verse. On this then I would hope all readers might be agreed: that in considering such a subject we are engaged in a consideration which involves all the formal aspects of Herbert's poetry, all that allows us to call it beautiful (a title we should certainly not allow to slipshod thought, either, however shaped). For who ever heard of expressing the quality of the heart's motions, or of apprehending that quality when expressed, without attending to the *form* of the expression? Only by the closest obedience to all the delicate indications in a poem—metrical, figurative, and the rest—can we come at exactly what is said in it on our subject; but there is no time here to point to all these unnumbered components of a poem's meaning. And perhaps no need. This is every mature and willing reader's own activity.

Such an examination of Herbert's ideas would be safer in the hands of a theologian; if there is a danger that the theology may not seem to be true criticism, there is a more important danger that the criticism may not be good theology. However, since all but some twenty of the hundred and seventy odd poems raise one or more of the many traditional questions which surround the problem of the nature of Christian love, and since Herbert addresses himself to it with a theologian's care and profundity and discovers to us answers that combine a poet's eloquence with a noble mind's humility, I have thought it more valuable than dangerous to make the attempt.

Our subject is not modest. It has engaged the best efforts of the greatest Christian thinkers during several hundreds of years. We shall not in a short article arrive at discriminations between Agape and Eros and Philia and Caritas, we shall not be able to point carefully to what is Bernardine, or Victorine, or Salesian, about the elements which attach Herbert's conceptions of love to mysticism, we may not stop to compare Herbert's phrasings with the cast of expression which differentiates, and with no trivial results, an Augustinian from a Thomistic grasp of some question in a poem. We shall have more than we can do though we deny ourselves an interest in the history of Herbert's conceptions to fasten upon the substance of them. Yet only some awareness of their long history can make us alert to their precise nature.

Herbert, like ourselves but certainly more deliberately, faced a whole set of questions concerned with love of God in relation to love of self—*amor Dei* and *amor sui.* We must try to observe whether love for God in his poems has the character of a soul's desire and search for its own good (a familiar emphasis in St. Thomas, and, with a difference, in St. Augustine; it is discussed, and accepted, by Hooker in Book I. xi). Whether Herbert's "love" does or does not bear this character, we may be sure that he has struggled with the ancient question of whether the soul's desire and search is thus reduced to a form, however spiritualized, of covetousness—love for reward, not (in the old term) love *gratis;* and, in being love for reward, sadly lesser than that noble disinterestedness which even pagans like Cicero could find in friendship, and pagans like Aristotle could see in benevolence. Facing another ancient question, we must ask whether Herbert equates desire for happiness, beatitude, with love for God. We might quickly insert, to clear one question, that at any rate he does not express this (as many have) as desire of the ever-changing for the unmoved; he means something else by his "Lord, though we change, thou art the same" in *Whitsunday* (59),[2] and he pronounces on a different problem of *amor Dei* in *The Pulley,* when he has God declare that He withholds the gift of "rest" from man in order that he should not "adore my gifts in stead of me, And *rest in* Nature, not the God of Nature" (159).[3]

Does Herbert distinguish sharply, as Augustine does, between *caritas* and *cupiditas?* If he does make this distinction with care,

[2] For the convenience of any careful student of these matters, who will wish to scrutinize contexts, I have followed every quotation from Herbert with the page on which the poem *begins,* in F. E. Hutchinson's edition (Oxford, 1941; italics usually mine). All Herbert's poems have been studied in connection with any emphasis indicated.

[3] The different problem is treated below, p. 202.

but if he moreover repudiates the wish to hold and possess as indeed a form of love but a degenerate form, we had best be careful how we interpret his own so frequent appeals to Christ, "O *come!*" It is usual nowadays to emphasize parallels between his songs of sacred love and profane love poetry, and hence to accommodate the meaning of such appeals to the meanings they have in the profane lover's similarly worded pleas. It would still stand to be examined whether the form of his distinction is a particularly familiar one: to see all love as radically one, *cupiditas* if directed toward the world, *caritas* if toward God. This Rousselot [4] exemplifies from Hugh of St. Victor; it is Augustinian, and underlies St. Bernard's famous fourfold description of the progress to a final love of all things, even ourselves, for God's sake and of God for His own sake. Or it may be that we are to read certain poems as if Herbert made the distinction and conclusion Hooker does in saying "it is not the *possession* of any good thing that can make them happy which have it, unless they *enjoy* the thing whereof they are possessed. Then are we happy therefore when fully we enjoy God . . . : so that although we be men, yet by being unto God united we live as it were the life of God" (I. xi).

Such phrasings, and the like or unlike ones we find in Herbert, cannot but bring us to another whole set of questions regarding the possibility and the nature of "love" between beings as disproportionate as are man and God. Does Herbert stress God's self-sufficiency? Certainly in no poem does he come so close as does his great contemporary St. François de Sales to saying that God's perfection needs man that it may be exercised (i.e. it seeks and enjoys satisfaction). It is equally pertinent to mark any stress on the indigence of love, Plato's old conception of Poverty as one parent of Love, which we find Christianized in Thomas and in Bernard. Does Herbert conceive of a true reciprocity in the love between God and man? Possibly instead he thinks of God's down-descending love as entirely "unmotivated" by any worth (rather, new-

[4] Pierre Rousselot, *Pour l'histoire du problème de l'amour* (*Beitr. z. Gesch. der Philos. des Mittelalters*, Band 6, Heft 6, Münster, 1908), p. 44. Rousselot's distinctions are criticized by Gilson, in the notes to *The Mystical Theology of St. Bernard* (transl. by A. H. C. Downes, N.Y., 1955), and indeed they do not hold for Herbert, though they serve to raise important questions concerning his understanding of submission of the will, which can be answered from his poems. Some discussion of oversimplifications of Augustine's understanding of *amor sui* is found in G. Hultgren, *Le commandement d'amour chez Augustin*, Paris, 1939, pp. 157ff; see also H. Arendt, *op. cit.*, pp. 20, 22, 25, 27, 34, 67–68.

creating a kind of "worth") in the loved creature—Nygren's definition of Agape in a now famous book; [5] if so, it is necessary to observe narrowly whether Herbert finds any "love" man can have in response, that should not rather bear the name "worship."

Here, where cluster the thorny problems raised by posing self-abandonment or self-love as opposite possibilities, is a center at which modern interest becomes intense, as we see in numerous modern discussions of the nature of Eros and of Agape. It is also apparent to any literary historian that the question is bound to arise here of possible similarities between these definings of man's love for God and the more idealized and esoteric refinements upon "courtly love"; the very phraseology inevitably used to frame our questions wakes echoes of secular literary counterparts. If we wish for illumination on whether we are apprehending a true similarity or just a blurring of distinctions in our modern minds, the place to fix our attention in Herbert's poems is upon their revelation of the nature of man's love of God. We have yet to inquire into the precise nature of the *relationship* which he thinks obtains. Is man's love almost synonymous with adoration or primarily gratitude; a vehement, or an ecstatic, or a not-on-earth-satisfied desire for union with the divine?

If the love of which Herbert writes so much be in truth the single soul's search for beatitude in God, we enter here upon a set of questions touching the second great commandment, the love of our neighbor. Herbert did not find them easy questions, saying in *Divinitie* (134):

> *Love God, and love your neighbour. Watch and pray.*
> *Do as ye would be done unto.*
> O dark instructions; ev'n as dark as day!
> *Who* can these Gordian knots undo?

[5] A. Nygren, *Agape and Eros*, transl. by P. S. Watson, London, 1953. Among the many books which seek to repair the tendentiousness of Nygren's arguments (though this flaw does not, I think, destroy the book's value and extreme interest), the most just and illuminating seems to me that by J. Burnaby (see n. 1). But the semantic study, *Agape*, by C. Spicq (Louvain, 1955) is very helpful, though he has not yet advanced systematically beyond O.T. uses. His expositions show up certain fallacies in Herbert's ideas about the two dispensations. But *Agape* even as understood from the 300-odd variants in the Septuagint would not suit with Herbert's definition of the Love that must obtain between God and his *un*profitable servant (despite Herbert's similar emphases on gratitude for goodness, on activity, as well as on tenderness and on joy or blessedness).

His answer to "Who?" is Christ on the cross and in the sacrament. Having called Christ's doctrine "cleare" and then corrected this by "At least" surpassingly "*bright,*" he typically finds only one sure and "not obscure" way to understand doctrine thus dark with excessive bright: "To take *and taste* what he doth there designe." Defining and dividing are not God's way of undoing the knots.

> Could not that Wisdome, which first broacht the wine,
> Have thicken'd it with definitions?
> And jagg'd his seamlesse coat, had that been fine,
> With curious questions and divisions?

The image of the seamless coat, commonly glossed as Christ's Love, confirms us in thinking that the theme of this poem is heavenly Love by which man understands *his* difficult way as the stars know theirs (in stanza 1), without the spheres men have "suppli'd"; that the title *Divinitie* has double reference to the science of divine things and to "*God* is *Love*"; and that "burn thy Epicycles, foolish man; Break all *thy* spheres" is not advice preferring the pious heart to the thinking mind, but a typical reminder that God, the creator and unmeasurable one, gave us a Manifestation of Love to *taste,* not a finite "skie" of Divinitie to "cut and carve" our own maps upon. (To be sure, it may seem ironic to continue this essay in the face of this judgment, but that we study here only *Herbert's* ideas of that seamless coat and broached wine, and must therefore continue to define and divide.) That Herbert did not range all writers of Divinity under the head of proud learning, which is the only kind he distrusts, is obvious from the amount he has learned from them.

Noting then, in this and other poems, Herbert's belief that men can fully comprehend the doctrine of "love thy neighbor" only through *imitatio Christi* and the "He in us and we in him" of the Eucharist, we have yet to see precisely how he found *his* way around the disastrously difficult problem of "love thy neighbor *as thyself*"—in response to which some have made love of self the pattern of all possible love of another (Augustine and Thomas), while others, turning in dismay, cast out all self-love as the very apple itself (Luther), and yet others so define "love of myself" that the words become a way of saying "a true discernment, as it were with God's own eyes, of what is my true and best end," and thereupon accommodate love of our neighbor to this self-love in various ways.

If Herbert's poems do treat with clarity the nature of a Christian love of other men, we should notice how he avoids, if he does, that element which produced the ominous phrase "do-gooders," and the heart-rending phrase "I don't want charity"; whether his Christian *caritas* can avoid that complacent magnanimity which taints Aristotle's noble conception, disinterested as far as overt self-profit is concerned, but, to a modern eye, in some of its forms inescapably condescending and hence impossible between equals, and in all its forms, including the highest, psychologically far from unselfconcerned. How indeed *do* we love "the creatures" in Herbert's view? Here we meet with the ideas most commonly entertained about his conflicts of will. Some assume him to have taken the position that we must quite reject such loves, for a better one (this would be the "retractation" so familiar in the courtly love tradition). Or, perhaps, seeing God "in" them we are to love only the divine in the creatures—that is, a highly motivated love of excellence in creatures, surely a good thing, but (when it stands alone) less an imitation of Christ's love of us sinners than an assumption of his inimitable role, of Judge. A related view is a Platonic love of the Good, merely beginning with its imperfect reflections in the creatures—in which case one must as one climbs leave behind one these mere "lower steps" on the Platonic ladder—but did The Country Parson do that? Herbert may have found another solution—Augustine's, seen in the famous distinction between use and enjoyment, with its figure of the pilgrims each journeying with the use and aid of all earthly good things and creatures to his true home. This view sees all things, all creatures here as good for mutual comfort, love, and use, but reserves for God alone true "enjoying," *fruitio Dei;* [6] in God alone the unquiet heart, the *cor inquietum* of the *Confessions*, can find its rest. This involves the difficult conception of loving "as referred to God" our neighbor and ourselves, but we may find in that much

[6] A doctrine of extreme importance, long after the close of the Middle Ages; see *De doct. Christ.*, Book I, *passim*, and the discussion in Burnaby, *op. cit.*, pp. 104ff, also *pasim* on *fruitio Dei.* A clear exposition of Dante's use of this conception of the love of creature and of Creator appears in C. S. Singleton, *Dante Studies I: Commedia*, Cambridge, Mass., 1954, pp. 24ff. On loving our neighbor "in God" see St. Bernard's *De deligendo Deo*, ch. viii.

light on those "Conflicts betwixt God and my Soul" which are in Herbert's poems. And in the sure distinctions with which he applies the great Augustinian emphasis upon God the *Creator,* we may find much light on what sets off his poetry, as it set off Dante's and as it sets off the treatises of the great mystics, from all literature and all theorizing that seems to assume fundamental likenesses between Christian mysticism and courtly love.

These are not questions fabricated for our purposes, of course. They are taken from the theologians I am confident Herbert knew, with the help of modern analyses by students of patristic and scholastic philosophy that especially study the problem to which we here direct our attention. Herbert is a theologian and as he writes remains one; moreover, it is of great moment to the critic of his poetry to appreciate the delicate sureness with which he walks upon the sword-bridge he lays over the swirling waters of controversial conceptions. For, in large part, the absence of mawkishness and the unerring mastery of a tone which befits his chief poetic subject, "Divinest love," is an effect of the subtle care which has been taken by an acute but an unselfcentered intelligence to think truly; with all his mind he has been to school to Heavenly Love to win the passionate honesty which draws us. His slow sure passage among obstacles and over them is of moment to us also because we can walk upon his bridge. Not only Anglicans, indeed not only Christians, have found it, being of tempered steel, though narrow so firm that one may jump some steps to a crossing. I wish now to look at a good many of Herbert's poems, not with the order imposed by our previous questions, and certainly not just to see "what is Herbert's position," although to read the man is to try what it is like to stand in that —"led by his music, so must we." I do not suppose we shall be able to separate from our literary pleasure in him the many things which happen in our minds as we see a clear-sighted, a saintly, and an eloquent man search out answers to questions still found pressing. Among the things that happen, although I shall seldom mention it, there may be something of that for which no one ever found a better phrase than Lord Bacon, lamenting after his trial that he was cut off from access to his books and counsellors—"to help out my wrecks." For certainly never was a world more loveless (as Herbert defines love) than ours, nor confusions more rife as to the nature and connections of the many affections which we try unsuccessfully to denominate by that single word. Never perhaps was so piteous a reduction of the infinite variety of the relations the word can denominate, and never, not in the first Christian centuries, a more untaught and undisciplined yet eager attempt to grasp the import of the Christian doctrine in this particular. To which undisciplined attempts I hope not to add one.

Herbert seems to write much more of God's love for man than of what man's love to God should be, we think after a first careful reading of all the poems. He is never for one instant unsure of the great security: *because He first loved us. A true Hymne* ends (168): "As when th'heart sayes . . . *O, could I love,* and stops: God writeth, *Loved.*" As he wrote *Jordan ii* (102), it is probable enough that Herbert heard mental echoes of *Astrophel and Stella* (1 and 3), for at least we find it hard to read either without thinking of the other. But the subject of *Jordan ii* is of a different order of magnitude altogether,[7] and in theme these poems are a world apart. Herbert's is clear from his crucial last stanza, following upon the familiar first two which describe how wrongly he had once sought to "deck" and "clothe" in words *heav'nly joyes,* those joys which so excel all others that they "trample on [the] head" of the sun, *this* world's very source of light.

> As flames do work and winde, when they ascend,
> So did I weave my self into the sense.
> But while I bustled, I might heare a friend
> Whisper, *How wide is all this long pretence!*
> *There is in love a sweetnesse readie penn'd:*
> *Copie out onely that, and save expense.*

When Herbert talks about "copying out" the sweetness revealed in God's manifested love (that is, in Christ), it is scarcely possible to believe that he could write the lines he has italicized without intending to speak of a greater subject than *poetic* imitation—man's imitation of the love of Christ. To copy out the sweetness in that revelation is to find the only, not the more restrained and

[7] Different from the "condemnation of elaborate modes of art," the search for simplicity, moving "from elaboration to restraint," which L. Martz points to, speaking of a "central theme of both Sidney and Herbert" in quoting from *A. and S.* 90: "And love doth hold my hand, and makes me write" (*The Poetry of Meditation,* New Haven, 1954, pp. 269, 261). I would not question many formal relationships to Sidney, from whom, as Prof. Martz has admirably shown us, Herbert learned much.

simpler, way of seizing the character of "heav'nly joyes," those things to be spoken of "not with *enticing words* of man's wisdom, but in demonstrations of the Spirit and of power." [8] The title of the poem is certainly not idly chosen, and its first line, "When first my lines *of heav'nly joyes made mention*" may indicate that Herbert's own way of phrasing the theme of a poem which deals with *the ineffable nature of divine love* might have been something closer to "the kingdom of Heaven" abiding "within us" as well as "those things which God hath prepared . . ."—things "spiritually discerned," but only if we "have the mind of Christ," and spoken of "not in the words which man's wisdom teacheth, but which the Holy Ghost [God's *Love*] teacheth." They were revealed in "Jesus Christ, and him crucified," certainly, but also in Christ's discourses on Love ("*my* joy") in such chapters as John 15, where the Friend that Herbert refers to gives the same injunction about copying his love, and says "Henceforth I call you not servants . . . but I have called you friends." As in all Herbert's references to love "penned" or "written," the new commandment of Love written in the fleshy tables of the heart is not far from his thought, and the poems turn out to be less about writing a poem than about living a life which copies out that love with which we first were loved. So, in *Sepulchre* (40):

And as of old the Law by heav'nly art
Was writ in stone; so thou, which also art
The letter of the word, find'st no fit heart
To hold thee.
Yet do we still persist as we began,
And so should perish, but that *nothing can*,

[8] This quotation and those which follow are from 1 Cor. ii. 4, 9, 14, 16; compare the whole subject of the chapter. The two *Jordan* poems are very generally treated as being primarily about finding a literary style, though J. Summers suggests something of the different theme I speak of (*George Herbert: His Religion and Art*, Cambridge, Mass., 1954, p. 111). The title in the Williams MS, "Invention," would have had its more general sense of "finding" as well as the specialized rhetorical one of discovering one's matter (and indeed the poem never had the title "Elocutio"). The *W* reading for the last line, "Coppy out that: there needs no alteration," emphasizing both heaven's-joy-*is*-Christ's-love and *imitatio Christi*, has been discarded for the further ellipsis of *expense:* loss, waste, total expending for nought. Much else in John 15 is pertinent, and the sun image supports the wider theme (see note 13 below for scriptural glosses). Covert allusion to N.T. phrasing is perhaps the most studied of all Herbert's "arts"; *The H. Scriptures ii* (58) tells us of his pleasure in the study.

> Though it be cold, hard, foul, *from loving man*
> *Withhold thee.*

Here is a love poet who never mentions, or implies, or fears, that his love is unrequited.

A strange love poetry, that cannot include the "complaint." Not only did God forestall the lover by loving him *first,* but in all the suffering involved with love God has forestalled him, "in all grief pre-ventest me" (from *Thanksgiving;* 35). This complete assurance that he has been, is, and will be, given the love he writes about constitutes a fundamental difference from other love poetry, yet it does not mean that Herbert is not often and poignantly aware of a disharmony in the relation—we suppose then in his own inadequacy to it. In loving him God loves his foe; *Antiphon ii* (92) runs: "Praised be the God of love," who was not *sans merci* "to his friend" say the Angels, "to his foe" say the Men. And when it continues "He our foes in pieces brake" the sentence refers to God's protection without losing its reference to the singers themselves. The title of *Miserie* (100) in the Williams MS is "The Publican," a figure used in art as the stock antithesis to pride hypocritically masking as "love of God," and its writer knows he loves like a Pharisee; but this "Miserie" is not that of one who because of his follies and selfwill fears he may be unloved.

> No man shall beat into his head,
> That thou within his curtains drawn canst see: . . .
>
> [Men] quarrell thee, and would give over
> The bargain made to serve thee: but *thy* love
> Holds them unto it, . . .
> *Not suff'ring those*
> *Who would, to be thy foes.*

Since the loved one addressed in this poetry cannot fill the usual role of "sweet enemy," lovable but insufficiently loving, we may ask ourselves whether Herbert does not merely switch things about and make a love-complaint about himself as the unrequiting one. Strange platform as this would provide for the speaker of a love lyric, I shall answer the point presently, while we might notice here that the disharmony is not resolved, as in other love poetry, by the hard-hearted beloved's at last yielding favors—only by being made able to receive them. The joyful poems do not differ from the joyless ones by virtue of portraying a more equal exchange. Something of the unique and paradoxical character of this relationship about which it is impossible to write a love-complaint is seen in the *Christmas* poem (80), inevitably one of Love's "Coming" to the beloved. Weary with pleasures and taking up in an inn, he found Christ "readie there   To be *all passengers* most sweet relief."

> O Thou, whose glorious, yet contracted light,
> *Wrapt in nights mantle,* stole into a *manger;*
> Since *my dark soul* and brutish is thy right,
> To Man of all beasts be not thou a stranger:
> *Furnish & deck* my soul, that thou mayst have
> A better lodging then a *rack or grave.*

The forms and attitudes of secular love pleas are little use as models in a situation where the partner who pleads is also the partner who is unready. Courtly love complaint persuades a will, and might be thought to have some skill in the situation man-*will-not*-serve-thee, but not a word can it muster in answer to the deadlock of

> Man *cannot serve thee;* let him go,
> And serve the swine: there, there is his delight: . . .
>
> A sick toss'd vessel, dashing on each thing;
> Nay, his own shelf:
> My God, I mean *my self.*
> (*Miserie,* 100)

The transformed will is outside the logic of complaint.

Indeed Herbert is so entirely convinced and aware of a boundless love received from the one he loves that this is a *datum* in the most unhappy, the most tormented of the poems. It is not only in happy poems like *Easter Wings* (43) that he says "Affliction shall advance the flight in me." And tranquil poems like *Even-song* (63), which ends "And in this love, more then in bed, I rest" are as likely as the torn and rent ones to admit: "What have I brought thee home   For this thy love? . . . I ranne; but all I brought, was fome." He has God answer, "*It doth suffice:* Henceforth repose . . ."—but the poems which do not reach this repose contain also its idea about un-repose: "I muse, which shows more love . . . the gale, [or] th'harbour."

We must strictly avoid any connecting of the love of suffering often pointed to in the courtly love tradition with the welcome to affliction which is found in Herbert's poems by that name. "The sigh then onely is A gale to bring me sooner to my blisse" (*Affliction iii;* 73); "We are the trees, whom shaking fastens more" (*Affliction v;* 97). The basis for the difference is not seen only in the idea which concludes the poem called *Repentance* (48), "Fractures *well cur'd* make us more strong," though it is obvious that the courtly lover exulting in the suffering imposed by love could not be interested in this cure which does not seek to alter the fact that "life . . . Is one undressing, A steadie aiming at a tombe," though it therefore made *these* broken bones, "Full of his praises, Who dead men raises," sing "in a *well-set* song." Another difference, though still not the great one, lies in the fact that (as in *Sighs and Grones;* 83) God with whom he pleads "O do not bruise me!" "O do not grinde me!" is asked to "*reform* And not refuse" him. For the key to this poem addressed to a loved one who, like many a *domina,* is both "*Cordiall* and *Corrosive,*" both "feast and rod," is that its speaker is a most well-beloved one asking help against self-caused suffering, not an unregarded servant in love with submission. Sacred poems which exalt loving submission—a different subject in sacred and in profane poetry—exult in the feast, not in the suffering, and the mystic loves life, not death. Some rods, being sceptres (see *Affliction iii;* 73) bring men to a feast, but not this one in *Sighs and Grones* —the Judge's rod, before which the well-beloved must change, not embrace his pain.

The basis upon which the differentiating factors rest, possible to no courtly love *Liebestod,* and defining the nature of God's love rather than obsessively concerned with the lover's state, is indicated in *Affliction iii* (73):

> Thy life on earth was grief, and thou art still
> Constant unto it, making it to be
> A point of honour, now *to grieve in me,*
> And *in thy members suffer* ill.
> They who lament one crosse,
> Thou dying dayly, praise thee to thy losse.

The best glosses to this and other appearances of the conception of God in each man bearing again the sin of the world upon these uncounted crosses, and in man sanctifying the suffering, are not parallels from secular love poems, even the most idealized mediaeval courtly-love welcomings of pain borne for love, but certain Pauline chapters, with verses such as:

> . . . Who now rejoice in my sufferings . . . and fill up that which is behind of the afflictions of Christ in my flesh for his body's sake, which is the church: (Col. i. 24).
>
> We are troubled on every side, yet not distressed; we are perplexed, but not in despair; . . . cast down, but not destroyed; Always bearing about in the body the dying of the Lord Jesus, that the life also of Jesus might be made manifest in our body. (1 Cor. iv. 8-10)

"I knew that *thou wast in* the grief," says Herbert; or, in *Affliction v* (97), whose first stanza concerns that "firm . . . floting Ark" the church:

> At first we liv'd in pleasure;
> Thine own delights thou didst to us impart:
> When we grew wanton, thou didst use displeasure
> To make us thine: yet that we might not part,
> As we at first did board with thee,
> Now *thou wouldst taste our miserie.*

Or see *Affliction ii* (62): "as *thou art* All my delight, so *all my smart:* Thy crosse took up in one, By way of imprest, all my future mone." Herbert's bits of "broken pay," even if he were to "Die over each houre" of a life as long as Methuselah's, would be but idle, as repayments for "thy one death for me"; since "by way of imprest" that payment in advance, which sealed the tie of exchanged allegiance, took up all "moan" to come—then "Kill me not ev'ry day." The old mystery of "the scandal of the Cross" is behind the "What is this strange and uncouth thing?" which begins *The Crosse* (164). Since all the described crosses, frustrations of his design for doing God's will, are Christ's own cross, may that will be done, as He did it, in the Father's way—in four words of Christ's become his words, instead of in the glorious ways he had designed.

> Ah my deare Father, ease my smart!
> These contrarieties crush me: these crosse actions

Doe winde a rope about, and cut my heart:
And yet since these thy contradictions
Are properly a crosse felt by thy Sonne,
With but foure words, my words, *Thy will be done.*

The use of the prayer to the Father in Gethsemane to conclude this analysis of an incomprehensible situation indicates to us what conception it is that has ordered the rebellion in Herbert's mind,[9] and it has again the same basis as that which differentiates all these poems of suffering from secular love complaints: the unique character of the divine love for man, which came down to dwell in him and bear what he could not.

These varying situations and statements are not put forward as many statements of "the same idea"; I point to a basic ground of difference which makes the relationship unique when the love exchanged is between God and man, so that the identical words and similar phrases of profane poetry cease to bear a comparable significance. This does not mean that all comparison is unprofitable, but that the popular assumption that "sacred and profane love poetry" treat the same *subject* is unwarranted; and that where subjects differ, themes of poems differ, and those single elements which are a component of meaning (even formal ones when they so operate) "differ" though they are outwardly similar. These difficulties are very familiar in iconographical study.

Affliction is still affliction, and not a way of loving death; but if Herbert does not get out of his affliction by self-annihilation in the passivity of suffering, neither does he ever get out of it by

[9] I do not believe Herbert would have used the words of Gethsemane (his italics) if this conclusion were the "whiplash of self-control" used at the climax of a piece of self-analysis. This is surely a poem in which "the whole edifice of self-will collapses," as Martz well says (pp. 133, 135), but I would admit more of painful struggle still showing in the poem itself, than this critic; there is something unlike Herbert in the picture of a poet manipulating tensions to a predetermined end. Herbert was a great artist, perhaps because he nursed no tensions he could foreknow the resolution of; they were sins to him, keeping his Savior on the rack. A "picture of [a] spiritual Conflict" *is* written after not during it, yet truth to an experience which led to an end is not the same as driving conflicting elements with steady hand towards a known end. "Betwixt God and my Soul"—Herbert's Adversary alone brought steady control to this conflict; our age (for I do not lay this at Prof. Martz's door) is perhaps over-ready to view a poet's struggles as chiefly those that can end with an aesthetic victory. The "wrastling," "combate," are like Jacob's; the "threatnings" those for which "I bent my bow."

self-excuse and the return of a sense of merit. It is not *that* which leaves his "Conscience" not a word, "not a tooth or nail to scratch" or carp at his actions. He *fights* grief, but with *God's* love (for him): "The bloudie crosse of my deare Lord Is both my physick and my sword" (105). Herbert's emphasis upon the absence of merit in himself and his stress upon *sola gratia* would have the savour of sound doctrine to many a Lutheran; of course we could show how ancient a Christian position he takes by quoting Bernard, Augustine, or others, for it is clear that, like Augustine, he thinks of our love for God as God's gift.[10] The idea is omnipresent and I shall only quote a stanza from *Grace* (60): "Sinne is still hammering my heart Unto a hardnesse, *void of love*: Let suppling grace, to crosse his art, Drop from above."

We find, then, that Herbert celebrates in poem after poem God's love for man, Agape, and the single complete revelation of it in Christ's Incarnation and Passion. Had I space for quoting whole poems, we could consider whether the profundity of *how* he speaks of the nature and manifold relations of that Agape must not be responsible for this curious fact: that Christians of every stamp and persuasion have read him, and now do, without that inner dissent which is so familiar an experience in reading religious poetry, and that this remains true even when these disagreeing groups read not only "in him" but read the whole corpus of poems (barring perhaps three, *The British Church* and two or three others). What is yet more remarkable is that the inner consent is made possible not by a large simplicity in the poet which leaves unstirred the subtleties beneath, but by phrasings so just and acute that they take account of and take care of each man's differing subtleties of interpretation. This sounds impossible; any reader may put it to the proof in a few years of wide comparison. The conception of Agape is in general markedly Johannine. The language or the particular strains of thought time and again call Paul to mind. The downward movement of Love—et propter nos homines, *Descendit*—is put into words (as it is so often put into the imitative music of the polyphonic Credos Herbert heard and sang) which stress descent, by image:

[10] *Amare Deum, Dei donum est* (Sermon 297, I); this universally familiar idea as found in Augustine is discussed with citations in Burnaby, *op. cit.*, p. 176, and some of St. Bernard's similarly memorable statements are in *De diligendo Deo*, chs. v, vii, xii.

When I had forgot my birth,
                And on earth
In delights of earth was drown'd;
God took bloud, and needs would be
                Spilt with me,
And so found me on the ground.
                (*The Banquet*, 181)

Or in *Discipline* (178): "Love's a man of warre, And can shoot, And can hit from farre. Who can scape his bow? That which wrought on thee, *Brought thee low*, Needs must work on me."

The remainder of each of these poems would exemplify how inevitably the consideration of God's love for man carries with it a consideration of the nature of man's love for God, and Herbert's treatment of the first great commandment is complex. He answers in poem after poem St. Bernard's first question in the *De diligendo Deo*, "Why should man love God?" usually with Bernard's first, and last, answer, "Because He first loved us," and hence with one variation after another upon the great themes of Incarnation and Passion. The strain of *adoration* sounds in a multitude of poems, oftenest perhaps the wonder-filled adoration inseparable from a love which the creature (twice-created) has for the Creator; an Augustinian emphasis upon this deliberately preserves the unique character of a love which therefore stubbornly resists attempts to see it as analogous to the "adoration" of courtly love poetry [11] (attempts particularly usual in treating of mediaeval poems). Man follows with all other creatures in the train of that love which moves the sun and the other stars. "Bright spark," he says to *The Starre* (74), "Take a bad lodging in my heart . . . Touch it with thy celestiall quicknesse, That it may hang and move After thy love"; "Get me a standing there" among the beams which crown Christ's face

[11] The latter emphasizes less a relation with one loved than qualities of love (boundlessness or intensity), and its natural mode is hyperbole. The same kinds of imagery do not serve in the two differing situations, and this is the formal factor which usually declares the difference. The so common stress upon the revivifying power of loving or being loved, based upon the common experience of it, differs from the above in the nature of its claims. Adoration and worship is not the note of this kind of praise, and differences between profane and sacred statements of it often appear analogous until the different nature of the revivification begins to appear (often, e.g., a difference between "revived" and "reborn").

That so among the rest I may
Glitter, and curle, and winde as they:
That winding is their fashion
Of adoration.

Or speaking of the sun, in *Christmas* (81): "We sing one common Lord . . . and both so twine, Till ev'n his beams sing, and my musick shine." Or, in *Man* (90), to the Creator of both micro- and macrocosmos: "Oh mightie love! . . . Since then, my God, thou hast So brave a Palace built; O dwell in it"; similarly, "Love built a stately house . . ." (*The World;* 84). Sometimes he stresses the difference between man and the creatures who cannot have man's consciousness of God's creative love, as in the bird of *Miserie* (100), who "Wonders and sings" but does not know "his power Who *made* the arbour." Sometimes "Man [as] the worlds high Priest . . . doth present The sacrifice for all"; man can thus give to (or else rob of) their fulfillment "a thousand" others of the creatures (*Providence;* 116); here Herbert sounds like Bonaventura.[12]

As in general Christian doctrine and as in the General Thanksgiving of the Prayer Book (only from 1662 onward), "We bless thee for our creation . . ." leads inevitably in many poems to "but above all for thine inestimable love in the redemption of the world . . .". This is the *basso ostinato* in all this music of gratitude, which to Herbert is truly a grace; and *gratitude* is in these poems the primary constituent of man's love for God. It is far more ubiquitous than an emphasis upon desire for the *summum Bonum,* or upon *quies,* rest or peace in God, or upon hope of ultimate full happiness, or upon mystical union—whether in the terms of the Song of Songs as in Bernard, of the God who seeks man as in François de Sales, even of the God whom man will "en-joy," as in Augustine. Much in Herbert does, however, closely resemble the *fruitio Dei* of Augustine.

There is not much of the luxuriating in this gratefulness which offends us in less intellectually firm verse. Herbert can exclaim, in *Ungratefulnesse* (82), "Lord, with what bountie and rare clemencie Hast thou redeem'd us from the grave!", but the stanza goes on to single out that inveterate tendency to which Augustine

[12] See Gilson's explanations of Bonaventura's discussion, pp. 438–39 of *The Philosophy of Saint Bonaventure;* cf. also (p. 446) "the hand which writes" and Herbert's "Secretarie of thy praise," *Providence,* line 8.

gives so many pages: man's ready substitution of the worship of a lesser light, when he has been granted the potentiality of *partaking* of essential light.

> If thou hadst let us runne,
> Gladly had man ador'd the sunne,
> And thought his god most brave;
> Where now we shall be better gods then he.

Since I have quoted this, I may interject that it contains, I believe, the sole reference to anything resembling deification through the love of God (or even resembling a modified conception like the soul becoming "deiformis" in Bonaventura's word).[13] Usually the temper is more like the end of *Gratefulnesse* (123): "Till I a thankful heart obtain Of thee: . . . such a heart, whose pulse may be Thy praise." Man's love has so much of gratitude that he "in heart . . . ever kneels"; he who does not feels "Neither sinne nor Saviour" (*Businesse;* 113). However, Herbert indeed means his word, when he calls man's ungrateful failure to realize and repent of sin not by some self-hating epithet of disgust, but "idle." "*Foolish* soul," he says, "Who di'd for thee?"

Herbert's emphasis upon the vanity rather than the foulness of sin is a concomitant of the centering in his theology upon the nature and operation of love. He is aware of, and he avoids, all the subtle psychological difficulties which accompany the presence of extreme *gratitude* in any *love.* He is perfectly clear about the unique aspects of Agape which make this possible. When he celebrates them, it is usually with gaiety, or else with serious confidence. "Thou art a day of mirth," he says to *Sunday* (75); we put

[13] St. Cyril's word also, according to Donne, in the Second Sermon preached before King Charles, on Gen. i. 26 (no. 29 of the *Fifty Sermons;* ed. Simpson and Potter, IX, 86). Moreover, Herbert's "shall *be* better gods" should have Hutchinson's gloss, Dan. xii. 3, and the echo of it in Matth. xiii. 43 (that the redeemed shine "as the sun in the kingdom of their Father" is their supernatural light). A straightforward and usual use of the betrothal figure in the next stanza underlines the "everlasting pleasure" in the union in heaven between "the work of thy creation" and "thy self," essential light—which only man's dark sin of ingratitude can preclude. Ungrateful, he instead closes himself in his dark grave-like box of sin, within his "poore cabinet of bone" which *can* in the grateful man be "just such another" as God's rare betrothal-jewel cabinet, the Incarnation. The other cabinet is the Trinity; the imagery stresses alluring love in the one, inaccessible light in the other.

on that new robe, Christ's new testament of love, "That was re-quir'd to make us gay, And fit for Paradise" (the Sunday of the Resurrection supplanting the old rest-day of the Law which would leave us in our sullied robe). He knows its relationship to Friday's "drops of bloud" (our new robe is "at his expence"), but he in many poems directs himself to look rather at the joy with which Love spent itself, leaving no sting of guilt in the gratitude when "a thankfull heart" ceases pining and crying to look at the *victorie* which to Christ was the only meaning of the *death*: "Do not *by hanging down* break from the hand, Which as it riseth, raiseth thee," "Arise sad heart . . . doe not *withstand*" (*The Dawning;* 112). Herbert knows quite as much about joy as about affliction. Firm doctrinal positions are as typically the substructure of his gay poems as of his analytical ones, and when he sees through man's incorrigible folly the wit and the mirth come not from obscuring the seriousness of it but from confidence in the remedy for it. "See how thy beggar works on thee," he says in *Gratefulnesse* (123), which begins, "Thou that hast giv'n so much to me, Give one thing more, a gratefull heart." Since all these poundings and hammerings, sighs, "Perpetuall knockings at thy doore"—*all our noise*—are the best sounds we can send up, God makes music then of them, hears them as prayers for grace; not that He has not "still" (ceaselessly) in heaven

> Much better tunes, then grones can make;
> But that these countrey-aires thy love
> Did take.

God's participation by love in the *whole* affair—affliction, joy, blame, groans, songs, delight—he stands upon. He is entirely aware that he is "behinde" in love, but makes clear not only *that* it does not ultimately signify, but why; and though he makes many statements on the famous problem of whether man's love to God can be *gratis*, perhaps all bear some relation to one I quote only partially from *The Reprisall* (36):

> I have consider'd it, and finde
> There is no dealing with thy mighty passion:
> For though I die for thee, I am behinde; . . .
>
> O make me innocent, that I
> May give a disentangled state and free:
> And yet thy wounds still my attempts defie, . . .

Yet by confession will I *come*
Into thy conquest: though I can do nought
Against thee, *in* thee I will overcome
The man, who once against thee fought.

The title of this poem in the Williams MS is "The Second Thanks-giving."

The love Herbert portrays is then a love between two very unequal participants. "O let me still [i.e. continuously] Write thee great God, and me a childe" (*H. Baptisme ii;* 44). Nevertheless, self-abasement is not the note of his poetry—much oftener instead we hear "Blest be the Architect, whose art Could *build so strong* in a weak heart" (*The Church-floore;* 66). Gratitude is less for dignity conferred, benefit procured, deliverance ensured, than for the revelation, open and indubitable, of Agape, a pattern of a love otherwise unconceivable (in two senses) by man. Of course this way of speaking of the Incarnation and Passion is traditional and universal, but when it comes to man's participation in or imaging of the revealed divine Love, we simply find missing in Herbert some of the important ideas of mediaeval Catholicism, in their Aquinian formulation particularly. We might look long for actual proofs that Herbert disagreed with St. Thomas, but I do not believe that he had the same philosophy of nature, or that certain therein-included conceptions of man's nature specifically are congenial to his thought. There is clear accord in many statements about grace, and in the universally accepted conception of Caritas as impossible to natural man without the infusion of grace, but we hear little in Herbert of "participation" or of man sharing God's beatitude, creatureliness being always pre-eminent in all his creatures. This reticence is matched by his abstaining from phrases which would claim reciprocity in the love between God and man, or the mutuality stressed in Bernard's treatment of the relation. Herbert face to face with divine Love revealed is more likely to find another way than this to lay aside his sense that he is too "Guiltie of dust and sinne" to receive and return the love of God. In "Love bade me welcome" (*Love iii;* 188), the consciousness that he is not "A guest . . . worthy to be here" is sharply present:

I the unkinde, ungratefull? Ah my deare
I cannot look on thee.

The answer "Who made the eyes but I?" simply removes the question of "worth" from the relation of love between Creator and creature, as the next question, "know you not . . . who bore the blame?" removes the burden of shame from the creature who "marr'd" those eyes. He is an unworthy servant; the matter is not to come in question, let him sit down as the guest at the banquet, for he shall be the one served. Herbert writes of a love that removes every obstacle to a return—obligation, inequality, deserts, mastery-or-servitude, disproportion; he is fully known for what he is and he is the well-beloved one, he is welcome.

The poem is one we cannot read to our satisfaction. The tone in which the most solitary inner loving spirit speaks to God Himself is one we have to be saints to manage, and we are also as likely to damage God's own speeches here as when we import our own niggling self-righteousness into the majestic or the tender utterances in *Paradise Lost.* There is no hint of human condescension in this lover, "sweetly questioning, If I lack'd any thing," because the one great fact that "quick-ey'd Love" is God Himself makes it different from every human welcome for which it may be the pattern; and the ending, "So I did sit and eat," is neither passive and self-abasing, nor self-gratulatory, but filled with joy and strength because of what Herbert thought it meant for man to taste Love essential in the Eucharist. His conception of the in-dwelling love of Christ in the heart which is both temple and altar, of being "rooted and grounded in love" (Eph. iii. 17), or of "putting on Christ" (Gal. iii. 27), recalls sooner or later all the great Pauline passages, and these are the immediate context for his understanding of "participation," as for his understanding of the meaning of "affliction."

This must be remembered when we remark upon the fact that Herbert, when he defines the nature of man's love for God and relates it (as he consistently does) to the revelation of the nature of Agape in Incarnation and Passion, turns naturally not to reciprocity in the usual sense but to *imitatio Christi.* It is not a disclaiming so much as a revision of the idea of reciprocity, even in *The Thanksgiving* (35), our most obvious example. "Oh King of grief! . . . Shall *I* then *sing,* skipping thy doleful storie . . . ? Shall thy . . . thorns [be] my flower?" "But *how then* shall I imitate thee?" After his twenty lines of attempted ways of learning Caritas—almsgiving, mending his ways, forsaking the world

—he says, "Nay, I will read *thy* book" and find "*Thy art of love* which I'le turn back on thee"—but the Passion puts him to a full stop; and the next poem is that *Reprisall* which ends "*in thee* I will overcome The man, who once against thee fought."

It is significant that Herbert throws away all the works of philanthropy as an insufficient way of pursuing the "imitation of Christ," as showing an insufficient understanding of divine Agape, but it is not significant of what Palmer thought the poems exhibit:

> The relations between God and his own soul are what interest him. Like Bunyan's Pilgrim, he undertakes a solitary journey to the heavenly city, and concerns himself little about his fellow men, except to cry aloud that they too are in danger. Any notion of dedicating himself to their welfare is foreign to him. . . . Usually his responsibility is to God alone; and this . . . is the farthest point to which his self-centred piety carries his verse. . . . To Herbert . . . the personal relationship of the soul to God is the one matter of consequence.
> (*Life and Works*, II, 111)

This is one of the most inexplicable remarks ever made about Herbert, and that it should come from a devoted editor, who knew the poems better than most of us ever shall, we can only explain lamely by remembering the preoccupations of Palmer's own time and place. Herbert's wellnigh perfect understanding of what it means to *love* our neighbor is assuredly visible in his poems, and it is firm, just, clear, subtle, bearing fruit inescapably in constant actions of high generosity and a humility so based as to rehabilitate the very word *charity*. We should know this even without the testimony of his life. We do not need *The Country Parson* to know that Herbert's theories on love and gratitude for it extend straight *through* a social philosophy which negates the idea of a "private good," and that he would in helping others be able to believe as well as write that not he but "*God* [should] be praised . . . that so the thanks may go the right way, and thither onely, *where they are onely due*" (245). His expositions of the operation of God's love for man and man's to God inevitably enclose the second great commandment, as most great thinkers on the subject have seen to be the case, from the scriptural "the second is like unto it" onward. His most overt reference in the poems to charity in the narrower meaning occurs significantly in one addressed to God and entitled *Unkindnesse* (93; the titular word has still its link with "ingratitude," not natural).

I could not use a friend, as I use Thee. . . .
Would he have gold? I lend it instantly;
But let the poore,
And thou within them, starve at doore.[14]

To Herbert, acts of love to fellow men are not acts deserving of gratitude, but acts *of* gratitude. Both his poetry and his life testify to how a right definition of Caritas removed those psychological tensions with which we are familiar through experience and theory, from "the love of one's neighbor as oneself."

It would have been interesting here, and entirely possible, to show Herbert's sound understanding of "love of self," [15] though like Augustine he finds it no great embarrassment, avoiding and showing us how to avoid some of the great mediaeval difficulties. But lacking space I shall rather draw to an end by rapidly relating all these matters to what Herbert said his poems portrayed, "the many spiritual Conflicts . . . betwixt God and my Soul, before I could subject mine to the will of Jesus my Master."

I think we must decline to assign these tensions, though much talk about Herbert does, to the lusts of the flesh or the delights of the world, all that inveterate love of the creatures to which man is prone. This despite words like "The propositions of hot bloud

[14] This is related to the description of the Last Judgement in Matth. 25, but to much else; it is naturally eminent in a writer like Herbert who so stresses Christ's indwelling love in every "neighbour" that every act of charitable love is done to Him, in loving and modest return. Among all the poets of wit, the hot-tempered Herbert stands out as the one incapable of scorn; his conception of the dignity of others is based upon the conceptions we have been examining. The familiar idea of God's presence *in pauperibus suis*, a favorite theme of mediaeval sermons, is treated for example in Augustine's Serm. 60, 9ff. Quotations which especially recall the attitude Herbert takes (often after considerable struggle and pain) towards "giving" anything to God are to hand in Burnaby, *op. cit.*, p. 134; e.g. "He has need of nothing . . . Yet that our works might have direction even to him, he deigned to be hungry in his poor." See both this sermon (60) and 61, in Vol. I (nos. x, xi) of *Sermons on the N.T.*, Libr. of Fathers of the Holy Cath. Church, Oxford, 1844.

[15] The conversation described by Herbert in *The Holdfast* (143) is an acute opening up of the problems involved in "We must confesse that nothing is our own," and his answer is no less characteristic for being familiar: "That all things were more ours by being his" (some phrasings seem close to St. Bernard, *De dilig. Deo*, ch. v). So also, in the treatment both of love *gratis* and of "participation" in *Clasping of hands* (157), the paradoxes show Herbert's answers to the difficulties raised, e.g., by Rousselot's major distinction concerning "finding" or losing" the self in love of God (see n. 4 above).

and brains," as in *The Pearl, Matth. 13. 45* (88); this poem treats of a more ancient and a deeper subject than "I wittingly gave up a good deal for God's love; high-priced, but I see its comparative worth, and am paying the price, if not without a certain lingering regret for what I might have been." The cost-and-value figure comes of course from the merchant who "sold all that he had" and bought the pearl of great price—the Kingdom of Heaven. The refrain is "Yet I *love* thee," and it answers to "I *know* the wayes of Learning . . . I *know* the wayes of Honour . . . I *know* the wayes of Pleasure . . ."; "I know all these, and have them in my hand," he says, and we have not a portrayal of renunciations, but a disclosure of that overpowering motive which made "*all that he had*" a mere nought to be thrown to the winds. A situation familiar enough in human love, but what he adds to this declaration of something done with open eyes and for love is that he was *led* and *taught how* to love the Kingdom of Heaven [16] only by heaven's "silk twist let down . . . to me" ("by it To climbe" [17]). That is, by God's love whence he learned his own, and he puts aside as useless "groveling wit," that

[16] Besides the fact that traditional interpretations of "the pearl" were commonplaces (e.g. *scientia Salvatoris,* in the *Glossa ordinaria;* Herbert describes what it is to *know Christ,* the true "Way"), and in line with his characteristic rejection of *vain* learning, these three "wayes" he knows and declines (Learning, Honor, and Pleasure) look to me a good deal like the famous great Three Temptations. Augustine's explanations of *Curiositas, Superbia, Lascivia* (lusts of the eye, pride of life, lusts of the flesh) are typical enough, in Serm. 34, 7. On the first one, see H. Schultz, *The Forbidden Knowledge* (N. Y., 1955), and on various ways in which these three from I John ii. 16 were accommodated to Christ's triple temptation and to "World, Devil, Flesh," see E. M. Pope, *Paradise Regained,* Baltimore, 1947, ch. v.

[17] The image seems to be a combination of *scala coeli* and the clue in the labyrinth; the first more traditional figure, familiarly related to the descent, in the Incarnation, of Christ by whom we climb, would allow the connection with *Love* coming down from heaven to conduct and teach—confirmed by the refrain. Ryley characteristically thinks of the clue as God's Word; his theological milieu and emphases are so different from Herbert's that his comments seldom help, though all have been scrutinized (transcript in the Harvard Library of Bodl. MS Rawl. D. 199).

In connection with this image, which appears in many authors in forms that can be illuminated by iconographical parallels, we may add a general note touching such connections. Theological conceptions of this degree of subtlety do not lend themselves to iconographical tradition; accordingly the distinctions are falsely neat in R. Freyhan, "Evolution of the Caritas Figure," *JWCI,* XI, 1948, 68–76.

proved no clue in these labyrinths, all his comparing, troublesome attempts to act on grounds of superior commodity; that did not decide it.

Struggles with fleshly desire or the pride of court prestige are on the hither side of the real conflicts. Consciousness of sin is accurately depicted in Herbert's poetry, but there is no disgust with the body, no loathing or self-hatred; the sins which provide such lurid passages in many other writers seem oftenest caught up in a phrase like "folly" or "vanity" or "a bubble"—*Poore silly* soul, says Herbert, with its "flat delights" that creep and grow on earth (*Vanitie ii;* 111). With perhaps two exceptions, those poems are oftener serene than troubled which speak of "This worlds delights," or which admit that "The world an ancient murderer is," with "her enchanting voice."[18] Similarly I would withdraw from the emphasis, popularly so stressed, on the conflicts Herbert had over entering the priesthood. As Canon Hutchinson so wisely notes,[19] the Bemerton poems do not show the earlier struggle with ambition but question rather the utility than the rightness of the decision.

But I should like to redefine the "ambition" with which Herbert struggled. I do not believe that what God willed, and Herbert could not, has very much to do with his giving up the secular for the clerical life. For one thing he rather portrays the difficulties of definition and acceptance as any Christian encounters them —for certainly Love as God defines it is outrageous to the natural man; but also his conflicts do not usually gather and break because of any professional decision and yet from the beginning are concerned with that "utility" of which Hutchinson speaks. Where others fight "ambition," Herbert fights that last outpost of the human will, the desire seemingly indigenous to all Love, to give his devotion where it is needed. Herbert detects the finest and

[18] This is no mere matter of date. The untormented poem quoted, *Self-condemnation* (170), about "loving amiss," is not in the Williams MS, but no more is *The Collar*, in which I find one of the exceptions (though the chief struggle is against the injustice of "no harvest"). And the earliest *Affliction* poem has all the conflicts over the nature of love which I presently point out.

[19] Introduction, p. xxxvii; all Hutchinson's corrections of Palmer in related aspects are particularly just and fit, and one cannot measure the debt of Herbert studies to this editor's commentary and introduction. From his renewal of attention to the inter-relationships and order of the poems there result many tacit corrections, of special importance to the subject we discuss.

subtlest deceptions that mask as "love of God." In *Frailtie* (71) he surmounts with ease those temptations which prevent men from seeing that honor, riches, fair eyes, are but "guilded clay," dear to foolish man but only "Deare *earth*." But he looks at splendor and power and then at the "simplenesse" with which God's rule (the other of the two "Regiments") has to get along, and thereupon in jealousy for God's honor "That which was *dust* before" rises and pricks his eyes. It is Herbert's ambition for God not for Herbert that he fought with longest. The striking thing is his recognition that this, which looks like love, is in fact the proud sin of distrust of God. This is a refined and spiritual kind of "Babel," as he terms it, for man to raise; but not only in this poem but many of his others there rises up this same old sin of the pride of life, as Milton's Christ met it in the wilderness when Satan asks him how such a one as He expects to establish a kingdom, a country youth from Nazareth with a few days' occasional experience in Jerusalem.

The poem in which Herbert sees through himself with most humor is fitly entitled *Submission* (95): "Were it not better to bestow Some place and power on me?" So many of the phrases are blandly and delightfully monstrous that Herbert's own amusement at such a "designe" is quite obvious; he is here well past struggle, though he records one. His mind "would be extreamly stirr'd" for missing *his* design—but that God is his "wisdome" and has both his eyes; the poem has the New Testament contrast between the two wisdoms, and the problem is not how to submit but how a will is supposed to choose—to act and do—when it has made over the eyes of the understanding.

I will no more advise:
Onely do thou lend me a hand,
Since thou hast both mine eyes.

Th next poem, in which Sin *the hand* hath got (*hand: power*, a regular synonym from the cliché "God's hand"), is very different in tone: "I cannot skill of these thy wayes." But it is named *Justice* (*i*; 95), and after the contrast between the powerful climbing antitheses describing God's actions and the frustrated contradictions describing his own, he has sadly to turn his verse with justice against himself: "I cannot skill of these my wayes." Or see *Praise i* (61): "Man is all weaknesse," a verse or two is all his praise, but "Mend my estate in any wayes, Thou shalt have more"; help out the short arm with a sling and he will fight Goliath, "O *raise me* then," who have a work to do. Or that poem filled with pain, *Home* (107): "We talk of harvests; there are no such things, But when we *leave* our corn and hay: There *is* no fruitfull yeare."

Ill health becomes a crux in this debate over man's "utility" to God; he asks often, what kind of a "service" *is* this? It is one thing for Christ to take the scandal of the Cross, the manger and the rest, but here is mortal man to take it too—not allowed to be a small thing yet given for God's glory, but made into a no-thing to reenact in his own person the no-glory given to Him he loves and honors. Two of the fullest delineations are in *The Crosse* (165) and *The Dialogue* (114). In the first—"things sort not to my will, Ev'n when my will doth studie thy renown"—he finds his answer in the nature of God's love which came down and met (and meets) his contradictions, and his title and his use of Christ's words show that it is not "resignation" (see above, p. 181). In the second, one of his contributions to a centuries-long series of dialogues between God and His beloved the soul, his difficulty is again a soul "not worth the having"; God's answer the inscrutableness of divine evaluations:

What, Child, is the ballance thine,
        Thine the poise and measure?
If I say, Thou shalt be mine;
        Finger not my treasure.

But natural man does not *like* God's plan; nor does Herbert want to be "a treasure" in this way. "The way is none of mine: I disclaim the whole designe." The answer is again love as revealed in the Incarnation and Passion; it is the way I took, Christ says. The creature learns the Creator's definition of "resigning."

Herbert is entirely aware that the root of the matter is his inability to love God *propter se,* with no admixture of "for man's own sake." He would like to love what he can benefit—God needs none. He would like to give himself—he is not his own, even to give. He would like to bring flowers and sweets to straw Christ's way (*Easter;* 41); but he knows that Christ was up first and brought His sweets along with Him. He knows that when the heart says "O, could I love!" it is "sighing to be approved" (*A true Hymne;* 168). It is the ancient problem, of the creature ready to love and bestow and be approved in the intelligible, self-concerned, self-willed, natural way—and faced with this "way" in which God's Love is to *be* its *will,* and even its will toward other men. After an exact delineation of such resentful doubts, the first *Affliction* poem (46) ends, "Let me not *love* thee if I love thee not." The thorn in all of them is that the world of nature can make nothing of the way love is understood in the world of grace; Herbert, poor natural man, is "A wonder tortur'd in the space Betwixt this world and that of grace" (*Affliction iv;* 90). This I think is the "stretch" he speaks of in *The Temper i* (55) and elsewhere; although he has to say "Yet take thy way; for sure thy way is best," such a tempering is anguish: "Will great God measure with a wretch? Shall he thy stature spell?" When his love, that has to be conceived in a mere human heart, is to take perfectly the similitude of *God's* love which *is* His "way" and therefore Herbert's—"O rack me not to such a vast extent."

This is why all the anguished poems are about a *hard* heart, why "*Cold* Sinne" always forces God's love in the heart to retreat (*Decay;* 99), why we "*freeze* on" in warm resentment at being fruitless (*Employment ii;* 78); and this is why he finds no way out but to cry "come, come" (as he does in *Deniall;* 79, in *Longing;* 148),[20] since he knows that only divine Agape in the heart can by grace enable a crumb of dust to love, which will be to will, as God does. That this could happen—transforming man's entire relationship to other men into one of love, and making all his service to Christ "freedom"—he does believe, and his poems seem to me to record how man loves when it does. Though I dare not take up here the staggering problem of whether and how man can love God in the way of Agape, Herbert's conception of how man having Christ in his heart loves Him "freely" and loves all creatures as His creatures, is his way into it; far from unrelated to what we experience in human love when that is unselfregarding, it is yet enabled to transcend human frailty by what Herbert calls "imping my wing on thine" (*Easter-wings;* 43). There is a major difference in all this from the "come, come" of profane love

[20] "My soul . . . untun'd, unstrung . . . O tune my heartlesse breast"; and in *Longing:* "My heart is wither'd . . . To thee *help* appertains . . . My love, my sweetnesse, heare!"

poems. So also of course an "abandonment of will" in profane love is very different from the transformation of all man's loving and willing in the union of wills Herbert wishes for (see *The Search;* 162, on the love from which nothing can separate us, "Making two one"); a new self is far from a self abandoned, or even a self "unregarded." Sometimes he adds, to his cry of "come," "O *fix* thy chair of grace," because every day that world in his heart, unlike the other, must be fresh created, the stuff for the second creation being bent with the fatal unruliness of mutability (*The Temper ii;* 56). Sometimes he sees through his irrationality in laying his coldness to God's will for him, "as cold hands are angrie with the fire And mend it still" (*Church-lock and key;* 66); sometimes, but seldom, he is merely like the tempests, which simply know God's hand "And hold it fast, as children do their fathers Which *crie and follow*" (*Providence;* 116). In the extremely rare poems which cry "come" but meet with "no hearing," "all lockt . . . no key," the answer and the key are nevertheless half caught within the compass of the poem, to stand forth clear in a following one (*Complaining;* 143, *Deniall;* 79, *Longing;* 148). It is to be noted that these rarer desperate poems always retain some shred of nonacceptance of the hard thing he phrases in *The Method:* "Gods eare . . . needs not man" (133). He did learn the distinction between love and the desire to be valuable, and learned it by becoming willing to *be* loved *propter se,* for his own so poor sake. Thus to match God's Agape [21] stretched the poor crumb. Herein lies the secret, and it is matter of course, of "the saintly Herbert's behavior to the other crumbs.

Herbert makes an answer to the quite different ideas of the source of valuableness which are held by the secular natural world, one in which (for it is our own) it simply does not seem reasonable to love God, least reasonable of all to love His will. Such an answer is in *The Quip* (110), when Beautie twits him for not picking her rose, and Money laughs at his simple-headed tune, and Glorie puffs by—and his answer is not, "but I have *God.*" Instead God answers for him, and the answer is, as it was in *The Pearl,* "He *is mine.*" This is a reasoned and reasonable answer, which Herbert makes often in Augustinian terms (for he ex-

[21] See St. Bernard, *op. cit.*, the end of ch. iv, for similar use of the figure of the grain of dust and God's inevitably outstripping us in love.

plores more deeply than any fleshly sinner what it means to be a "creature"). It is not, and no poem of Herbert's is, a prostration of the will.[22] Nor do passionate feelings direct him to his answer, though these prevent self-deception in the clear hard thinking which did direct him to it, and are responsible for the ardor with which he proclaims it. In secular natural man within himself, as in the world with its quips, he sees the same blindness of self-sufficiency, and proud unwillingness to belong to the God who created him; the title of the poem *Nature* (45) is exact.

> Full of rebellion, I would die,
> Or fight, or travell, or *denie*
> *That thou hast ought to do with me.*

Later poems show the multitudinous meanings, theologically quite precise, of the second creation asked for—a new heart for his "saplesse" one which is a stone fit only to hold "my dust," grace transforming nature. Sometimes he uses the ancient and complicated figure, "Yet Lord *restore thine image* . . . And though my hard heart scarce to thee can grone, Remember that thou once didst write in stone" (*The Sinner;* 38).

This, the plea for the restoration of God's image in man, is the key to the *theme* of *Dulnesse* (115), rather than the parallels with secular love songs which are recalled, and quite properly recalled, by his "Where are *my* window-songs?" "Thou art my lovelinesse . . . *Pure* red and white." Herbert does not use here a situation of profane love poetry (it would make an odd one, the lover lamenting the dullness of his love, and would surely cause the situation to worsen), and he certainly declines its devices—quaint metaphors to curl o're again *his* Love's curling hair. Those are suitable enough to the loves they celebrate; Herbert does not campaign against secular love poetry, though he has a larger definition of what human love could be than most love poems. But

[22] Touching this much-discussed matter (closely related to much we have already brought forward) one very clear poem is *Obedience* (104). The sixth stanza defines Agape ("a strange love to all our good"—good of all of us, the old genitive); st. 4 clarifies with fineness the relations of God's *love* to man's *will,* Herbert's characteristic reconciliation of submission with freedom. It is interesting to watch him time after time miss—again avoiding reduction of the human personality—a related stumbling-block; sees man a sinner, yet does not sum man up in his sinfulness (e.g. *Praise ii;* 146: "Though my sinnes against me cried, Thou didst cleare me; And alone, when *they* replied, Thou didst heare *me*").

here, in his asking God why he is a duller lover of *perfection* than courtly lovers are of imperfection (of not-pure red and white, imperfect love and innocence), there lies a tough theological problem, and he answers it. He knows the relation of Sansjoy to Pride as well as Spenser did, and his recognition of the accidia which gives him his title is accompanied by quite usual self-accusations, that he has become "all earth," without the "quickening" spirit which that was given. Not the profane lovers mentioned, but the sacred one, is "lost in flesh." This poem uncovers situations (needs and remedies) which cannot come into secular love poetry, and to which its special devices would be quite unequal, though its words cannot but occur. For he is writing about his inability to *see* the very form of perfection and therefore praise it with joy, about the dimming of God's "gift"—a "minde" that was His own image in his creature, enabling him to apprehend, though in a glass darkly, something of God's nature, which is Love.[23]

Sure thou didst put a minde there, if I could
Finde where it lies.

Lord, cleare thy gift, that with a constant wit
I may but look towards thee:
Look onely; for to *love* thee, who can be,
What angel fit?

I have quoted this poem last because it brings to mind the fact that various recent books on the subject relate the much-discussed mediaeval literary tradition of courtly love or *fin' amors* to contemporaneous conceptions of *amor Dei*, Caritas, Neo-Platonized Heavenly Love, man's love to the Deity purified of *amor sui*. The interest and popularity of such connections often shows up in seventeenth-century studies in certain assumptions which lie behind the interpretation of "love poems" by Herbert and by others. This final poem also seems to me to show the radical differences which have made the most discerning among recent books disclaim a real relationship, either of indebtedness or profound similarity, between courtly love and the mystics' love of God, each the subject of some of the best of Western literature. In lit-

[23] Even small reading will disclose how Herbert's care prevents his belying the extreme complication of the theological problem of *God's image in man*—e.g. in Augustine (*De Trin.*), or Thomas, or Bernard (*op. cit.*, ch. ii), or see on Bonaventura, Gilson, *op. cit.*, pp. 432–44.

erature each has many variants which we may not separate with rigor from their extremest forms.

Quite aside from the question of whether Herbert deliberately paralleled the devices and situations of secular love lyrics, and from his use of the figure of the Spouse, we look in every such thinker (or any human being, I suppose) at the relations made between sacred and profane love; these relations are certainly as important to proper definition of the first as to "virtuous" management of the second. These matters now lead us into a quite different area of studies, and I must simply assume a recognition of the importance of the problem, and a responsible rather than a casual or argument-seeking concern with the chief literary works that show it—Dante's *Vita nuova,* the *Roman de la rose,* Chaucer's *Troilus and Criseyde,* Petrarch, Chrétien and the French lyrics and mediaeval romances generally, or at a farther remove Spenser's *Faerie Queene* and *Fowre Hymnes,* and the English sonnet sequences.

As everyone knows, the courtly lover of eleventh-century Provençal poetry, like his descendants thereafter, was the *servant* of a *domina* whom he often lauded in the terms usually accorded only to deity; this service, only possible through her grace, was grounded on her merits and assumed his complete radical unworthiness, and particularly a complete subjection of his will to hers, and the sufferings necessarily involved in such a relation were to be embraced with joy both as proof of his love and in some cases as a kind of fruition of it. As everyone also knows, the language of this devotion employs religious terminology (or vice versa), both for images and concepts, so wholeheartedly that courtly-love parodies even of religious services like matins and mass become quite elaborate by the thirteenth century, and devotion to mistress or to the Blessed Virgin is similarly expressed. In its idealized form, courtly love is in a high degree unselfregarding, and as subtly deliberate in its exclusion of *amor sui* on the servant's part as is the attempted "love gratis," by the human creature, of God. It is virtuous love, whether extra-marital or not, in that from it as from a fountain spring all virtues (notably the chivalric virtues), and it is herein a reasonable more than an irrational appetite. Moreover, it can be a highly spiritualized rather than sensuous relationship, to which the bodily presence of the beloved is not essential, *l'amour lointain* being a typical, even necessary phenomenon; more than this, *amor purus,* which would be contaminated by physical union, according to courtly love's famous clerical theorist Andreas Capellanus and others, is perfected not despite, but through, being unconsummated.

The seeming parallels made obvious in my summary are as obviously connected with another question—not the possibility of a likeness, but the problem of a conflict, between such a secular love and the love of God. And though that conflict shows most acutely in the thirteenth century, in Jean de Meun or in the Old French *Queste del Saint Graal,* we are familiar with the recurrent phenomenon of a retractation, a declaration that the lover will give up all such phantom deceptions for the true heavenly love to be offered to God—in Chaucer, Petrarch, Sidney, less obviously in Spenser. Many might see such a retractation in Herbert's boyish sonnets sent when he was about seventeen as a New Year's gift to his mother, which call women worm's-meat, or even (as I do not) in *Love i* and *ii* (54), which marvel that "onely a skarf or glove" can warm our hands to write of love, and ask that the "greater flame" of Heavenly Love should "attract the lesser to it." [24]

But I am chiefly interested in so stating what made courtly love a "problem" that we can see whether in Herbert's pictured "Conflicts" we are shown the problem and the issue to it (to his problems, as we know, he found an issue). In the first place, a distinction between love and lust chiefly beclouds, and does not take care of in the least, the "problem" of courtly love. Nor is it to be stated as chiefly a problem of adulterous sterile love over against legitimate, natural, productive love in marriage. The *major* problem of courtly love is not solved in Spenser's figure of Britomart by virtue of our agreeing with the now quite common statement, "Britomart is *Married* Love." Possibly all her actions, most of them not in relation to Artegall, make her an answer, but the true

[24] The two boyish poems are published from Walton by Hutchinson, p. 206, and there is little if any other evidence that Herbert favored a deliberate attempt to displace secular love poetry by sacred love poetry (he does frequently deplore men's confusions and idolatries—scarcely a singularity, in writers on his subjects). It is dangerous to allow the content of these early efforts to circumscribe the meaning of the two mature sonnets, nor do I know the evidence for Martz's treatment of them as recastings. *Love ii* especially is clarified by application of the Augustinian conceptions found elsewhere in the mature poetry regarding love of the creatures, the *usurping* "dust." At seventeen he had not thought out "Roses and Lillies speak thee," nor realized that "Worms may chance refuse" even young men.

problem is no more answered by marriage than it was by Petrarch's forgetfulness of self or by Guenevere's causing knightly virtue in Launcelot. When in the *Queste* the virgin Galahad, prototype of Christ, can achieve the Grail, and Launcelot-Adam can barely approach the threshold, the answer involves not virginity as such but that chaste fidelity which impels the questing "knights of Christ" to virginity—though the Cistercian mysticism of the *Queste's* author can see that *fidelity* as sufficiently pure only in this *condition.* Neither in unlustful, nor in virtuous, nor in "natural" love is there a solution to the problem of courtly love.

Herbert does give the problem's answer. It is close to Dante's solution in the *Vita nuova;* there alone, Singleton claims, we find a resolution within the tradition. Dante's is not the solution of a *donna angelicata;* though, for an example, Sidney claims this as a solution in *Astrophel and Stella,* he, like Dante, saw through it early. Dante's solution is the displacement of the courtly God of Love by a Beatrice really *operating* as Caritas—but I may not follow out the Dantean terms for the solution, though Singleton applies with special clarity the distinction I also wish to introduce from Augustine.

What Herbert sees and shows is that tendency in all man's "loves" which is responsible for the really tough problem in courtly love, as in other similar affections of the human spirit: that like much men call love it is not a sin of sensuality primarily but a sin of disorder in love, of idolatry, the inevitably frustrated attempt to deify (two) creatures by a relationship which is only possible if it obtains between the Author of Nature and a piece thereof. A major strength in Herbert's definition of "divinest Love," conscious as he always is of the radical differences between Creator and created, is his evident understanding of the distinction Augustine makes by use of the terms *use* and *fruition.* This is a distinction between the love that "uses" and the love that "enjoys," between the good and lovely things which we pilgrims see on our journey and can not rest in but rather love "as referred to" or "according to" or "in" their yet lovelier author—between these, and God, whom alone we are able to take joy in as the end of our being. The distinction is not, of course, the one we should have in mind if we spoke of God as end and creatures as means; our usual use of such terms (e.g. to "use" one's friends) points to something Augustine calls not "use" at all but "abuse." We "enjoy" the human beings whom we love (*De Trin.* ix. 12) but enjoy them "in the Lord"—a relation to them which a true *love* of Him inevitably includes.

Augustine's inherited Ciceronian terms of *frui* and *uti* were forced, and are even more difficult for us,[25] but we may swiftly exemplify with two images from Herbert a simple form of this difference between man loving God and a creature loving another creature. From *Mattens* (62):

> Teach my *thy love* to know;
> *That* this new light, which now I see,
> May *both* the *work* and workman show:
> *Then by a sunne-beam I will climbe* to thee.

This is not simply the ordinary "see God in his works" and thereupon love and praise Him; the poem attempts the subject of how a man's heart is "wooed" by God through His other creatures. And from *Mans medley* (131):

> Not that he may not here
> Taste of the cheer,
> But as birds drink, and straight lift up their head,
> So he must sip and think
> Of better drink
> He may attain to, after he is dead.
> But as his joyes are double . . .

No explanation of a love of creatures (and being loved by them) "in God" is so clear as the presence of it in great numbers of Herbert's poems; it is impossible to read his statements about the love of God, from Him and to Him, without noting how it made "loved" and valued and indeed lovable to him a whole natural universe, of men and all creatures. This is the difference between

[25] They came to seem unsatisfactory to him, Burnaby says, who calls this the central principle of Augustinian ethics; see above, note 6, and Arendt, pp. 21, 27–28. The basic Augustine reference is *De doct. Christ.*, Book I, but the idea is frequent in the *De Trin.* There is a helpful semantic note in App. A in J. F. Bonnefoy, *Le Saint-Esprit et ses dons selon S. Bonaventure*, Paris, 1929. Singleton's discussion of courtly love is in *An Essay on the Vita Nuova*, Cambridge, Mass., 1949, esp. ch. 3 and the important notes. One of the few theological authors we know Herbert to have possessed was Augustine, and it is obvious from my frequent references that I have found the likenesses striking in the area studied. Beside most such indications of likeness one might have named in the margin three or a half-dozen other poems.

The Flower (165) and any usual sermon-in-a-stone. One is to remember that with human beings it goes both ways; one looks also to be so loved, both as "the work" and the beloved creation of "the workman"; and Herbert looks out upon a universe of creatures of whom we feel him to be one, and in their status as "fellow"-*creatures* takes joy in them, in *relation* to the relationship all share as beloved creatures of God. He applies the distinction to himself as to all creatures, striving to accept his faulty self "as referred to God," accepting pain without making a religion of it, denying no good thing respect and denying no creature love, but learning what kind of love-to-God made a freedom of the only "*service* of Love" which affords freedom. At least this was the purport of his last known utterance on the subject.

His answer is, like Dante's, really a solution, not a retractation. Just as he does not substitute heavenly love for profane love but refers the second to the first, so one must look with unease at any attempt to accommodate his love songs to those of the secular tradition, even (or especially) as substitutes. Not for Herbert the syncretistic accommodations of an earlier age—Ficino's, or Spenser's throughout his poetry; equally not for him either the imitation or the replacement of courtly love's poor praises with similar ones directed heavenward.[26] Of course he would replace lust ("foolish lovers" who "love dung"; 176) with love, and he

[26] In this connection we should call attention to his reshaping of a secular love poem of (?) Lord Pembroke's (also attributed to Donne), which Herbert himself entitled *A Parodie* (183). The verbal relation is very close for one stanza only. I am not satisfied to interpret this *title* as indicating what the poem does not—a wish to substitute sacred for profane love, or some other oblique comment on the less valid secular content of the original. Yet "turning the sense," and therefore, as in our common usage, something to be shown (if not necessarily shown up or mocked) by the turning of it, seems too firmly fixed in the seventeenth-century definition of *parody*, whether English or continental, to be disregarded. With one exception: the use in connection with music, in which a "parody" indicates that the new words have been written to fit an already known tune with other words. The older and strictest musical use (not quite as in *missa parodia*) had been established by a practice hundreds of years old and as familiar to Herbert as to all students of fifteenth- and sixteenth-century sacred music: the use of the *musical* material of a secular chanson or a motet to furnish *musical* material for a mass. I think that both the puzzling title and the relation of imitation to original can be explained, but not here in small space, and shall publish a note elsewhere. [See below, pp. 207–51.] The poem is not, I think, a tacit comment on the folly even of courtly love, though Herbert surely thought *that* "love" a folly.

knows men's fond tendency to worship a fire usurping the heart's temple-of-Love-Incarnate, and to call the fire love. I think he does not scorn the kind of "flame" which men feel in earthly beauty knowing its relation to heavenly beauty, that it is "a flame But borrow'd thence to light us thither" (*The Forerunners;* 176). But men's words—the "Hony of roses," "Lovely enchanting language" used by men who write of lust, of the borrowed light, of love's essential light—these words used of divine love simply mean, like the mystical images,[27] something else. But Herbert makes their necessarily different meaning and their inner change quite clear; as he says, when we lead them from the doors of stews and brothels to other doors, we wash the best phrases we had, and bring them to Church. I have attempted in treating *Jordan ii, Dulnesse,* and "Love bade me welcome" to exemplify this radical difference, when a quite different "love" as theme makes even phrases quite familiar in profane love poems so different a language that the outward similarity ceases to be significant thematically.[28] The phenomenon is familiar in mediaeval literature; one should also emphasize the fact that the history of these

[27] I do not take up the more specialized problem of the relations of courtly love writings to those of the mystics because Herbert largely abstains from the language of the great tradition of mysticism for expressing the love between God and the soul. Gilson's chief arguments in App. IV of *The Mystical Theology of St. Bernard* seem to me incontrovertible, and he properly brushes aside E. Wechssler's thoroughly uncomprehending parallel-passage points showing how both loves are engrossing, transfiguring, require *Askese* (*höfische* or real), and the like (*Das Kulturproblem des Minnesangs,* Halle, 1909). Herbert's distinctions would immediately dry up these false alignments, but neither would he stop long over the traces of similar conceptions of Caritas to be found in far more careful expounders; see even M. Lot-Borodine in *Mélanges . . . offerts à M. Alfred Jeanroy* (Paris, 1928) on similarities of terminology, and on Bernard, or cf. the idea of a unitary conception of love as necessary to explain similarities between Provençal poetry and Christian mysticism, in L. Spitzer, "L'amour lointain de J. Rudel," Univ. of N. C. Stud. in Rom. Lang. and Lit. 5, 1944. Two popular and influential books I have not directly cited, the first especially tinged with these ideas, are D. de Rougemont, *L'amour et l'Occident,* Paris, 1939, and M. C. d'Arcy, *The Mind and Heart of Love,* N. Y., 1947.

[28] Like other writers, L. Martz makes much of the mentioned poems when he speaks of "Herbert's use of the devices and situations of popular love-poetry" (*op. cit.,* p. 186). It seems necessary to speak here of Martz's stress upon "Herbert's *all-pervasive* art of sacred parody" (p. 271), though there is so much helpful commentary on Herbert in his volume that it is misleading to single out this point, vitally connected as it obviously is with the larger question discussed in my last

matters would probably lead one to think of the imitation as going in the other direction, from sacred to secular writings, at the time when the imitations were most common. This is not likely to happen in Elizabethan and seventeenth-century writings, but by that time authors had a long and living tradition to imitate in both kinds, and did so.

Constantly in his poetry Herbert declares also for another language still, "that Hermogenes never dream'd of," though it must be heard through that which men use—"my Master . . . let me

---

few pages. The word *parody* is troublesome, for if by "I use the word in *the neutral sense*" (186 n.) a non-tendentious imitation be meant, this is belied even by Dryden's half-century later definition cited as "an example of *this neutral usage*," for that talks of "Verses patch'd up . . . and turn'd into *another Sence* than their Author intended them," and is far from "neutral" in context (ed. Ker, II, 52). And as we should expect, there creep in with the use of this word considerations of parallel theme, of author's intention to "convert" to a better use, or to point silently to profane parallels, or make some such tacit comment on or use of the *sense* which he has turned. On the other hand, both the word in its familiar archaic sense, and such considerations, seem proper touching the truly parodic Spanish tradition presented in E. M. Wilson's interesting article, "Spanish and English Religious Poetry of the Seventeenth Century" (*Journal of Eccles. Hist.*, ix, 38–53); and enough such writings in English, especially popular writings, may come to light to alter points made here. But, touching the practice of so theologically sophisticated and subtle a poet as Herbert, the assumptions which need to be questioned are: that Herbert too was in truth (Martz, p. 279) "attempting to ultilize the arts of profane love in the service of religious devotion" (he used any useful art he could lay hands upon, including formal arts learned from any kind of *poetry*, but the situations and fundamental poetic subjects "of profane love" being thematically so far from his own deeper ones, the relationship seems in no clear and useful sense parodic); that "the Song of Solomon provided poets with their prime justification" for doing this (but they did not think the Canticles did this, nor do such words fitly describe what occurs in *allegorical reading*); and that Herbert, so motivated, "transformed" devices, as, for example, "the popular love-dialogue of Elizabethan poetry" into the dialogue between Christ and *anima* (pp. 286–87). But Herbert consistently uses language, images, conventions, and subjects which had been those of religious devotion long before Elizabethan love poetry came into being. Hence we must also consider whether things are altered by the fact that the poet himself must have thought that he was (or was also) using the language, imagery, and conventions of the New Testament, the Fathers, theological discourses, and earlier Christian poets, to write about the situations and problems these had treated. The question is more than historically important; assumptions about models direct a reader's grasp of theme. On the other hand, parallels and echoes which illuminate a poet's education in artistic form are as important to notice in secular poems as in religious literature, and here our debt to Martz's careful study is very large.

hold my peace, and doe thou speak thy selfe; for thou *art* Love" (*The Country Parson,* p. 233). This idea in all its multitudinous forms and relations so mastered Herbert's thoughts on the subject that the mentioned language or "Character," that of "Holiness" —which he thought his sermons should show ("he is not witty, or learned, or eloquent, but Holy")—is often the "Character" his poems show, as though he had indeed held his peace while a greater author spoke through him. At the root of this strange success, so far removed from the calculated effects of applied literary theories, there surely lies his long-held conviction that God is the source as well as the object of the only love in which man meets and "enjoys" relationship with the divine, his true "fruition"; sacred poetry, the poetry of Agape, differs fundamentally by virtue of this belief about the uniqueness of its subject. What Herbert would not allow to us moderns is our hope that we may be allowed to make gods either of ourselves or one another. He was chary even of the thought that God Himself could make one of him. Man's attempt to transcend his nature, by love, *within Nature,* was a problem he met and fought too, and it is the root problem of courtly love. That a considerable number of writers within recent years attempt to answer the falsities of courtly love by exalting fertile natural love, the natural principle, as Jean de Meun also did, may have some relation to the fact that thirteenth-century Paris, our own times, and Herbert's were all eras in which to make a religion of naturalism, or to erase the difference, was tempting. Herbert was little attracted to *libertin* thought, and would be as little taken in by this. But there is a related modern desire—for like him and all human beings, we would like well to have it turn out that "love of God" could be the-same-as loving the Good in some adored Beloved, such as ourselves—and this he avoided by a theology of love showing extreme intellectual fineness no less than humility. He would not have accepted our praises. "Praise *God,*" he would have said. Like generations of writers on his themes, he thought he must learn the arts of Heavenly Love from the author of it.

Sacred "Parody" of Love Poetry, and Herbert*

SOME conceptions held by Herbert and his predecessors of the relations between sacred and profane love poetry are the matter at issue in this essay—yet it is particularly directed to the attention of two kinds of special students not likely to be especially interested in that issue. I wish it might be read by those who know unpublished Renaissance music, and those who work with semantics and early dictionaries in various European languages. It is written with the hope that someone else may run across an unfound musical setting, and that someone else may adduce earlier uses of a puzzling word. Its main concern, however, is to present certain materials and ideas of rather broader interest to students of Renaissance poetry.

Herbert gave the title "A Parodie" to a poem addressed to God, beginning:

Souls joy, when thou art gone,
And I alone,
Which cannot be,
Because thou dost abide with me,
And I depend on thee;

Yet when thou dost suppresse
The cheerfulnesse
Of thy abode,
And in my powers not stirre abroad,
But leave me to my load:

O what a damp and shade
Doth me invade! . . .

Prof. William Dinneen of Brown University has given musical assistance to the author, who would like to acknowledge this debt and thank him, without implicating him in the errors or omissions which very probably remain in a field where the writer can claim no special competence. A similar gratitude is due to Miss Nancy Donohue and Dr. F. W. Sternfeld for the helps and suggestions whose incorporation they will recognize.

* Reprinted with permission of the Renaissance Society of America from *Studies in the Renaissance* 8 (1961), 249–90.

He has imitated a secular lyric addressed by one lover to another and early attributed to Donne,[1] as recent editors of both poets have observed. Another attribution, to William, third earl of Pembroke, is that preferred by Grierson, and I shall call the original piece "Pembroke's poem" to save awkward reiteration.[2] It begins:

Soules joy, now I am gone,
And you alone,
(Which cannot be,
Since I must leave my selfe with thee,
And carry thee with me)
Yet when unto our eyes
Absence denyes
Each others sight,
And makes to us a constant night,
When others change to light;
O give no way to griefe,
But let beliefe . . .

But Herbert's title will not bear the meaning which the word *parody* has in seventeenth-century dictionaries of the learned or vernacular tongues, nor does it square with Latin or Greek or English or French usage of the word in literary contexts. These, like our own use of the word, stress the element of mockery, bur-

[1] Herbert's model was printed by Grierson among poems attributed to Donne, in *The Poetical Works* (Oxford, 1912), I, 429, with the heading "*Song.* Probably by the Earl of Pembroke." Herbert's poem begins on p. 183 of F. E. Hutchinson's edition of *The Works* (Oxford, 1941).

[2] Chambers thinks it Donne's. No more than did Hutchinson do I venture a sure attribution, not having access to all relevant data, but Chambers' arguments are not of a kind to convince us unless there is a clear case on other grounds for denying the poem to Pembroke. It is printed as Donne's in editions 1635 through 1669 (see Grierson, II, cxxxv), is not in 1633, but is in the important O'Flaherty MS (see *Divine Poems,* ed. H. Gardner, p. lxxi on the character of *O'F*). Because the Dobell MS at Harvard (Engl. 966.4) was not used by Grierson, nor, I believe, Engl. 966.7 (formerly Norton 4620*), I examined—without finding "Soules joy" in any of them—these and other Harvard manuscripts containing or ascribing poems to Donne: Engl. 626 F* (formerly Phillipps 13187), Engl. 966 (with Coleridge notes), Engl. 966.2 (eighteenth-century copy from *O'F*), as well as Stephens, Carnaby, the newly acquired Gell Commonplace Book, and Engl. 686, a commonplace book formerly Phillipps 9235. The poem's ascription to Pembroke depends upon Lansdowne 777 and on its appearance (labeled "P.") in *Poems* by Pembroke and Sir Benjamin Ruddier, ed. by Donne the younger (London, 1660); it appears without ascription in Stowe 962.

lesque, or at the least some sidelong denigrating comment on the original author's sense; something on the order of Ben Jonson's "a *Parodie!* a *parodie!* . . . to make it absurder then it was" (*Every Man in his Humour*, V.v.26), or on the order of N. Pasquier's "parodier, parodiant" in a violently polemical letter answering a detractor of his father's who had written scurrilously, and scoffing at that user of these words. For an actual dictionary definition, the early English-only dictionaries do not provide us with evidence (see below, note 9). The earliest citation in von Wartburg's *Wörterbuch*[3] of the French substantive, 1614, confirms the meaning of "travestissement burlesque," and when we consult, *faute de mieux*, the later seventeenth-century French dictionaries—Furetiére, Richelet—we find the same elements of "raillerie" or burlesquing of "ouvrages serieux." [4]

Its derivation in modern tongues from Greek παρῳδία, probably by way of Latin *parodia*, is agreed upon in the historical dictionaries. The word in classical Greek apparently kept to the kind of connotations just given (see Liddell and Scott); and in sum the *Oxford Classical Dictionary*'s articles on *Parody: Greek* and *:Latin* seem to cover the matter: exaggeration and incongruity (often through the use of high language for trivial things) are essential elements, and examples show that what we might call a "take-off" is the root idea, whereas exaggeration to bring out "salient features of an individual's style . . . was seldom attempted by the Greeks"; while in Latin usage we find both pastiche ("caricature of manner without adhering to the original words") and parody proper, in which "distortion" of an original with but few verbal changes provides a new sense "often incongruous with the form."

[3] *Französisches etymologisches Wörterbuch* VII (Basel, 1953). The Pasquier use of the verb is given the date *c.* 1580 (cited in von Wartburg, Hatzfeld-Darmsteter, *admis* Academy 1718); I used the 1723 *Oeuvres*, where the passage —in the long *Lett.* x. 5—may be found in col. 1422. In *The Optick Glasse of Humors* (London, 1607), p. 35, T. W. clearly intends a travesty when he prefaces Latin lines on the sad effects of surfeit with "all which in a parode, imitating *Virgil* we may set downe."

[4] Though obviously used in the sixteenth and seventeenth century, the word is not in Cotgrave (1632 or 1673), not in Nicot's *Thresor* (1606), or in Monet's French-Latin *Inventaire* (1636), or in Miège's French-English one (1679), and is not listed in Cayrou's *Français classique*. Incidentally, the Spanish equivalent is not in Covarrubias, 1611 (with add., 1674; ed. Martín de Riquer, Barcelona, 1943).

Not any of these descriptions accurately describe the relation Herbert's poem bears to its original, though he has declared the relation to be that of "A Parodie." Obviously he is not mocking Lord Pembroke's poem in any usual way, nor caricaturing its manner, nor distorting or exaggerating its sense, with a view to the humor or irony of an incongruity we are expected to notice either in his original or in his imitation. To explain the anomaly of the title, Herbert's editor Hutchinson offers Dryden's definition of parody in the "Discourse concerning . . . Satire" in the *Juvenal* (1693). This is repeated by L. L. Martz, when in an extended treatment of "Herbert's art of sacred parody" he adds that the poet's title is an illustration of "this neutral usage" as defined in Dryden.[5] But quite aside from the two-thirds-of-a-century gap in time, an examination of Dryden's context shows that if Herbert were neutral after Dryden's fashion, his so-called neutrality would be what Dryden finds in "songs, which are turned into Burlesque and the serious words of the author perverted into a ridiculous meaning." Herbert scarcely intended such an effect when he so turned Pembroke's phrases that they decorously suit an address to God, and Dryden's other example of Ausonius' joke on the modest Virgil is quite as malapropos. For Dryden's definition and usage are neither one neutral; he is discussing the satyric *silli*, "full of parodies," of scoffing and petulancy and invective. And Herbert is not doing any of the things Dryden describes.[6]

So far as I can discover, in seventeenth-century literary usage, if an imitation of a poem was "parody," it was not neutral. The vital point here is whether or not we can take Herbert's title as proof that he has intended a series of sidewise derogatory comments on the ideas and theme of Pembroke's poem. The answer is

[5] *The Poetry of Meditation* (New Haven, 1954), p. 186n; this is a note to the statement that "Sacred parody of love-poetry plays *an essential part* in much of Herbert's best work"—a preoccupation which points the way to "a fundamental relation" between him and Southwell (my italics).

[6] The extracted and supposedly "neutral" clause is: "Verses patched up from great poets, and turned into another sense than their author intended them" (*Essays*, ed. Ker. II, 52). But this contains the same element which prevents all the other definitions from explaining Herbert's "neutral" use—that the imitator's eye is primarily fixed on the sense and intent of the original author, upon which his imitation *constitutes a comment*. Travesty, which, it is universally agreed, is not present in Herbert, is but the extreme form of this. The issue is whether Herbert's attention is not otherwise engaged.

of some moment, in our whole understanding of Herbert's attitude toward sacred and profane love. Neither do I know (some one else may) *examples* of such subtly covert literary parodying, that is, of imitations neither burlesque nor yet truly innocent, which would furnish evidence of a *practice*—however silent the dictionaries are—that could be responsible for Herbert's title. There are examples in plenty of something close to this: for there is another reason than raillery, or mockery of a style, for writing sacred imitations of secular poems—substitution. Both scholars I have mentioned claim it as part of Herbert's intention. Shoals of poems were written in Europe with this intent, before and just after Herbert. Was he in truth following in the path of "Southwell's campaign to convert the poetry of profane love into poetry of divine love" (Martz, p. 184)? If so, Herbert's use of the word *parody* is no more innocent than would be the case if his poem exhibited the constant mocking parallelism of travesty or burlesque; no attitude toward another man's work is much less neutral than an intention to displace it entirely.

An interest in this displacement of the profane by the sacred has been widely accepted in modern times as a prime motivation for much of Herbert's writing of religious poems, and few are the treatments of him which do not mention the tensions which thence accrue, especially if the poet is thought to be not quite ready, himself, to make the substitution of one love for another. It is not impossible that this is a peculiarly subtle form of the fallacy of attributing a certain character to poems in order that they should suit with an intention which we would find psychologically interesting in their author. Their purport and bent is deduced from an assumed intention, whereas criticism properly uses the latter rather as a hint to try out hypotheses about meanings. We can never know the answers to such questions with certainty, but we can look for evidence. If we look first at the poem in hand, we find that the seemingly tendentious title stands almost alone as proof. (The text of both poems is given at page 239.)

Herbert seems to drop anything we could call a paralleling of ideas concerning profane and divine love after the first stanza or so. Lord Pembroke's poem is a forthright secular love lyric concerning the powerlessness of absence over true love. But Herbert's is not even "a sacred love poem" except insofar as any poem about man's relation to God is a poem about love. There is no indication that he disbelieves what Pembroke says about absence being for mutually true human lovers a wound only sense-deep (whether we read Pembroke as serious or as over-easy); nor is there any comparison between Pembroke's human lovers and God who is by definition always spiritually present (a foolish comparison). He neither says nor implies anything about the validity of Pembroke's different kind of claim; it is simply clear that this statement about absence and mutual human love was a point of departure for his thoughts about the damps and cold which invade him when God's light seems to be eclipsed. He leaves quite behind him the ideas about love, over against which modern interpreters say he intended to set a sacred parody on a parallel theme, to consider instead the treachery with which his sinful lying mind denies the constant abiding presence of God. Editors of course have perceived his departure from his model, but nevertheless both Grierson (II, 267) and Hutchinson (like Martz later) attribute to Herbert the "aim" or "intention" of turning the muse "from profane love verses to sacred purposes," meanwhile commenting that the parody does not extend beyond the opening lines.

This, however, is untrue. There is a parallelism between the two poems extending throughout their length, but it is not conceptual, and I think had little to do—in origin or intention or effect—with "turning" another poet's sense and thus obliquely commenting thereon, or with the intention of substituting good loves for bad by displacing naughty verses.

One kind of *parody* really did include a neutral relation of imitation to original. The first meaning in Hatzfeld-Darmsteter is: "couplets composés sur un air connu"; recurring in the eighteenth-century Academy dictionaries, and familiar from Littré, this common musicological term, in several European languages, for an ancient practice is hard to date precisely. In Apel's article in the *Harvard Dictionary of Music* the term's use, earlier, to denote simply "replacement of text for a known tune" is explicitly distinguished from later musical usage with a necessary connotation of caricature. Herbert may have confused the early practice (*contrafactum*) with parody, as others did; moreover we must remember that the seventeenth century used many musical terms with more flexibility than do modern scholars. The really often-met early musical use is the related one in *missa "parodia"*; the great number of parody masses, and their great beauty, may quite possibly have been known to Herbert. He was a musician of such competence as to elicit contemporary remark even in days when such abilities and tastes were common, certainly among men of his kind of family,[7] education, and pursuits, and his special zeal for ecclesiastical music is common knowledge, as are Walton's references to his composing and his bi-weekly rides into Salisbury to sing after services in a "private Musick-meeting." That cathedral's music and roster of singing-men had its ups and downs, but its not undistinguished annals show us during Herbert's time names like Thomas Lawes, the father of the two brother composers, Francis Sambrooke, and Giles Tomkins of the Cambridge and west-country musical family; and Herbert knew the music both of Cambridge and the court. The longish development of parody masses came to its peak just before Herbert's lifetime; his liturgical sympathies make it the less likely that he was ignorant of them, and their very names, unmistakably references to secular originals, advertise their character; moreover other works show that England did know the parody technique. The older and simpler phenomenon of musical parody mentioned first in this paragraph, was yet more everyday, whatever a gentleman musician of the 1620s called it.

It is properest to think first about this simpler musical kind of parody (whatever the term), the supplanting of a text set to music by fitting the melody to new words. In the edition of Pembroke's and Ruddier's poems wherein the original "Soules joy" is printed, headed "*Song.* P." (i.e. by the Earl of Pembroke), the younger Donne's prefatory remarks "To the Reader" run thus:

> In the collecting of these poemes (which were chiefly preserved by the greatest Masters of Musick, all the Sonnets being set by them) I was fain to send to Mr Henry Laws, who furnishing me with some, directed me for the rest, to send into Germany to Mr Laneere, who by his great skill gave a life and harmony to all that he set.

[7] His brother Edward, Baron Herbert of Cherbury bequeathed his lutes and viols to his daughter-in-law, the sister of the Lady of *Comus;* in 1626 this Mary Egerton married Richard (later second Baron of Cherbury), and their son Edward was Lord Edward's favorite; with her sister Alice she received the dedication of Lawes' handsome 1653 publication. The much-travelled Lord Edward also was interested in the Roman liturgy, as remaining books of his show, and on his personal collection (largely in his hand) of lute music and his compositions (now in the Fitzwilliam), see T. Dart, "Lord Herbert of Cherbury's Lute-book," *Music & Letters,* XXXVIII (1957), 136–48.

Surely it seems very likely that there existed a musical setting for William Herbert's "Soules joy, now I am gone," to which music George Herbert, his cousin, who knew him and frequented his household, composed the new set of religious words in "Souls joy, when thou are gone"—in strict accordance with the musical usage noted above for "a parodie."

I cannot find out exactly when this term came to be applied to this habit. The inclusion of special uses is not to be counted on in early dictionaries, and the absence from them of this sole use showing the "neutrality" which would best explain Herbert's own use does not mean much more than the absence of the word itself from so many of them. As I have pointed out, known occurrences (as in Jonson), literary practice, and gradual dictionary appearance with the "burlesque" meaning show this to have been its *literary* connotation. The commonly known musical treatises in English [8] do not treat the term or the habit, and roughly contemporary English dictionaries (Cooper, Bullokar, Blount, Phillips) are of small use on the whole matter.[9]

IF IT IS HARD to run down the earliest date for use of the *term* "parody," for new words framed to a melody, it is certainly not hard to find hosts of examples. One important point is that as soon as the element of music is involved in the imitation the pleasure becomes far less dependent upon mockery or "showing up."

[8] Treatises of sufficient circulation to find place in musical histories or books on the relations between poetry and music (such as B. Pattison's *Music and Poetry of the Renaissance,* London, 1948; C. Ing's *Elizabethan Lyrics,* London, 1951; M. C. Boyd's *Elizabethan Music and Music Criticism,* Philadelphia, 1940). Grove's *Dictionary of Music* (5th ed., ed. E. Blom) treats only *missa parodia,* but Apel in *The Harvard Dictionary of Music* gives both, implying that the simpler use of the term is earlier. The usual definition cited is from Rousseau (1768). There is considerable information to the purpose in F. W. Sternfeld, *Goethe and Music: a List of Parodies* (N. Y., 1954; also in *Bull. N. Y. Publ. Libr.* LIV, 1950; especially p. 108 on derivation, and numerous examples later seen to be pertinent, e.g. no. 9, no. 52, *et al.*).

[9] The likeliest ones lack the word *parody:* Cooper, 1578 (thus covering Elyot); Cotgrave, 1632 and 1673; Bullokar, 1641; Blount, 1656; Edward Phillips, 1658 (I give the date of the copy consulted, and omit precise titles, which may be found in Starnes and Noyes, *The English Dictionary from Cawdrey to Johnson,* Chapel Hill, 1946). Only late editions of Rider-Holyoke were seen, but in both 1639 and 1640 *parodia* occurs in the Latin list only, defined as "a turning of a verse into another signification by altering of some few words." Yet both *NED* citations and the French dictionaries show the vernacular word to have been in use despite neglect of it by English lexicographers.

Strictly formal imitation pleases. Common sense observes also that sung 'parodies' are less likely to show ironic, refined, or thoughtful oblique commentary on the ideas in an original text than those written to be read. Quite aside from the added formal hurdles to be cleared by an imitator, there is not time for either a singer or his auditors to catch esoteric relationships between two *texts*, only one of which can be present to the ear. The main source of the pleasure and interest lies elsewhere. Indeed one has only to sing successively Marlowe's, Raleigh's, and Donne's words to the tune for "Come live with me and be my love" which Chappell gives,[10] and many of the fastidious comparisons between those much-discussed poems will explode and disappear. The Elizabethan and Jacobean habit of writing vastly different lyrics to be sung to the one air should temper some of our too-meticulous claims about the intended strategies touching the "tone" of this or that poem—unless music has naught to do with mood. And if any persons at Wilton, or a mile and a half away at Bemerton, heard both poems beginning "Souls joy" sung to one setting, it is difficult to believe that their reactions would indeed have had the character of serious responses to a serious attempt to supplant profane loves with divine and turn the devices of secular art to better because more pious uses.[11]

Of course country or language makes no difference when it comes to the musical use; what I hope some one will add to this information is precisely when, in any of the used tongues, this meaning of composing new words to a known air (usually employing a few of the original's phrases) could receive a first citation under the term *parody*. Herbert is not given to coinages. To be sure, the link, or the confusion, is all but made by the commonness of the practice itself plus the used term *missa "parodia."* G. Reese's first citation of the latter *term* is 1587 (*Music in the Renaissance*, N. Y., 1959, p. 202). The indication by frequent inverted commas that I refer to *practices* by the use of *terms* which may have arisen later becomes so awkward that I must beg the reader to observe my reservations on this point and apply them himself as he reads.

[10] *Popular Music of the Olden Time* (London, 1859), I, 215; an earlier tune, printed 1612. In various examples which follow, I do not attempt research into the historical accuracy of matters like "original tune," "first setting," and the like—not my affair here, and not relevant to my points so long as chronological limits and possibilities are regarded.

[11] This is quite simply not what one hears when one listens. There is no reason to disbelieve the claim that Herbert set songs to music of his own composing, and sang them. This habitual exercise puts a different complexion on his probable interest and pleasure in the musician's form of parodying, as well as his skill and interest in what that requires of the writer of song-texts.

That there were such serious attempts is of course questionless. There is a truly huge corpus of "parodies" in the sense we are examining which are not "neutral" imitations of their originals in the way I think Herbert's was of his. There was indeed a time when men systematically transposed great numbers of secular songs into spiritual ones as a deliberate move in a campaign of substitution—but the great flowering time for this phenomenon was the time of Luther and of Marot and of Bourgeois. It may quite well be that with Southwell's "Epistle Dedicatorie" "the aesthetic of the Counter Reformation establishes itself on English soil." [12] But as far as this special element—the diverting of men's minds from profane to sacred poetry by using the former's arts—is concerned, the aesthetic was shared by individuals of a considerably different color of thought, and if such a zeal is to distinguish for us a tradition running from Southwell through Herbert to Vaughan, we shall have to bear with the awkward results of the fact that the tradition and the aesthetic are attached at the farther end to (for example) Coverdale or *The Gude and Godlie Ballatis* and the immediate circles of both Calvin and Luther. An aesthetic which is uncompromisingly "Reformation" before it is "Counter Reformation" is likely to be imputed to Herbert with considerably less ardor. These ideas and the practice of "sacred parody" with substitution as an aim [13] can have been no news to the England of the 1590s, though the ferment and excitement of concerted efforts in this direction had been continental.

It is well known that Luther and his immediate followers took the music for their hymns from wherever they could lay hand upon songs known to the people; since the fairly restricted number of thoroughly familiar melodies for Latin hymns, adaptable for congregational singing, could not take care of the tremendous output of vernacular compositions, they used secular tunes, popular melodies, as well as the modified liturgical chants and extant hymns Latin and German. In countries where Puritanism was to

[12] See Martz, *op. cit.*, pp. 184–85, and following.

[13] It is said by Martz to have "remained central to Herbert's poetry" from the time of his two sonnets written at 17 (Hutchinson, p. 206) until the time he refers to his grey hair in "The Forerunners." I see in the former typically youthful and jejune conceptions of both kinds of love (and both kinds of poetry), which Herbert certainly replaced with profound and humble ideas. I should think he must have turned—much as we do—an eye of mirth upon these fiery and arrogant compositions as he rejected them for his *Temple*.

be strong, and in the history of the Huguenot psalter and its descendants and translations, we encounter as a declared purpose in prefaces the intention of substituting sacred songs for ribald or frivolous ones,[14] stated in terms often resembling Southwell's. Singing was as well recognized a means of spreading the ideas and the renewed devotional fervor of the reformers as was preaching; the virtue of the borrowed secular melodies was that they were well known and singable, and new words framed to them sprang up in a huge and fertile crop. The far from neutral intention—substitution of sacred lyrics for secular—of *such* "parodies" is directly attached to the governing purpose of the men who wrote them: the reforming of a faith. A similar intention has much to do with the later efflorescence of a similar practice among authors of the Counter Reformation. This is shared by a Southwell, but only very little if at all by a Herbert. In case we are determined to find such substitution so important to his poetry, I suppose that we might conceivably attribute to him a general aim touching the improvement of men's moral sensibilities, but Herbert was not concerned to remake the faith of Anglicans. His own attachment to that communion was serene. Convinced "sacred parodists" anxious about the substitution of the sacred, to the best of my knowledge, have either such reformers' aims or else the narrowly moral fervor of puritanical piety, Catholic or Protestant. Herbert's religious verse smacks of neither.

It is not that the reformers had gone about to do any new thing; musically, the procedure had been common practice for

[14] The tunes meanwhile being flatly taken over from the frivolous songs; see O. Douen, *Clément Marot et le psautier huguenot* (Paris, 1878), II, 363 for, e.g., Calvin's preface to Marot's psalter (1543 preface in English in Oliver Strunk, *Source Readings in Music History*, N. Y., 1950, pp. 345–48). The emphasis is less usual in Lutheran materials. Coverdale, in his *Goostly Psalmes and Spirituall Songes*, says to his book: "Geve them occasyon" to "thrust under the borde | All other ballettes of fylthynes," and to the Christian reader: "would God our minstrels" had nothing else to play and our ploughmen nothing to whistle "save psalms, hymns, and godly songs" like David's; he adds a sharp reference to women who as they spin can sing nothing but *hey nony nony*, *hey troly loly*, and more in like vein (*Remains*, Cambridge, 1846, Parker Soc., XIV, pp. 534, 537). On the other hand, it is obvious that such motives did not dictate publication of all the "pieuses alouettes" and "rossignols spirituels," using *airs mondains*, which became popular (see Douen, I, 689). The mere practice of "parody" does not tell us an author's motive.

some centuries. What they did was to use a musical practice to fulfill intentions they had as religious leaders; the intention does not inhere in the practice and we cannot use the latter to support guesses about Herbert's intentions. The writers of mediaeval *contrafacta* and the numerous composers who had built sacred motets for liturgical use on secular *chanson* themes did not intend either to kill the *chansons* or wake the people to a "Reformation." It seems to me just as difficult to believe that Herbert wished oblivion to overtake Lord Pembroke's innocent small song, and although to be sure he grieved over the way men willfully allow their worldly loves to usurp all place in hearts that should turn even through those to the source of all love, it is a grief he shares with all serious Christian thinkers. This is not to be cured by a substitution; the Country Parson would perhaps have spoken rather of putting on Christ. It is a different thing from cutting out secular songs, or human love. Those who are ready to whip human love out of the heart are commonly very sensitive to the idea of an ineradicable incongruity between earthly and heavenly loves. We must ask for a considerable body of evidence before we attribute this, either, to Herbert.

When it comes to the presence or absence of self-consciousness or tension concerning the use of secular models, the "spiritualizing" of secular songs during the mid- and later 1500s shows an especial likeness to the mediaeval practice of *contrafactum* which preceded it; the likeness is shared by the already prominent somewhat different technique of the *missa parodia*. For in them all it is apparent that the *musical* part of the imitation was truly felt as neutral. The term *contrafactum* refers to a vocal composition framed to a new text which is substituted for the old one, and although the setting of a new sacred text to existing secular melodies is common, the replacement can go either way, trouvère *chansons* being fashioned for example upon liturgical plainsong melodies.[15] Neither in this mediaeval conversion of secular music to religious use, nor in the closely similar widespread sixteenth-

[15] See G. Reese, *Music in the Middle Ages* (N. Y., 1940), p. 218, one example, the drinking song set to the Christmas sequence *Laetabundus;* note also his point on p. 219 concerning the importance, to interpretation, of knowing both music and words, and cf. below pp. 234–35. But the volume of "spiritual" parodies is truly vast; K. Hennig (*Die geistliche Kontrafaktur im Jrh. der Reformation*, Halle, 1909) calls the sixteenth century the *Blütezeit* for the writing of sacred songs on secular models (using both words and tune), throughout Germany, and not only by the reformers. Since his extremely long list of analyzed

century practice which provided the large literature of Protestant hymns and influenced the psalmody of Huguenot countries and others, nor in the *cantus firmus* mass which resembles *contrafactum* (in that a monodic borrowing, often from a secular *chanson*, provides the tenor) do we find any nervous indication that incongruousness was felt between *the known* secular provenance and the new religious use. The singers knew both uses, and listeners are very generally expected to recognize the secular originals; their attached names usually serve as identifying titles, or as indications of what tune to sing to, where songs are printed without music. And in *cantus firmus* masses and motets portions of older secular text show how the musical structure was contrived and were evidently sung by some of the voices. Like florid descant, this confusion of texts (*of two sacred texts as well*) was felt to be an evil, and both were censured at various times during the fourteenth and fifteenth centuries; Pope John's famous bull is primarily concerned with purely musical decorum, but confusion of texts was prohibited at the Council of Trent, in 1562.[16]

Sir Richard Terry's claim that "in the sixteenth century the sharp line of demarcation between 'sacred' and 'secular' music did not exist" [17] could well be pondered when we consider the interchanges and borrowings of other similar "arts" and "devices"

---

pairs of examples frequently quotes stanzas of text from each, it is especially easy to find corroboration of points I make later with English materials (especially that touching the transformation of images, p. 223).

[16] On these matters of double texts and simultaneous singing see G. Reese, *Music in the Middle Ages,* p. 315 (that motets incorporating bits of original secular motet-words were probably not intended for church services); p. 357 (Pope John's bull, 1324/1325, virtually banning polyphony, but in abeyance before very long; translated in *Oxford History of Music,* 1920, I, 294–96). See very many references in G. Reese, *Music in the Renaissance* (N. Y., 1959), especially, p. 55, the motet-chanson as written by Dufay (secular French text for two upper voices and Latin text for lowest part); p. 89, *incipits* of a rondeau by Binchois that survives with both a secular and a sacred text; and *passim.* For the canon of 1562 see pp. 448–49; it is important to have a clear idea of the kind of musical excesses which provoked it.

[17] In his edition of *Calvin's First Psalter* [1539] (London, 1932), p. vii; he recalls the popularity in Francis I's court of Marot's psalms set to popular airs, the Huguenot adaptation of known tunes, and the use of Lutheran chorales, of which some of the best were "originally secular songs," reminding us that equally "the 'popish' origin of a tune" was no obstacle to its use. There are comments in H. C. MacDougall, *Early New England Psalmody* (Brattleboro, Vt., 1940), p. 17, and some corrections of Terry's edition in W. S. Pratt, *Music of the French Psalter of 1562* (N. Y., 1939), p. 15n.

and techniques—those rhetorical arts which govern the musical management of verse whether it is secular or religious. The sense of sharp demarcation may belong more, as it does in the musical historians, to the nineteenth century than it does to the sixteenth and seventeenth.[18] Clearly we cannot apply our common notions about felt incongruities between profane and religious "worlds" to times when even a Beza himself expected men to sing his translation of the canticle "Voici que dit David" to an air he chose and set, "De retourner mon ami je te prie"; when the 1540 Flemish psalter directed men to sing Psalm xxvi to the tune of "Ick weet een vrouken amoreus," or the Antwerp psalter of 1541 set Psalm cviii to "Faulte d'argent c'est douleur non pareille"; when it was entirely in line with long-followed practice to fit a "Kyrie eleison" to the initial portion of the madrigal "Reviens vers moi," or to sing Luther's "Nun freut euch lieben Christen g'mein" to the secular tune he chose for it.[19] Nor should we attribute to insensi-

[18] Douen, for example, though his massive volumes are a basic piece of research, has both a musical prejudice common at his date ("ce deplorable tonalité gregorienne," II, 364) and a pronounced Protestant bias; he is anxious to claim that the Huguenot psalter introduced no secular melodies "telles quelles" into its pages, and to answer contemporary and later accusations concerning its lax and effeminate "Ionic" and "Lydian" airs, but he likes at one and the same time to score contemporaries who set German and Flemish and French *Catholic* spiritual songs to secular tunes, and he is very considerably shocked by some kinds of mediaeval Catholic *contrafactum* and parody masses. See both ch. 22 of I and ch. 24 of II.

[19] The Kyrie is Philippe de Monte's, the Beza example is taken from Douen (I, 664–68, 680), where examples abound throughout I, ch. 22 and II, ch. 24. The former chapter gives 30 of the first lines of secular tunes, one per psalm, singled out for use by the 1540 Flemish psalter, and they range from "J'avais fait choix d'un amant" (for Psalm xii) to "J'ai perdu la tête" (for Psalm xx; see pp. 682–83); cf. also other examples from the Antwerp psalter of 1541 (p. 712). Secular songs of Marot's own were reused (e.g. for Psalm ciii; see p. 687). Some of the examples most amusing to us with our own more rigid post-nineteenth-century ideas of decorum in religious music come from E. de Beaulieu's volume, *Chrestienne reiouissance,* 1546—paternoster set to "Les Bourguignons ont mis le camp," or the doubtful ingenuity of continuing a love song "Puisqu' en amours a si beau passe-temps" by adding the clause ". . . je veuil amer Dieu" (Douen, I, 704f, 708ff). A revealing example is the *quattrocento* Zachara da Teramo's conversion of his own macaronic *ballata* "enthusiastically" addressed to Pluto into a credo (Reese, *Renaissance,* p. 33). For references to the sources of information on Luther's chorale see the treatments of it indexed in H. Glahn, *Melodistudier til den Lutherske Salmesangs Historie fra 1524 til 1600* (Copenhagen, 1954), especially no. 58, p. 152, and no. 70, p. 181 (in the section "Verdsligt Melo-

tivity such absence of strain, touching the mediaeval religious use of formal arts or elements familiar in secular contexts, or touching the Protestant reformers' use of familiar music without hesitating at connotations either worldly or popish. A likelier explanation would be the sensible assumption by most of these men that formal elements in an art do not have a Protestant or a Catholic soul, a profane or a sacred "nature" except as their *formal* character provides tangible distinctions; and one would incline to the judgment that Herbert's or other poets' uses of rhythms, devices, and rhyme-groups with a largely secular history show a similar understanding of decorum. One halts before a godly stanza-pattern, or an unchaste feminine rhyme, as before a Christian vowel-quantity, or a Mahometan alliteration. As well say—as some one did—all that pale mauve is un-American.

Certainly the English and Scottish "parodies" of the sixteenth century show very little sense that formal borrowings would bring their secular flavor with them, to provide a secret ambiguity in men's responses. To our unaccustomed minds the "incongruities" arising from such imitation do often seem more like camels than gnats; yet, had they been strained at, the whole purpose of the reforming "sacred parodists" would have been set at nought. It is not possible to call in question the singlemindedness with which men were able to accept the spiritual songs in, for example, the *Gude and Godlie Ballatis.* This much reprinted book, though it contains translations of psalms and canticles, is not a collection of hymns used in services, rather of sung religious lyrics. Yet the historian of the Scottish psalter calls it "a book which, next to the Bible itself, did more than any other to further in Scotland the Reformation cause."[20] These are sung, not read, lyrics, though

distof"); this advantageously recent study is helpful because citations and corrections of earlier work on the various tunes are full and convenient, and melodies with variants are transcribed in part II.

[20] M. Patrick, *Four Centuries of Scottish Psalmody* (London, 1949), p. 5. Of the book commonly known as *Gude and Godlie Ballatis* (here abbreviated *GGB*) I use the Scottish Text Soc. edition of the 1567 ed., *A Compendious Book of Godly and Spiritual Songs,* ed. A. F. Mitchell, with copious notes and appendices (Edinburgh and London, 1897). In the examples which follow I deliberately keep to a few volumes—Chappell, the *GGB,* Rollins' editions of miscellanies—even though the nineteenth-century editors write without benefit of much information found since, and the character of tunes is sometimes belied in early reprintings. I attempt thus to make it convenient for readers to look at long

no music is printed, the secular tune being simply cited. Hence, a singer who knew what tune to use for the spiritual song I quote below did know the secular song at the left. Thence, for example, it was present to the mind (if not at the instant of singing) that the melodic phrase for I-the-pined-lover-of-my-lady now fits itself to Christ-the-pined-lover-of-mankind, and evidently this fact did not carry with it the sense that earthly and heavenly lover could both be suggested, with the disturbances of tone and temper that would result.

Into a mirthfull May morning
As Phebus up did spring
I saw a May both fair and gay,
Most goodly for to see!
I said to her be kind
To me that was so pyn'd
For your love truly.
(*GGB*, p. 270)

In till ane myrthfull Maij morning,
Quhen Phebus did vp spring:
Walkand* I lay, in ane garding gay,
Thinkand on Christ sa fre:
Quhilk meiklie for mankynde,
Tholit to be pynde,
On Croce Cruellie. La. La.
(*GGB*, p. 137; *variant "Waking")

Without the least attempt at disguise of provenance, men were expected to (and hundreds did) sing "Grievous is my sorrow," a long lyric of the kind called Christ's Complaint to Man, to the music of a song which Ritson reprints as "The Dying Maiden's Complaint." Hers too begins

Grevus ys my sorowe,
Both evyne and moro,
Unto myselffe alone,
Thus do I make my mowne, . . .

—but with the last clause we change to "Thus *Christ* makis . . ."

. . . Thus Christ makis his mone,
Saying, Vnkyndnes hes killit me,
And put me to this paine:
Allace! quhat remedie,
For I wald nocht refraine.
(*GGB*, p. 151)

. . . Thus do I make my mowne,
That unkyndnes haith kyllyd me,
And putt me to this peyne,
Alas! what remedy
That I cannot refreyne!
(Ritson, *Ancient Songs & Ballads*, ed. Hazlitt, p. 171)

texts, and at portions of secular originals, or to test out the music—for points about incongruity and the like may not be accepted on the basis of a stanza or two. More up-to-date examples would not affect my points, and unless recent information and research would so do it is not cited. Music for the example next following ("Into a mirthful . . .") is found in Forbes' *Cantus* (2d ed., 1666, sig. A2); only the secular words appear.

The secular song as an ultimate source for the theme and characteristic structure of such a religious poem is out of the question; this is not strictly a *populе meus* poem, but the details of the "unkyndnesse" suffered during Christ's life and Passion contrasted with the "Kyndnesse" of the Atonement, are usual in this small poetic kind.[21] Nevertheless, to those who knew both well enough to sing both, the identity of commencement, refrain, and melody could conceivably be constant reminders that the author seemed, at least, to be simply translating a profane into a heavenly love; moreover, images using the same terms occupy the same musical place (the heart, the tomb, the bequeathing) and frequently show an identical series of rhymes. The types of rhetorical formal relation are very like those which attach Herbert's poem to Pembroke's, though closer and more frequent. But nothing in Herbert's imitation shows the interesting effect below:

(the maiden's complaint)	(Christ speaks)
O harte I the bequyeth	Go, hart, I the bequyeth
To hyme that is my deth,	To hir that was my deith,
Yff that no harte haith he	Mannis Saule is scho [she] trewlie,
My harte his schal be;	My hart hir hart sall be,
Thought unkyndnes haith kylled me,	Thocht scho maist unkyndlie slew me,
And putt me to this payne,	And put me to greit paine:
Yett, yf my body dye,	ȝit thair is na remedie,
My hertt cannott refrayne.	My hart will nocht refraine.

Despite precise verbal imitation, these are not the same image at all. The prior existence of the traditional spouse image allowed the adaptation, but the sense in which Christ's bequeathed heart "*hir* hart sall be" quite alters the function and nature of the figure, and the same thing happens because of the special theological meanings of "unkindness" (in a special way un-natural and in-grate), as the changes are rung on this in the fifth line of each stanza. The same real transformation, not imitation, of *meaning*

[21] See the present author's *A Reading of George Herbert*, part I, especially pp. 32ff. The tomb image is probably immediate imitation of thought as well as form, whereas the motifs of "if there be any sorrow like unto my sorrow," of "love bought dear," and the testament image, show the kinship with Good Friday complaints. It is quite possible that the secular complaint, composed late, had imitated some other religious poem of this special small "kind," for the refrain fits best the familiar attitude of Christ in the religious *planctus*.

occurs in the changing relevance of the refrain—both melody and words meanwhile providing a strict formal identity. This phenomenon furnishes us with the reason why "incongruities" were not felt as such, for they are apparent, not real. The question of congruity does not arise where subjects are not parallel but, simply, different.

This is also the reason why it is superficial to speak as if parodic imitation in which the secular is converted to the sacred *of itself* brings in a baroque tension or ironic dissonance between two "worlds." Form can straddle two worlds without tension; it is conceptual identifications (within images, for example) which bring in the likelihood of ambiguous doubleness, and our tools for detecting such identifications in users' minds (let alone readers' minds) are very blunt. If we met, in a poet whose date led us to expect such complications, the use of an *aubade*, tune and all, for a religious "parody," voices would not be wanting to call attention to the witty doublenesses surely intended by one who would use the situation enclosed in that particular small form for a sacred lyric.

The thissel-cok cryis
On louers vha lyis,
Nou skaillis the skyis:
The nicht is neir gone.

As the parody below advances beyond the initial identical lines, we see that when in it Christ has become the cock announcing "dawn," then that dawn takes on a meaning which totally ousts the usual *aubade* situation. The warning voice of a cock in an *aubade* wakens lovers so that the idyl need not come to a violent end but may continue when jealous day in its turn is near gone. But Christ has not become *that* cock, and *night* has turned into a *figure*, making an "identical" line an utterly dissimilar line:

Hay! nou the day dauis;	Hay now the day dallis,
The jolie Cok crauis;	Now Christ on vs callis,
Nou shroudis the shauis,	Now welth on our wallis
Throu Natur anone.	Apperis anone:
The thissel-cok cryis . . .	Now the Word of God Regnes: . . .
The nicht is neir gone.	The nycht is neir gone.
(*GGB*, p. 289) [22]	(*GGB*, p. 192)

[22] In the notes on p. 289 the editor dates early references, though the secular text quoted is late and there is much controversy about the tune. My points

This parody could, but does not, pull over some of the original point of the warning voice which wakens lovers in the *aubade;* it could, but does not, thereby introduce baroque dubieties, as though the author were implying some sorriness that the "night" (here, of ignorance, often of sensual love) was brought to a conclusion by Christ's "reign." I am not sure how a later religious poet with a different type of sensibility would manage to convey the notion that he was not quite ready to be so delighted that his night of natural sensuality was brought to an end by Christ's wakening cry. But I am sure that such ambiguities, in baroque poets either, should not be claimed on verbal identity alone, but depend on their retaining, provably, some of the original's *reason for using* the images of cock and night. In our instance, those images have been displaced; the new cock, and the night whose going is unequivocally welcomed (as "Christis flock singis" what they are taught by the "Word" of God who is "King of all Kingis") are new images.[23]

They happen also, of course, to be very old ones. The ancient Christian symbolism of Christ as cock, thence priest or preacher as cock, perhaps started this poem (it is a criticism of clerics) on its way; but it is not very important to it. Only so much of a symbol is "in" a poem, even a poor one, as can be seen to serve some end there. A different situation appears in another song related to the *aubade* form, one of the "spiritualizations" written to the prodigiously popular sixteenth-century tune of "The hunt is up." The symbolic figure of Christ the king-huntsman, and the resulting figures playing on *his deer—his dear,* are sustained through eighteen stanzas. They tell of God's creation and enclosure of his grounds, of how the deceiver caused God's chosen Dear to leap the pale, how He

hold no matter what variants of the conventional mediaeval *aubade* images came directly under the eye of the parodist.

[23] I would attach a warning against the idea that what is here noted is "same *form,* different *content.*" The entrance of figurative meaning is equally a formal element, and both have altered. What we have yet to devise is ways of distinguishing the differing kinds of contributions made, by formal elements which differ within their sameness, to meaning. We shall thereby arrive at firmer notions of what constitutes *evidence* for claims made on the basis of the true general statement, "Form is a component of meaning." I would anticipate that the best route to this is careful historical study of poems, for it is only too easy to claim that some component we hope is there is "in the form."

. . . sent his owne soone,
Who strongly begoon
To hunt both hill and playne;
No one kynd of payne
But he dyd systayne,
To wyn his deare agayn.

And of how He then enclosed a "park," and taught twelve "To blow so just a note" as brings all deer within it; and the poem ends with injunctions to keepers, and promises to those who will "be his deere for ever." There were many sets of secular words, so familiar that I quote none, and similarly this is only one of the "moralizations" written to the tune.[24] Indeed, "a hunt's-up" became a substantive, and what witty ambiguities might we not introduce into the godly parody when we learn from Cotgrave's Renaissance dictionary that the synonym for French *resveil,* a morning song *for a new-married wife,* is "a hunt's-up"? But for the fact that there is no evidence that it was intended, this connotation could provide an intersting shock in the final use of that anima-spouse image which of course is present throughout:[25]

The hunt is up,
The hunt is up,
Loe! it is allmost daye.
For Chryst our kyng
Is cum a huntyng,
And browght his deare to staye.

It seems worth while to remind ourselves frequently that "music is at the bottom of it," in this establishment of a widespread habit of "sacred parody"—widespread long before we can expect, or find, anything at all close to a baroque sensibility demonstrated in the parodic relation between secular and sacred texts. To be sure, plenty of music of this same period has the habit of pointing secretly at some hidden doubleness of meaning,[26] but its

[24] See Chappell, I, 60–62, and another appears in *GGB,* p. 174, notes on p. 283. John Thorne's text which I have described was printed by Halliwell, *The Moral Play of Wit and Science* (1848, *Shakespeare Soc.,* II).

[25] The provision of such an interesting shock often seemed the chief reason for some of the interpretations offered during that decade or so when the Elizabethans were permitted to have no word which simply meant "die: to expire."

[26] I refer of course to the extreme form of musical double meaning in which abstractions, veritable concepts, are suggested by truly musical means—the riddles

characteristics are not shared either by that which arose from the quite usual mediaeval practice of *contrafactum* or that which we trace during the sixteenth-century wave of borrowing tunes for sacred songs. But for the still-maintained ancient tie between lyric poem and music, we might have had very little of the phenomenon of parody, so far as the English poetic scene exhibits it; its far greater seventeenth-century strength in some other countries may support very different conclusions from those I have stressed.

One point should be recalled: that early "popular music" had a character so different from that of popular music as we have been accustomed to it since the eighteenth century, and was formally so much more truly suitable to sacred themes and moods, that nothing but singing two texts to a melody shows how natural the interchange was. Luther's "Nun freut euch," like other chorales less universally recognized as popular tunes, takes and has kept its place in the most dignified of all hymnologies with no sense of alienness; it was one of those Coverdale reproduced with the music, and translated, in his attempt to introduce into England words and music from the Wittenberg and other chorale books from 1524 onward.[27] England shared least in this enrichment of eccle-

---

and hidden references apparent to a coterie of highly trained musicians. But even the two simpler forms of musical translation of texts—word-painting, and the suiting of pattern to mood—could not have been much attended to by composer, singer, or listener in the really popular borrowings. Only in case we find Pembroke-Herbert music can we examine the possibility of a composer's intended relations to Pembroke's text (of any of these three kinds familiar to musicians), and it would still be difficult to prove that Herbert ironically made capital thereof, *and was so heard.* But I am interested to demonstrate the existence of an interchange between secular and sacred sung texts so habitual and so unselfconscious that we should need just such proof before we should have a right to conclude that Herbert's own imitation of secular lyrics was ambiguously significant. Yet this conclusion is taken for granted in Herbert criticism, and is what makes critics of the whole period think of "sacred parody" as baroque. On the possibly different situation in other literatures, see E. M. Wilson's article in *Jour. of Ecclesiastical Hist.*, IX (1958), 38–53, "Spanish and English Religious Poetry of the Seventeenth Century."

[27] His *Goostly psalmes & spirituall songes, c.* 1543 (STC 5892) was ordered burnt in 1546; see *English Music*, Bodleian exhibit of 1955. For a musical transcription and an examination of the unique copy at Queen's College, Oxford, I owe thanks to my friend James Dalton, fellow of Queen's; "Be glad now all ye Christen men" occurs at ff. 13^{v}–15^{v} (sigg. Di^{v}–iii^{v}). Words are given at p. 534 of *Remains of Myles Coverdale*, ed. G. Pearson (1846, Parker Soc., XIV). See n. 19 above; in Thomissøn's *Den danske Psalmebog* (ed. of 1569) "Nu fryder

siastical music through deliberate borrowing; even Protestant France, though less eminent and less alive musically, benefitted more, through the Huguenot psalter of 1562 and its predecessors for which Bourgeois found and arranged so many magnificent settings for Marot's vernacular metrical psalms. One may sing through the whole without noting flaws in decorum attributable to provenance, and usually only the asterisk affixed by an editor would apprise one of secular origin. Wynkyn de Worde printed in 1530 this sacred song with its music:

> And I mankynd haue not in mynd
> My loue that mornyth for me for me.
> Who is my loue but god aboue
> That born was of Mary . . .
> That king of blys my loue he ys
> That mor*n*th so sor for me.

The melody is almost certainly from a secular song of which these words are a parody, but it is entirely suitable to its present text.

Only occasionally can one pass off the practice as a revivalist device—suitable to naïve singers, musical stuff for Flemish weavers. This does seem to me to fit the remaking of the famous song "Who is at my window, Who? Who?" The tune had an interesting history of instrumental settings. Chappell's text of the sung tune is rather a jingle, *formally* suitable instead to its original secular words, and we need not ask ourselves seriously why those who enjoyed singing such a parody felt no formal incongruity as they went through the long dialogue-song. "Ane wratcheit mortall" sings verses which end "Se Quho is at thy windo, quho," and his "Lord Celestiall" sings those which end "Go from my windo, go" (the refrain later shifts to a series of changes rung on "In at Thy door let me go" [". . . at My door thou shalt go"]). The conception of the deity's nature is as relaxed as the tune, but apparently nothing very early remains [28] to give us an actual sec-

---

eder" appears on f. 51ᵛ (Glahn's index no. 109, p. 225; see also no. 58, p. 152). For the Wynkyn de Worde song mentioned in this paragraph see a page of music reproduced in App. III of *GGB*, and the sacred text given at p. 271 (compare that on p. 140 from the 1567 *GGB*); the British Museum copy is K.1.e.1, where the song begins on sig. Hiᵛ and is attributed to John Gwynneth at the end on H4ᵛ.

[28] I have not thought it worth while to search beyond the reprinted "godly ballad" in *GGB*, p. 132, and Chappell, I, 140–42; but for Richard Allison's set-

ular text for comparison save other "real" parodies (take-offs) in various snatches in plays. In the main however, there is singularly little in this whole sixteenth-century exchanging of melodies that encourages us to check up the entire affair to the same account as "*OH* come, *to* the church in the wildwood | *THE* lit-tle brown church in the vale." Even for "Who is at thy window," as also for the pious text to the tune of "John come kiss me now" (*GGB*, p. 158, and Chappell, I, 147), we should doubtless remind ourselves that this Scottish collection was a book of songs for household hearths and for jogging about, not for church and service.

For many sacred parodies we have only the names of original secular texts which served to identify the tunes—evidence of the practice but of no use for judging of relations. Or we have the numerous references to "a moralization of" this or that, entered in the Stationers' register, references such as are scattered through the pages of Chappell and which attest to the habit of "spiritualizing" secular songs whose texts we possess, but which can tell us nothing of the nature of the imitations. On the other hand, the long text of the extremely well known "Nut Brown Maid" can be compared stanza after stanza with the parody in which it becomes a dialogue between Mary and Christ the "banished man" (*c.* 1520: printed by E. F. Rimbault, *Ancient Poetical Tracts,* 1842, Percy Soc., VI, pp. 33ff; chiefly alike in rhyme-words preserved).

In stressing religious-from-secular borrowings only, for their obvious pertinence to our special questions, I have introduced a division into categories which does not stand out so sharply during the periods concerned. It is also pertinent to recall the large amount of parody in which a secular text replaced another secular text, since we are interested in gauging the extent to which melodies were felt to be a divisible formal element, not inescapably tied to one kind of meaning or another. This should shed light on the extent to which certain other formal devices were similarly re-

---

ting with elaborate variations see Sydney Beck, *The First Book of Consort Lessons* (N. Y., 1959), no. 12, and Reese, *Renaissance*, pp. 874–75 and index. But if we wish to sing it, the godly words are scarcely to be preferred to those well known ones in the *Knight of the Burning Pestle* III.v: "Go from my window, love go: | Go from my window my dear, | The wind and the rain will drive you back again, | You cannot be lodged here. | . . . Begon, begon my juggy, my puggy, begon my love my dear. | The weather is warm, 'twill do thee no harm, thou canst not be lodged here."

garded. Recalling that parody involves deliberate modeling (though of course singers as well as authors can be parodists), one still has only to leaf through the row of Elizabethan miscellanies for examples; in *A Gorgeous Gallery* (1578): "The Lover wounded with his Ladies beauty craveth mercy. To the Tune of where is the life that late I led," i.e. "If pitty once may mooue thy hart" (p. 39); [29] or "Not light of loue lady" (p. 38), "To the Tune of Attend thee go play thee"; or "Passe forth in doulfull dumpes my verse" (p. 31), "To the tune, when Cupid scaled first the Fort"; or "The glyttering showes of *Floras* dames" (p. 26), to the famous tune of "lusty Gallant." Singing it to that tune (in Ward, pp. 176, 170), one may enjoy the exercise of seeking any comparable element which made the tune seem suitable also to "Fain would I have a pretie thing, to giue vnto my Ladie," in *A Handful of Pleasant Delights* (1584), p. 57. One may also try to imagine how a "moralization" can possibly have gone onward following the first line we have from its 1566/1567 entering, "Fayne wolde I have a *godly* thynge to shewe unto my ladye," and how it can have used the engaging part of the tune that goes with this part of the song in the *Handful:*

> I name no thing, nor I meane no thing,
> But as pretie a thing as may bee.

But these citations could go on for pages, showing us how usual a thing was "parody" (whether called by that term or not) in the first and simpler musical sense which we set out to examine.

Much more could be presented. My object has been simply to indicate the existence and extent of a practice which descended to seventeenth-century "parodists" without break, a long history of formal imitation and exchange, unselfconscious and ordinary, provocative neither of ambiguities nor ironies. This long development has to be taken into consideration when we wish to determine *what* precisely allows us to think of seventeenth-century reli-

[29] On the ballad and tune "Where is the life . . ." see *A Handful of Pleasant Delights*, p. 88. For all these miscellanies I have used Hyder Rollins' editions, with his helpful notes and cross references. On the third example, from p. 31, see *Tottell's Miscellany*, II, 283; a "moralization" of the latter printed by J. P. Collier (*Old Ballads from Early Printed Copies*, 1840, Percy Soc., I, p. 29) treats of the fight against the papists for "God's Fort." John Ward treats the "Music for *A Handefull of Pleasant Delites*" in *Jour. of the Amer. Musicological Soc.*, X (1957), 151–80; on "Lusty Gallant" and "Fain would I have . . ." see pp. 169, 176—cf. Chappell, I, 92; 16 of the tunes are now recoverable (p. 155).

gious uses of secular formal elements as something characteristically baroque, something related to the marriage of two incompatible worlds, with all the unresolved tensions, the ambiguities and oblique double intentions which thence accrue. If it be the presence of ironic dissonances that allows this categorizing, our readiness to find these must depend on something other than the mere practice of "spiritual parody" itself, for scores of examples of the spiritualizing of secular poetry are not baroque at all in this respect or others. The practice alone of "spiritual parody" is fairly generally accepted as a criterion for such categorizing, but the category itself breaks down if we include what the criterion would admit.

Touching Herbert in particular, these details of literary history are evidence for the fact that even if numerous forms of converting the secular were more important in his poetry than they are, this would not declare to us the nature of his motives or the kind of attitude he took toward secular arts and profane love. It would be no more legitimate, and no service to him, to substitute—for an alignment with a Counter Reformation Southwell on grounds of shared aesthetic—an alignment with the Coverdales and Wedderburns and Sternholds whose motives were more typically puritan. We must look elsewhere than to his "sacred" use of the formal arts and devices of profane love poems for evidence that he condemned their subject. He had many predecessors in the practice who also shared these reformers' habit of borrowing without sharing their puritan or pietistic reasons for doing it. Surely it somehow lessens Herbert as a poet to conceive of him as nervously and tensely anxious to convert whatever hinted at the power and interest of love between human beings to pious uses. If this be true, it has very real connections with his theology, particularly with his conception of the definition of the love of God, the center of a Christian life as of a Christian theology. Such interpretations do not seem to me to square with the rest of his poetry, nor with his notably sane and balanced understanding of the close relation between heavenly love and all the many kinds of human love which he dealt with, knew, and apparently wove into a life distinguished for its practice of loving-kindness.[30]

[30] For more careful examination of such relations and definitions with evidence from the poems, see the present writer's "George Herbert and *Caritas*," *Jour. of the Warburg and Courtauld Inst.*, XXII (1959), 303–31. [See pp. 167–206 above.]

Yet once at least he indubitably did remake an extant secular poem into a sacred one, and his title "A Parodie" constitutes *his* definition of what he has done. But instead of assuming, from his act, a campaigner's intention, should we not rather follow his title's suggestion and relate the poem to the history, including the musical history, of such remakings? They were *formal* imitations; they were not ways of declaring a position through oblique commentary upon another text whose different *concepts* were thus derogated, or whose concepts were the source of hidden ambiguities because these were felt to be still present in the borrowed *form.* Where reformers used parody for their special intentions, it is abundantly clear that the formal elements borrowed are not the carrier for these. However, though one may be convinced that Lord Pembroke's *Song* was sung, and that Herbert followed a musical convention of some centuries' standing in writing a "parody" of it, the only way to make sure that that conviction stands upon a fact would be to find the piece of music. This I have not succeeded in; and because I hope some one else will, I shall set down with some exactness just how and where I have looked for it.

Because of the younger Donne's reference to Lawes and Laniere (thought to be Nicholas, 1588–1666), in the 1660 edition of Pembroke and Ruddier containing "Soules joy," one would seek first in them. One would expect a later public appearance of such an air, not one contemporary with Pembroke and Herbert—always provided it were thought to be worth publication. The printed collections were examined, beginning with those mentioned in Grove's *Dictionary* as important for Lawes; this is made easier by the fact that the several collections printed for Playford [31] are indexed in Day and Murrie's first-line index of *English Song-Books 1651–1702* (1940), with a check made possible by the more recent *Music at the Huntington Library* by

[31] *Select Musicall Ayres and Dialogues* (1652, 1653, 1655, 1658, 1659, with slight variants in titles); the 1699 *Treasury of Musick* is important for Lawes. Both Lawes brothers' names and Laniere's appear on the title page of the handsome 1653 ed. (the 1652 printings being without Lawes' consent). See the interesting article by E. Ford Hart, "Introduction to Henry Lawes," in *Music & Letters*, XXXII (1951), 217–25, 328–44; and on various matters concerning him, Willa Evans, *Henry Lawes, Musician and Friend of Poets* (N. Y., 1941). We now have, in the relevant volume (1960) of *Die Musik in Geschichte und Gegenwart*, V. Duckles' article on this composer.

E. Backus (1949).[32] The knotty problem of music still in manuscript is not taken care of by the first-line indices which fortunately exist (for the British Museum, for manuscripts at Christ Church, Oxford, and at the Music School, supplemented for Oxford by the first-line card-index of manuscript poems in the Bodleian, in process [33]); there is still the matter of manuscripts acquired since those listings. This is easier to handle for Lawes, and in particular the important privately-owned "Lawes Autograph MS" often mentioned in connection with work on the *Comus* music is now at the British Museum (B.M., Loan 35) and was examined. But despite the helps like the British Museum class catalogues and Bodley's slip-catalogues, my checking of Laniere seems uncomfortably inadequate.[34] At this point, however, one may recall that all we

[32] Nevertheless, considering the use of airs slightly altered for different sets of words, it seemed wise to look at copies when possible (B. M., Bodleian, Yale) to see if manuscript notes would add information; and for the same reason to look as often as one could at the manuscripts themselves in the case of indexed but unpublished songs. In any "first-line" index, there are five possible headings for "Soules joy" (each stanza or half-stanza, and the refrain), the manuscript musical miscellanies especially being content to take tag-lines from any of these places. Hence the request on my first page that musical students looking for other things will keep this text in mind.

[33] By Miss M. Crum; to be added, for Bodleian music, is the music index in the Upper Reading Room. Hughes-Hughes' *Catalogue of MS Music in the British Museum* (1906–1909, and supplements) lists both by composer and first line; the *Catalogue of Music belonging to the Music School* (1854), and Arkwright's *Catalogue of Music in the Library of Christ Church* (1915) cover the most important Oxford collections not in Bodley. Squire's *Catalogue of Printed Music at the Royal College of Music* is by composers, hence that collection and the manuscripts at St. Michael's Tenbury (catalogued in 1924 by Fellowes, but predominantly church music) were inadequately covered. The B. M. Manuscript Students' Room has a recent accessions handlist, and music manuscripts therein were looked at; but any hiatus in the Addit. and Egerton MSS between the latter and Hughes-Hughes' date is uncovered, since of course no ordinary manuscript catalogue can take care of this type of problem.

[34] Laniere's music even for a masque by Jonson (Pembroke's friend), *The Vision of Delight*, has only recently been brought out into view, by J. P. Cutts in *N. & Q.*, n.s. III (1956), 64–67. It is in MS Egerton 2013, which says nothing of our song, but I attach this scrap of "parody" (in all senses): the famous "Hence all ye vain delights" (f. 3v) from Fletcher's *Nice Valour*, with its ending "Then stretch our bones . . . Nothing's so dainty sweet as lovely melancholy" has its attached *L'allegro* on f. 5v: "Come all you deare delights . . . then stretch your selves uppon the Taverne Benches, there's nothinge dainty sweete but wine & wenches." Images are travestied throughout; musical settings are related but not the same.

know from Donne's preface is that Lawes and Laniere are good risks—the song may be anyone's. To meet such a problem, we have only things like Fellowes' numerous publications, such collection listings as go by first line rather than composer, and the possibility of covering through reading-room handlists such recent acquisition as the extraordinary huge two-volume MS Egerton 3665. There is still, so to speak, a hole between Fellowes and Playford [35]—and I hope Lord Pembroke's song is in it.

The musical literature, and particularly the manuscripts, which contain much that can never be got into print completely (like the format of lyrics), can illuminate many of the questions and possibilities which make difficulties for the critic of lyrical writing. This is especially true for poems written for extant music (as compared with those merely set by a later composer). One learns much about such matters as relations that cross language barriers, including the importation of lyric patterns (many manuscripts are half Italian, or sprinkled with French texts; a song of course is borrowable from any model). Or about special "kinds" like the dialogues, secular and "spiritual"; about conventional metaphors given more durability by the popularity of kinds of settings (for example the lady as besieged fortress, set from the fourteenth century to the seventeenth in the style of battle pieces; see Reese, *Renaissance*, pp. 12, 56). Or about the particular type of parodic composition paired with its original as an "answer"; about the popularity of pieces, often to be attributed to a musical setting, and the changes in them to suit later tastes and later musical styles; about the repetition of portions as "refrains," and other subtler ways in which the contour of poems affects our judgments of their structure; and about conceptions of formal fitness, especially of what formal elements are assumed to be largely indifferent to the mood or conceptual content, hence to be changed or exchanged at will.[36]

[35] In which lie, for example, Porter, Peerson, Filmer—I have not seen the last. The F. Sambrooke whom musicologists will connect with the last-named Egerton MS, 3665, and with N. Y. P. L. Drexel 4302, was a chorister, in his forties, at Herbert's funeral (Aubrey); Herbert presumably knew those he went twice weekly to hear.

[36] Touching music, the assumption would arise largely because actual experience shows that auditors vary greatly as to their translation of musical elements into this or that mood. This practically necessary neutrality of music (and for similar reasons of many rhetorical effects) must be taken into consideration when

It is no easier for a student of music to recognize the possible solution of literary cruxes, unless he knows the lyrical works of several decades almost by heart, than it is for a literary student to perceive—as he reads some setting—that a contemporary musician is overturning some of our most orthodox assumptions about literary decorum, touching tone perhaps, or tempo, or the contribution of rhetorical devices (repetition, inner rhyme, assonance). I allow space to the perhaps overprecise bibliographical materials above partly to emphasize the difficulties and pitfalls which come in the way when literary or musical students need to ask, of the others' expert knowledges, answers to their own respective kinds of questions. And partly to suggest how much remains to be done before we shall have a true sense of what the living reality was that corresponds to the literary phenomenon we refer to as the development of the seventeenth-century lyric.[37]

One aspect of this is small but it is unlikely to receive comment in any other connection: the extent to which the numerous minute facts brought to light in these slow and desultory ways affect our notions of the groupings and exchanged influences between authors. The web of interrelations between writers, and between works, which the living men experienced, would not look at all like our set of logical and schematized critical divisions. The musical popularizing and transmission of texts provided a different kind of viability, and influences unlike those of printed whole editions; the single poem, and not always the most characteristic or "best" poem, is more important, and moreover what men learn from others' poems depends on what form they meet them in. (This holds for literary critics as well.) A network of ties we are largely unaware of made poets answer each other's poems, try out each other's new modes, proclaim improbable admirations and dis-

we interpret parodic writings, for the incongruities and tensions we care about are those that can be apprehended (in the Herbert example, those that would be inescapably detected by hearers who knew both songs).

[37] Only one small facet of this is apparent in the fact that virtually no editor thinks of reprinted music as a necessary part of annotation, though none would dream of editing without providing variant readings. But the first can under certain circumstances present as important a line on the author's original conception as the second. Only one of the sixteenth-seventeenth-century lyrical writers can conveniently be taught by singing him; yet an easy test of the difference this makes to critical response can be made simply by confining all illustrations in a discourse on that one poet—Campion—to *sung* musical quotations.

likes, pay the compliment of imitation to attractions we do not see, produce a sudden spate of "blackamoor" poems or pastoral invitations, pursue some motif to an early, final, and absurd death. Of this network we once had only fairly gross notions—on the order of "Herrick, son of Ben," "young Herbert and young King, inside the dean's circle," "Browne, Spenser, Daniel: another world." Biographical research has confused our once neat critical alignments, and particularly some of the old assumed antipathies have had to go; the allowed patterns would be further shaken by a detailed history of musical settings.

Odd single relationships can sometimes afford a safer glimpse into special "influences" and the judgments men made of each other than our ideas of what would be plausible. Who could easily say why, of all the poems Herbert might have imitated, he chose to leave us this one close echo? Not that we lack evidence of connections between the two cousins. We have fairly continuous evidence of the friendly relations between the several Herbert brothers, including Edward and Henry also, and their fourth cousin William Lord Pembroke, and of his favors to George. Pembroke's close friend Ruddier (commonly paired with him touching authorship of poems long before the joint editing of the two in 1660) is the Sir Benjamin Ruddyard to whom Herbert says he is writing for support of his candidacy for the oratorship, as well as to "my Lord" (pretty certainly Pembroke; letter VIII in Hutchinson, p. 370). Ruddyard was returned for the borough of Wilton, "again," in June 1625. Herbert evidently owed his own seat as M.P. for Montgomery to Lord Pembroke and his brother Philip (1624; Herbert's term overlapped that of his important earlier patron, for he was not succeeded in the seat by his brother Henry until 1626).

It is a little difficult to disentangle actions in his behalf by the two Lords Pembroke, especially in the matter of the Bemerton living, the deed of presentation of which (16 April 1630) is dated six days after William's sudden death made Philip fourth earl. The story in Walton of King Charles, the Earl of Pembroke, and Laud, at Wilton or Salisbury, together persuading Herbert to acceptance, is properly called in question, but Hutchinson accepts the statement that Pembroke "requested the King to bestow it upon his Kinsman *George Herbert*" (it was a living in the earl's gift, but fell to the crown this time through promotion of the incumbent). All Herbert's movements center in Wiltshire for several months around these dates. We may not fix a precise date for the late poem "A Parodie"; but close connections with Wilton, with the Herberts who came and went there, and with the interests of that third earl who was so well known a patron of poetry and music, do not have to wait for residence at Bemerton. Nor need they depend on whether Herbert was chaplain at Wilton House (as Aubrey says), or on his good friendship with its famous later mistress, Philip's wife Anne, countess of Cumberland.[38]

Lord Pembroke's interest in music is a little less well known than his patronage of poets.[39] Lawes and Laniere most likely did their settings of numerous pieces by him and his friend Ruddier during a connection of long standing—a kind of patronage-partnership which is not unusual, and all the more natural given Lawes' Salisbury boyhood and continued connections there through his father Thomas, vicar choral.[40] The incomparable Dowland

[38] The facts about Herbert's connections with Pembroke and Wiltshire may be found in Hutchinson's admirably succinct presentation in his introduction and his commentary on the letters, supplemented by J. H. Summers' also admirable account. Those on Ruddyard, of whom much more of interest could be told, have here received additions from J. A. Manning, *Memories of Sir Benj. Rudyerd* (London, 1841). Of special interest, in 1628, in connecton with alleged similar ideas of Herbert's, is *Sir Benj. Rudierd his Speech in behalfe of the Clergie,* printed at Oxford, arguing vigorously for better-paid livings, and commenting on the shame of the fact that clerics are scorned for their poverty, and churches not maintained in dignity. Herbert's activities in the repair of both Leighton Church and Bemerton are well known; he evidently received £50 help, possibly double that, from Pembroke.

[39] His poetic patronage has now been properly studied by Dick Taylor, Jr., in a series of articles, 1955 to 1959; titles may be found in that on "The Masque and the Lance" in *Tulane Stud. in English,* VIII (1958). "The Third Earl of Pembroke as a Patron of Poetry," in the same *Studies* for 1955, although I had not seen it until my text was written, is especially welcome, gathering together the extremely numerous references to this famous patron and dedicatee of so many poets and dramatists, and confirming our realization that Herbert as poet could not have taken lightly such a kinsman's friendship. Taylor takes no stand on the attribution of "Soules joy," but see in addition to my previous remarks Summers, *op. cit.,* p. 205.

[40] See W. M. Evans, *Henry Lawes,* ch. I, also pp. 30, 37, with dates which support the assumption that Lawes the elder remained at Salisbury quite through Herbert's time. A preface by Henry Lawes in the 1653 *Ayres & Dialogues* shows that he got his texts from their authors directly (one of Pembroke's is included). His pupil and dedicatee Mary Egerton married Herbert's nephew (see note 7 above).

set a song of Pembroke's. Tobias Hume, that strange and finally piteous character, would no doubt have liked to have set one too; his dedication of his *Musicall Humours,* 1605, sounds too formal for the friendship we sense in the Lawes connection, and by 1642 he is thanking a later Lord Pembroke for "a meal's meat" now and then.[41] Other musicians testify to Lord Pembroke's interest in music of other kinds than songs of profane love; Thomas Tomkins' dedication to the earl of his *Songs,* 1622, after alleging ties with him as another west-country man, speaks of his "often frequenting and favorable attention to the Musicke in the Chappell," music which raises the soul above the body (this would be in the court's Chapel Royal). *The Just Mans Memoriall* is a printed sermon preached by "T.C." (his London chaplain?) "before the interment of the Body" at Baynard's Castle, the earl's London house where he died suddenly on 10 April 1630; its description of "my dead Master," including his daily attendance at prayers, suits ill with the bad reputation Pembroke has had, falsely it now seems, in some modern comment.[42] It takes no flight of the imag-

[41] Dowland's songs is in Fellowes, *The English School of Lutenist Song Writers,* vol. XII. On Hume, see P. Warlock's *English Ayre* (London, 1926). A useful book on the network of connections not present to the memory of a literary student is W. L. Woodfill, *Musicians in English Society* (Princeton, 1953). J. H. Summers' chapter on music is welcome for general connections with Herbert. One's hope that scraps of Herbert's own, or contemporary, settings of his verse might turn up in the manuscript indices I have mentioned is met with disappointing silence, though wordless tunes so often have a just recognizable tag that only scrutiny of the manuscripts is sure proof. When the Christmas anthem in dialogue mentioned in H. Davey's *History of English Music* (London, 1921), pp. 228, 211 as "by Herbert" and set by Ford, is pursued, it turns out to have rather the words: "Look shepherds, look! | Why? where? | See you not yonder, there! | . . . *The Angel:* Fear not, Shepherds . . ." (spelling modernized; from Bodleian MS Rawlinson poet. 23, f. 151; also in Ashmole 36–37, f. 255 and Harl. 6346, p. 175). As this goes to press, I am grateful to be told by Mr. Vincent Duckles of six three-part polyphonic settings by Jenkins of poems by Herbert (parts of *Christmas, The Dawning, Ephes. iv. 30, The Starre*) in Christ Church MS 736–38.

[42] The derogatory commonplaces are controverted by Dick Taylor, Jr., in "The Earl of Pembroke and the Youth of Shakespeare's Sonnets," *SP,* LVI (1959), 26–54, and another essay therein cited. I do not know who was Pembroke's chaplain at this date, not at any rate the one of 1624 whose epitaph adjures us to "Know! thou that treadst on learned *Smyth* inurn'd"—that man is but an unreversible hour-glass. I quote this from the most trustworthy of the manuscripts containing "Soules joy," Lansdowne 777, f. 55. Its connections with William Browne would reward inquiry, for Wood and others stress his close

ination to think that the alleged author of the first "Soules joy" was a congenial friend as well as helpful kinsman of the author of the second, and that both amateurs of music and of poetry did not live in the same county so many months of several different years connected only by letters and the memory of past obligations. A poem with or without music, in manuscript at Wilton when Herbert came at the earl's persuasion to live so near by,[43] is enough to explain why a good musician should write "A Parodie." It is a disappointingly common sense explanation compared with the picture of a Herbert torn by anxieties and determined to turn all secular love into sacred channels, but it suits the man better.

Much of this information, like so much information, simply changes our expectations a little. For the chief support for understanding the poem in the matter-of-fact way I have suggested lies in the nature of the relation between it and its model. It is a formal imitation.

I reproduce the two poems in a format which allows easier comparison.

Song

Soules joy, now I am gone,
And you alone,
(Which cannot be,
Since I must leave my selfe with thee,
And carry thee with me)

Yet when unto our eyes
Absence denyes
Each others sight,
And makes to us a constant night,
When others change to light;

O give no way to griefe,
But let beliefe
Of mutuall love,
This wonder to the vulgar prove
Our Bodyes, not wee move.

A Parodie

Souls joy, when thou art gone,
And I alone,
Which cannot be,
Because thou dost abide with me,
And I depend on thee;

Yet when thou dost suppresse
The cheerfulnesse
Of thy abode,
And in my powers not stirre abroad,
But leave me to my load:

O what a damp and shade
Doth me invade!
No stormie night
Can so afflict or so affright,
As thy eclipsed light.

association with Wilton from 1625; some doubt of Browne's autograph in it is registered in the B. M. copy of the catalogue. A certain "T.C." copied a well known music manuscript, Addit. 11608, containing much Laniere and Lawes but not our *Song*. Whoever the T.C. of the sermon was, he calls himself, in a phrase oddly like the motto of Bemerton's parson, "I the least of all the least," "minimorum minimus as Bernard speakes."

[43] That the train of requests and persuasions which ended in the Bemerton presentation deed of 16 April was started by William seems likelier than a rapid

Let not thy wit beweepe
Wounds but sense-deepe,
For when we misse
By distance our lipp-joying blisse,
Even then our soules shall kisse,

Fooles have no meanes to meet,
But by their feet.
Why should our clay,
Over our spirits so much sway,
To tie us to that way?

O give no way to griefe,
But let beliefe
Of mutuall love,
This wonder to the vulgar prove
Our Bodyes, not wee move.

Ah Lord, do not withdraw,
Lest want of aw
Make sinne appeare; [cleare,
And when thou dost but shine lesse
Say, that thou art not here.

And then what life I have,
While Sinne doth rave,
And falsly boast,
That I may seek, but thou art lost;
Thou and alone thou knowst.

O what a deadly cold
Doth me infold!
I half beleeve, [grieve,
That Sinne sayes true: but while I
Thou com'st and dost relieve.

The usually careful and meaningful format in Herbert is not disturbed, except to point up by deeper indentation how the parallel third and sixth stanzas would have been sung to what was probably set as a refrain in Pembroke's, twice following upon ten lines (two identically patterned fives). We do not know the format of Pembroke's *Song*. Grierson evidently takes the format, in two ten-line stanzas with an italicized refrain separating these and recurring at the end, from the 1635 Donne (and parallel later editions). In neither of the two manuscript copies (Lansdowne 777, Stowe 962) nor in the 1660 edition of Pembroke is there any indication that the five lines "O give no way . . ." are a refrain[44];

---

business assigned all to Philip—initiated, concluded, and officialized within the six days that included his brother's death and burial. Herbert's stature as a poet was known to his friends by 1630, yet no one stresses the fact that congeniality of tastes may have motivated the patron earl as well as the accepting parson; something of this sort probably lies behind Walton's overwritten story. Acceptance must have been at least expected when the deed was dated. Philip was a poor exchange, to anyone who had thought the environs of Wilton would be frequently graced by William and by Ruddier.

[44] Lans. 777, f. 73, the MS with the crucial ascription to Pembroke, writes five unindented five-line stanzas in a series, thus completing the text but giving no hint that the seeming third stanza is repeated as a refrain. Actually, if there is music, this is how we copy too; we simply get down all the words. Stowe 962, f. 226, ends with Grierson's line 15, and here also there is no indication that the "refrain" was felt as other than a third five-line verse. Other texts in this MS are poor. But as an example of "parody" in the sense we are not using it, I subjoin

but if the edition (a bad text) is a careless copy from a music manuscript, this "refrain," if it is one, might have been sung after each five, not each ten, for the lines appear as the second five.[45] But there is no trusting this editor. The 1635 Donne probably got this poem, as it got other additions to 1633, from the O'Flaherty MS (now at Harvard), for that carefully arranged text gives us a two-stanza song, each of ten lines, with refrain (to repeat at end) as in Grierson, with the additional care, as in Herbert, of showing by lesser indentation that the fourth line, in each stanza and in the refrain, is a longer one. But its verbal blunders are only a little less absurd than those of 1660, and Grierson had to correct them from the Lansdowne MS (see Grierson, II, xcviii). Syllabically, each stanza (or half-stanza) is 6–4–4–8–6, and the same music will suit the same completed song, whether in six separate fives as in Herbert or two tens with inserted and final refrain as in Pembroke. This explanation was necessary in order to see that Herbert suits a text to a pattern, not a text to a text.

The conceptual structure of the *Song*, quite different from Herbert's, allows the parallel ideas about absence in stanzas one and two to be laid at rest each time by the asseveration repeated in the identical "refrain," truly one in this respect at least. The thought of "A Parodie" is not built like this; it proceeds in one line from the impossibility of God's absence, to His seeming absence, to "O what a damp and shade" that induces, to a plea not to seem absent, to the dangers that involves, to a climactic final five lines that begin *formally* (and with great propriety musically) "O

---

one on Jonson's famous lyric: "Have you seene but a blacke little maggott Come creepinge over a dead dogg | Or an old woeman with a fagott Smotheringe of an hedghogge . . . O soe blacke, o soe rough, o soe sower is shee."

[45] It is there presented, however, as a two-stanza piece, labelled "I" and "II." But the indentation is not careful, lines 16–20 are missing entirely, and errors make some lines senseless. Its editor, the younger Donne, either got it from the composers as he says he got many, in his preface, or from a source that was not the one which put it among the Donne materials, and not either MS mentioned in note 44. Of course he might have taken a longer text from the 1650 Donne which he had had connections with, but this would have included the embarrassment of finding out whether his father wrote it. Copying from music manuscripts would explain some of the vacillation copyists show, about what its stanzaic form is and what place to give to the five lines "O give . . ." Unlabelled refrains are not visually clear to rapid copyists of song-words from music manuscripts, and there is also some excuse for shuffling a form to make it clear as a read poem.

what a deadly cold . . . ," as before, but end *"Thou com'st* and dost relieve." Conceptually there is and can be nothing in Pembroke's poem for this thought-structure to be a "parody" of, neutral or otherwise. It is not a parody of ideas or style; it is the use of a strictly formal pattern to write one's own poem to. Whether there was music or not, or whether both poems were sung to some music for a third which we therefore do not find in our searches, Herbert's poem is set "to" the form, in the way words are set "to" music. Herbert does not "leave" Pembroke's subject; he has never picked it up. His poem is on a different subject, which is not the nature of love.

This statement may sound foolhardy in the light of five lines of near verbal identity between the two poems. But concepts do not build up with words as with bricks, and even closer verbal identity would not make the same idea out of "my self left with thee" said of a relation to another human being, and "thou abiding with me" said of God's relation to the soul. Change of referents changes the meaning even of identical words, and this interesting aspect of the relations which obtain between form and meaning provides part of the pleasure in all types of parody. But instead of watching how Herbert talks about seeming absence without talking about Pembroke's subject of seeming absence, we may more profitably follow with some care the formal echoings which relate the two poems well beyond the point where verbal parallels cease.

In doing this I shall make several references to the technique of the *missa parodia.* This is illegitimate in that music alone can show the technique. For any poem is, like a song, monodic, whereas the whole burden of a good deal of fairly recent work on the parody mass is to show its difference from its ancestors, the practice of *contrafactum* (also monodic) and the *cantus firmus* mass, and the difference lies in the fact that a parody mass is based on a polyphonic model and uses its borrowings polyphonically. The *missa parodia* borrows not just a line of melody, augmenting and inverting it and treating it contrapuntally, but borrows consonances, harmonic phrases and entries, polyphonic interweaving of melodic elements. Obviously this can have no precise literary analogue. Yet the effects thus gained, and their obscured but present relations to their model, are more useful to bear in mind than straightforward monodic imitations when one looks at the way combined literary elements of vowel and consonant quality, accent, rhythm, and echo produce a texture related to an imitated texture. In addition, because we need not doubt that Herbert had an ear made alert to this contemporary technique through singing and listening, and because even if he did not know such masses the parody technique was otherwise known in England (see e.g. some of Morley's madrigals and canzonets),[46] and because *missa parodia* may be the term which gave earliest currency to the *term* used in his title, it is proper to make some references thereto. It remains true that his probable confusion of *contrafactum* and *parody* may account for his name, thus harking back to a yet more common technique.

The definite and recognizable use of the original for the opening is universally characteristic. As in "Souls joy," this is an imitation, often very close, of a largish formal portion, a near-quotation. Every Kyrie in a mass showing either the earlier or the later kind of imitation "states," as does Herbert's beginning, its parodic character, but it is just as much a Kyrie for all that, and no notion can really enter of a reference to the *ideas* the composer had to hand in his secular musical models, in "L'homme armé," "Fortuna desperata," "Malheur me bat," "Douce memoire," "Ite rime dolenti," "Ultimi miei sospiri," "Cara la vita mia," "Puisque j'ai perdu," or whatever else. I simply take names of extant masses by the best-known composers of sacred music;[47] these do not differ in their "spirituality" from other masses by the same writers

[46] On works by Morley parodying compositions by Croce and others, see J. Kerman, "Morley and 'The Triumphs of Oriana,'" *Music & Letters*, XXXIV (1953), 185–91, especially p. 188; there is further information in Reese, *Renaissance*, pp. 824f, with citations (especially to Kerman's *The Elizabethan Madrigal* [N. Y., 1962]). I use without direct citation the following treatments: R. B. Lenaerts, "The Sixteenth Century Parody Mass in the Netherlands," *Mus. Quar.*, XXXVI (1950), 410–21; J. Schmidt-Goerg, "Vier Messen aus dem xvi Jhr." [by Palestrina, Lupus, Clemens, and le Roy, all on one motet by Lupus Hellinck], *Kirchenmusikalisches Jb.*, XXV (1930), 76–93; and P. Pisk, *Das Parodieverfahren in der Messe des Jac. Gallus* (Wien, 1918, Studien zur Musikwissenschaft). It would be impossible to cite all the relevant information in Reese, and the reader is referred to the rich presentation of pertinent materials throughout that volume.

[47] About half of the large number of Palestrina's masses and more of di Lasso's are parody masses, and all names I later include are important representatives of the practice. The four masses analyzed by Schmidt-Goerg were published in 1590, 1532 (Lupus's own), 1570, 1585; others were publishing at later dates, though the parody mass declined during the seventeenth century.

based instead on sacred motets[48]—and the same is true if one compares Herbert's "Souls joy" with his independent or liturgically based sacred poems. Where masses seem "secularized," as is sometimes said of di Lasso or Victoria, there are formal reasons for it—declamation, "skipping rhythms," and so on—not this practice of parody which they share with Josquin, Clemens non Papa, Philippe de Monte, Gallus (Handl), Palestrina, and others renowned for their deeply religious quality. Several of these were notably devout men, and if they thought possible the intrusion of secular connotations through formal likenesses, they did ill in usually choosing secular models made famous by recent or noted settings. Taverner's mass founded on and called after "The Western Wynde" uses *cantus firmus* rather than parody technique, the reworking thus being all the more eminent, but it would be equally idle to suppose that he either feared or desired any tensions set up in his auditory by the fact that in his Benedictus the trebles sing "qui venit in nomine Domini," in the Gloria the tenors sing "peccata mundi," in the Credo "Patrem omnipotentem" —to that part of the melody every one knew was occupied by "Christ, that my love were in my arms | And I in my bed again."

The formal parallelism between Pembroke's *Song* and the "Parodie" is again peculiarly marked where "O give no way to griefe, | But let beliefe | Of mutall love . . ." is echoed by Herbert's "O what a damp and shade | Doth me invade!" and "O what a deadly cold | Doth me infold!" This would be a natural way to make the most of a musical phrase, in case Herbert wrote to a setting composed for a text whose "refrain" had this accentual pattern (therefore occurring twice). The textural likenesses (they are in contrast to his own other fives) are apparent in tempo, shifted accents, falling cadence after the first "O," long and heavy words, with long vowels in rhyming positions—though the feeling and meaning of the two five-line units are simply not related, not even op-posed.

In musical parody, the fact that one formal structure is being used to bring another one into being results in the appearance of a great many small semi-quotations of partially parallel motifs—

[48] Of J. Gallus' 20 masses printed in 1580, 16 are parody masses, and Pisk's analysis indicates no such differentiation in feeling between the 9 based on sacred motet, 3 on German songs, 2 on madrigals, and one with a combined *chanson*-madrigal base.

ranging from harmonic coloring to *Nebentheme,* sometimes a figure quoted with a slight but transforming change in rhythm or in the time, a lengthened or contracted near-repetition. These are not true analogues to what we find in Herbert's or any literary imitation except that a similar effect of a likeness that is not quite a likeness results from the numerous all-but-parallel rhetorical effects: the same poised hesitation before a cadence in several lines, near-assonance and parallel endings in each 14th line ("this *won*d*er* to the *vu*lg*ar* prove"; cf. Herbert's alliteration and final consonance in slightly altered accent-positions in "Can so afflict or so affright"; similarly both 21st lines: "*m*eanes to *m*eet"; "li*f*e I ha*v*e"); the same high slow emphasis ("Éven then . . . ," "Sáy, that . . . ," both lines 20), continuing into a row of fastidiously separated syllables. These relations, like the subtly similar winding of the run-ons, are quite different in effect from outright repetitions like "Yet when . . ." (6), or the mere clang of rhyme-words in the memory which is most likely responsible for the last stanzas' "griefe . . . beliefe": "beleeve . . . greeve." The contour of "Lét not thy wit beweepe" (16) is reflected, though with a pebble just moving the image in the pool, in "Áh Lord! do not withdraw" (16), but they share nothing conceptually except a wordless sense of the mental posture of pleading. One does not think these planned tricks but the result of a sensitive ear accustomed to notice and take pleasure in artistic imitation, accompanied by a disposition to regard formal imitating as a thing quite separable from following the line of another man's thought.

Perhaps it is necessary to remark in concluding this comparison that its relevance does not depend on our envisaging England as full of men singing foreign polyphonic masses. To be sure musicians—going either way—did not stop at the channel, nor the tastes of cultivated men pull up short before popish music like pledge-signers, and musical Englishmen were not at this epoch writing or listening to native wood-notes wild; also, in a time of such unusual mobility among performers and composers no great household or cathedral town (or even Cambridge) can be safely placed in the category "just out in the provinces." But this is not the essential element in my reason for noting these comparisons. They demonstrate usefully the nature of a parodic relation which imitates *form,* and is unarguably divorced from the interest in evoking conceptual ambiguities which we attribute to practically all literary interactions of the sacred and the profane, especially in the seventeenth century.

That Herbert is one for whom the musical comparisons are particularly apt because of his special interests and competences is so much extra good fortune. It should not need to be said (but experience shows that it does) that the idea of Herbert setting himself to compose "Souls joy" as if he were writing a parody mass or a parody of a polyphonic canzonet would be a laughable one. Rather we realize that he was used to what it meant to "parody" formally, and that he had an exquisitely sensitive ear, with complete integrity as far as keeping his eye on his own subject was concerned.

I would suggest that this was his attitude also with respect to the more inclusive matter of his use of arts learned from secular poetry, and that his poems support it. This is not to deny that tensions and wry ironies accompany men's attempts to relate or combine what is sacred to them and what is not, and that these are sometimes expressed in ambiguous juxtapositions or a bizarre relation between form and *raison d'être* of a work of art. That such tensions were peculiarly acute in the early seventeenth century is true, and there is no doubt some virtue in taking over the art historian's terms to call such expressions baroque.[49] Such analogous terms have come to limit overmuch our ideas of what authors can be like, nailing them down often to the insights of their lesser contemporaries. Obviously if a particular practice or a way of using secular arts in sacred art works has had a long history, being used by men who subscribed to a variety of aesthetic positions, its mere presence in an author can tell us little about his particular aesthetic. To ignore this is simply to assume intentions for an author and proceed as if he had declared them. It is necessary to find the declaration of them in the nature of his peculiar expression, and it is hard to find poems by Herbert wherein his uses of arts learned from secular poetry operate as a cause to produce a baroque ten-

[49] The nature of distinctions made as this general parallel is forced to take care of divisions into Mannerist, early Mannerist, late Renaissance, Rococo (to give but one example, W. Sypher, *Four Stages of Renaissance Style*, N. Y., 1955, touching Milton), has so far at least seemed unsuitable to the peculiar relation between concept and form in a verbal art like literature. Where distinctions are *by their nature* inadequate to embrace the complexities of that relation, criticism has no hope but to remain naïve and often totally blind, so that I merely recognize here that many such attempts exist.

sion born of straddling two worlds and giving up neither. Or giving up either.

That other men of his date so wrote and had such intentions is only to the purpose in that it warns us to scrutinize his carefully. An author's date can never declare what he meant. Any good writer (and to some extent any writer, and any man) has the freedom of all the history he knows. The history of how other men of other dates used practices he uses is again only to the purpose in that it moves us to careful scrutiny. We have seen that Herbert in turning secular arts to sacred purposes and specifically in writing "parody" is doing something many generations of men had done before him, and yet that this is not evidence for thinking either that he must share the intentions of the puritan reformers or must resemble in style the pious parodists.

One does not use history to discover uniformities, but possibilities. It is dangerous nowadays to call attention to likenesses between artistic events or habits in different historical eras, since some one always arises to declare that the events are not identical. One thinks of this as a point of departure so accepted that intelligent men do not remark upon it to each other. Artistic expressions are incurably single. It yet remains necessary to demand that writers' differences should be found in that wherein they differ, not in that which they share. Herbert's great differences in style and feeling from his predecessors should not throw dust in our eyes concerning his differences in some elusive but basic ways from his contemporaries. A poet shares much with these, like all men, perhaps more deeply and more variously than most. If he is a good poet he is different from anyone—and also if he is a good poet an enjoyment of his uniqueness is inseparable from the sense of his transcendence of it.

This transcendence of their uniqueness and their unique historical moment is not peculiar to poets but to men. It is not the historian among critics who is likeliest to put an author into the strait jacket of a "time" or a "milieu" or a "tradition," but the critic or reader who by reason of a false sociology does not see writers as men who make choices.[50] Their freedom from time in this respect

[50] That men have this freedom will always make it impossible to equate literary works either with "the history behind them" or "the expression of their times." Yet modern fear of these equations sometimes results in another variant of the confusion between poetry and history. Hence it seems to me the duty of anyone

they communicate directly to us who share it. This does not mean that we need retreat to the obscurantist and at bottom sentimental position that merely by being men—and a poet one who is "a man speaking to men"—we shall straightway understand all. It is rather when we know enough history not to impose ephemeral distortions (its creator was able to elude them) that a poem reveals to us both its historical uniqueness and its nonhistorical permanence, and this caveat applies generally to Herbert's and many others' close relation to several kinds of earlier traditions; we hear in Herbert's poems the arts he learned from others, even the words he copied from others, but as it was not these—his history —which finally determined what he made, so also it is not his own historical uniqueness (a true and valuable thing) which alone makes him valuable to us in ours. These very borrowed things themselves in any art speak with a voice that was unique and yet is not silenceable in the way everything unique is silenced.

In parody, an extreme and deliberate form of imitation, this can be all the more apparent. I shall now append a parody of my own. It is a tour de force, and not satisfactory, but it will show that borrowings do not account for the things they help to make, that the long history behind a relation between two poems helps

---

dealing even with small examples where all these principles come in question, to proclaim their relation to the ideas which are at stake, and to disregard the risk of overloading a small craft. The tendency to retreat from the intellectual rigors of historical criticism has taken on so many complicated forms during recent years, gaining strength and unexpected forms of adherence across the Atlantic while it weakens somewhat on this side, that one cannot but feel alarm for the future of literary criticism if, as the older forms of rebellious subjectivity fade, we face the growth of an ancient kind of literary pietism, staggered by the problem of relating history to poetry and ready to settle for inner voices (there are many signs of this). It is an evil to substitute knowing the history of something for apprehending it in its living intrinsic essence, and most good historical critics of late have tirelessly pointed out the danger, as they have pointed out the similar abuse of mistaking the irresponsible tracing of "patterns" of symbolic imagery for the discovery of poets' meanings, and as they have pointed out the manifest impossibility of our somehow through history getting out of our time into another to apprehend first hand an author's true quality in his habit as he lived. These are all forms of shrinking down poetry into history, and all are common. But it is the anti-intellectual and Romantic form of the same evil to let the uniqueness of artistic events obscure all subtler understandings of how authors, and indeed all men, are "in history" but yet are *not* caught and pinned in their own unique moment of time—in other words produce something that is not only history.

us to see what it is and the limits of it, and that the ways in which parodic relations are interesting and pleasurable are too varied to be assigned to any single simple intention in a poet. Lacking a setting for "Soules joy," I have appropriated and adapted an originally secular composition remade to a sacred use, before 1561, by "the continuator of Bourgeois," who completed the latter's work on the settings of the Huguenot psalter.[51] The reader is asked to perform this with all the secularity of which he is capable, singing Lord Pembroke's words. And then to see whether, as he sings Herbert's words to the same music, he does not find that a formal imitation is the sole relation between the secular work of art he first produces and his own production of a sacred Parodie.

[51] Bourgeois, before he quitted Geneva in 1557, had set all but 62 psalms of the Huguenot psalter during the gradual process of its translation by Marot and Beza. Psalm XCVI had been among those sung to a twice-used tune (to CXVIII) until the unknown continuator found or wrote melodies for these. The music here given is adapted from Goudimel's 1565 setting of the Psalter melody for Psalm XCVI; there is no modern reprint of his 1565 settings, but it may be found in a New York Univ. master's thesis by August Ruut, *The Genevan Psalm Melodies set by Claude Goudimel in Chordal Style,* 1956. (There is a modern harmonization of the tune in J. Ver, *Le psautier Huguenot harmonisé,* Réalville, 1918.) W. S. Pratt (*op. cit.* in note 17), giving in modern notation the tune as in 1562, for text by Beza, notes its secular origin; see Douen, I, 726, 716, where the initial phrase from its supposed original is given. This is found, ascribed to J. Arcadelt, in *Chansons nouuellement composées . . .* (*Sixiesme livre,* Paris, Le Roy and Ballard, both 1556 and 1559). The melody was very considerably altered; the secular words begin: "Le saint serviteur eshonte, Qui abusant de la bonté De sa dame, une autre pourchasse N'ha il merité qu'on le chasse? . . ." Were the scheme of the Pembroke-Herbert stanzas not so extremely rare, I should have found music more capable of enhancing both sets of words, but this is perhaps sufficient to the restricted purpose of demonstration which it here serves.

8 Pembroke 1.Soul's joy, now I am gone,__ And you a - lone, (Which
4.Let not thy wit be-weep__ Wounds but sense deep, For
Herbert 1.Soul's joy, when thou art gone,__ And I a - lone, Which
4.Ah Lord! do not with-draw,__ Lest want of awe Make
can-not be,__ Since I must leave my self with thee,
when we miss__ By dis-tance our lip-joy-ing bliss,
can-not be,__ Be-cause thou dost a - bide with me,
sin ap-pear;__ And when thou dost but shine less clear,
And car-ry thee__ with__ me)__ 2.Yet when un-
Ev'n then our souls__ shall__ kiss,__ 5.Fools have no
And I de-pend__ on__ thee;__ 2.Yet when thou
Say, that thou art__ not__ here.__ 5.And then what
to our eyes__ Ab-sence de-nies Each oth-er's sight,__
means to meet__ But by their feet. Why should our clay,__
dost sup-press__ The cheer-ful-ness Of thy a - bode,__
life I have__ While sin doth rave, And false - ly boast,__

And makes to us a con-stant night, When oth-ers change
O-ver our spi-rits so much sway, To tie us to
And in my pow'rs not stir a-broad, But leave me to
Then I may seek, but thou art lost; Thou and a-lone
REFRAIN (in Pembroke)
to light; Pembroke 3./6. O give no way to grief,
that way?
my load: Herbert 3. O what a damp and shade
thou know'st. 6. O what a dead-ly cold
But let be-lief Of mu-tual love, This won-der to the
Doth me in-vade! No storm-y night Can so af-flict or
Doth me in-fold! I half be-lieve, That sin says true: but
vul-gar prove, Our bod-ies, not we move.
so af-fright, As thy e-clip-sed light.
while I grieve, Thou com'st and dost re-lieve.

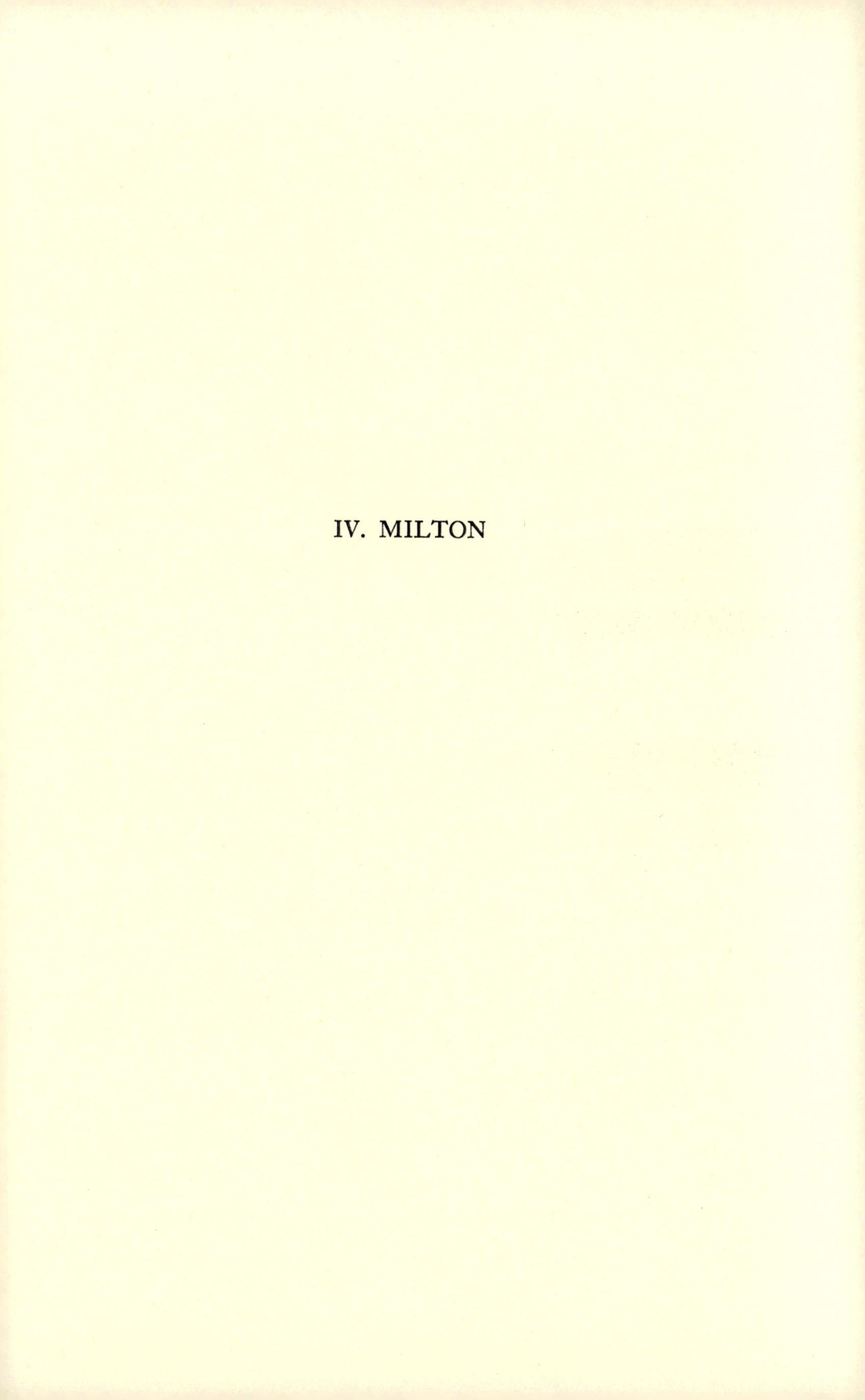

IV. MILTON

New Approaches to Milton*

I HAVE tried in vain to find some reason why the matters I wish to discuss should take to the air in 1958. No one I shall mention was born in 1558 or 1758 or 1258, nor died, nor took a wife, nor arrived at a pole, nor named a chrysanthemum; and I am reduced to the admission that I do it because I was asked. At least everyone listening has done twenty things today for the same reason, and perhaps our common condition can take the place of that timeliness which the air seems to demand if there is no convenient controversy to hand. It is true that the name I shall mention oftenest is that of John Milton, and he is a subject who in the ten or fifteen past years has been famous in my country as the subject likeliest to call out any latent animosities which your countrymen harbor against mine. If I noticed any such family animosities and national differences I should minimize them—so far, that is, as my pronunciation will allow. (For the one great bastion of his independence no American can, or should, give up is the transatlantic roll of his sentences, and the speech with which philological history has provided him.) That great exception aside, I shall find small place for national differences. For like most American students of English literature who have walked through the open doors of English libraries and universities to spend the most delightful hours of their lives among those freely offered books, my liveliest emotion in England is gratitude. A state of mind so common among Americans that they hesitate to put it into as few words as any Briton would find necessary. This is a typical form of American reserve, and as good a way of concealing deep feelings as any.

If I should appear to say that Americans have escaped from certain too constricted 19th-century ways of considering the work of John Milton rather more rapidly than some of their English contemporaries, it might easily be merely the reserved American way of praising one of the greatest of all Englishmen. In America Milton has never died (not even recently)—perhaps because he

* Transcript of a BBC broadcast, July 23, 1958. Reprinted in *The Listener* 60 (1958), 312–13, under the title "Rosemond Tuve on John Milton."

can be chiefly a poet there; his politics do not touch our daily thoughts, nor press against our daily pieties.

I was faced some three or four years since by a request to read and analyze all criticism of the imagery of *Paradise Lost* from 1800 to the present. This turned out to mean all criticism involving interpretation of his ideas, for the detachment of the imagery of any author from his thought makes a fatal division. What it kills is his poem. I met with two surprises. One was the unanimity with which the great crowd of 19th-century writers turned their attention—their most admiring attention—to the almost purely descriptive qualities of Milton's images: how huge Satan was, how loud the Thunder that bellowed through the vast and boundless deep, how swarmingly numerous the bad angels, like the locusts that hung over Pharaoh's realm in a "pitchy cloud," how red the Lightning and how mysteriously black the gloom, how plenteous and sweet the roses of Eden—in a word, "Milton's pictures."

The other interesting consistency among these writers was their almost militant secularism—as the century progressed a more and more valiant (even strident) attempt to read *Paradise Lost* without feeling obliged to take its theology seriously.

Now the first of these, the pictorial power and grandeur of the images, is certainly a proper thing to attend to in literary imagery. But it is a severe limitation on the nature and power of images to assume (and here I use, as very typical phrases, the influential ones of Macaulay on Milton) that an image chiefly "does by means of words what the painter does by means of colours," that it should primarily provide an "illusion," usually "a picture to the mental eye." This suits some literal sensuous detail, but only some aspects of some literary subjects ask for it. Certainly very few figures—Milton's complex ones least of all—serve an end so restricted.

Pleasure in splendor, mystery, and picture, in and for themselves, ruled out attention to Milton's extreme care for fitness, which reached down to take thought for the evaluative force of every shadowy association. God's thunder "bellows" because Satan, who is speaking, cannot but cast resentful aspersions, with that bestial verb bellows, upon the Author of the thunder. Satan's hugeness, like that of the prone Leviathan to whom he is compared, is that of power which is suspect from the start, inimical. And the locusts in a "pitchy cloud" associate defilement with the bad angels because they are not a picture of locusts, but of those special locusts which "darken'd all the land of Nile" as God's curse must darken the Egypt that is the enemy of his chosen people; when they (and the bad angels) "hang like Night" this is a spiritual and moral night such as no painter can depict (unless he too uses some such known story of a spiritual darkness).

For if you will observe closely Milton's images, or some other poet's, or tomorrow's conversations, you will find this fact to be true, though I have never seen it stated outright: authors and speakers use plain particulars when images are to suggest sensuous experience; they use figures when we are being covertly swayed to embrace or reject something (are being attracted, being repelled, brought to think well of, think ill of). The slightest element of metaphor brings into the images the factor of directed evaluation. We admire, we despise, we share amazement, share horror, we share a judgment of scorn, of pity, of praise. I do not know what to call this other than the evaluative functioning of figurative speech. It is the meanings of narratives that figurative language assists.

But the marvellous precision and restraint with which Milton slowly commands our attention to large complexes of meaning through images perfectly suited to their task, as a wind will blow unseen over a prairie and show itself only in the obedient bending of the grasses—neither the precision, nor the restraint, nor the suitability are the staple of 19th-century comment. Fulsome praise was given to Milton's "phrases of towering port" (I am quoting now several critics), to his forms "exaggerated to gigantic dimensions, and veiled in mysterious gloom," to his "loading sweets on sweets," to his "magnificent similes that dilate the imagination." It is no wonder that when the narrow range of accomplishments which were isolated and admired in Milton's images came rather to rouse antipathy, or seem inadequate, praise turned to blame. Modern detractors are just the reverse of the 19th-century medal; earlier praise shows the same disregard of Milton's care for the decorum of his images as does the modern dis-praise (of his magnificence, of his vague mysterious gloom, of his loaded sweets). Especially as regards comment on images, the Milton decried in recent controversy is almost comically the 19th-century Milton—a reversal such as we know in comedy, when a thing has one meaning upside down and another downside up.

But this is a wave whose force is spent. There is a newer wave which is just gathering its force, a 20th-century form of praise of Milton which bids fair to provide a 21st-century crowd of readers, differently blind to the special power of images as he chose to write them. Anyone who teaches knows that there has been a revolution within the last fifteen years in the attitude which students take toward the symbolic element in images. Where an earlier century demanded almost literal pictorial language, we now find readers who will spin out of the smallest suggestion, or no suggestion, a series of symbolic meanings—often fantastic, and often highly subjective—for images which purport, at least, to be concrete portrayals. The rehabilitation of myth, the interest in so-called depth psychology and in Freudian and Jungian symbolism, and the example of contemporary or rediscovered writers who use various languages of symbols (Yeats, Eliot, Joyce, Melville, even Henry James)—these currents have provided readers who see Eden as The Archetypal Garden before they have taken pleasure in more than the first of the flowers with which Milton provided it.

No one would give up this new readiness to read with constant openness to the metaphorical profundity of large images. And that Eden is The Archetypal Garden, and that Milton put there certain symbolical meanings we refer to by that tag, is not to be questioned—yet what he put there is not taken care of by our tag.

There are two dangers to poetry here. One is apparent to anyone who reads and listens to modern criticism—the daily flow, in journals, classrooms (both on the platform and below it), current comment. There is developing a sort of symbol-hunting which finds the expected plums and cries "ha"—and this is utterly opposed to the proper action and the artistic power of symbolical imagery, which is used because it is necessary and beautiful not because it is a good game for classifiers.

The second danger is more damaging to great poems. The reading of images for their archetypal or "mythical" significance can so concentrate on the universal meanings of images that that is all we have left. All quests become one Quest, all gardens one Garden, all hells one Hell. These are not images but faceless abstractions. Where one century, interested in Milton's pictures and "characters" and biographical footprints, was in danger of leaving a permanently serious total significance unread, another century interested in the psychological basis of universally familiar images is in danger of reading one serious total significance forever and ever in all works ever penned. The final situations in each epoch look curiously alike; both waste much Milton. These are not necessary results; they appear only because in each case the unique form of the poem's real seriousness is disregarded.

For works of art are irrevocably born one of a kind. The way *peculiar to him* in which a great poet uses a common archetypal image or a familiar symbol is part of that uniqueness. We do not take in his special form of the common figure just by staring at it. This is because such great images *symbolize;* they do not just "stand for" some idea which we carry around with us by nature, and hence always know enough to appreciate fully, wherever we meet it. Milton's Paradise—the Eden man was in and had to leave, and the Paradise within him happier far—does not just "stand for" whatever notions we and all men approach the poem with, concerning the Perfection which so differs from the place of our exile. Symbolic imagery depends on a good many other things besides man's psychological make-up, and this is one of the reasons why each century finds it easy to take its own way of "disregarding the unique form of the poem's real seriousness."

I should like to hark back to the second general observation made about 19th-century appreciation of Milton. Raleigh's *Milton* shows, with much grace and wit, a way of reading *Paradise Lost* which once seemed to lose least of value from the poem, and his phrase "a monument to dead ideas" will do as well as any, to remind us of a point of view that had decades of currency. The trouble about poems as monuments to dead ideas, for a student of images, is that if an action is not serious the images cannot be figuratively read; they have nothing to figure. Sensuous particulars still give pleasure, and human characters react and interact interestingly even in meaningless situations. But the richest suggestions pall if they suggest only other suggestions; and if figures carry us toward a dead meaning we are angry. As the 19th century gradually found acceptable the idea that it was unrewarding to pursue Milton into the recesses of his untenable system of thought, it could not but shrink up the functions of his imagery. One cannot remake a poet's subject and expect his images to reflect anything just and satisfying, and *Paradise Lost* as a secular drama has no images of any great profundity. For Milton chose to make his poem inescapably theological, to make creatures' actions and their consequences reveal a deity's nature. This means that the great images of Christianity appear and work together not merely with dramatic power but bearing their full symbolical and theological import; that is their character because that is how they function in Milton's poem.

But Milton is very careful about where, and how soon, he allows the full theological purport of his greatest images to come through to us, and it is as falsifying to shout "Symbol!" too soon as to try hopefully like an earlier century to read over and escape embarrassing depths of intention in serpents and apples. Unlike the Light of God, and the Garden, the Serpent is kept less-than-symbolic until the great explosion of meaning in Book X where all the demons perforce change their shape. Were Satan fully symbolic too soon, we could never understand the subtleties about freedom and its nature and its loss, which make the contrast between the *character* Satan's eternal fate, and Adam's. And we could never discover with the same shock as the serpents had, the ashen nature of the symbolic Fruit—time and again tried, and time and again spat out with writhing jaws, eternal defiance eternally frustrated. We do not *know* what the apple was, we *learn* it, with Adam. As vision follows vision, Adam learns what *was* the knowledge he ate, good and evil twinned, never seen apart again. Never but once, and with Adam we are slowly instructed in the meaning of the Bruise upon the Serpent's head. Only Michael's long and gradual revelation of the workings of love in history can make us see, instructed as Adam was in the full meaning of the symbolic bruising of Satan, where we belong in that slow victory which we are not to dream of "As of a duel, or the local wounds of head or heel." "O goodness infinite!" says Adam, when he begins at last to understand the images of the Paradise he lost.

But we have to be as ready as Adam to listen to the archangel. And it is in this respect that there has been an astonishing shift in the second quarter of our century in ways of approaching the study of images in *Paradise Lost.* The willingness to take Milton's theological theme seriously entered general criticism most brilliantly in the work of Charles Williams and C. S. Lewis. Because this is an area where we are likeliest to grasp "the unique form of a poem's seriousness" if we follow its author with humility and care, our primary helps lie in the great series of scholarly investigations of Milton's thought and doctrines in their historical context, most of them done in the last forty years and many by American scholars both in the United States and Canada—Hughes, Bush, Kelley, Barker, Woodhouse, Clark, Haller, and others less well known in this country, but all merely part of a real change in both countries in the study and thence the criticism of Milton.

Yet although the way is open for a deeper appreciation of Milton's imagery than has been possible I think since the 17th century, there are some beams in our eyes, as well as the many motes in our neighbors'. There is a good deal of loose complaint about the uncritical nature of historical studies. The books are written but they are not read, or read in isolation from the poem, and with no mind to make them of use in reading it. There is much interest in theology, and much less in Milton's theology, especially among younger students. This moment when the prestige of historical studies is at a low ebb, and the discipline required for them unpopular, when everyone may cast his arrow at the aridities of scholarship, and criticism without footnotes is an idol in the schools—this moment may turn out to have been an unfortunate moment for a pronounced revival of interest in symbolic imagery and in the literary power of religious themes. There are signs that the excitement of a new fashion is producing chiefly a new jargon and a new obscurantism.

But, at worst, these will last only a hundred years or so, a mere incident in the life of *Paradise Lost.* Art is long, and only critics die. The worst die young; good reading will drive out bad. And as 19th-century contributions outlasted their incompleteness, so too may ours.

Baroque and Mannerist Milton?*

IT HAS BECOME thoroughly conventional during the last ten years to speak of Milton as a baroque artist. When any label for a major figure is no longer simply a provocative term used by knowledgeable critics to suggest relations, or when a cliché in the easy-going journalism that likes to pick up such labels for the great becomes a cliché of the schools as well,[1] then it is valuable for as many serious students as possible to consider its usefulness, before the ticket begins to remake the poet. As is usual, terms beget terms, and the unfortunate tendency of every poem to differ from others has forced an extension into the Mannerist category to account for *Lycidas* (*Paradise Lost* being Baroque, and *Comus* being left to fill up "Renaissance"). Thus far, the equally awkward tendency of poets to differ from each other, so that a baroque Donne writing short *libertin* love poems is hard to square with the Milton of *Paradise Lost*, has been taken care of by careful choice of what to look at in the epic, or by devising verbal formulae which can somehow stretch to include differing things under a similarity. All comparisons and all classifications require some of these shifts. But if a category is to become fixed, the need is to make sure that terms which align—usually by differentiating from a third thing, in this case usually "the Renaissance"—can in truth align validly and differentiate surely.

One way to examine this is to look at the basis upon which each of the criteria used to delimit these categories is erected. The great desideratum in words which help us characterize and thence

* Reprinted from the *Journal of English and Germanic Philology* 60 (1961), pp. 817–33.

[1] Clichés about the greater poets are a more important matter than they seem. Milton has held a reading public better than most, but the last hundred years have seen changes; of the vast majority of those currently reading *Paradise Lost* in the English-speaking countries, the average age must be around 19, and the average age of those instructing the readers, around 29. Present "scholars" may be safe from clichés; the ones to come are at their mercy. They commonly penetrate rapidly down into the school handbooks; misconceptions created by the invalid ones (especially if they classify) are to be rooted out largely by the college instructor, and with difficulty, as everyone knows. Graduate-school clichés are thus endowed with an all but heel-less immortality.

classify, is that they should point to the presence or absence of something sufficiently observable that men may agree about its being importantly in one thing and not in another. Despite wild variety on the fringes, the innumerable discussions [2] are enough alike to furnish a set of criteria or characteristics which recur faithfully. No violence is done by taking up singly these familiar differentiating traits, for discussions persistently fall into the pattern of putting this or that author into the category by finding them in

[2] It would be idle to point to the users of each term or idea I take up; they overlap, and often differ chiefly in ingenuity of phrasing. Treatments are prodigiously numerous, and affect Milton study almost equally whether they mention him or not, in the latter case of course being all the less conscientiously applied by disciples; but I try to take locutions or paraphrases from those who bring Milton in directly. I am released from the necessity of space-taking citation by the chief bibliographical help, which is still René Wellek's "Concept of Baroque in Literary Scholarship," *JAAC*, V (1946), 77–109, if one adds the special number of the *Revue des sciences humaines* devoted to the subject (n.s., nos. 55–56, July–Dec. 1949), Helmut Hatzfeld's "Clarification of the Baroque Problem in the Romance Literatures," *CL*, I (1949), 113–39, and the notes in O. de Mourgues, *Metaphysical, Baroque and Prècieux Poetry* (Oxford, 1953). For characterizations applicable and being applied to Milton, the most important forms of statement in recent years have been the numerous French treatments, by Lebègue, Raymond, Buffum, de Reynold, Rousset, and others, cited in the book which tries hardest to make the necessary distinctions of Baroque from neighboring categories (that by deMourgues). Wölfflin's treatment is still fundamental, despite its virtual confinement to art history. But except for the form given to the problem by Curtius on Mannerism (ch. 15 of *European Literature and the Latin Middle Ages*, tr. Trask [New York, 1953]), German discussions are less important now than they were to the question of Baroque as a term applied to English writers (unless we except also for a very different reason—his notable caution—A. Esch, *Englische religiöse Lyrik des 17. Jahrhunderts* [Tübingen, 1955]). On the other hand, Croll's influence is pervasive; as with a few early or carefully delimited works like Austin Warren's on *Richard Crashaw* and Mario Praz's several essays, definitions are extended and traits widely applied by others, though the earlier writings were deliberately suggestive rather than dogmatic (and I suppose no one would deny Crashaw's baroque traits). Sometimes the application reaches Milton, as in Roy Daniells' "Baroque Form in English Literature," *UTQ*, XIV (1945), 393–408, or he takes a larger place as in M. Mahood, *Poetry and Humanism* (New Haven, 1950). But the book by far the most dogmatically and persistently concerned to fit Milton into these categories, is W. Sypher, *Four Stages of Renaissance Style* (New York, 1955), which I therefore use most for examples, or when a phrasing will delineate a criterion (without cluttering the text with references, since points are reiterated throughout the clusters of relevant material at pp. 1–5, 19–25, 104–19, 174–75, and Parts II and III of the section "Baroque").

him. This is perhaps a necessary feature of a classification borrowed from other arts, just as analogy is an inescapable method in the attempt to make the differentia applicable to literature.

The division made (p. 88) in Wellek's remarkably clear, inclusive, and temperate analysis still holds, and critics still adduce two sorts of criteria—touching stylistic elements or touching attitudes of mind. Somewhat to one's surprise, the first of these is not the staple of discussion in attempts to find Milton baroque. Actually, it is natural that great numbers of attempts to fasten the term on particular authors either slight the question of style, or else are highly impressionistic, or rather elementary, or tied to a passage or two, in their treatment of it. For although the original use as a category in art criticism had the great merit of being based on definite stylistic elements provably in a monument or painting, these elements must all be translated before they can apply to form as literature shows it. Most remain only metaphorically intelligible (open and closed form); many stubbornly resist any but an impressionistic application (linear, painterly; absolute and relative clarity).

None depends on the presence of any isolatable verbal device such as the rhetorician can describe, and most tangle with difficulties raised by the inescapable conceptual dimension of words. From this attribute of the medium arises the fact that an author can control the relevance, more surely than the form, of the images we make: he does so especially through fairly precise indications of their relation to a poetic subject. Thus Sypher's statement, "If a Spenserian sonnet is 'linear,' Milton's vistas in *Il Penseroso* are 'painterly,' " turns out not to be a comment on style but an announcement of the fact that vistas are painterly, obscuring the further fact that Milton, whose poetic subject involved portraying, through concrete "circumstances," the nature of an abstraction governing a chosen kind of life, could do it with help from vistas, whereas Spenser's sonnets do not usually reflect about matters that can use any. Few sonnets do at this date and stage of the fashion, and neither adjective can be responsibly used about Milton's to Lady Margaret Ley, or either sonnet to Cyriack Skinner, or that on his blindness or on *Tetrachordon,* while if we become too ready to pause on what might be painterly in the Nightingale on the bloomy spray we are soon set right by the last two lines—as we are if we overstress what we "see" in "Methought I saw. . . ." This is not to say that "sonnets cannot paint"; many do, but in Keats and Wordsworth too, as in Donne, the nature of the poetic subject will be seen to be causally related, and the picture-evoking words will be seen to be too complicated as to connotations and conceptual significance for us to agree on any counting up of which is stressed, line or "paint."

Such problems about the presence of qualities and effects, even the simplest, thus turn into problems about decorum. Indeed, it was soon seen that Curtius' attempt to call literary pieces Mannerist if they *used* hyperbaton, *annominatio*, periphrasis (a thing we can indeed determine and agree on) provided no criterion; for all literature does so, and for a hundred reasons. This cannot even separate *Lycidas* from Drayton's *Mortimeriados*, to say nothing of severing a Mannerist "Nativity Hymn" from a Renaissance *Comus*. Curtius himself moved toward one of the ways to make this observation of something ubiquitous into a criterion that can differentiate, by implying that it was the presence of very many or too many such devices which could bring a work under the rubric of Mannerism. But most critics have perceived that whenever we erect a criterion upon quantity, in any art, we run into the plain fact that quality makes much more difference to effects produced, and that one effective periphrasis will unaccountably seem like "more" use of periphrasis than five vapid ones.

Of course the moment "*too* many" comes in, our criterion is no longer based upon the presence of something determinably there, but upon a norm in the mind or sensibility of the judge. One's discomfort about this is not due to an unwillingness to admit evaluation as part of criticism (probably there is no criterion of any importance which does not draw in evaluations (—but an unwillingness to depend on evaluations referable chiefly to a reader's impressionistic report of his reactions. People can agree that there is "too much" of something, but usually they do so not because firm evidence can be brought to bear, but rather because their tastes click and their linguistic sensibilities are similar.

That one among Curtius' criteria which is most oblivious of this danger is the one which has lived longest in later discussions; he claims seemingly with no qualms that far-fetched metaphors ("manierierte," "studied") distinguish a Mannerist. This famous distance traversed by a mind fetching the second term of a comparison is not a measurable journey, as is obvious from constant disagreements, but critics continue to speak as if our quite different mental speedometers could be expected to agree, and put forward as criteria both "strain" and "incongruity" in the images, as well as "superabundance" of metaphors. The first is a very stubborn form of subjectivity, for readers seem unable to learn to experience connotations which are not their own by early unconscious habits of association, and the old remarks about Donne's "mechanical" or down-to-earth compass image roll on, no matter how much we learn about its seventeenth-century associations with symbols of perfection and of divine creation. In much the same way Crashaw's fires and perfumes are obstinately felt as primarily sensuous, though centuries of their history had shortened their "distance" from the spiritual states signified; it is as if we were to insist that "bread and wine" *must* seem as much closer to lunch than to heavenly love, to Herbert, as to Omar Khayyam.

No matter how adroitly it is phrased, or how persuasively it appears as a way of recognizing the "distorted vision" or "deformation" critics put forward as differentiating characteristics of Baroque, it is obligatory upon us to recall that unless we look at how close the link in a metaphor may have seemed to the man who "fetched" it, we merely point to what seems to us strained, distorted, or extravagant. This is one of the most famous wax noses in history. Almost anything can melt it—linguistic fad, small changes in environment, developments of any and every kind, from railroads to eschatology. Every change in mental furniture changes connotations and mental linkages; it is all but impossible to know any author's or any time's linguistic world this fastidiously. "Mannered metaphor," and other criteria having this environmentally regulated instrument hidden within them, could well be discouraged among those making the elementary decision of classifying, as requiring too much knowledge now impossible of discovery, a criterion largely suitable to those with absolute conceptions of "justness" in language or life.[3]

[3] As usual, a warning is necessary: this is not to say that there are no strained metaphors, or that linguistic wrenching does not characterize some authors and times, but that keeping in repair the proper equipment for recognizing them requires a scrutiny of such meticulousness as to be defeating. So far in literary history "common sense" has not proved enough, though it lasts during the time that our form of it is what is common. Supersemantics and detailed social history should not be asked of those trying merely to group authors in classes.

The superabundance of images, which Lebègue and others adduce (talking of richness not selectivity, of minuteness of description and details accumulated in a comparison), has the same difficulty of a subjective norm—that in the critic necessarily differing from that in the author, for, of course, no poet decides to put in too many or too much. This is less a difference in aesthetic than in simple judgment as to what will suffice. It is no accident that the criterion is generally employed as a whip, one of those chastising uses of the car-horn that someone has named "the pedagogical toot." But despite these difficulties it continues to be used as a differentiating characteristic; "baroque profusion" is a commonplace, usually illustrated by image-filled passages without special regard to whether a subject needs images; one critic speaks of profuse emblems, metaphors, conceits, another of jeweled richness.[4] But I do not find treatments of Milton which carry this point forward in two possible ways which could set a control on its subjectivity. One is to relate it strenuously to the author's conception of "decorum according with the subject" as we can detect that from his entire poem, and the other is to group metaphors more reliably according to their *formal* nature and according to how this fits their observed working. It might be possible thus to separate out the embarrassing intruders into the Baroque category whose profusion also seems "too much" but who assuredly are not baroque.

It is no wonder that through so open a door the wrong people have come in; while one theorist wears a distressed smile at the entrance of Lyly, another greets Marlowe without unease, and yet another asks him to leave. On what precise basis do we distinguish Eden's profuse "accumulation of sensory impressions" as baroque plenitude, and Comus' spawning seas and strangling fertility as "Renaissance"? The latter more like, we must suppose, to the "busy illustration" in a (quite truly) "busy," and poor, Spenser

[4] De Mourgues can distinguish Metaphysical from Baroque, controlled equilibrium from an orgy of metaphors, by looking for those whose intelligence has put a check on sensuous visions and love of decorative imagery. Hatzfeld can divide multiplicity of figures in *secentismo, marinismo* from Baroque richness by assigning the first to "lack of discipline," thus by use of the same ground providing us with precisely opposed groups under the label. Some will agree, some will not, but agreement in either case involves the double subjectivity: a standard located in a critic's mind, with which we agree when we too find figures overused, and an inferred attitude in an author's mind, which we find ourselves able to label "self-indulgence" or "discipline," respectively.

sonnet, or to the "decorative naturalism" of the *Prothalamion.*[5] We can of course avoid asking the question by somehow fishing out the *personage,* Comus, as a "baroque element" in a Renaissance piece (though to be sure his naturalistic argument is classical, mediaeval, Renaissance, and seventeenth-century). But then we have lost the merit which this criterion stressing sumptuousness, redundance, powerful simplified rhythm despite apparent crowding, and the like, had in the original formulation concerned with nonverbal arts: that the quality was experienced in demonstrable relation to unity of effect, though meanwhile no one could deny that the redundant elements were present. Differences of opinion as to how dangerously Comus topples over Milton's unified argument in praise of Temperance, and as to whether Comus' description of Nature's instructive fertility contains lush redundancies or just observation of natural fact, correlate suspiciously with a given reader's receptivity to *libertin* arguments. If anyone could argue that compounded orders and double domes and numerous *putti* were sometimes these and sometimes something else, things would be harder.

But there is a more usual way out of these confusions between one writer's profusion and another's, between enough and too much, between Renaissance fussy surface vitality, Mannerist virtuosity and contrivance, and Baroque plenitude and energy. The way out is, generally: to inquire whether, or not, the superabundance (of rhetorical devices, of image and conceit, of any observable stylistic element) is there because the writer wishes to surprise and startle. Curtius is only too forthright and simple: the Mannerist "wants to surprise, to astonish, to dazzle. While there is only one way of saying things naturally, there are a thousand forms of unnaturalness" (p. 282). Of course his bias is obvious,

[5] Examples are from Sypher (pp. 192, 92, 88). He relates the *Prothalamion* passage to Spenser's Renaissance "fractional seeing"—which in turn is useless for Comus' descriptions, that are as tightly argued as the Elder Brother's equally crowded ones, with each of the lavish images following veins in the old argument-systems. But the critic neglects all the *reasons* for the kind of "vision" in *Prothalamion,* just as his next comments on the disunity of the "anecdotal" *Faerie Queene* and its ornate "processional movement" show entire lack of interest in the complex kind of unity of *FQ,* with its hundreds of intertwined, never quite severed, threads. It would be easy to describe accurately the unity of *FQ* using solely the phrases popular in discussions of baroque form (which would place it in a very false category).

and we are not far from the grand Sophomore division of all literary styles into Flowery and Sincere. Nevertheless, the emphasis on the author's *wanting* to dazzle has never been lost; it was ancient before Curtius as a principle of disapproval but not as a ground for a literary category, and it appears in all kinds of phrasings, pejorative or not, according as the critic admires or dislikes baroque (or mannerist) artifice.

The overintellectualism, contrived ingenuity, and frigid learned niceties that can go with self-consciousness as with trying to astonish are generally attached now to Mannerism, for by many this term is uneasily kept as a kind of last box to house what could once be disliked in Baroque—though Curtius' charge of affectation is often simultaneously denied. We must with Sypher see these listed qualities as preeminent in *Lycidas,* taking our pleasure as best we may in Milton's inexplicable private willfulnesses, in the disconcerting shifts being expressive, and in the fact that the poem is complex (and, though false, inflated, frigid, callow, and erratic—"great"). Similar dissociations and shifts (not disconcerting as in *Lycidas*) we must see as dictating a different categorization for *Paradise Lost* (which is Baroque, not Mannerist) by perceiving that here Milton is not awake to "the contradictions between his baroque sensuousness and his Puritanism," but has naïvely surrendered to his images, and hence does not suffer from the tensions inherent in them (as Donne each instant does, and the author of *Lycidas*).

But what is disturbing is not the high price (a "self-seduced" Milton, ethically and theologically diddled) we here pay for a way out, when we must label a stylistically discoverable characteristic in one piece Baroque and in another Mannerist, and in one aesthetically satisfying, in another transcended with difficulty. What disturbs us most is not even the manifest difficulty of applying such a differentiating principle to a conceivably mannerist Carew or a debatably baroque Herbert. What is most disturbing to anyone who wishes to use a criterion to distinguish reliably is that this one is grounded in knowledge about the state of mind of an author which we can never have. We can suffer from what we see as contradictions, but we know less about whether an author did, or so saw them; we can tell whether we are surprised, or dazzled, but how high up this came in the author's motivations is a secret, except to those who like Curtius know exactly what the "one way of saying things naturally" would be. And with the latter, though at least we look at poem not poet, the subjective standard is in the critic's inner being, whereas in the statement "he chiefly wanted to astonish" we effortlessly enter the author's. (Even an occasional Marino who so declares his end would be hard to find in England.)

Criticism properly discusses such matters, but neither as a first step nor without safeguards touching evidence. Some intentions of an author can be reliably deduced from the nature of a work we have before us. But motivations in him inferred from the nature of our responses are something different, as also expressed meanings are a different thing to look for, from unconscious psychological needs or self-deceptions. De Mourgues' demonstrations of distortion and lack of balance as a distinguishing characteristic of Baroque show authors enthralled with the excitement of surprising primarily themselves, and stopping at nothing to indulge themselves in it; but in the use of a criterion based on knowledge of the motivation and overpowering psychological pressures behind profusion, over-plus, and extreme amplification of fancy, these demonstrations similarly classify according to what we can only think we know with sureness.[6] An unexpected embarrassment turns up with keeping authors *out* of a category so based. Suppose Spenser's *Daphnaida* shows a man obsessed with death trying to indulge himself in it but failing to induce in us a similar obsession? Then we are at a loss where to put him; is he proto-Baroque —like Chaucer in the *Duchess?* We have, moreover, to measure the extent to which a man desired to startle or was impelled by

[6] The chief knowledge demanded in the application of de Mourgues' criteria is that we should know what is a balanced view of the universe. Since we try to know this whenever we read a book seriously, I do not mock it (even in Curtius' version—that Mannerists ought not to wish to say things abnormally but normally). Yet these necessarily self-flattering assumptions regarding eternal norms seem unfortunate as bases for knowing a baroque poem from another one. They seem peculiarly unhappy when we are awakened to a lively sense of history; there have been times when it was a mark of unbalance *not* to be impressed by the "disorder on a colossal scale" which would precede the Last Judgment. After all there are the Fifteen Signs, with all their history in OE, ME, and early Irish before they ever decorated the margins of xvi.c. *Horae*, and there are II Peter and Revelation. Can one be balanced and Metaphysical in one's time and get into the Baroque category later when one is seen to have been looking at an "unreal problem"? This would be the situation of many mediaeval lyrics on death and of most ME sermons on the Judgment.

psychological needs. Renaissance confession literature would be unmanageable; indeed, from the old difficulty of St. Augustine onward to Montaigne and Greene the problems germinate, multifarious, the data for solving them irrecoverable.

Certain older tests for knowing whether a thing we held in our hands was to be called Baroque, like Croll's "portraying in one's style exactly those athletic movements of the mind by which it arrives at a sense of reality," and once implicitly believed in, begin to seem more difficult to apply as the subdivisions multiply, and as modern literature has taught us more about what is produced when this "highly self-conscious simulation of the mind's actual operation" is indeed attempted. This was so attractive a thing to find in an author in the 1920's and '30's that it is only as the years pass that we realize we do not actually come upon statements by English "baroque" authors that they are trying to do precisely this (famous declarations by Montaigne and Burton do not regard total thought processes reproduced as by a recording instrument). It is significant that later writers on the Baroque have borrowed chiefly from Croll's remarks about this Senecan motive or desire, rather than from the analyses which accompanied them. It is also significant that one critic can adduce prose from Milton to exemplify this simulation of the movements of thoughts, while another quotes Milton's disapproval of, and analyzes his differences from, the style which the criterion aims to distinguish. I believe that one's gradually increasing sense of discomfort (experienced also as the years distance us from Daniells' suggestive descriptions of "baroque" exploratory prose) arises chiefly from the same element seen in other criteria, of inescapable conjecture and inference, increasingly distrusted as one attempts over the years to distinguish which authors are "trying" to do something, and which are not.[7] For these are not intentions concerning meanings, which

[7] Croll did not come out for the classification "Baroque" until his latest appearing article of the famous five (from that on "Attic Prose," in *SP*, XVIII [1921], I use some phrases above, as from Daniells' essay cited in note 2). It is of some significance that George Williamson does not find the classification useful in the book which pursues, orders, and refines upon Croll's treatments with real care: *The Senecan Amble* (Chicago, 1951). Before one finds it easy to call Milton's prose baroque, or to separate seventeenth- and sixteenth-century styles, one must consult Williamson's careful working out of relations usually left to impressions and tastes, such as those between Euphuism and later styles; he also consistently demonstrates writers' ties with what they themselves would have thought

can be sought, and found with considerable sureness, within a work.

As so often, difficulties come especially when one is keeping people out of some category; one has too often to avert the face from a criterion and simply "know better" than to let in what it would admit. In the very descriptions categorizing them as "Baroque," later authors who shared Bacon's or Lipsius' desideratum of a plain style, but whose zeal for honesty came out in the broken, loosely articulated style we confront in their works, are characterized stylistically through sets of phrases which suit point for point much earlier prose (Malory or some earlier Middle English writer). Though one would never confuse the two writers or periods, the offered descriptions do not separate them, as they have not in practice separated off Milton. For separation we must resort to the factor of the self-consciousness in later writers as they meticulously followed the trail of subtle thought; the earlier writer has to be assumed to be either naïve (mediaeval) or interested in his rhetoric rather than his thought (Elizabethan). These are all three suspect presuppositions; they belong to the end, not the beginning, of a critical examination.

Almost the same difficulty arises with the criterion of artistry "for its own sake." This used to seem simple applied to Lyly, but not if it covers as well, though with a difference in motive, mannerist writers and (to some theorists) baroque writers. Here again the differentiating factor depends on our knowing what *produced* an author's preoccupation with virtuosity—and the predilections of critics are ill-disguised as they assign orders of merit. One might have some success in examining whether technical cleverness functions toward a work's recognized end. But this turns out not to be a relevant point, for a differently based decision has instead to be made, in relation to antecedent decisions by which we suspect Renaissance virtuosity of being, unconfessed, its own end (Lyly), know Mannerist virtuosity to be the visible sign of unresolvable inner dissonance (*Lycidas*), and enjoy Baroque virtuosity as *Lebensfülle* or honest report of complexity (Donne, Browne). Locatable qualities in pieces or how these function are no longer the

---

to be the sources of their characteristics: numerous varieties of classical practice and theory, rather than baroque ways of seeing reality. Of course men see reality differently; it is our detection of this in their syntax that is too crude to use for categorizing them.

point; our decisions turn upon why these have been attempted. It is difficult if one uses litmus paper not to go by whether it turns pink but by whether the subject tested intended to produce acid. One would like to call theatricality by that name even if baroque stylists produce it by mistake through zeal for "lifelike" delineation, would like to be enabled to differentiate qualities of prose, not be required to detect when and when not an intention to be direct unexpectedly produced effects that are spiral. In particular, "significant darkness" needs to be reliably differentiated, as to instrument and form, from the Renaissance *clarté* (luminousness, not the explicitness into which it is mistakenly translated—only *some* Renaissance poets made the mistake before us, the poorer ones). The styles differ, but not the aesthetic desideratum of "illumination"; hence the criterion which opposes a belief in significant enlightening "darkness," to content with unmeaningful noonday visibility, is a red herring.

It is that eminent baroque figure E. K. who claims, in the Preface to Spenser's *Shepheardes Calender,* that in the most exquisite pictures "they use to blaze and portraict not onely the daintie lineaments of beautye, but also rounde about it to shadow the rude thickets and craggy clifts," and maintains that, "I knowe not how" (this is the familiar *je ne sais quoi* in baroque strangeness-in-beauty) he takes "great pleasure in that disorderly order." All his maintaining cannot add one mannerist dissonance to his literary character, but the sleight of hand of looking sometimes at writers' desiderata and sometimes at their performance must be allowed to complicate matters all along the line, instead of merely where we are ready to consider a split between motive and resulting quality proper to the dissonance of the times.

These half-hidden difficulties in criteria touching stylistic matters seem all but trivial compared with those we meet in the second great division of criteria which enable us to classify works, and Milton's among them, as Mannerist or Baroque—those erected directly upon our conceptions of the author's state of mind. There is no treatment of the matter which does not use these as touchstones. The insecurity which one feels in observing their application can vary greatly. Exuberance, *Lebensfülle,* dynamism, energy, do seem observable in literary form, and in Milton's formal elements of style; and splendor, triumph, grandeur, do look like characteristics of themes, including Milton's themes.

On the other hand, all security disappears before the appalling problem of applying as a difference-finder between poems the Mannerist's sense of not being "at home in the world," which causes him to distort space, light, color, and contour and to take refuge in abstract art. The last being closed to the poet, and *formal* analogues to the first not possible,[8] critics have universally looked for characters not "at home" or speakers in moods of alienation, and difficulties naturally multiply. There is the fearful matter of men's changing views and moods; one cannot live without knowing that this particular stone "troubles the living stream" as it "changes minute by minute," and men's work has to be atomized to get the criterion to fit. A narrative's needs are a fatal complication. We must decide whether Chaucer agreed with Egeus, and if so how much of the *Knight's Tale* is mannerist. We have also on our hands some dozen centuries when *exules filii Hevae* and *hoc exilium* was doctrine seriously held; if we apply the differentiating factor as it has been applied to Milton, even saints would be hard to sort into, respectively, Baroque because they resolved the problem or Mannerist in case they suffered grievously under it. It is so basic a power of literature to portray attitudes progressively during imagined passing time, that from the spectacle of a man resolving such problems we cannot isolate the evidence which proves to us that a work of art's design does or does not do so.

"Disturbed balance" is the key to most phrasings of Mannerism, and many of Baroque, as a classification. In literature one does not only (or even chiefly) deduce, but is directly presented with, conceptually indicated balance and imbalance, and *in* persons' minds, whether characters or writers. It is uncomfortable to line authors up according to the "position" they take on such questions posed in their books; we have the alternative of turning

[8] Analogues not purely formal, concerning distortion of actuality, are especially subject to confusion with the literary problem of probability-improbability. Moreover, happy and confident fairy tales distort most notably of all. Figurative speech makes distortions mean something totally unconnected with strain or alienation; the dragon's three-furlong tail which disturbs Sypher (p. 89) in *FQ* is a *probability* when a man is portraying the conquest of quintessential evil. But the whole Renaissance problem of finding a place among the learnings for the feigned truth of poetry becomes merely the "Renaissance" "tyranny of probability" in this critical discussion. Several examples in paragraphs following this one have been taken from the same critic (see above, end of note 2).

reading into one long inquiry into the unrealized psychological state of poets. We are consulting the worst evidence in the world, an artist's deliberate reordering. It seems folly not to *expect* that a lyric which hopefully invites a lady to put a kiss within the cup will "have a stability lacking in" one whose theme is the ineluctable shortness of the moments of enjoyment of a coy mistress. One (only one) is *about* instability.

It is a fatal shortcoming of all these criteria based on attitude and state of mind that in literature, a continual direct presentation of these through a conceptual medium, the criteria must immediately count on perfected decisions concerning the most problematic and the last thing we know about any work, the full nature and import of the entire poetic subject. Marvell's own invitation to love has a Jonsonian stability: "The grass I aim to feast thy sheep, The flowers I for thy temples keep." When Damon's next words show us that the subject is not what we expected, we move from the "stability" (it is not erased) to something else in a progressively discovered subject. No formal distortion marked the change; that was possible but not necessary—a naughty, confusing attribute in "evidence." The "troubled" *Lycidas* is Mannerist; it is hard to find a poem about the pain of early death and seeming unjust heavens, that is untroubled. Quite aside from the aesthetic doubtfulness of turning poets into mere sheaths of their subjects, we are stranded with the alternative of claiming either that only some eras have such attitudes (doubtful) or deal with such subjects (impossible), or else that any poet who does is mannerist out of his time. It must be noticed that we have only been saddled with the vast task of considering everything from *Job* to *In Memoriam,* or led toward any conceivable confusion between the pieces, because we sought the aid of this criterion, to classify—we should never confuse the things themselves. This is only the beginning, for we must ask of all these troubled pieces just *how* they are troubled (but here at this heart of the matter impressionistic phrases appear which aid us to no distinctions, because they commonly describe one item, usually one we are trying to classify, e.g., *Lycidas*). And if the essence of the criterion be that there is some special form of suffering under the way inescapable conditions impinge on men's wishes and their peace, we must find formal characteristics that reliably distinguish that form from all the others. We have further to discover, in all the other genres such as dramas and novels, whether it be the author who is tormented and torn, or his created characters—his own attitude being a thing to be otherwise discovered. All this comes close to making classification an end in itself merely by virtue of how long it takes. It can be rapid only if we deny authors the right to present trouble as troublingly as they can, or measure their sufferings and their resolutions against our incapacity to share them.

With every example we seek to classify, we are dogged by this intimate relation in literature between poetic subject and the decorum of the piece, complicated by the fact that words have meanings, though meanwhile *we* shape the forms we are asked to imagine. *Comus* is serenely "Renaissance"; but if it is difficult to see how a tormented treatment of Temperance could recommend it, it seems equally unfortunate to erect poetic categories on whether men are "for" or "against" a virtue. Who shall not be a Tenebrist, or has not been, who really set out to depict Hell? though with words the medium, capacities to respond with imaged *tenebrae* both differ with persons and alter with time. If we proceed to a Heaven without shadows we are uncertain whether that should slip the poem into another classification. Milton's description of Eden is quoted that we may observe its fleshly abundance. One would look long for a pre-Fall Paradise that had meager instead of rich groves, unripe not burnished fruits, jungle-hot recesses, and an Adam and Eve not eminently naked. Though we could tell a Spenserian paradise from Milton's in an instant, this is because we look elsewhere for differentiating characteristics than to the abundance which all Edens must possess.

That the innocence of prelapsarian fleshliness is part of Milton's quite orthodox Christian point is apparent from his different post-lapsarian fleshly lost-paradise; the Milton studies which make his theological sophistication so clear could easily induce it in any critic who finds the innocence of the flesh so out of square with Milton's "Puritanism" that unconscious loss of his convictions must be called in to explain it. Far from deserting his tenets for his images, it is through the images that he makes sexual *temperance* his point; but it is the same Christianized conception of temperance as in the "Renaissance" *Comus,* defined (as a long history had made possible) with respect to its consonance with worshiping God rather than the flesh which He had "created good" but not to take His place. To lock up a thoughtful author, with a whole language and all the conceptual refinements language can get into images at his command, into the few large oppositions which can be unambiguously the *conceptual* burden of nonverbal works, is to give ourselves difficulties of interpretation at every turn. Milton's Eden certainly reminds us of baroque rather than Renaissance or mediaeval painting. Yet when the classification "Baroque," instead of giving us a name for certain indefinable likenesses, imposes upon an author a pattern of thought derived from other examples in the classification, our poems have become tools to protect our categories.

This can happen with any classifying. But perhaps it happens with special ease when the criteria are drawn over from arts in which form can only imply [9] a state of mind in a creator, into an art where such implications are obscured or short-circuited by the preeminent capacity of words: that they say meanings outright, counting upon an antecedent, very rough, resilient agreement on what these are. This capacity takes precedence over everything else, when we are watching the decorum with which style makes poetic subject manifest. If "Il Penseroso" is an example of "open form," and if open forms "imply . . . that there is no stable order in the world," so that the hermit at the close quite simply has nothing to "rightly spell," however old his experience—we have the choice of calling its form Milton's mistake, or questioning the applicability of our criterion. If we are willing to do the latter, we shall find that the peculiarly literary formal elements lead the poem toward the end he gives it with an almost perfect decorum. If Spenser's flower catalogue in *Prothalamion* has the "fractional seeing" of the Renaissance, and the *Lycidas* flower passage similarly taken alone and out of context has the same fastidious perception of single flowers despite the poem's mannerist "proximate seeing," it is possible that we should give up isolating and attributing a fixed significance to these images we have made and are "seeing," in favor of attending to literature's preeminent way of apprehending what it is we "see." That will lead us, in these two whole poems, including every flower and every other image, to "see" the difference of life from death. Dead flowers could not do it; they can say resurrection as easily as death, if

[9] In the merely apparent exception—when "images" or formal motifs have a history that makes their conceptual burden clear—it is natural and significant that we speak of "a language of images."

asked to. If one wishes to classify with delicacy, it is better to use criteria which do not ignore, but take full cognizance of, the peculiar capacities of the medium of what one is classifying. Absolute clarity and relative clarity have a similar inadequacy; clarity in arts which use words is implacably connected with clearness as this is had by things to which shape, color, light are (except metaphorically) indifferent: ideas, impulses, notions. Criteria grounded in what our phenomena cannot possess can only be partial.

The bases of differentiating principles, that we have uncovered, do not make the outlook very cheerful for attempts to use "Baroque" or "Mannerist" as categories through which we will group poems more reliably and understand them more fully. In all this I have left out one great further difficulty. Nothing makes one more uneasy in reading applications of these classifications to literature than to allow one's knowledge of literature of other periods to be at all awake. It is especially necessary to throttle all ghosts from the Middle Ages, and resolutely disallow that movement of mind which sees how neatly criteria as described suit writers who clearly do not belong with those being discussed. That the experience is painful is obvious from the exceptions others have taken. Alanus pops up at us out of one description; Adam of St. Victor agreeably inhabits another, Chaucer flies through all three time-divisions, his traits subsumable under the characterizations, though we know he belongs in none (we may be the last to know it); Augustine will not stay put unless we turn a deaf ear, deafened by his great history and by keeping away from numerous sermons, the *Enarrations* and the *Confessions;* the radical images of a *Somme le roi* or the subtle sustained metaphors of a *Queste del Saint Graal* insinuate themselves as the best possible examples of some described criterion identifying a category, inclusion in which we know would make the works misunderstood; lyrics on the Last Things or the Charter of Christ or the deceptions of *saeculum* beat through the brain; Chrétien's disputed *sen* and ambiguous comic ironies find yet another rubric and unsafe dwelling place; Jean de Meun, especially in his character as a master of extended ironic dialectic in large figurative sweeps covering thousands of lines, winks like a will-o'-the-wisp in and out of the descriptions of differentiating traits; both stylistically and as to psychological preoccupations, sermons (Latin and vernacular) are incorrigible uninvited guests; and Carolingian pastorals are a plain nuisance. I am not speaking of characteristics we can "find" in pieces, but of the traits we should have to describe in trying to come at their true quality.

It may be this kind of experience, finally, which makes one think: since one would not confuse the works themselves, nor the styles or themes of any of them with those of a mannerist or baroque Milton, however much the descriptions of wherein he is mannerist or baroque pull these unlike works into his company, would it not assist clarity and save time to avoid the machinery of categories so unable to isolate the true quiddity of a great poet's works? It is not only that this seems to elude the describing phrases, but that the categories which carve Milton up often differentiate what seems to matter least about literature: some dead man's problematic but possible, or temporary, state of mind which has little to do with what makes his poem memorable, some private motive or need that impelled him toward ornateness or spareness or profusion, but has little effect on our enjoyment of the ornaments or the brevity or the plenty, because his motive is not the subject he is writing about and has used these means to illumine. Meanwhile the categories, or the criteria advanced to help us put men into them, do not differentiate except by virtue of the antecedently sure taste of the most experienced critic, between things it is critically vital to distinguish; profound terror gets into the same drawer with melodrama, restraint into the same drawer with smothering of screams, poise with frigidity, truth of revelation with self-obsession. This is not true of the arts to which the criteria are directly applicable, for form is a supremely delicate carrier. But literature does not have forms in this sense; we make them out of meanings, suggestions, relations. The infinite complexity and stubborn uniqueness thus provided may be the reason why we have the uncomfortable sense—when we have ranged literary works under categories not merely arbitrary like chronology, but purporting to indicate a view of reality—that we have merely stuck names on them like tickets. And the names belie and circumscribe, rather than illumine, the nature of the thing we have labeled. To come out with names for things is one way of classifying; it does not order the phenomena.

This is not to say that our previous habit of using these categories to make suggestive relations with other arts was mistaken; I should be no more willing than another to forego the stimulation and insight into qualities of works which the series of such treatments has provided. If every critic past or future who has called attention (or will) to baroque elements in seventeenth-century poetry or Milton were to find that here attacked, a disservice to criticism would have been done. Dogmatic categorizing and the attaching of labels seems a different thing, and the more popular it threatens to become, the more different. It is moreover true that this may be one of the numerous ways in which English literature is less amenable to some kinds of arrangement than other literatures; the question at issue here is solely that of the usefulness of these criteria and categories for the literature to which Milton belongs, and for Milton's several works. It would not be the first time that John Milton, *Anglus,* resisted all efforts to get him whole into the order that justly suited others, and he would not be the first Englishman to show that recalcitrance.

A BIBLIOGRAPHY OF ROSEMOND TUVE'S WRITINGS

Arranged Chronologically

"The Sixth Sense in Danish Ballad Poets," *The Minnesota Quarterly*, Winter 1923, 12–16.

Review: "Music Notes, RT," *Fritillary: Magazine of the Oxford Women's Colleges*, March 1929, 17–19.

"The Red Crosse Knight and Mediaeval Demon Stories," *PMLA* 44 (1929), 706–14.

"Guillaume's Pilgrim and the *Hous of Fame*," *Modern Language Notes* 45 (1930), 518–22.

Carroll Marion Crame and Rosemond Tuve, "Two Manuscripts of the Middle English *Anonymous Riming Chronicle*," *PMLA* 46 (1931), 115–54.

Seasons and Months: Studies in a Tradition of Middle English Poetry. Paris, J. Gamber, 1933.

"A Mediaeval Commonplace in Spenser's Cosmology," *Studies in Philology* 30 (1933), 133–47.

"Spenser and the Zodiake of Life," *Journal of English and Germanic Philology* 34 (1935), 1–19.

"Spenser's Reading: the *De Claris Mulieribus*," *Studies in Philology* 33 (1936), 147–65.

"Spring in Chaucer and before Him," *Modern Language Notes* 52 (1937), 9–16.

"Spenser and Mediaeval Mazers: with a Note on Jason in Ivory," *Studies in Philology* 34 (1937), 138–47.

"Ancients, Moderns, and Saxons," *ELH, a Journal of English Literary History* 6 (1939) 165–90.

"Spenser and Some Pictorial Conventions: with Particular Reference to Illuminated Manuscripts." *Studies in Philology* 37 (1940), 149–76.

Review: Brooks, Cleanth. *Modern Poetry and the Tradition.* In *Modern Language Quarterly* 2 (1941), 147–50.

"Imagery and Logic: Ramus and Metaphysical Poetics," *Journal of the History of Ideas* 3 (1942), 365–400.

"A Critical Survey of Scholarship in the Field of English Literature of the Renaissance," *Studies in Philology* 40 (1943), 204–255. Published under the direction of the Committee on Renaissance Studies of the American Council of Learned Societies; written at their request as one of a series covering all fields of study in the Renaissance.

Elizabethan and Metaphysical Imagery: Renaissance Poetics and 20th Century Critics. Chicago: University of Chicago Press, 1947.

Palingenius's "Zodiake of Life." New York: Scholars' Facsimiles and Reprints, 1947. Facsimile edition with critical introduction.

Review: Eric Bentley. *The Playwright as Thinker.* In *Journal of Aesthetics and Art Criticism* 5 (1947), 326–27.

"More Battle than Books," *Sewanee Review* 55 (1947), 571–85.

Review: E. Catherine Dunn. *Concept of Ingratitude in Renaissance English Moral Philosophy.* In *Modern Language Notes* 63 (1948), 427–28.

Review: Moody Prior. *Language of Tragedy.* In *Journal of Aesthetics and Art Criticism* 6 (1948), 349–52.

"On Herbert's *Sacrifice*," *Kenyon Review* 12 (1950), 51–75. Included in *A Reading of George Herbert.*

Review: Josephine Miles. *The Primary Language of Poetry in the 1640's.* In *Modern Language Notes* 65 (1950), 60–62.

"AAUW Fellows and their Survival," *Journal of the American Association of University Women* 44 (1951), 201–208.

Review: R. Kirk. *Joseph Hall's "Heaven upon Earth"* and *"Characters of Vertues and Vices."* In *Modern Language Quarterly* 12 (1951), 364–66.

Review: Milton Crane. *Shakespeare's Prose.* In *Journal of Aesthetics and Art Criticism* 10 (1951), 181–83.

A Reading of George Herbert. Chicago: University of Chicago Press, 1952.

Review: George Williamson. *The Senecan Amble.* In *Journal of English and Germanic Philology* 52 (1953), 112–15.

Review: E.M.W. Tillyard. *The English Renaissance: Fact or Fiction?* In *Modern Language Notes* 68 (1953), 421–23.

Review: Erich Auerbach. *Mimesis: The Representation of Reality in Western Literature.* In *Yale Review* 43 (1954), 619–22.

Review: J. H. Summers. *George Herbert: His Religion and Art.* In *Journal of English and Germanic Philology,* vol. 54 (1955), pp. 284–85.

"The Race Not to the Swift," *Journal of the American Association of University Women* 49 (1955), 23–27.

Review: Louis Martz. *The Poetry of Meditation.* In *Modern Philology* 53 (1956), 204–207.

Images and Themes in Five Poems by Milton. Cambridge, Harvard University Press, 1957.

Review: W. S. Howell. *Logic and Rhetoric in England, 1500–1700.* In *Modern Language Notes* 73 (1958), 206–211.

"Rosemond Tuve on John Milton," *The Listener* 60 (1958), 312–13. Reprint of most of a talk entitled "New Approaches to Milton" in the Third Programme, British Broadcasting Corporation. See discussion of this talk in *Times Literary Supplement,* 5, 19, 26 September 1958, pp. 497, 529, 545.

"George Herbert and *Caritas,*" *Journal of the Warburg and Courtauld Institutes* 22 (1959), 303–331.

"Sacred 'Parody' of Love Poetry, and Herbert," *Studies in the Renaissance* 8 (1961), 249–90.

"Baroque and Mannerist Milton?" In *Milton Studies: in Honor of F. H. Fletcher.* Urbana: University of Illinois Press, 1961, pp. 209–225; and *Journal of English and Germanic Philology,* 60 (1961), pp. 817–33.

Commencement Address [at] Williams Memorial Institute. New London, Conn., June 10, 1963.

"Notes on the Virtues and Vices," *Journal of the Warburg and Courtauld Institutes* 26–27 (1963–64), 264–303, 42–72.

"Spenserus," *Essays in English Literature from the Renaissance to the Victorian Age, Presented to A. S. P. Woodhouse,* ed. Millar MacLure and F. W. Watt. Toronto: University of Toronto Press, 1964, pp. 3–25.

INDEX